MONEY

MONEY

5,000 YEARS OF DEBT AND POWER

MICHEL AGLIETTA

In collaboration with Pepita Ould Ahmed
and Jean-François Ponsot

Translated by David Broder

VERSO
London • New York

This English-language edition first published by Verso 2018
First published as *La monnaie. Entre dettes et souveraineté*
© Odile Jacob 2016
Translation © David Broder 2018

1 3 5 7 9 10 8 6 4 2

Verso
UK: 6 Meard Street, London W1F 0EG
US: 20 Jay Street, Suite 1010, Brooklyn, NY 11201

versobooks.com

Verso is the imprint of New Left Books

ISBN-13: 978-1-78663-441-2
ISBN-13: 978-1-78663-444-3 (US EBK)
ISBN-13: 978-1-78663-443-6 (UK EBK)

British Library Cataloguing in Publication Data
A catalogue record for this book is available from the British Library

Library of Congress Cataloging-in-Publication Data

Names: Aglietta, Michel, author.
Title: Money : 5,000 years of debt and power / Michel Aglietta.
Other titles: Monnaie. English
Description: Brooklyn : Verso, 2018.
Identifiers: LCCN 2018024563| ISBN 9781786634412 (hardback) | ISBN
  9781786634443 (United States E Book) | ISBN 9781786634436 (United Kingdom
  E Book)
Subjects: LCSH: Monetary policy. | Money – History. | Economic anthropology. |
  BISAC: POLITICAL SCIENCE / Economic Conditions. | SOCIAL SCIENCE /
  Anthropology / Cultural. | POLITICAL SCIENCE / History & Theory.
Classification: LCC HG230.3 .A3913 2018 | DDC 332.4 – dc23
LC record available at https://lccn.loc.gov/2018024563

Typeset in Minion Pro by Hewer Text UK Ltd, Edinburgh
Printed in Great Britain by CPI Group (UK) Ltd,
Croydon CR0 4YY

Contents

Acknowledgements

This book brings together thirty-five years of studies on money. I would like first of all to thank Pepita Ould Ahmed and Jean-François Ponsot for their partnership through this whole adventure. Their help, through our discussions and various drafts of the text, has been essential. I would also like to thank André Orléan and Catherine Blum for their attentive reading of the trickiest parts of the manuscript.

Finally, I would like to thank Sophie de Salée, who formatted this voluminous and complex book with incomparable skill.

The *Institut caisse des dépôts pour la recherche en sciences sociales*, directed by Isabelle Laudier, provided financial assistance for the writing of this book.

Introduction

In mid-September 2008, the financial crisis that had been sweeping across the Western world for more than a year reached its climax. The whole of the Western financial system was collapsing, with nothing to hold back the tide. At this critical moment, the most important figure on the planet was Ben Bernanke, chairman of the Federal Reserve. The dramatic decisions were taken over the weekend, when the financial markets were closed. This was itself symptomatic of the sudden loss of confidence in these markets. When a senator asked Bernanke what would happen if the central bank did not carry out its rescue package, he replied, 'If we don't do this, we may not have an economy on Monday.' Finance and the Western economy were saved by money.

This reality contradicts the liberal *doxa* of financial efficiency. Following a quarter-century of financial liberalisation, this ideology today sweeps all before it. Of course, the knowledge that it provided was unable to foresee the global financial crisis. At its theoretical core, it ruled out the very possibility that any systemic crisis could develop. But, graver still, it was unable to learn from what had happened and to reform itself accordingly. The financial lobby was saved by the central banks. After that, the regulatory authorities, acting under G20 auspices, did timidly attempt to impose a few mini-reforms to avoid a repetition of what had just occurred. Yet the international financial lobby knows nothing of gratitude. It shamelessly sought to torpedo the new regulations, or to find some other way around them. The corrupt financial practices that had built up with the real estate speculation bubble would in fact take on much greater proportions after the crisis. These practices were facilitated by the collusion of the major international banks, who manipulated prices on the world's two most important money markets: on the one hand, the LIBOR, or benchmark interest rate between banks, and on the other hand the dollar exchange market. Those responsible for these attacks on law and morality were immune from any criminal responsibility.

Yet, more seriously for the advancement of our understanding, the academic world that spreads the good word of finance has remained unperturbed in the face of the cataclysm. Finance is still assumed to be efficient. This 'truth' is taught in the departments of finance of all the major universities and business schools, with a haughty disregard for any doubts that the financial cataclysm must surely have aroused in any researcher enamoured of scientific methods. Alas! The dogma of the efficiency of finance has triumphed in economic policy. So, in Europe, where the inability to contain the Greek crisis has caused a protracted economic quagmire, so-called 'orthodox' economic policies blame the labour market for the continent's inability to return to the path of growth. This imperfect labour market, which in fact has nothing to do with the crisis, is held to be the cause of all our post-crisis ills. Finance, for its part, is once again imagined to be blameless.

Worse still, it is now barely possible to pursue an academic career without wedding yourself to this same credo. This is particularly the case in France. There, a warning from a single economist – one decorated with a Nobel prize, it is true – was enough to make the government abandon its decision to diversify the field by creating a department designed to put economics back into society.

This intellectual poison is a serious matter indeed, in an era in which our inability to rediscover the course of progress can be felt everywhere. This is particularly the case in finance. Indeed, as was announced in a press conference on 21 September 2015 by the governor of the Bank of England, Mark Carney – who knows what he is taking about, London being home to the world's largest financial trading floor – the rhetoric of the financial lobby and the financial theory that supports and justifies it rests on three lies.

The first lie is that if finance is entirely free, globalised and unregulated, it will develop instruments to insure against risks (derivative products), rendering impossible the spread and intensification of the blaze. After two decades of stable inflation and financial liberalisation, the financial community, the media, and the political establishment loved to proclaim that systemic crisis had now become impossible ('this time it's different'). But the impossible did happen. This owed not to some external mega-event but rather to the fact that speculation had eroded from within any sense of reason and any barrier to the appeal of greed. This first lie is also the basis for the other two.

The second, then, is the claim that financial markets spontaneously find their own equilibrium. This lie concedes that the markets can be thrown off their equilibrium by shocks. But it is also imagined that these shocks are external to the markets' own logic. Market actors are wise enough to note any divergences; it is in their interest to act in a way that reduces breaches. After all, such actors have an apparently infallible compass: namely, knowledge of the 'fundamental' values of the financial securities traded on the markets, which is to say the 'true' long-term values of companies. This same compass allowed Milton Friedman to claim that the only speculation that can be successful is that which restores equilibrium: speculation that brings a return to the fundamental value whenever the market price departs from it. Yet, ever since the birth of market finance in the thirteenth century, the whole history of finance has been punctuated by bubbles of speculation that end up bursting and causing the debts that financed them to implode. With the return to financial liberalisation in the 1980s, the most devastating crises have been real estate crises. Indeed, real estate assets are the biggest single element of private wealth, and financing these assets requires taking on debts. Real estate is founded on ground rent, which is income from a non-produced asset – the soil. For this reason, it has no equilibrium price, and thus no fundamental value. The same is true of all non-reproducible natural resources. The competition to appropriate these resources brings only a rise in rent, whose sole limit is buyers' monetary capacities. The financial dynamics of the real estate sector are moved, therefore, by the logic of momentum – by the spiral of interacting rises in credit and prices – and not by the return to some predetermined equilibrium price. Eventually, there will come a point at which such momentum is reversed. Yet given that both the climax and timing of this turning point are radically unpredictable, the actors who feed the bubble in real estate values have an interest in holding onto their positions indefinitely. This only ends when their fictitious and self-generated values implode, followed by a state of 'every man for himself'.

The third lie is that financial markets are moral. This lie claims that the markets' functioning is itself transparent, whatever the ethics of individual market actors. The markets' functioning should bring any deviant practices out into the open, so that the social interest will always be safeguarded. It follows, according to this ideology, that the only thing able to perturb the markets in a lasting way is inflation, since inflation is created by the state. This claim would be laughable if it were not so tragic. The biggest financial crises, including the one whose effects we are still shouldering today, have taken place during periods of low inflation, which have encouraged financial risk-taking. We have already mentioned the large-scale, organised corruption that has come to light since the crisis. These corrupt practices contravene the notion that the market disciplines its actors. For the markets to work in society's interests, what is needed is an institutional framework that is itself a public good: one imposed by political will, and which is intrinsically linked to money.

PUTTING MONEY BACK AT THE HEART OF THE ECONOMY

Once we have acknowledged these three financial lies, we must, at a minimum, take a rather more critical approach. Yet such an approach must also delve into the fundamentals of what is known as economic science, or in other words, the theory of value. For it provides the foundations in which each of the three lies takes root. These foundations are not innocent, for they contribute to an intellectual project that has been ongoing for more than three centuries – and one, moreover, that was originally known as the 'natural order'. This project consists in the total separation of economics from the rest of society. The so-called economic science that drives this project has no link with the disciplines known as the social sciences. It is a theory of pure economics whose unifying concept is that of the market. And it displays one essential characteristic: it downplays the significance of money.

The fundamental theorems of financial efficiency are theorems of an economy without money. Money is either ignored entirely or it is grafted onto a predetermined system of efficient prices said to guide economic actions. In the second case, money is assumed to be neutral. While some would add that it is only really neutral in the long term, as we see in Part I, this caveat changes nothing about the essential proposition of the theory of value: the market totally and exclusively coordinates economic exchange. This coordination owes nothing to social relations and nothing to the political arena. And yet, debates on the nature of money and its role in the overall movement of the economy date back to the origins of modern economic thinking in the sixteenth century. The opposition between a notion of money as a particular commodity – as a simple appendage in an economy coordinated by the market – and money as an institutional system that binds the economy together traverses economic thinking. This book seeks to give full expression to this second tradition, which allows us to insert economics into its properly social context.

As members of society, we daily experience the interconnection of the economic and the social, especially through the haunting omnipresence of money. We can only be astonished, then, when a theory that purports to explain social behaviour simply neglects the question of money. But we must dig deeper. Money is an essentially political animal. It is not by chance that a theory that exalts the market as the exclusive principle of economic coordination excludes money. Indeed, it is precisely through this exclusion that it can establish the ideology of a 'pure' economy separate from the political sphere. Conversely, if we consider the economy as a subset of social relations, then we need a political economy founded on money. Here, money is the mode of coordination of economic acts. However, the manner in which this coordination operates does not make equilibrium the alpha and omega of economic understanding. On the contrary, we have to think of economics in terms of resilience, fields of viability, crises, and forks in the road. Coordination by money makes crises possible as an endogenous characteristic of its own regulation. This coordination refutes the three lies about finance. It makes it impossible for economic theory to deny its political element, because money is itself political. The question is thus posed: why is money seen as legitimate, in the practices of those who use it? What is the source of confidence in money? These questions call firstly for a theoretical response, which is examined in Part I of this book.

THE HISTORICAL DEVELOPMENT OF MONEY AS A CONDITION OF ECONOMIC REGULATION

Money is not an immutable object. It is an institutional system that develops across history. This point is of primary importance to any monetary conception of the economy, because the transformation of money influences the way it acts on the economy. If money is a mode – or series of modes – of economic coordination, these modes themselves have historical characteristics. It follows from this that any empirical investigation into the monetary modes of economic coordination must be based on data that span the course of history. The metamorphoses of money interact with the transformations of political systems, and this very interaction enables us to verify our hypotheses on money as a mode of economic coordination.

The second part of the book ventures, then, into the extended *longue durée*. Anthropologists teach us that money has existed at least since human populations first became sedentary and the division of labour first appeared. Further, money acquired the capacity to express value in the form familiar to us today – that is, it defined a space of equivalence called accounting – once the state had centralised sovereignty over its members. The invention of writing and the invention of money as a unit of accounting go hand-in-hand. Starting out from this basis, we search here for an interpretative thread that provides, in very broad terms, an overview of the historical trajectory of money. In so doing, we ground our study in the most salient lessons of historical research.

Our analysis follows two interconnected lines of interpretation: first, the historical links between money and debt, and therefore between money and finance; second, the historical links between money and sovereignty. In following these threads, the preponderance of the political over the economic will become visible, as will the ongoing tensions between financiers and sovereigns, and their transformations across historical periods. We will pursue an investigation of the dynamic interdependence between monetary doctrines and political forms of sovereignty. We will emphasise how different forms of democratic sovereignty in Europe shape conceptions of monetary governance. At a more fundamental level, we will examine the way political and cultural differences between nations take root in different interpretations of citizenship – for money, as a social contract, indeed plays a part in citizenship. Taking account of these differences offers another perspective on Europe's present difficulties, as well as on the reasons why Britain distanced itself from the euro. In our investigation of the current malaise of democracy, we will also take a look into the future, to examine the virtual currencies that appear to escape from sovereignty and the local currencies that signal its fresh transformation.

MONETARY CRISES IN HISTORY, THEIR LINKS WITH FINANCIAL CRISES, AND THE POLITICAL MEANS OF AVERTING THEM

In Part III, we show that monetary crises have been observed by contemporary historians ever since money first acquired a fiduciary character in Asia Minor and Greece in the sixth century BC. Appearing in this same period were monetary policies, or rather decisions taken by a sovereign power, which sought to reconcile the state's financial needs with the concern to maintain confidence in money. Insofar as money is the general mode of economic coordination in societies cohered by states, it has an ambivalent character. On the one hand, it is a system of rules and norms established for the purposes of realising economic coordination by way of payments; on the other hand, it is a privately appropriable (concrete or abstract) object that we call liquidity.

Why does this ambivalence give rise to the possibility of crises? Because behaviours generated by conditions of liquidity violate the hypothesis that equilibrium is sufficient to coordinate exchange. Indeed, there is no limit to the private desire for liquidity: liquidity cannot be saturated, for it is a pure social relation, with no use-value other than the power to act upon society by virtue of the universal acceptance of money. It follows that each demands liquidity because the others demand it. For the market to function, it is absolutely necessary that individuals' behaviours with regard to their objects of desire are separate – that is to say, that each individual has their own desires, totally uninfluenced by other people's. If this separation is put into doubt, then an interdependent system of equilibrium prices cannot establish itself, and market coordination, which is to say coordination by equilibrium prices, vanishes. Two opposing crises result. There are financial crises, in which the desire for liquidity takes hold because the continuity of financial relations, and therefore the structure of credits and debts, is thrown into doubt. Then there are monetary crises, in which the form of liquidity established by the state, which normally resolves all other debts, is rejected due to a loss of confidence in the monetary order.

This interpretative key will allow us to analyse the great monetary crises in the long course of history, including the difference between the financial crises of antiquity and those of capitalism, and the invention of monetary regulation in the different eras of history. Part I of our study thus illustrates the contradictory relations between finance and sovereignty. It shows that monetary crises are always also social and political crises. Citing Lenin, for whom subverting money was the best means of destroying the capitalist system, John Maynard Keynes noted that a loss of confidence in money weakened the ethics of social belonging and citizenship. The resolution of monetary crises can result in transformations of the political system, or at least in changes of government and a re-establishment of the norms that govern the monetary order. Monetary crises teach us, therefore, that monetary systems are mortal. But they also teach us that as a society persists, the monetary system *qua* social contract must constantly be reconstituted.

THE ENIGMA OF INTERNATIONAL MONEY

From its origins at the time of the Crusades, capitalism has been a financial capitalism of global ambitions. As Fernand Braudel has shown, it was only much later that capitalism came to dominate material life, and this domination became complete only thanks to the Industrial Revolution. For the logic of capitalism is the unlimited accumulation of value in the pure form of liquidity. Yet value can express itself only in monies legitimated by political sovereignty. The expansion of capitalism thus entails the confrontation between different forms of money. How can this confrontation be regulated? What acceptable principles can be imposed by sovereigns? The tension between finance and political sovereignty reaches its climax in the international arena. It is thanks to the financial elite's capacity to internationalise capital in liquid form that this elite is able to bring states to their knees. This was precisely what happened to Greece in recent years. Across history, this tension has all too often degenerated into political crises and wars. What can be done to prevent this from being the case forever? Such questions regard the definition of the international monetary system, the theoretical problem that this system presents, the historical forms it takes in developed capitalism, and the investigation into its future in the twenty-first century. These questions are the object of Part IV of this book. Here, we show that there is an irreducible contradiction between capitalism's claim to universalism and the insurmountable plurality of sovereignty in the historical era under which it develops. The always-precarious conciliation between the two takes the form of an international monetary system, which organises the confrontation between monies according to the principle of convertibility. We will study in detail the principles, the norms and the conditions of acceptability of two international systems: namely, the gold standard, which lasted for four decades, and the Bretton Woods system, which lasted for two. We will examine the endogenous conditions for these systems' deterioration and ultimate destruction.

The lesson that can be drawn from this is that these systems rely on a key currency: one currency is superior to the others in that it provides the basis for international liquidity. Money is thus organised in hierarchical fashion and set under the leadership of a hegemonic country. This only holds true so long as this hegemon is not challenged, meaning that it is able to give economic, political and military advantages to the other countries who participate in its system, and that these advantages remain more important to these countries than the disadvantages that stem from their subordination to it. Systems degenerate at the moment when the key currency issuer's hegemonic system deteriorates at the economic level, even as the financial advantage of issuing the key currency also allows this country's financial institutions to continue to dominate international relations.

Here, we will analyse the evolution of international monetary relations after the 1971 disappearance of the Bretton Woods system and the 1976 Jamaica Accords. We will analyse these developments as a form of degenerated system, known as the dollar semi-standard. This system persists through inertia, on account of the lack of an alternative and because of the advantages the United States gains from financial domination. But it does not provide the common good that we would expect from an organised and accepted international system, which is to say, monetary stability for all participating countries.

This analysis allows us, finally, to pose one of the great questions of the twenty-first century. What will happen if the current developments persist? The United States' relative economic weight can only continue to decline in the face of the emerging continental powers. China has recently announced a strategy of loosening its monetary peg to the dollar to assist its companies to become global actors. Chinese finance remains largely under state control, and by no means does it toe Wall Street's line. As for the euro, given the flaws in its governance, it remains an incomplete currency. The financial markets of the euro are fragmented, and there can be no eurozone foreign policy, including in the monetary domain.

The dollar's dominant position has survived thus far because American unilateralism has been validated by the asymmetry of finance. The disturbances that US economic policy creates in the rest of the world do not rebound on the United States' own economy. But China's changing strategy could challenge this asymmetry. Will the forces that are now at work lead us to a multipolar monetary system, structured by regional monetary zones? If no international monetary coordination emerged, we would be left in a dangerous situation. Indeed, if it turns out that the key currency principle belongs to a historical era now condemned to the past, then it will be simply impossible to avoid the problem of creating a worldwide monetary organisation. The enigmatic problem of international money must be resolved by a principle of coordination based on the issuance of a fully supranational ultimate liquidity. If not, financial globalisation can only retreat, as it has done repeatedly in the past.

Part I

Money as a Relation of Social Belonging

Those beliefs that bind us to one another and underpin our lives – God, the nation, justice, law and civic ethics, as well as money – are essential objects for the social sciences. Delving into the knowledge accumulated by the social sciences on these subjects helps shape our questions regarding the human condition, of which these beliefs are a vital part. However, in this quest to better comprehend our experience, few of us would turn to an economics textbook. We would find nothing in its pages to calm our anxieties. It is almost as if economics were not part of society. In economics, there is no notion of the social bond. The only exception is in the concept of equilibrium, where this bond takes the paradoxical form of a complete harmony between individuals and society: as each individual realises her desires independently of others, she contributes to the perfect harmonisation of society. Indeed, the knowledge condensed in these textbooks, which is taught as the absolute fundamentals of economics, presents its fundamental concepts independently of any hypothesis as to the nature of social bonds.

Here, the question of money becomes intriguing. For who could claim that money is not part of economics? It is omnipresent in our daily lives. We are all obsessed by money. When we cannot access it, we are excluded from society, or at least subject to humiliating social palliatives that make our existence a matter of survival rather than living. Yet nothing in economic theory, which conceives of society as a self-sufficient system of markets, guarantees universal inclusion in this system. Market theory stands very far from common sense. It claims that everyone will find a job, but not that the resulting income will allow us to live decently – at least according to any acceptable principle of justice.

Another way to gauge this malaise is by asking what contribution pure economics has made to the question of sustainable development, which is the emerging theme of the twenty-first century. Even to formulate the question demands that we take account of the economic relations between social groups and nations, and the links between the economy and nature. These themes stand outside of the dominant economic theory. But they are nonetheless integral to any pertinent conception of an economy understood as something that exists within society. It is money, defined as a fundamental social bond, that allows us to draw the links between all of these themes. But such links can be drawn only by rejecting economic science's pretention to be an autonomous discipline.

Let us look back at our own recent experience: namely, the financial crisis and its after-effects, which we are continuing to live through. This has been a crisis of devastating consequences. Yet it cannot be understood or interpreted within the logic of the general equilibrium of markets. For this logic ignores money, reintroducing it only after the fact as a peripheral object that is essentially neutral with regard to the system of 'real' economic exchanges. Understanding the current crisis demands that we grasp the relationship between money and finance, which is indeed a strong one. This fundamental interconnection constitutes the basis of this book.

Societies endure over time but can do so only if they are capable of producing and renewing the material bases of social life. It is these bases that capital, as it is normally understood, serves: a set of infrastructures and material means, competences and techniques in service of production. Here, we must take as given a notion that we will later challenge: namely, that there is a substitute for social bonds called 'the market'. The market determines the prices that ensure a coherent relationship between that which existing capital can produce – a capital principally embedded in business – and the demand from the isolated individuals called 'consumers'. A market period is the time required between the discovery of equilibrium prices and the actual realisation of exchange. This is, in a sense, a *causal* time. When the prices that balance producers' possible supply with consumers' needs are known, companies know what they have to produce. If the price system is perfectly coherent, then it can be supposed that the conditions of production that transform inputs into products for consumption are entirely objective. These inputs (the use of machines, the employment of a workforce, the consumption of raw materials and intermediate products) are combined according to what we call a function of production. Within a certain time, the supply derived from the production mechanism will meet its demand: this is the period of production and exchange. Hence, to say that production and exchange processes unfold according to a causal time is to say that they unfold in a single direction.

But what happens beyond that? How will capital be renewed? Should it be accrued or not? In short, how will the 'producers' invest? If the economy is stationary and all the actors in this economy know it, there is no problem. Economic time is then made up of a succession of identical causal periods. The problem arises when the economy is part of a society that desires change, and the individuals who express these desires are unable to communicate them through social bonds – after all, the conception of market economics assumes that individuals bear no relation with one another. How, then, do producers decide where to invest? Investments require another kind of time: a time of expectation. This future time cannot be the repetition of the past, for the future will be moulded by all manner of innovations. These innovations concern not only methods of producing but also lifestyles and political mutations, which are radically unpredictable. Indeed, innovation is by definition whatever is not part of the ensemble of knowledge issuing from past experience. Hence, this future time can only be subjective, which is to say, it can only be constituted by beliefs. How do these beliefs structure the future by informing decisions in the present?

According to mainstream economic theory, the answer is finance. Finance operates on the basis of the future. This is not to suppose that the future can act causally on its own past – which is to say upon the present. Causality necessarily respects the direction of time. All present action rests on an objective substratum left by the past:

actions taken in the present prolong or develop interactions whose origins lie in the past. Conversely, the future has an effect precisely by means of social actors' beliefs. Yet there exists no objective base that pre-exists these beliefs. For this reason, where beliefs about the future influence present actions, we see an inversion of time. For those societies that do not project themselves into the future through collective action, such an inversion is indispensable if they are to evolve and not simply reproduce an eternal present. But this inversion is heterogeneous to causal time. We might, then, say that the influence exerted by beliefs corresponds to a *counterfactual* future time.[1] If I think that such and such event could take place in the future, then I will act in such and such a way in the present. But if I think that another event could take place instead, then I will act differently. Yet I have no objective basis to distinguish the one possibility from the other. By its very nature, the time of belief is subjective. How does finance remove this indeterminacy, enabling companies to invest in such a way as to satisfy consumers' future (and thus unknown) desires?

The theory of market economics claims to answer this question by making beliefs into objective facts. In this view, beliefs are not subject to the uncertainty of the future, but rather insights into what will really take place, at least on average. The market then becomes something quite other than a forecaster with every chance of being mistaken – for indeed, no forecaster could claim to be rid of the radical uncertainty of the future. According to this theory, the financial market plays a quite different role: namely, that of the biblical prophet. If this is a 'real' prophet and not a usurper, then he will not be mistaken, for he knows the word of God. According to the theory of financial efficiency, the market is an anonymous prophet. He knows the 'true model' of the economy and reveals it to all. And if everyone follows him, then his prophecy will indeed be realised, just as the prophet's word is correct because all those who hear him believe that God is speaking through his mouth. To any reasonable and 'secular' individual, this can only appear as absurd. Such a hypothesis also does enormous harm to

1   Jean-Pierre Dupuy, *L'Avenir de l'économie: sortir de l'écomystification*, Paris: Flammarion, 2012, pp. 75–150.

economics' supposed scientific character, for it means rejecting what Karl Popper called the principle of falsifiability by experience: the criterion for an experimental science, as opposed to a normative dogma. It bestows upon the market the property of never being wrong, at least on average. Yet by this hypothesis, global systemic financial crises, followed by phases of depression, would be impossible. And the contemporary world has experienced three such crises in eras of so-called financial liberalisation, from 1873 to 1896, from 1929 to 1938, and from 2008 to . . .? Of course, the efficiency hypothesis does allow room for error. But this error is confined to the supposedly stochastic nature of disturbing events, which are treated as shocks. The efficiency hypothesis allows for only a limited notion of uncertainty, for it supposes that the 'future states of the world' are a matter of objective knowledge – and in turn of common knowledge, this knowledge being centralised by finance and incorporated into market prices. In this account, there would be nothing left to do except observe prices on the financial markets, in order to act in accordance with the most complete knowledge – which, as a bonus, is affirmed as 'true'. We are thus presented with a portrayal of the best of possible worlds.

Let us go further into the events of the crisis that we all remember (because we lived through it). After the collapse of Lehman Brothers, finance in the so-called advanced countries had entered into a process of self-destruction, lacking the capacity to stabilise itself by its own means. Finance itself produced the devastating contagion that was now spreading unopposed. Everything was unfolding as if the counterfactual horizon of the future had disappeared. Financial agents were exclusively driven by immediacy, which is to say, by the exclusive search for money – not in order to kick-start spending, but in order to protect themselves. This is the reason why finance was saved only through the coordinated action of the central banks, or in other words, by money. Economies nonetheless fell into a deep recession, which could be overcome only through an expansionary fiscal policy coordinated at the G20 level, and thus through the power of the state seeking to reconstruct a future at the level of the world economy.

Thinking through such phenomena poses several theoretical demands:

1. The economy is coordinated not by the figure of Equilibrium, but by payment relations which make cumulative and endogenous disequilibria possible.
2. The money that fulfils this coordination is the most general social bond; it is that which relates all the agents of exchange in a market society in which the same form of money is used. Money is thus the most fundamental concept of economics.
3. Money is, nonetheless, ambivalent. It is the desire for money that leads finance into deliria of collective hubris. But it is the power of money that re-establishes order in exchange and restores a counterfactual dimension to the future.
4. The role of state power is decisive in underpinning the monetary, economic and social order. Money is not a creature of the state, nor is it a public authority. It is the fixed point of a coordination process established outside of the knowledge of each person, despite involving the participation of all. The Law, as a constitutional order in democratic societies, nonetheless plays a central role in stabilising and regulating the objectivated form of money, or the system of payments. There are, therefore, organic links between the institution responsible for money (in contemporary societies, the central bank) and the state as an executive power.

Yet, if we are to establish these conclusions, and thus to enter into the secrets of crisis, we also have to provide hypotheses capable of discerning the nature of the money that lies at the heart of the social bond. We can do this only if we challenge the presuppositions of economic theory that render money a peripheral notion without any real impact on this theory's central message: namely, the proposition of a general equilibrium of the markets. In short, we can only rehabilitate the universally dominant place of money if we challenge the dominant theory of value, for this theory excludes money from the fundamental principle of market coordination.

1

Money Is the Foundation of Value

The challenge for the 'pure theory of market economics' is to conceive of a self-sufficient mode of economic coordination. In its view, money has no role in the formation of the equilibrium price system that holds the market economy together. How can it arrive at such a paradoxical conclusion?

THE NATURALIST HYPOTHESIS OF VALUE AND ITS CRITIQUE

What allows goods to be exchanged? According to the dominant theory of value, goods have a common nature – a common substance prior to any exchange – which allows them to be rendered equivalent in when exchanged with one another. This substance is called 'utility-scarcity'. This is the starting point of Léon Walras's fundamental work.[1] Material or immaterial things are useful to individuals, and they are only available in limited quantities. These two principles are sufficient for a definition of social wealth. Having defined value, Walras shows that the relations of value in exchange are equal to the relations of scarcity.

This is a surprising point of departure when we consider that, contrary to the vulgate of the 'neoclassical' economists, Walras was fully conscious of the importance of social relations to economics, and

---

1   Léon Walras, *Elements of Pure Economics, or, The Theory of Social Wealth*, London: Routledge, 2010.

attentive to the actions necessary in order to improve these relations. This definition of value as an objective substance separate from any institutional framing is a deliberate attempt to render 'pure' economics autonomous from social relations. Thus, Walras carefully distinguishes the social economy from pure economics, in order to be able to think through this latter on the basis of principles analogous to those of the physical sciences.

This is a starting point with enormous consequences. First of all, the hypothesis that value is a substance is a conceptual abstraction that clashes with our experience of everyday life, in which we constantly see that our desires are moulded by our relations with others. The incongruity of this hypothesis becomes particularly striking when we get to work. Indeed, in capitalist societies, where the huge majority of the population is made up of wage-labourers, work is the principal mode of social belonging. As Amartya Sen has demonstrated,[2] the possibility of involving ourselves in labour is our principal means of realising our capacities and life ambitions. Whether our capabilities are realised or not depends essentially on the institutions in which work takes place, which means, first of all, the enterprise. Against the substantial theory of value, we could even maintain that labour is nothing other than a social relation. But in the context of the substantial theory of utility, we can only consider labour as dis-utility, since it is opposed to leisure, a utility. It follows that individuals' desires are solely expressed through the negotiation between leisure and labour. According to this reading, individuals' sole motivation is to escape labour, which they accept only in order to acquire useful goods. Symmetrically, labour is nothing but a cost for the employers who purchase it.

The naturalist conception of value, then, corresponds to a naturalist conception of production. 'Factors of production' are combined in a 'production function' that is presumed to be purely technical in character. Now, if managers understand involvement in work to give meaning to individuals, the company's business model will make cooperation among employees the principal source of productivity. But when managers conceive of labour only as a cost and dis-utility,

2   Amartya Sen, *The Idea of Justice*, London: Allen Lane, 2009.

their only concern is to push down wages. The resulting governance practices are likely to undermine workers' motivation and, eventually, the conception of labour as a dis-utility will prove self-fulfilling, to the detriment of the economy as a whole.

The Problem of the Coordination of
Market Exchange without Money

Let us consider the way in which market coordination operates in an economy without money, in order to better grasp the problem raised by this coordination. The theorists of utility value call such an organisation of exchange pure economics. The mode of coordination is not money, but prices. This is not a question of decentralised 'barter' transactions, but of the centralisation of supply and demand in what we call markets. Right away, we can see that this is a question of self-organisation. In order to centralise supply and demand, we need prices to aggregate them as values. Yet prices result from the comparison between aggregated supplies and demands. This is what the theorists of pure economics call the search for a fixed point. This is a logical problem whose solution is far from self-evident. For if individuals seek to enter into exchange in full knowledge of what their preferences are, no prices exist to communicate these preferences to others. Since these individuals do not know each other or speak to one another, they are forced to speculate on what others are thinking. But this is not enough, for it is also necessary to speculate on what others think each person is thinking. The result is an infinite race to the bottom.

No equilibrium price can come about through this infinite game of mirrors that reflect one another to infinity. The most effective way to break open this indeterminacy is with the hypothesis of *price fixity*. But how can each person take prices as being fixed, and thus external to their free will? How can a society that is supposedly based on the sovereignty of the individual transform into its opposite – into a dictatorship of the market? The answer comes by way of a hypothesis that transforms supposedly decentralised exchanges into their opposite: a hypercentralisation of exchange. This hypercentralisation operates under the aegis of a metaphorical entity that Walras calls 'the auctioneer' and Adam Smith 'the invisible hand of the Market'. This hypothesis holds that no market actor has any influence on prices. Everyone buys at the prices that the auctioneer announces. And yet this latter is nothing but a metaphor!

Why do market actors take prices to be fixed? It would make no sense to reply that they are too small to influence prices. There are actors of all sizes on the market, and indeed there are actors who form coalitions. Moreover, we can hardly justify a fundamental theoretical hypothesis by resorting to incidental empirical considerations. If the hypothesis of price fixity – indispensable for the claim that the market itself is the mode of economic coordination – rested, as most economists believe, on an *ad hoc* hypothesis of this type, then the pure market hypothesis would fall into insignificance. This is not an empirical question, but an axiomatic one. Lacking this essential hypothesis, the theory of pure economics makes no sense.

Jean-Pierre Dupuy offers an enlightening reading of this enigma, framed in terms of *the self-transcendence of prices*.[3] What is hiding behind the auctioneer is the project of pure economics. Market actors must not exhibit strategic behaviour, for this would refute the hypothesis as to the absence of social relations between them, and in turn the whole edifice of value-substance. Strategic behaviour would thus have to result from a game of mirrors between actors who have to make their decisions by asking themselves what others think, what others think others think, and so on, in the infinite regression we have discussed. The very basis of the theory of value – understood in terms of individuals' intrinsic preferences for goods, unaltered by their observation of others' preferences – would thus be violated. The fixity hypothesis stipulates that the regression stops at the level of prices. Indeed, in order to make choices on the market, individuals necessarily make counterfactual hypotheses: how satisfied would I be if I chose this, rather than that? If these choices influenced prices, their counterfactual calculations would put them in strategic interaction with other actors' counterfactuals. The determination of a fixed point would be impossible, because the strategic game of mirrors has no single solution. A fixed point is only possible if actors hold prices to be independent of their actions.[4]

----

3 Dupuy, *L'Avenir de l'économie*.
4 Ibid., p. 81.

If we assume that prices are external to actors' decisions and created solely by the auctioneer prior to any exchange having taken place, it is possible to show that equilibrium configurations do indeed exist. But here we have supplemented the naturalism of value with a hypothesis that allows equilibrium prices to be known prior to exchange. This hypothesis allows for a mode of coordination that is compatible with the independence of actors' choices. The market has become a coordinating convention. It follows from this that the theory of the pure market has absolutely nothing to do with any notion of barter, for prices are determined before exchange takes place. The market is a self-organising entity that establishes the price system as the unique coordinating principle. The metaphor, for this, is Walras's auctioneer.

It is paradoxical to claim that this mode of coordination respects actors' freedom even while it renders impossible their reciprocal negotiation and thus their ability to influence prices. However, this is only a slight loss of freedom. Utility is, of course, beneficial – and certainly, greater utility is derived from the greater consumption of more of any given good. But this extra utility, which we call marginal utility, grows less as the quantity of goods consumed increases. At equilibrium prices, all marginal utilities on all goods exchanged are equalised; this is the condition for market actors' ability to maximise their utilities. Indeed, if this were not the case, they would improve their wellbeing by consuming more of certain goods and less of other goods. Prices would not be at an equilibrium, and the search for this equilibrium would continue.

It is evident, therefore, in what sense equilibrium is a coordinating principle. Each person calculates her supply and demand by taking prices as fixed. Yet the supply and demand incorporated into the prices announced by the auctioneer have a causal effect on prices. At equilibrium, the prices that are realised are those that market actors had individually taken to be fixed. Coordination takes place exclusively by way of equilibrium prices. By the time this fixed point is known, everything has been decided already. The realisation of the transactions is now of no importance, since it apparently takes place without any cost. If this were not the case, the fixed point that is the system of equilibrium prices could not exist.

But there are more surprises in store for the honest reader unfamiliar with the arcana of pure economics. So far we have given a static picture of the theory of prices. But what becomes of the equilibrium over the course of time? How can we take future prices as fixed? What is an intertemporal equilibrium? As we mentioned in the introduction, we all know that the object of finance is the economic future. But we also have the intuition that finance is intrinsically linked to money. That is not the case for the theorists of the pure market, who consider finance to be independent of money if it is efficient. This theory realises the *tour de force* that is coordination by the future.

Financial Efficiency and Coordination by the Future

The essential question for understanding finance is the following: How is it that present actions, and therefore the present situation, can be determined by behaviour regarding the future? As we emphasised in the introduction, actions cannot be causally dependent on the future, for any causal relationship must respect the march of time. The reflexive effect that the future exercises on the present is necessarily counterfactual. This counterfactual reflection in turn causally determines the future that is to be realised. This is what we call a self-referential loop.

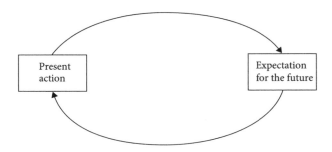

It follows from this that when finance produces a common belief regarding the future, it sweeps aside all the other possible futures. How does a collective belief like this take shape? For what reasons should this self-realisation be said to be an equilibrium? The fixed price hypothesis is again essential to justifying the counterfactual dependence of the present on the future. For the future cannot have a causal effect on its past. It is the power of self-organisation that allows us to consider the future's reflexive effect, but this inversion of time is necessarily subjective. As we mentioned in the introduction, the financial market is cast in the role of the prophet: it takes individual beliefs and transforms them into a common belief that market participants hold to be external to themselves, even though they have themselves produced it.

What we might call finance's self-transcendence is, quite simply, its efficiency. But as history has repeatedly shown us, the future thus produced can be extremely harmful for society. Indeed, this has been the case ever since the financial markets developed as a form of mediation in the production of economic time. The self-organisation of the financial market produces vast collective infatuations, speculative bubbles followed by crises and depressions. How can the theorists of pure economics deny the enormous financial fluctuations of the last three decades – fluctuations well attested by the Bank for International Settlements[5] – and lay claim to a different conception of efficiency? They do so by declaring that finance produces the 'true' model of the economy and that this model is an equilibrium, thus generalising the equilibrium price model to the future. This is what they call strong efficiency, a term which makes the reflexive action of future belief on present action into a causal relation. Economic time is thus homogenised. By eliminating the radical alterity between causal relations and counterfactual ones, the so-called strong efficiency model makes economic time into an eternal present from which all uncertainty has been banished. This fundamental characteristic is not altered by the existence of contingent hazards, for these are presumed to be identifiable and objectively measurable.

In a sense, the financial market does indeed take the place of the prophet. It does not settle for fixing a projected course which is then confirmed because actors in turn follow it. If it were just a matter of prediction, then no prediction would be truer than any other, in any

5   The BIS research studies the cyclical character of finance and its strong circumstantial instability over the last thirty years and more. See Claudio Borio, Craig Furfine and Philip Lowe, 'Procyclicality of the financial system and financial stability: Issues and policy options', *BIS Papers*, no. 1, March 2001, pp. 1–57; and Claudio Borio, N. Kennedy and Stephen Prowse, 'Exploring aggregate Asset price fluctuations across countries', *BIS Economic Papers*, no. 4, April 1994.

more fundamental sense than the fact that it is indeed self-realised. In that case, the economy's trajectory across historical time would be nothing but a path-dependent process. It could not, then, be characterised as an equilibrium in the sense that pure economics means it: as a system of prices that optimises the wellbeing of all market participants. No, the prophet does not just make predictions. He speaks the 'Truth', because he speaks the word of God. He does not bring convergence around a fixed point on the basis of a prediction. Rather, he brings into being the very order of things that must be. As unbelievable as this may seem to any reasonable individual, the theory of pure economics says that there does indeed exist a 'True' economic model, and that the financial market reveals this model to all market participants. This model is what must be: it goes by the name of a general and intertemporal Equilibrium. The future prices of goods and services associated with this equilibrium are called fundamental values.[6]

A Dogmatic Cathedral: Pure Economics

The strong efficiency theory is thus the most extreme point of academia's domination by what Kuhn calls 'normal science', which is nothing but dogma. It is wholly wedded to its logic. Its domination is maintained and consolidated by the monopoly exercised by the academic institution on 'acceptable' research programmes.

The theory of pure economics emerged in the 1950s and matured in the 1970s. This was a period in which the rise and the enrichment of the salaried middle classes allowed for an increase in their savings. Managing these savings, with a view to building up financial wealth for their retirement, became a social demand – and therefore a concern for the financial institutions that collected these savings. This concern prompted research programmes. A theory of the optimal allocation of financial wealth emerged. It was Harry Markowitz who made the intellectual breakthrough in 1952, as he generalised the theory of utility optimisation by transposing it from consumption onto wealth. Instead of searching for the structure of consumption that would

6   For a detailed critique of the hypothesis of objective financial asset prices underlying the notion of 'fundamental value', see André Orléan, *L'Empire de la valeur. Refonder l'économie*, Paris: Seuil, 2011, pp. 31–50.

optimise their wellbeing, individuals were searching for ways to invest their savings so as to optimise their wealth.

A combination of investments constitutes what is termed a portfolio of financial assets. Since choices regarding the future are a lot more complex than choices regarding present consumption, savers entrust the search for these future investments to intermediaries. These latter are charged with determining the optimum portfolio for savers, taking into account their age, professional situation and other characteristics. Markowitz showed that the optimal investment of the savings entrusted to the financial institution was a portfolio with a diversity of asset categories. This resulted from the optimisation of a utility function of financial wealth whose variables are yield and risk. His approach consisted of demonstrating the existence of an optimal portfolio by taking account of shadow prices. This approach, and the determination of the associated future prices, represented a generalisation of Walras's theory of equilibrium prices. Just as these equilibrium prices expressed the marginal utilities of present consumption, shadow prices represented the currently anticipated marginal utilities of future consumption. That is why they were called 'shadow prices'. The optimal portfolio was thus conditioned by the fact that future prices were the marginal utilities of future goods as compared to present goods. In the 1960s, the practical consequences of this theory were further developed. William Sharpe made an essential step forward for financial management when he identified Markowitz's optimal portfolio with the market portfolio.[7] According to this theory, market coordination does indeed extend into the future. This advance would result in the famous Capital Asset Pricing Model (CAPM) used by asset managers around the world.

The following problem is subsequently posed: how does the market organise information to make this identification possible? The indispensable author on this question is Eugene Fama, who outlined a range of possible forms of efficiency. Owing to the self-referential loop explained above, the market's self-organisation produces a weak efficiency. All the information provided by the economy's past evolution

7   William Sharpe, 'Capital Asset Prices: A Theory of Market Equilibrium under Conditions of Risk', *Journal of Finance*, vol. 19, no. 3, 1964, pp. 425–42.

is contained in the future prices declared by the financial market today. No one can 'beat the market', because the market condenses the expectations of each and every actor. This justifies Sharpe's proposition. Since Markowitz's optimal portfolio is the market portfolio, the best method of financial management is benchmarking. But Eugene Fama goes further.[8] He defines a semi-strong form of efficiency in which the market is supposed to condense all public information and, most importantly, a strong form in which the market condenses all the information 'liable to be known'.

What does this actually mean? What relation is there between strong efficiency in Fama's sense and the 'True Economic Model' that determines the fundamental values of future goods and services? It was up to the rational expectations revolution to accomplish the theory of pure economics that would establish this link. The foundational text in this respect was John Muth's 1961 work.[9] Muth wholly embraced the position of the prophet. The theorist of pure economics speaks the 'Truth'. He speaks the Word of the Equilibrium which is the God of the economy. The self-organisation of the financial market transmits the Word to the actors, whose anticipations realise themselves within it. It follows that for any given set of information, encompassing all the information liable to be known in a stochastic universe, economic agents' expectations will be distributed exactly according to the objective probabilities contained in the 'true' economic model. On average – as a mathematical expectation, we say in theoretical jargon – the agents who implicitly conform to this model by following the market price cannot go wrong.

The final stage was achieved by Robert Lucas,[10] who adapted macroeconomics to the rational expectation hypothesis. Since all agents have access to the true economic model in the form of a mathematical expectation, they are all the same. We can hypothesise that the economy taken as a whole is itself a single individual – the

8   Eugene Fama, *The Foundations of Finance: Portfolio Decisions and Securities Prices*, New York: Basic Books, 1976.

9   John Muth, 'Rational expectations and the theory of price movements', *Econometrica*, vol. 29, no. 3, 1961, pp. 315–34.

10   Robert Lucas, 'Expectations and the neutrality of money', *Journal of Economic Theory*, vol. 4, no. 2, 1972, pp. 103–24.

representative agent. Moreover, the true economic model has no historical temporality: it extends infinitely. In this model, the macro-economy lacks any autonomous existence. It is entirely determined by its microeconomic foundations. Since the equilibrium is always optimal, there is no room for macroeconomic policy even to exist, for it has no influence on the true model. The only policies with any sense are those which alter the structural parameters contained within the fundamental relations. These are the famous 'structural policies' to which the European leaders as well as the European Commission are so partial.

But where should we locate the uncertainty that produces empirically observable economic fluctuations? These fluctuations can be found exclusively in innovations in the structural parameters of the economy, such as they are incorporated into the 'true' model. Indeed, innovation is all that eludes the strong-efficiency domain of information. We can thus simulate models that produce cyclical fluctuations called 'productivity cycles'.

This is the dogmatic cathedral called pure economics. But here we are faced with a considerable paradox. In this entire elaboration regarding equilibrium, ranging from the transcendence of prices to the transcendence of the future and from this latter to rational expectations, there is never any question of money. Pure economics is entirely moneyless. Yet, as economic subjects, the presence of money is our obsession. It is universal and a part of our daily experience. It is the object of dedicated policies, and the subject of a multitude of forecasts. But if rational expectations were to conform to the true economic model, they would be required to act as if money did not exist. So how does this theory deal with money?

The Neutrality of Money

The neutrality of money is a *sine qua non* condition of pure economics' existence. This latter is defined, as we have seen, by the concept of equilibrium. The pure economy is by nature always in equilibrium. Say's law operates on all markets simultaneously: supply and demand must be equalised through the equilibrium price. The logic of the markets' self-transcendence means that prices are always in equilibrium; money must not be able to disturb them. As Robert Lucas declares, counter to Milton Friedman, rational expectations imply that money is neutral – full stop. In pure economic theory, there can be no distinction between the long and short term. The time of the equilibrium is eternally homogeneous. The claim that money is active in the short term, even if it is neutral in the long term – a highly questionable proposition, as we shall see – belongs to an entirely different theoretical field. And that is the field of monetary economics, the object of the present book.

As far as the general equilibrium model is concerned, for money to exist, some utility must be found for it as a supplementary good – the $(n+1)^{th}$ good – and the price that results from this utility must have no influence on the price of the n other goods. The economist who threw himself into these acrobatics was Don Patinkin.[11] If money is to have a price, then it must have a use value. It must supply services to the economy, without which the equilibrium would not be achieved. So, the realisation of transactions poses a problem even after the equilibrium prices are known. According to this reasoning, time must have a certain density. The realisation of the equilibrium concerns a period during which there is a desynchronisation of expenditure and receipts. Since exchanges are decentralised, the availability of money re-establishes the adequation of supply and demand within the markets. In Patinkin's view, the problem is thus resolved. A new good supplies a service that comes downstream of the formation of equilibrium prices, and thus does not change them. Yet this good itself has a utility and thus a price, because it enters into the utility function of market participants.

Of course, this effort is a failure, and barter comes back to haunt equilibrium theory. If exchanges are decentralised and if there are costs involved in realising them, then these costs necessarily make up part of price formation. There can be no logically sound dichotomy between prices independent of transactions' effective realisation, and an $(n+1)^{th}$ good which is parachuted in to absorb these same costs. Money cannot be integrated into pure economics. For it is impossible to show that money could have a positive price at equilibrium in the market self-organisation that produces the self-referential loop that

11   Don Patinkin, *Money, Interest and Prices*, New York: Harper and Row, 1965.

defines the system of equilibrium prices. If we want to have an $(n+1)^{th}$ good to echo the mass empirical reality within a theory that excludes this reality, then we have to postulate as much through an *ad hoc* supplementary equation. This latter is analogous to an equation of supply and demand, determining what is called 'the value of money'. The postulate of monetary neutrality is thus advanced, but without money being integrated into equilibrium theory.

Another means of modelling decentralised exchanges by overlaying them onto pure market theory is the 'cash in advance' hypothesis.[12] This theory postulates that exchanges are monetary so that they can be decentralised: there are non-equilibrium exchanges. The parties to private exchange, then, must dispose of reserves of money in order to be able to participate in sequential non-equilibrium exchanges. This transaction structure provokes a demand for money. In these conditions, money has a positive price. The existence of money is thus presupposed from a functional point of view, without it being related to any theory of value.

If, on the contrary, we want to introduce money on the basis of the decentralised realisation of transactions, we will have to show that the behaviour of the decentralised agents seeking to minimise costs drive the creation of a good unanimously accepted as a means of transaction. This brings into play a particular branch of the monetary economy, namely, search models. These models cast light on the demand for means of transaction, based on a game of coordination between market actors who seek a common transaction vehicle in order to realise decentralised exchanges.[13] They can integrate multiple

12   Robert Clower and Peter Howitt, 'Taking markets seriously: Groundwork for a post-Walrasian macroeconomics', in David Colander (ed.), *Beyond Microfoundations: Post-Walrasian Macroeconomics*, Cambridge University Press, 1996, pp. 21–37.

13   Nobuhiro Kiyotaki and Randall Wright, 'A Contribution to the Pure Theory of Money', *Journal of Economic Theory*, vol. 53, no. 2, 1991, pp. 215–35. So-called search models belong to an evolutionist theory that proposes to demonstrate the possibility of decentralised exchanges. Indeed, the common acceptance of a form of money results from a bootstrap effect, as the result of a non-cooperative game. Money is the result of a Nash equilibrium. Just as there exist a multiplicity of such equilibriums, including a moneyless economy which thus has no exchanges (an autarchic equilibrium), there remains a fundamental indeterminacy over the means of exchange.

equilibria, and thus competing monies, but also equilibria without money. This endogenous determination of money is a way of overcoming the conundrum posed by barter. But the hypothesis of price fixity in the search for the fixed point – which, as we have shown, is constitutive of the single competitive equilibrium – no longer holds. No longer is there monetary neutrality. We can no longer rule out the role of strategic behaviour in price formation. The question is how the introduction of money brings these behaviours under control.

We will not continue along this same route. For we think that money plays a much more fundamental function in the economy than transactions alone. Indeed, the above attempts to define money all do so in functional terms. Money is not conceptualised as a principle of economic value. The naturalist theory of utility value and – consubstantial with this theory – coordination by the market must be rejected, so that we can get to the fundamentals of the monetary economy. If money must be linked to a theory of value, it cannot be an object derived from the market; rather, money is the market's logical foundation. Two fundamental propositions flow from this: *logically speaking, money precedes market relations*;[14] and *money is a more fundamental social bond than the market*.[15] This is the conception of value that we must now try to conceptualise.

MONEY AS AN INSTITUTION OF SOCIAL BELONGING

The theory of pure economics is an impressive cathedral of dogma. But it is of little use in deciphering the world. We have already covered the reasons for this over the last few pages. As we have seen, this theory has built itself on the basis of its systematic isolation from society. Hypostasising the market comes at a very high cost. It subtracts all meaning from the collective, from the pursuit of power, and from the conflicts that produce innovations in society. It ignores all the mediations of the institutions that interfere in the economy. This is true of

14   Michel Aglietta and André Orléan, *La violence de la monnaie*, Paris: PUF, 1982.

15   Michel Aglietta and Jean Cartelier, 'Ordre monétaire des économies de marché', in Michel Aglietta and André Orléan (eds), *La monnaie souveraine*, Paris: Odile Jacob, 1998, p. 131.

the most fundamental institution, the most generalised social bond: money. For this reason, the challenge to pure economics must be a radical one. An economic theory in which money is nonexistent – or at least amputated, appearing only in the simulacrum-form of neutral money – has nothing in common with a theory in which money is the relation at the foundation of the market economy. To abandon pure economics and think through the monetary production economy demands that we return to our fundamental hypotheses.

By abandoning the naturalist theory of value, we can rid ourselves of the hypothesis of pure market coordination and study the markets for what they really are: namely, spaces in which private actors – the prospective parties to exchange – meet and come into confrontation. These actors can realise exchanges only via the medium of money. Every exchange implies payment. Economic coordination is realised not on the market but through this payments system. Yet this coordination will not inevitably produce an equilibrium. For an exchange to take place, it is not necessary that the individual action meet with the implicit agreement of all. In any case, the auctioneer could only obtain such an agreement if it was hypothesised that prices were external to actors' counterfactual choices. Since every exchange has, as its counterpart, a movement of money, and since money is unanimously accepted, the economy can be simultaneously both decentralised and integrated.[16]

Defining Money: The Language of Numbers Institutes the Value Form

Money can be defined as a relation of belonging: a relation that links each member of a social group to the whole. At this level of abstraction, money resembles a language. It produces meaning for others. This meaning is *value*: an abstract space of measurement in which the diverse activities that take place within a human group can be exchanged. In other words, it is the signifier of commodities' values, allowing goods that are incomparable in qualitative terms to be designated in terms of identical units. The operation through which such goods acquire a value is *payment*. It follows from this that the

---

16   Orléan, *L'Empire de la valeur*, pp. 148–52.

value of the objects committed to exchange does not pre-exist this exchange. Exchange for money – that is, payment – is what produces value.

Money institutes value because it is a norm that is the same for all. We can thus propose an initial definition of money: *money is the means by which society gives back to each of its members what it judges each of them to have given to it.* This definition makes clear that money is an institution external to economic actors, who have various strategies for accessing it. Money provides the power to be a member of the market society, at the level of the amounts of money that can be mobilised according to the prevalent logic within that society.

All of the prospective parties to exchange are included in the coordination by money, following the principle of commensurability that establishes money as a unit of account. Since money is the means of access to exchange, when it is unanimously accepted, no one has an interest in rejecting it. Like language, money is a pure form, a common principle of coordination, because it is indifferent to the personality of the economic subjects and the nature of the goods exchanged. The potential uses of goods do not define value. Use value is distinct from value, just as in language the signified is distinct from the signifier. The separation of the signifier and the signified is the very principle of the human relation that takes the form of language. The great philosopher Hegel remarked that the concept 'dog' does not bark. Just as the relation of communication through language mobilises grammar in order to make itself understood, value mobilises the grammar of numbers known as accounting in order to secure its social recognition. Just like in language, in the payment that institutes value there is a detachment between the signifier (money) and the signified (the market object). This is how money operates as a principle of commensurability and equivalence: this detachment is the condition of mediation. Even in his time, Aristotle remarked that money is pure law. That is to say: money has no value, because it is the principle of value. The value bestowed by money is the common sense of commodities. During production, the commodity is a private thing; it must meet with the desire of the other if it is to become an object of consumption. It thus bears a tension between the private and the social, a tension which itself results from the separation between human activities in society. Money brings together what is separate. It enables the satisfaction of the desire of the other, and it validates the activity of the producer through payment, providing this activity with social recognition.

More accurately defined, money is a social contract objectivated in a common medium. In the act of payment, the collectivity that uses this medium gives back to each of its members what it judges it has received from that member through her activity. Value is recognised and established by way of the logic of money.[17] Money is the institution which, through payments, gives a social value to the private initiatives taken with a view to producing commodities for others.

Accounts and Payments

It is important to define two different theoretical levels: the foundations of the monetary economy, and the monetary system's *modus operandi* once these foundations have been defined. Accounting articulates these two theoretical levels. The monetary economy is first of all an economy that records economic operations in terms of accounts. This is why money's essential function is to establish the unit of account, and thus the space in which value is commensurable. The exchanges between actors in the market economy are above all accounting relations, which operate under the aegis of money. Every exchange is double-recorded in the accounts of the two parties to the exchange, as a flow of market objects whose counterparty is a flow of money. This double-entry recording does not mean that two pre-existing values have been equalised, but rather that a value of market objects has been created and validated by a flow of money. This is the sense in which money is the operator of value.

Accounting is the quantitative representation of actors' position in the economic system in relation to other actors. Actors', companies' and households' individual accounting is integrated into national accounts, which are in turn integrated into a global system of accounts. The language of money thus extends across the whole world through the convertibility of units of account and the transposition of

---

17   Michel Aglietta, Pepita Ould Ahmed and Jean-François Ponsot, 'La monnaie, la valeur et la règle', *Revue de la régulation*, vol. 16, no. 2, Autumn 2014.

accounting rules. It is just like the conversion between languages by means of translation. Economic interdependencies are observed through the flows of money between agents across a given time period. During an accounting period (a day), each actor records flows of expenditure and receipts, expressed in money. These flows are synthesised in a balance: a varying level of assets or debts. This balance is added algebraically to the stock of assets and debts that existed at the start of the accounting period. The balances of payments that result from the double-entry recordings link the operating accounts of the period concerned to balance sheets, which both bear the memory of the past and lead onto the future.

Together, the accounts of all actors constitute a system. This owes to the mirrored recording of the decentralised exchanges between actors, following the principle of double-entry bookkeeping. Each exchange has a double record: a record of the flow of payment, and a record of the equivalent value of the object transferred. It follows from this that agents' accounts balance out. Exchanges are decentralised, but at the same time they have a unity. This owes not to prices, but to the flows of money that circulate between accounts. The bookkeeping of the system records the memory of all the exchanges made during a given period of time, by way of the payment system. This latter is designed in such a way that the entire economy forms an integrated whole. Later on, when we study the payment system, we will see how the coordination of the whole economy is realised through the *finality of payments*. This involves using money to settle the debts resulting from exchanges in a given period, or else deferring them over time in the form of financial assets and commitments. Finance is imbricated in the logic of money.

We have seen that in the conception of market coordination held by the naturalist theory of value, the fixed price plays the role of a norm produced through self-transcendence. What does this have to do with money as it is understood here – that is, as an institution that produces the norm of payment through which market objects' value is realised? The norm establishes a value because it is a prescription that acquires an objective signification. And the payment obligation makes money a generalised norm. This owes to the fact that payment is a social judgement that operates independently of its recognition by whoever has to pay. For the value judgement resulting from the payment is pronounced by the society's other members. The norm applies to all. The question is then posed: how can the transcendence of the monetary norm, the foundation of the market economy, be established? For a foundational norm does not directly follow from the authority of a will, even that of a state. Self-transcendence will emerge as a real problem, because the basic norm has to be presupposed by all those to whom it applies, which is to say, by all the prospective parties to exchange. As we search for the common referent that institutes value, how can we avoid falling into an infinite regression?

THE LOGICAL GENESIS OF MONEY: THE MIMETIC MODEL

Counter to the substantialist theory of utility-scarcity, the relational theory of value stipulates that value makes sense only in relation to other people. Value is not a relation between isolated individuals and 'things', but a relation between subjects that participate in societies in which there reigns a norm called money. This norm is, as we have seen, a principle of equivalence objectivated in payment. Societies governed by this norm are called market societies. It follows from this that money does not have the same theoretical significance in other societies that anthropology has studied. We will later have the opportunity to see this.

The question is, therefore, the theoretical genesis of this basic norm.[18] Of course, this is not a historical genesis. For individuals living in a market society, money is always-already there. The armature of social institutions precedes the individuals learning their roles within society. This, indeed, is the conceptual problem we run into. If we take the existence of money as self-evident, then we can only define it in functional terms. It is said that money is defined by three functions: it exists as a unit of account, as a means of realising transactions, and as the reserve of value. Yet these functions are modes of operation united in a single system. What is the essence of this system? And what, then,

---

18 On the ontogenesis of money, see Aglietta and Orléan, *La violence de la monnaie*.

is individuals' position with regard to it? Once we have rejected the hypothesis of a naturalist conception of value, we find that this system is the mode of coordinating economic activities. Individuals' desires and preferences are not predetermined facts. Rather, they are the results of social interactions that link their bearers to one another. In this model, desire and disappointment are the two inextricably linked faces of the indeterminacy of preferences.[19] They are perpetually redefined by social interactions. Correlated to this is the fact that objects are not the 'natural' bases for exchange, but rather the stakes of exchange. The mimetic model expresses the type of relation that logically produces this representation of society. This model of social interaction flows from the hypothesis of a radical non-fulfilment of desire.[20] Desires for objects are strategies for social recognition. They can only be defined by the other people involved in this same existential quest. The games of mirrors that result from this extend across the whole spread of subjects, for they are all subject to this same incertitude. What object should I desire? What will secure me other people's recognition? This mimetic model's strength is that it reveals the emergence, from amid this general confusion, of a polarisation around one single object of desire recognised by all (see Box 1.1).[21]

What are the theoretical properties of such a solution? The society of market subjects, who are supposedly all endowed with means of production, is a society of equals. In the theory of coordination by the market, this is expressed in the hypothesis that all subjects accept prices that they hold to be exogenous. In the theory of social interaction, subjects uniformly seek a form of wealth that is immediately an object of social recognition: namely, liquidity. This unanimous focus thus results from subjects' common and undifferentiated desire for liquidity. But the self-referential process produces a multiplicity of possible results. Desires polarise around one or another of the initial beliefs as to what the liquid object might be. Indeed, liquidity is not a

---

19   Albert O. Hirschman, *Bonheur privé, action publique*, Paris: Hachette, 2006.

20   In its anthropological dimension, the mimetic model is expounded in René Girard, *La Violence et le Sacré*, Paris: Grasset, 1972.

21   This model is from André Orléan, 'Monnaie et spéculation mimétique', *Bulletin du Mauss*, no. 12, December 1984, pp. 55–68.

Box 1.1
Theorem of mimetic convergence

In a population of N agents (i = 1, N), on date t each person has a belief $u_i(t)$ regarding the debt that represents absolute liquidity. i chooses his belief in t+1 by copying an agent j at random, with the probability p_{ij} for j = 1, N. So we have $P_r\{u_i(t+1) = u_j(t)\} = p_{ij}$ with $\Sigma p_{ij} = 1$ for each i.

The mimetic interdependency is formalised as a Markovian stochastic process defined by the matrix

$$P = \begin{bmatrix} p_{11} \cdots p_{1j} \cdots p_{1N} \\ p_{i1} \cdots p_{ij} \cdots p_{iN} \\ p_{N1} \cdots p_{Nj} \cdots p_{NN} \end{bmatrix} \text{With the vector of beliefs } U' = [u_1 \ldots u_i \ldots u_N]$$

Such that the dynamic process is written U (t+1) = PU(t)
The theorem shows that
- If the graph associated with P is strongly correspondent (matrix P does not break down into independent sub-matrices);
- and aperiodic (the process of revising beliefs is not cyclical);
- the mimetic contagion converges towards unanimity around a belief, which can be any of the initial beliefs.

There is a probability q_i expressing the power of influence that i has over the group in its totality, that the process converges towards $u_i(0)$, and thus that U = $\{u_i(0), \ldots u_i(0)\}$.

Source: André Orléan (1984), 'Monnaie et spéculation mimétique', pp. 55–68.

predefined substance to be discovered; it is the unintentional result of this polarisation itself. In any case, the final state of the mimetic process is self-fulfilling, for once a common belief has emerged, the imitation takes the form of the repetition of this belief.

This object of desire is a convention, which expresses whatever is recognised as the common form of the absolutely desirable. Thus, the polarisation produces a unanimous desire for an object called money. This object does not pre-exist the social interactions among the

prospective parties to exchange. Rather, it is the product of these interactions. To put it another way, the object of desire is established by the
interaction between a society's members, which is driven by each
person's search for recognition. Placing a limit on this generalised
rivalry, money is the object of a unanimous desire for wealth. This is
why it is the common reference point according to which all other
objects of desire are measured. Hence, the essential quality sought for
in money is absolute liquidity: a liquidity that is unanimously acceptable. *This is a collective good that results from the non-fulfilment of
subjects' desires.* This common referent is a collective institution that
no doubt results from self-organisation, but is not an equilibrium. For
this reason, it is necessary for institutionalisation to go beyond
self-organisation.

After all, a convention that is produced by polarisation can be a
fleeting one. Such is the case for the price of a financial asset, which
results from a polarisation of beliefs among market participants.
Looping together a set of intersecting influences, the market convention is vulnerable to shifts in perceptions of the future, which distort
the conditions in which subjects intervene. For this reason, the
convention is volatile. In order for the monetary convention to serve
as the anchor of value, it must be validated by a process of institutionalisation. Society, as a collective power, must make the monetary
convention external to the mimetic relations of interdependence
that bring it into being. As we shall see, this collective power is the
sovereignty that sets the seal of legitimacy on the chosen common
belief.[22]

Of course, not all desires for recognition proceed by way of the
monetary medium. Market societies are societies in which the desire
for recognition is expressed through the exchange of objects with
any kind of subjects. What makes market society possible is a desire
for wealth common to all and focused on a single object – money –
on the basis of which desires for particular objects can be fulfilled.

---

22   The election-exclusion process of money outside the world of commodities, thus allowing for its circulation to be regulated, was first addressed by Marx. He
considers it in analogous terms in Chapter 1 of *Capital.* Karl Marx, *Capital: A
Critique of Political Economy, Vol. 1*, trans. Ben Fowkes, London: Penguin, (1992
[1957]).

But whether they are 'goods' or 'services', these objects cannot exist without having been produced. This is true both of objects produced through acquired skill and those produced through the simple capacity to work, which also has to be reproduced. We have to produce what we imagine others will desire in order to confront the test of payment. We also have to draw resources from society in order to produce, even without knowing if this activity will be validated in money. We hope to pay for these resources through the payment derived from our product – a payment which is itself uncertain. Drawing resources from society in this uncertain way is called taking on debt. Thus, *market recognition is a recognition of debts*.

From this, we can deduce that money is not just any mode of recognition, but one in which relations between individuals take the form of debts. Monetary recognition is a resolution of debts through payments. This is only possible if there is a homogeneous principle of equivalence. Thus, the unanimously shared object of polarisation is a debt by which all other debts are measured and settled. We call this higher form of debt absolute liquidity. The desire for wealth is, therefore, a *desire for liquidity*. And because market circulation is a circulation of debts, it takes the form of a payment system. This payment system is a public good which gives money a grip across all market society and consequently institutionalises the monetary convention, which becomes a set of rules codified by public power. The important thing now is to understand how these rules, and not Walras's auctioneer, frame market exchanges.

Before entering into this analysis, it might be useful to summarise the theoretical results that we have obtained thus far. Table 1.1 presents a synthesis of these results.

DEBT, MONEY-CREATION AND PAYMENT SYSTEMS

Market relations are constituted by debts. No matter what motivations or obligations have given rise to these debts, they are validated by society itself. The fact that such debts constitute a system is thus fundamental to the debt relation. For society, the system of debts is inextinguishable. If all debts had to be settled simultaneously, society would

Table 1.1

Alternative views of the genesis of money

	Theory of perfect competition General equilibrium model	Evolutionary theory Models of prospection	Institutional theory Mimetic model
How is exchange conceptualised?	– Individual subjects which are autonomous and endowed with their own utilities – Goods' characteristics are common knowledge – Centralised exchanges – Coordination by the invisible hand	– Same hypotheses on utility as in perfect competition – Decentralised exchanges – Coordination by the search for a means of exchange	– Utilities depend on social relations – Exchanges are reciprocal debts with a view to the acquisition of the society's resources – A search for liquidity regulating debts
How is money introduced?	– $(n+1)^e$ commodity in individual utilities – Or money = exogenous constraint (cash-in-advance) – Non-monetary equilibrium exists	– Means of exchange can emerge as the result of strategic interactions – Liquidity results from mutual acceptance – Possible plurality of means of exchange – Moneyless exchange is possible	– Mimetic rationality – The mimetic dynamic converges towards a common belief on absolute liquidity – This polarised form of belief is transformed into a social institution (payments system)

Table adapted from Michel Aglietta and André Orléan (2002), La Monnaie entre violence et confiance, *Paris: Odile Jacob, p. 95.*

disappear. That is why we can only properly understand money's social nature by addressing the question of the payment system, through which the settling of debts takes place.

Whoever speaks of 'debt' in a market society is referring to a constraint on the solvency of whoever bears that debt. It is money that clears a debt or defers it in time in a manner that society recognises as legitimate. It is the payment system that makes this social constraint operational. The logic of debt validation – the settlement obligation – operates independently of the reasons for the debts' contraction. Here, we will strictly examine the logic that structures economic exchanges, saving for the following chapter the more general principles of society's sovereignty over its members by way of money. To identify the logical architecture of the payment system is to elaborate the economic theory of money – inextricably bound to the theory of value as a social bond, explained above – and the theory of the legitimacy of money, which will follow in the next chapter.

At the most general level, a payment system entails three minimum components: a *common unit of account* that allows the expression of economic quantities (prices or individual wealth); a *principle of money creation* that is the prior condition of decentralised action by individuals; and a *principle of settling balances* that explains how equivalence in exchange determines economic quantities.[23] The articulation of these three rules forms the market mechanism. These rules make up an indivisible whole, fundamental to the integrity of the payment system. This is the only known structure that permits the reconciliation of the two dimensions of a market economy: the decentralisation and interdependence of market actors. This definition has nothing to do with the functionalist conception of money, in which the three functions are juxtaposed. Such a juxtaposition allows them to be tacked on to empirical observations, but fails to demonstrate any necessary link between them.

The Common Unit of Account

The common unit of account is the first condition of a quantitative expression of social relations. The numbers expressed in this unit are the presuppositions of values. The unit of account can be purely abstract, and its permanence is not guaranteed. It poses a problem of collective confidence, which we call its nominal anchoring in society. All the same, this unit is the necessary presupposition of any

---

23   Aglietta and Cartelier, 'Ordre monétaire des économies de marché', 1998, p. 131.

monetary theory of the market: a monetary space is a space in which there reigns a single unit of account. The fact that there are multiple units of account in the world economy is characteristic of the fragmentation of money, a fragmentation that mainly (but not exclusively) conforms to the boundaries of political sovereignty.

Money Creation

If individual producers and consumers are to be able to act on the market, they need to have access to a certain quantity of means of payment (expressed in units of account). Money creation is a generic term that indicates individuals' modalities of accessing such means of payment before the market opens. Once means of payment are made available, this allows individuals to set in motion an activity of production for the market (such as buying raw materials and spending expected income).[24] Sales levels will confirm whether this activity was well founded or otherwise.

Concretely, money creation takes the most varied forms, depending on the payment system. In a strict metal-standard system, only the possession of metal allows individuals to obtain the means of payment; namely, the metal coins that circulate as units of account at an official rate. The creation of money takes place through the monetisation of the metal brought to the mint. The destruction of money results from wear and tear and the melting of coins.

In a credit system, it is the banks that create money. But whether money is metallic or scriptural, it is fiduciary. It is always and everywhere a reciprocal debt between society as a whole – as represented by the payment system – and its members.

---

24   General equilibrium theory reduces the description of the market to a direct or indirect exchange of an initial endowment of factors of production. In so doing, it singularly reduces the traditional representation – from Smith onwards – of the market division of economic activities. This hypothesis is indispensable if we are to wish away any reciprocal dependency among market participants. A good available in the future is considered in the same way as any other good, enabling the hypothesis of fixed prices – a hypothesis indispensable to coordination by the invisible hand of the market – can be extended into the future. The anticipated price of a good available at a future date is called the fundamental value of the real future asset that produces this good.

Table 1.2
Making metal into money

Creation of metal money without seigniorage

Metal holder		Mint	
Unminted metal −100		Assets in metal + 100	Minted money +100
Minted money +100			

Creation of metal money with seigniorage

Metal holder		Mint	
Unminted metal −100		Assets in metal + 100	Minted money +95
Minted money +95			Seigniorage + 5
Tax: +5			

What determines individuals' capacity to act on the market is therefore the amount of capital used as collateral and (or) its liquidity (in the case of a negotiable financial security). For an individual to be able to reimburse a sum of money m in the oncoming period, she must have a cash-exchangeable wealth $m/(1+i)$, where i is the interest rate at which this sum can be borrowed from a bank. The mode of evaluating this wealth – that is, the actualised value of a flow of future incomes – defines this wealth as *capital*.

One means of accessing the market is through bank debt. These debts remind us that, in order to be able to sell, we must previously have had the capacity to buy, and thus to have contracted a debt. Here, in the initial act of contracting the debt, the intermediary is a bank. But, as we will see when we look at the functioning of the payment system, the economic subject's debt is, in reality, contracted from society as a whole. Obtaining means of payment that are accepted by everyone has, as its counterparty, a debt with regard to everyone. The destruction of money is the opposite of its creation: its counterparty is the transfer of assets and debt securities by the banks, or the repayment to the banks of the credits granted to borrowers. For banks cancel out on the liabilities side of their balance sheets the deposit that was the counterparty of the asset coming off the balance sheet.

Table 1.3
Creation of bank money

Creation of money by overdraft advance:

Borrower		Bank	
Bank current account: + 100	Borrowing: + 100	Loan: + 100	Agent's current account: + 100

Creation of money by sale/purchase of a financial security:

Agent selling the security		Bank	
Financial security: −100		Securities portfolio: + 100	Agent's current account: + 100
Bank current account: + 100			

The market economy is portrayed here as a matrix of payments (see Table 1.4). Individuals' spending is arranged according to its destinations. The columns determine the receipts that individuals draw from the market. The payments matrix is the exhaustive representation of decentralised exchanges across a market period – for example, a day. Since spending is decided in a decentralised way, no one is master of his own receipts. Individuals' monetary balances ($s_i = r_i - d_i$) are generally not zero. They define net credits and debts which are not recognised by society. This is where the third fundamental rule of the payment system has to operate: the rule of the settling of accounts, which truly constitutes the *monetary constraint*. Only at the end of this phase can it be recognised that value has been created for society and that payments are final.

The Principle of Settling Balances: The Finality of Payments

Let us consider exactly how the exchange between two goods in a monetary economy works. This is an exchange between two individuals, one of whom possesses a good G and the other a good G', who want to exchange these goods. In the naturalist theory of value, these goods can be directly exchanged if they are considered to have a common value in terms of utility-scarcity, which is revealed to the two parties by the discovery of the equilibrium price *before the exchange*. This is an imaginary procedure that we have called the self-transcendence of prices. As we have seen, according to this logic, value is derived from the formation of the complete system of equilibrium prices that encompasses the whole market economy. In this case, there is nothing in principle to oppose the use of barter – that is to say, the exchange of products against one another – in order to realise exchanges.[25] But barter does not itself make the exchange possible; rather, what makes it possible is the formation of equilibrium prices through the determination of a fixed point within the whole ensemble of exchange. The bilateral transaction through which products are exchanged between two parties itself contains the general equivalence of values, or the transaction G-G'.

In a monetary economy, the selling or buying of a good for money is not an exchange. An exchange is constituted by the selling and the buying *taken together*. Money does not buy goods because it has a value equivalent to their own. Rather, it confers on goods a value that did not previously exist, by supplying the power to buy other goods or to clear the debt that was contracted for the expenditure necessary for the good's production. The matrix of the exchange is G-M-G', where M is the quantity of value that attributes the goods G and G' a common value.[26]

But it makes no sense to say that exchange is validated by each of the transactions included in the matrix of payments. Rather, it is validated in the settling of transaction balances, which implicates the whole payments matrix, and thus in the clearing of accounts at the end of the day or in their postponement over time in the form of validated debts and credits, constituting a financial structure of debt credits. Only the finality of payments proves that there is an equivalence in exchange, and thus that socially validated values have been produced.

---

25   Opposed to this are the transaction costs (information in order to understand the possible counterparties to the goods which each party wants to exchange, transport and insurance, verification, etc.). Hence the need for commercial intermediaries. But it is important to distinguish the question of the discovery of equilibrium prices from the question of the conveyance of the objects of exchange.

26   The theory of the payments system entirely conforms to Karl Marx's theoretical elaborations in the first section of *Capital, Volume I*, which regard the indispensable mediating role that money plays in the circulation of commodities.

Table 1.4
The matrix of payments

Receipts / Expenditure		Agents						Total	Balances
		1	2	....	i	....	n		
Agents	1	0	d_{12}	....	d_{1i}	....	d_{1n}	d_1	s_1
	2	d_{21}	0	....	d_{2i}	....	d_{2n}	d_2	s_2
	⋮	⋮	⋮		⋮		⋮	⋮	⋮
	i	d_{i1}	d_{i2}	....	0	....	d_{in}	d_i	s_i
	⋮	⋮	⋮		⋮		⋮	⋮	⋮
	n	d_{n1}	d_{n2}	....	d_{ni}	....	0	d_n	s_n
Total		r_1	r_2	....	r_i	....	r_n	V	0

Legend:

dji are j's money expenses j = 1, ... n, towards i, whose total makes up the receipt ri

dij are i's money expenses towards agents j = 1, ..., n, whose total is the expenditure di

The sum of ri's = the sum of di's = flow V of monetary value crossing through the payment system

Balances si = ri – di, which are > 0 or < 0 depending on the agents.

They must be settled in money or deferred in time in the form of credits and debts.

The algebraic sum of balances is nil: $\Sigma si = 0$.

For this reason, bilateral exchange – be it in money or in kind – does not in itself constitute a realisation of value. Value is only realised under the auspices of society as a whole: through the equilibrium price system, in the theory of pure economics, or through the finality of payments, in the theory of monetary economics.

We now understand that the payment system is the social institution through which money operates as the foundation of value. This implies a relational and not a substantial conception of value. For the accounting system that records payments, economic agents exist only as volumes of wealth acquired during a market period (be they positive or negative). They exist only by virtue of the simultaneous conclusion of accounts across the monetary space at the end of the day, which takes the name of the clearance and settlements procedure. What we still need to uncover are the forms in which this procedure plays out.

In a pure metallic system (such as a full gold standard), a hypothetical system in which money exists only in the form of a unanimously accepted ultimate liquidity, money creation conforms to Table 1.2. Balances are settled automatically. Indeed, if a participant in an exchange has a surplus of receipts over expenditures, then this is, directly, the acquisition of liquid wealth within the market period. Individuals who have a surplus of expenditure over receipts suffer a loss of liquid wealth within this same period. Their monetary assets are reduced. Those who have a surplus of receipts over expenditure increase their monetary assets. At the level of the whole monetary space, and thus the entire society that uses this payment system, aggregate expenditure is limited by the amount of metal assets. The monetary constraint thus comes into effect directly, in its most intransigent form. No matter how the unit of account is defined in terms of the weight of metal, economic activity is limited by the quantity of metal that has been made into money. As we will see in Part II, ancient economies were haunted by shortages of the metals that could be minted. They had no experience of debt transferable to third parties, which is to say of scriptural money.

When money is issued with a counterparty in credits or the monetisation of financial securities (Table 1.3), which we call capital-money creation, the finality of payments is much more complex. Firstly, the process of money creation is very different. A purely metallic system creates money on the basis of a pre-existing and prior source of wealth: the metal that has already been extracted from the ground. On the contrary, the creation of scriptural money by issuing debts transferable to third parties is only valid if these debts can ultimately be settled. They will only be settled if the issuer has acquired some value that allows it to honour the debt. Money is thus created on the basis of anticipated future wealth. Additionally, multiple symbols are issued as means of payment, and balances are not necessarily settled in the ultimate liquidity within a market period, for they can also be deferred over time. This delay results from financial operations that construct a more or less complex structure of financial assets. Equivalence in exchange nonetheless continues to exercise a constraint, in the form of the intertemporal solvency of the credit and debt structure. This also implies the intertemporal solvency of the value of the assets that sustain these debts and credits, which is to say, their capacity to be converted into liquidity. Here we enter into capital's monetary economy. This is one of the two foundations of capitalism, the other being the separation of labour and capital by way of the private appropriation of the means of production. Capital's monetary economy, however, is the essential focus of the arguments that we elaborate in this book.

For now, we will show how day-to-day settlements work, and thus how the finality of payments operates, when money appears in a multiplicity of banking signs issued as a counterparty to credits. The theory of money expounded above has shown that a money is a money only within a given monetary space. It follows from this that the monetary signs issued by banks, which allow the circulation of commodities, are interbank balances which also have to be settled if payments are to be final. Indeed, the transactions between economic agents realised through bank payments change the holders of deposit accounts and create interbank credits and debts. We can say that there is a circulation of scriptural monies, through payment signs that bear the marks of the different banks. Therefore, there must exist some single form of ultimate liquidity accepted by everyone, and thus a monetary institution vested with the power of society as a whole, on whose books bank debts are settled. In contemporary monetary societies, this institution is the central bank. The finality of payment becomes a hierarchically organised process whose highest stage is the clearing of interbank debts, in the form of the liquidity issued by the central bank and held by the banks: this is what we call bank reserves (Table 1.5).

The settlement of interbank debts can be net, which is to say that it takes place at the end of the day after multilateral clearing. Thanks to electronic technologies, it can also be gross, which is to say that it takes place continuously across the day. This demands that the banks dispose of an adequate cash flow of central bank money, on a continuous basis. It thus implies the need for intraday credits.

The central bank controls the payment system by regulating the amount of bank reserves on a day-to-day basis. It does this through its interventions on the money market, which it is able to make due to its higher position in the payments hierarchy (Figure 1.1). Three techniques are possible here: rediscounting bank credits, buying high-quality financial securities on the money market, or entering into temporary repurchase agreements. In these latter operations, the central bank temporarily repurchases securities possessed by the banks against its own higher liquidity, with a discount on the securities' value. That is why the day-to-day interest rate on the operations through which the central bank provides liquidity is considered the policy rate that guides the interest rates of the money market. Indeed, through its pivotal role in the payment system, the central bank extracts information about tensions emerging in bank liquidity, and thus about imbalances affecting the monetary economy as a whole.

Readdressing the Illusion of Barter

As we go on to study the historical evolution of monetary systems (in Part II) and monetary crises (in Part III), we will show that the hierarchically organised system appearing in Figure 1.1 did not always exist, and that it can be destroyed in times of monetary crisis. In such circumstances, there exist fragmented monetary systems or 'monetary pretenders': groups of actors who are dissatisfied with the dominant monetary norm and who thus create new monetary reference points valid in market spaces that better conform to their own interests.[27] These new reference points may be goods that replace the official liquidity for settlement purposes. Superficial observers wrongly see in such situations a return to barter.

Thus, in 1990s Russia, the shortage of liquidity forced companies to exchange goods for other goods or for debts, within the framework

---

27   Orléan, *L'Empire de la valeur*, p. 167.

of inter-enterprise clearing agreements.[28] These were thus payments in kind. Such payments are, in fact, not so rare in international commercial exchange, outside of the domain of convertible currencies. These exchanges are nonetheless monetary ones, in which certain goods play the role of means of payment for other goods. To suppose that the opposite is true would be to confuse the principle of payment for the modalities of payment. In any case, money – as the principle of commensurability that we call value – precedes the market exchange. It is this principle of commensurability that allows agents in certain payment systems to use their goods – entered into the accounts in monetary units recognised by all – to settle their debts. If this act of payment is recognised as having redeemed the debt, then the exchange is, without doubt, monetary in nature.

Table 1.5
The circulation of scriptural money through the interbank payment system for the sale of a good, from A to B

Level of payments by non-bank agents, in bank monies:

Agent X hands cheque to A		Agent Y pays cheque issued by B	
Good – 100		Good + 100	
Bank current account A + 100		Bank current account B – 100	
Bank A		**Bank B**	
Credit issued on B: + 100	Current account of X: + 100		Current account of Y: – 100
			Debt toward A: + 100

Level of payments by non-bank agents, in bank monies:

Bank A		Central bank	Bank B	
Central bank reserve account + 100	Current account of X + 100	Reserve of A + 100	Central bank reserve account – 100	Current account of X - 100
		Réserve of B - 100		

We have a more ambiguous situation when there is no single principle of commensurability. The fragmentation of money runs deeper here, because it affects the unit of account and thus the space of measurement itself. Nonetheless, an agent X can pay an agent Y with his commodity C only if X and Y recognise by common agreement that the payment of C has redeemed the debt. In accepting C from X, Y recognises that the debt X has been resolved. The debt relationship between X and Y is thus closed. But what will Y do with C? If C is a use-value for Y, the settlement of X's debt is the end of the transaction for Y. If that is not the case, then Y will try to use C in a transaction with some third party. The commodity C used as money must have a power to redeem debts throughout a chain of circulation, up until an agent Z takes it for its use value. Along the chain of transactions, uncertainty weighs down on whoever holds C.[29]

Such a payment system, having a multitude of partial equivalents, is bound to be fragile. We have called this a fragmented market order.[30] Each participant in these exchanges attempts to valorise their good as an expression of value. This is what we find in the model of the genesis of money presented in Box 1.1. Any of the objects possessed by the prospective parties to exchange can become the means of payment around which actors polarise. This fragmented monetary order is particularly unstable. Indeed, this is why we have underlined that the polarisation of actors around a specific means of payment must be consolidated by a much stronger institutional armoury. We have also shown that the importance of this institutionalisation consists of the fact that it gives form to the ultimate liquidity that should remain permanent and stable in the face of economic shocks.

LIQUIDITY AND CONFIDENCE IN MONEY

Liquidity is absolute wealth because it is the unanimously accepted debt issued by the central bank. Between money and the other forms

---

29 Pepita Ould Ahmed, 'Le troc: une forme monétaire alternative', in Frédéric Lordon (ed.), *Conflits et pouvoirs dans les institutions du capitalisme*, Paris: Presses de Sciences-Po, June 2008, pp. 143–71.
30 Aglietta and Orléan, *La violence de la monnaie*.

Figure 1.1
Hierarchical organisation of payments

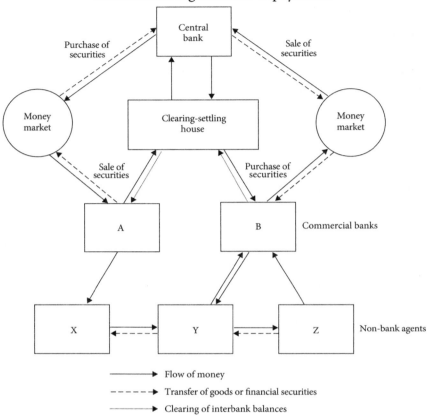

Flow of money

Transfer of goods or financial securities

Clearing of interbank balances

of wealth, there is a difference of nature and not of degree. Indeed, whoever holds liquidity can obtain means of payment without submitting themselves to the market. Conversely, holding any other form of wealth requires a sale on the market, which may be more or less easy or uncertain. Real assets, like real estate assets, have low liquidity. Selling these assets, including transferring their rights of ownership, involves cumbersome and expensive legal formalities. Their sale also requires buyers who are able to borrow, so it depends on these buyers' own solvency. Financial assets' degree of liquidity is determined by the possibility of selling these assets without capital losses. This essentially depends on the existence of organised 'secondary' markets. These latter must be large in terms of volumes of negotiable securities, deep (prices are less sensitive to fluctuations in sales orders and individual purchases during the day), and resilient (there exist market markers that cushion price fluctuations). Financial assets are thus more or less liquid according to the degree of efficiency of the secondary markets on which they can be traded. Conversely, money issued by the central bank has an infinite degree of liquidity. To hold liquidity is thus to have the capacity for absolute autonomy from the market. This is why liquidity inspires unlimited desire, unbound by any conception of utility – for liquidity is power over the whole of the society that expresses a desire for money.

The Ambivalence of Money: The Achilles Heel of the Monetary Order

Here we grasp the paradox of what we have previously called the ambivalence of money.[31] Money is the social medium *par excellence* of market societies. Yet this social relation is objectivated in liquidity. Liquidity is thus the object of universal desire. In the market world, it is the possession of cash that confers freedom. For the market economy to function correctly, it is necessary for money to be a public good. We have just studied the unity of the rules that structure the payment system; it is this unity that money embodies. Yet the finality of payments shows that the pivot of the system is liquidity, which is in itself the object of all private desires for appropriation. This contradiction between money as a public good and the possibility of its private appropriation, which constitutes money's ambivalence, can lead to a massive demand for the conversion of other forms of wealth into money. Later on, we study the forces unleashed by monetary crises. Such crises occur when collective psychology considers, rightly or wrongly, that the structure of financial assets and the corresponding debts are unreliable. That is why the viability of market economies depends on an enigmatic relationship between the members of the market society and the society as a whole, understood in terms of *the confidence in money*.

It is worth outlining why the question of behaviour regarding liquidity is of such fundamental importance. In the naturalist theory of utility value, every desire for an object has a marginal utility that decreases with the possession of more of this same object. This form

---

31 Ibid.

of utility function is indispensable for showing that there exists a single equilibrium price system. Yet the demand for liquidity as a form of wealth does not display this same characteristic. This, indeed, is why the theory of pure economics has to neutralise money. Given that the possession of liquidity creates a power over society, the desire for liquidity is unlimited. There is thus an externality of demand. I demand liquidity because others demand it. The functions of individual demands are not separable: we see as much in situations of uncertainty. It follows that the preference for liquidity, which motivates the demand for money, is particularly unstable. Indeed, since the liberalisation of finance starting in 1982, the Federal Reserve has ceased to consider this preference for liquidity a relevant indicator for guiding its policy interest rate. Such is the consequence of money's ambivalence. As history has amply demonstrated (Part III), money is a principle of economic coordination that is vulnerable to crises.

Confidence in money is a collective attitude, and thus an implicit institution, which drives away the corrosive forces of ambivalence. To have confidence in money is to recognise the lasting advantages of the payment system's rules to each participant of an economy governed by the monetary order. It is to recognise money as a public good. This imposes the need to ward off any frenzy of private liquidity appropriation. *To have confidence in money is thus to hold the monetary order to be legitimate.* Given that the monetary order taken as a whole is a public good, it is also political in nature. The question of confidence is therefore one of confidence in a collective. Fundamentally, it is an ethical norm that recognises the legitimacy of the institution that issues and regulates ultimate liquidity. How, then, does this norm operate?

The Foundations of Confidence and Its Forms

Confidence reduces uncertainty across all of those relations involving promises. This is because it replaces the prediction of uncertain yields with the choice between conforming or not to an obligation. If an individual can act in the confidence that others will take decisions to avert risks that she does not herself understand, then her economic environment becomes drastically less complex. Confidence means a reduction of the indeterminacy among different possibilities. For it means that we can assume that freely agreed monetary constraints conform to a standard that no one has deliberately distorted. That is why conforming to monetary rules is not a matter of costs and benefits. Rather, it is an internalisation of social rules.

The philosopher Georg Simmel aptly highlighted the theoretical traps hidden within the idea of confidence. These are traps that economists, as well as economic actors, completely conceal. They content themselves with asserting that we need confidence in order to keep business moving! This is unsurprising. After all, in the idea of confidence we touch on the mystery of the mimetic process of money's self-creation, unknown to the individual subjects who participate in it. As we have shown, this is an abstract process. But an excessive stress on the abstraction of the mimetic model, and thus on the 'arbitrariness' of fiduciary money, can itself unleash the forces of desire for money: forces which endanger the monetary order.

For Simmel, the foundation of confidence goes far beyond economic determination by money.[32] The very existence of fiduciary money depends on a belief in the free monetary order. Money is the symbol of modern civilisation: of its spirit, its forms and its thinking. The monetary order has a moral basis. Its virtue is in its capacity to contain the tensions, frustrations and rivalries that a competitive society of free individuals produces. Its virtue is that it avoids the formation of any arbitrary power; that is, the excrescence of financial powers that could subvert monetary discipline in order to create unearned income and finally destroy liberal society itself.

This moral conception of monetary legitimacy is shared by the whole of the Austrian school, which has exercised significant influence over monetary doctrine in the German-speaking countries since the end of the nineteenth century. For these economists, money is the pivot of the economy, and it must be morally internalised as legitimate. This is why these thinkers are violently opposed to the assertion that money is neutral. Ludwig von Mises saw the quantitative theory of money as a heresy, while Friedrich Hayek emphasised the falsity of the claim that changes in the quantity of money do not affect relative prices.

32 Georg Simmel, *The Philosophy of Money*, London: Routledge and Kegan, 1978.

Nonetheless, these economists denied money any political legitimacy. The Austrian current had its roots in Germanophone philosophical thought dating back to Immanuel Kant and Johann Gottlieb Fichte at the end of the eighteenth century. It continues into our time through German ordoliberalism. For this philosophical current, a society's most robust cohesive forces are those that have been internalised in moral commandments. These commandments are the cement of the monetary economy, for they are incorporated into individuals' beliefs and reactivated in the symbol of a people united by a culture forged through history. In Hayek's work, this moral conception of money leads to a radical critique of public monetary institutions. This is expressed in his advocacy of the free banking principle, and thus of the abolition of central banks. In this conception, the monetary hierarchy can be abolished as soon as the money's legitimacy becomes universally accepted. A higher form of money is, without doubt, indispensable; but it does not have to be managed by a central bank that stands above the banks in a hierarchy and imposes rules upon them. If the banks are moral, then any excessive desires for liquidity will be self-restraining. It is sufficient, therefore, to encourage the emergence of a higher form of liquidity that everyone accepts. Of course, this higher form of liquidity is gold. The demands for convertibility that creditor banks make to debtor banks will be settled in gold. So, is this sufficient? Is a system of free banks viable?

Simmel was pessimistic in this regard, albeit in a different sense to Keynes. The latter, as a citizen of the twentieth century, doubted that the free monetary order would be able to withstand the rise of two types of antagonistic social forces: the financial powers that sought the infinite accumulation of wealth through liquidity, and the social demands carried forth by new collective forces. For Keynes, the monetary order could not be safeguarded by money alone; it would require state regulation.

Simmel was a contemporary of the classical era of capitalism. He observed the development of technological civilisation made possible by the universalisation of money. Individuals become more and more dependent on the objective constraints of credit at the same time as their subjective universe explodes traditional barriers. The monetary abstraction allows everything to be quantified, because it denies the subjective and the singular. Money allows individuals to realise their own aims through impersonal means. But this creates an irreducible tension in the formation of desires: a tension between the singular and the universal, between the subjectivity of promises and the objectivity of constraints. From here emerges Simmel's imperious conception of ethical confidence, which he shared with Carl Menger and the Austrian school.

If money is not to appear as an arbitrary convention – and therefore an unreliable one, liable to capture by partisan authorities – the monetary order must be essentially ethical. A moral judgement on what produces social cohesion allows us to arrive at an explanation far better than any rational cost–benefit analysis. What is the performative capacity of a moral rule? A moral rule is an obligation that avoids the endless mirroring effect that results from the strategic interplay among different actors (I act in accordance with how I think you think I will act, and so on). Three conditions must be satisfied for this to work. Firstly, the rule must specify the appropriate conduct in situations specified by the rule. Secondly, the subject must feel obliged to follow the rule after identifying that she is indeed facing one of these situations. Thirdly, she must feel satisfaction in conforming to the rule, and dissatisfaction in not conforming to it.

Herbert Frankel attempted to reconcile the two conceptions of confidence: the ethical foundation, as according to Simmel, and the political foundation, as according to Keynes.[33] An author of the contemporary period, Frankel underlined the fact that the transformation of financial structures has itself driven considerable social change. The generalised rise in indebtedness seems irrepressible, and public finance has now assumed decisive importance. This poses crucial questions: can debt be infinitely accumulated, and can it be financed indefinitely through ultimate money creation by central banks? Do different principles apply to the settlement of public debts as compared to private debts? These questions make one thing clear: that we must unavoidably address the political dimension of all this. It is possible to draw a link between the moral and state dimensions of

33   Herbert Frankel, *Money: Two Philosophies: The Conflict of Trust and Authority*, Oxford: Blackwell, 1977.

money, which interact in the relationship between individuals and the nation. In order to make this link, we need to mobilise the concept of sovereignty.

In a previous collective work, we articulated the question of confidence in money by breaking it into three hierarchically organised forms.[34] The highest form is *ethical confidence*. This makes the monetary order a set of civic rights and responsibilities. It also expresses democratic sovereignty, which in turn establishes a *hierarchical confidence* in the public institution responsible for the integrity of the payment system. This second form of confidence reinforces the importance of individual conformity to the monetary order. Accepting this conformity simplifies individual choices, as is apparent in the routine or *methodical confidence* through which the promises arising from day-to-day credit relations are managed. Methodical confidence is founded on repetition. However, if we are to gain a proper understanding of the hierarchy between these three forms of confidence, we need to mount a deeper investigation of the concept of debt, and to grasp its profound relationship with sovereignty.

34 Aglietta and Orléan (eds), *La monnaie souveraine*.

2

Logics of Debt and Forms of Sovereignty

The first chapter showed us that money is a relationship between the individual and the collective, and that all money is a kind of debt. It follows from this that not all debts are of the same character. In studying money as a system of rules, we showed how the settlement of private debts is realised in the horizontal dimension of payments. But we also showed that in seeking to define confidence in money, we cannot overlook the vertical dimension of belonging to the 'social whole' – the dimension that we identified in terms of ethical confidence. If we assert that 'money represents the wholeness of society', to what logic of debt does this proposition correspond? In the introduction to a recent collective volume,[1] Bruno Théret re-examined the proposition that we had ourselves elaborated in *La monnaie souveraine* in 1998: that of a *life debt* which defines the relationship between a society's members and this society as a whole, considered as a sovereign power. This position has been sharply criticised by certain anthropologists.[2] It is important, therefore, to reassert how essentially important this hypothesis is to monetary theory.

1   Bruno Théret (ed.), *La monnaie dévoilée par ses crises*, Paris: Éditions de l'EHESS, 2007.
2   Notably Alain Caillé, 'Quelle dette de vie?', in *L'Homme*, no. 162, April–June 2002, pp. 242–54.

VERTICAL DEBTS: LIFE DEBT, INHERITED DEBT, SOCIAL DEBT

Life debt is inscribed in the course of time. In status societies that do not have a state, this is a debt transmitted through descent. In societies that do have a state, which postulate legal equality among individuals, it is a debt identified with citizenship. In any case, the debt is the counterparty to the attributes of the collective; it is a debt to the sovereignty of the 'social whole'. At an individual level, it exists from birth. It is a debt to the sovereign, and is contracted as the counterparty to the collective inheritance without which it would be impossible to live in society. It is also transmitted as an inheritance, passed on from one generation to the next. This debt is inalienable because it is a one-way street. It is impossible to pay this debt back to the generation that earlier bequeathed it. Society's wealth (be it material, cultural or cognitive) is always handed down from the generations of the past. This wealth is maintained and accumulated through the recognition of the active generations' own life debt, and then passed on to the generations that follow.

This debt is inalienable because it has its counterparty in the intergenerational collective that produces the one-directional social time from which confidence in the permanence of the society results. Throughout individuals' lives, this debt must necessarily be recognised. Its forms depend on the type of sovereignty prevalent in the society concerned: it can mean sacrifices to gods, offerings to the ancestral generations, taxes to the state, or the transfer of assets to the following generation, whether in the familial form of inheritance or the socialised form of retirement savings. Vertical debt is thus linked to the society's endurance over time.

It is precisely the fact that life debt is fundamentally inalienable that allows it to mediate the relationship between money and sovereignty. Life debt is aptly named, because it pledges allegiance to the absolute sovereignty that is death. Death is the absolute creditor of life debt, for every human recognises it as the supreme power. The political sovereign, on the other hand, represents the immortality of society in the face of the mortality of that society's members.

Vertical debt stands opposed to a horizontal debt, which is based on reciprocity. Horizontal debt is alienable, and thus it can be transferred to third parties in the form of gifts and counter-gifts, or commodities through the payment system. The distinction between the forms of exchange is of less importance than the opposition between the alienable and the inalienable. Moreover, the exchange of gifts and counter-gifts is always susceptible to transform into bargaining. Life debt allows us better to understand the symbolic sources of ethical confidence. The 'social whole' is a system of relations that confers protection on individuals, allowing them to maintain their living conditions; it is endowed with a productive power that perpetuates society over time.

Unlike horizontal debt, which is contractual, life debt is a pact devised in opposition to death. It stands at the foundation of sovereign authority. This is a pact that spans history. It is experienced as an authority that legitimises the power of the political and religious institutions that have the authority to order the repurchase life debt. This is a fundamental point. Even in secular, 'modern' societies that have broken with any belief in the link between the dead and the sacred, sovereignty nonetheless transcends the state institutions that it legitimises. Sovereignty, as we shall see, takes the form of a constitutional order that legitimises the state. Individuals experience this link to the sovereign – be it divinity, money or the nation – in the form of a symbol. This has very important consequences for our understanding of the monetary order. Because money emanates from sovereignty, it is not a creature of the state. Yet it does entertain close and organic relations with this latter.

The symbol, which is the source of ethical confidence, does not obey rational criteria. In this regard, it stands opposed to the linguistic signifier. The symbol is a focus of emotionally charged images, a field of metaphorical substitutions and analogies that must constantly be remade in order to demonstrate the otherness of the collective in relation to the individual. We can thus arrive at a deeper view of money's ambivalence. In the horizontal dimension of the payment system, the monetary constraint imposes the formal logic of equivalence. In the vertical dimension, in which one's relationship to the 'social whole' takes the form of absolute liquidity, what commands respect is instead the analogous logic of the symbol. As we accumulate absolute liquidity, we symbolically experience the feeling of possessing a fraction of the collective. This is a logic of disproportion, which can only be maintained if sovereignty is kept at a distance, by way of the rituals constructed and practised by political and religious institutions. Faced with the absolute desire for liquidity, monetary rituals – also called monetary doctrines – function according to the principle of repression [*refoulement* – that is, in the psychological sense]. However, during crises, as we will see, the weakening of monetary rituals brings back to the surface all that has been repressed.

VERTICAL DEBTS IN CAPITALISM AND IN ECONOMIC THEORY

How does contemporary economic theory treat vertical debt? Most modelling does not address it at all. We can just assume that individuals go on living indefinitely! The problem is left entirely to one side. Life debt results from the opposition between mortality and immortality. Immortal individuals can seal contracts *ad infinitum*. For such individuals, there exist nothing but horizontal debts. We can thus overlook the irreducibility of the collective – which is to say, we lose it in the forest of implicit contracts.

The models most often used to deal with the effects of economic policy have a single representative agent who makes rational predictions and has an infinite horizon. In order to give these models a semblance of realism in relation to the various situations to which they are applied, echoes of the collective are parachuted in, albeit without any theoretical justification, under the name of 'friction'. We end up with a theoretical concoction that can only be deemed conceptually absurd. For these models are constructed precisely on the basis of the hypothesis that the collective does not exist. This is what the theoreticians of pure economics call the microeconomic foundations of macroeconomics. For them, there is no sovereignty other than individual sovereignty. Is it really so surprising, then, that their models have proven incapable not only of predicting the financial crisis and its long-term repercussions on Western economies, but of analysing the latter?

More interesting are so-called overlapping generation models. These models recognise that individuals are mortal and analyse the economic relations between generations. Private credits cannot be transferred between successive generations, because the debt that an active generation contracts from a retired generation will never be repaid – for, by the time it can be repaid, the retired generation will have died away. Private financial relations are insufficient to making the generations overlap. There must necessarily be some non-contractual body able to stand in for the deficient contractual relations. And this 'technical' solution is liquidity. Young people sell the production surplus (relative to their present consumption), in exchange for money. When they are old, they buy the goods that they need. Money is thus the intergenerational bond that guarantees the immortality of society.

But what is the nature of this unanimous (and thus non-contractual) recognition, in an economy that is exclusively founded on contracts, precisely because it rejects the hypothesis that society pre-exists individuals (and thus their opportunities to establish contracts)? If one generation accepts money, then what certainty does it have that the generation will be willing to accept it? If the active generation expects that by the time it reaches old age the following generation may not accept money, then an autarchic economy will emerge, separating the generations. This is not, however, the case if there exists some sovereign authority to which all generations are indebted. Let us call this authority the state, as the provider of the public services that allow for society's continued existence. Adult individuals honour this debt in the form of taxes payable in money. The acceptance of money by all generations is thus guaranteed. But ultra-liberal theoreticians reject this solution, which presupposes the collective. Only one possibility remains: to admit the existence of an indefinite chain, spanning the generations, of belief that money will be accepted in the future. But by no means is this chain a contractual matter. The chain of belief is in fact market society in its totality. Liberal thinking, however, is unable to accept this possibility.

Overlapping generation models, constrained by the parameters of liberal thought, thus refuse to go this far. Instead, they purport to offer a technical solution. The indefinite acceptance of money, they claim, is an equilibrium that is justified by the self-realisation of beliefs. Once again, a self-referential logic is called into play. The desire for money is unanimously shared, without reference to any social body that stands above individuals. Money is just accepted ... because it is accepted! It corresponds to a counterfactual, reflexive time: 'If I know that money will be accepted in exchange tomorrow, it is in my interest to accept it today.' That all seems just fine. Yet if the acceptance of money is self-fulfilling, then so, too, is its rejection. A non-monetary equilibrium is equally possible. Simply to invoke the existence of a self-referential logic does not allow us to say why a monetary logic, as opposed to a non-monetary one, is realised. Indeed, this overlooks the fundamental point: what Jean-Pierre Dupuy calls self-transcendence. In overlapping generation models' monetary-equilibrium 'solution', money has to make its entrance at date t_0, as though parachuted in from the outside. This is indeed an absurd hypothesis if we refuse to accept that money is the institution of collective belonging that lies at the foundation of value.

Nonetheless, despite falling short in all these ways, the overlapping generation model does implicitly reflect one fundamental reality: the bond between money and death. Money is necessary because individuals die. Death introduces a distance between human subjects and society. This distance is the foundation of a hierarchy of values that asserts the primacy of the collective over individuals. Yet overlapping generation models are happy to make death into a banality: just another technical constraint. Because of death, individuals cannot all simultaneously be present on the market, even by way of their expectations. These models result, therefore, in a purely instrumental conception of money, and hence contribute nothing to what the naturalist theory of value already proposes. They are internal to its normative project of rendering the economy completely autonomous from society.

Now we can leave aside theoretical models, and concern ourselves with a question of much greater importance: namely, the modernity of capitalism in relation to so-called archaic societies. In these latter societies, offerings, sacrifices, and ceremonies held to mark socio-cosmic cycles express the collective force that enables life to continue. The living are thus obliged to purchase the conditions for their collective survival from the sovereign powers – which is to say, from their divinities and ancestors. But this series of purchases never pays off the original debt that constructs this sovereignty in the first place and

cements the social relations it underpins. In such societies, the hierarchy of values separating the human and the superhuman provides the
basis for society's existence and maintains its cohesion.

Capitalism inverts this order's values. Life debt continues to determine the foundations for our conceptualisation of money. But modernity does not recognise this. The unity of debt with regard to the
collective breaks down into two parts: private debts of an economic
character and a social debt of a political character. The social debt no
longer appears as a debt that the living owe to society's sovereign
powers, but instead as a debt that the state owes to individuals *qua*
subjects of law. In this order, individuals are bearers of social rights,
and thus creditors to the state.

The reason for this mutation is a centuries-long revolution in the
hierarchy of values. In traditional societies, the totality resides in the
principle of the reproduction of society. The superior values are collective ones, to which individuals are subordinate. In modernity, the ultimate value is the human person as a juridical entity. But the authority
on which this value is based – the universal community of human
beings – has no sovereign institution to represent it, and to ensure that
this universal community is recognised as a legitimate foundation.
This authority exists instead in the territorial space of nations, in the
form of political power framed by a constitutional order. Yet the space
in which private debts circulate does not coincide with the space in
which the rights representing the social debt are recognised.

Modern money is the primary mediator between the economic
and political logics that make up the two sides of debt. Money expresses
society's judgement on the wagers made by private agents in the
payment system. It is also the basis for transfers and deductions, which
themselves pertain to the political values of citizenship as a form of
social belonging. The dissociation between these two logics sets them
in conflict, which grants money as an institution a unique position.
On the one hand, it is allied to political authority, albeit without merg-
ing into it. On the other hand, it has to establish its own hierarchical
superiority over private finance, so that it can hold the desire for
liquidity in check. This particular position is juridically recognised
through the independent status granted to central banks. However, in
no sense does a juridical position equate to legitimacy. The answer

provided by overlapping generation models – namely, that of equilibrium – is of no practical consequence. Here again we find the need for ethical confidence and its symbolic roots, which have the virtue of making the 'social whole' opaque in the eyes of the members of society. This opacity sets the collective at a distant, higher level. This is the only strategy for holding back the corrosive power of self-referentiality unleashed by the desire for liquidity. Keynes's genius was that he drew the political lessons of money's ambivalent character.

LIFE DEBT IN ANTHROPOLOGICAL DEBATES

An incursion into political philosophy has provided us with the concept of life debt, which allows us to make sense of the individual's relationship with the collective. Let us remind ourselves of the essential conclusion that we have drawn. Because of its inalienable nature, life debt mediates the relationship between money and sovereignty. The sovereign is the representative of the immortality of society: it is the absolute lender of life debt, because every human recognises death as the supreme power. In the market universe, life debt (vertical debt), owed to the sovereign, is distinct from and opposed to the private debts (horizontal debts) that make up a system of equivalences. Money is the institution that mediates between these two kinds of debt.

There have been lively, even bitter, debates among anthropologists as to the nature of life debts. Why did Alain Caillé's fundamentally important reading of Marcel Mauss's *Essai sur le don* lead him to a virulent critique of the notion of life debt?[3] The reason was the preponderant influence exercised by Claude Lévi-Strauss for some four decades on account of his renowned work on the elementary structures of kinship. When Lévi-Strauss proposed that the prohibition against incest was a founding norm for humanity, he portrayed the exchange of women through matrimony as the principal relationship by which societies are structured. For Lévi-Strauss, the exchange of women was logically primary to the universal principle of gift and

---

3   Marcel Maus, 'Essai sur le don: Forme et raison de l'échange dans les sociétés archaïques', *Année sociologique* (1923–24), republished in Marcel Mauss, *Sociologie et anthropologie*, Paris: PUF, 1973.

counter-gift. His theory of matrimonial alliances opposed the theory of descent, and thus opposed horizontal debt to vertical debt.

It was Annette Weiner, in 1992, who re-established the duality of the debts produced by the social bond.[4] According to Weiner, ethnographic studies show that all known human societies distinguish alienable goods from inalienable ones. The former are traded, while the latter are transmitted from one generation to another.[5] Weiner emphasises that Mauss himself distinguished between two types of goods. Some goods were the basis for gift exchange – defined by him as the obligation to give, receive and return – while others stood outside of any exchange relation. Mauss did not push this distinction any further because he was purely interested in exchange.

In the context of the Melanesian societies observed by Weiner, inalienable goods do not leave the line of descent. Such goods provide the descent group with its identity, its ancestors, and its inheritance. Alienable goods, on the other hand, circulate. While inalienable goods are vertical goods, structuring the social relation of kinship between successive generations, alienable goods (including women in matrimonial exchanges) are situated on the horizontal axis of exchange. Relations of exchange and continuity, the basis for identification, together make up the social bond within which individuals move. In this research, Weiner returns to the late nineteenth-century origins of anthropological studies of kinship, in the writings of Lewis Henry Morgan,[6] to argue that lines of descent and marriage alliances make up part of the social bond. Each individual contracts a life debt with regard to those who have set her in a relation of descent. This is a vertical debt; it is a debt owed by subjects to the group. If this group is incorporated into a wider social structure united by sovereignty, then this life debt *is contracted with regard to the sovereign itself.* Life debt is the counterparty of a cultural and social inheritance, which is

4   Annette Weiner, *Inalienable Possessions: The Paradox of Keeping-While-Giving*, Berkeley: University of California Press, 1992.

5   This anthropological controversy is examined by Jean-Pierre Warnier, 'Alliance, filiation et inaliénabilité: le débat sur le don à la lumière de l'anthropologie de la parenté', *Sociétés politiques comparées*, no. 11, January 2009.

6   Thomas R. Trautman, *Lewis Henry Morgan and the Invention of Kinship*, Berkeley: University of California Press, 1987.

always-already there at the time the subject is born. No society can persist in the absence of this inheritance, which it must maintain and develop through the life achievements of its individuals. The life debt (or inherited debt), as we have seen, can never be settled, because it works in only one direction and because its counterparties are inalienable goods. It can only be honoured in the sacred rituals specific to the society in question, which are transmitted to the next generation. Life debt, therefore, structures the course of time. It integrates so-called archaic societies – that is, societies without a state – into the socio-cosmic cycle. The life debt inscribed in lines of descent distinguishes such societies from ones in which sovereignty is centralised in a separate political power.

There remains the question of the logics of exchange: the logic of gift and counter-gift, as against the logic of market equivalence. According to Stéphane Breton, the exchange of gifts and counter-gifts constitutes a form of service to the collective.[7] Here, money establishes social value by way of status. It is, indeed, the symbol of a social relation. But the acts thus signified are not thereby stripped of their multiplicity. On the contrary, they come to bear the social attributes of individual persons. Fetishism resides in the hypostasis of symbols. When the social bond is obscured by personal prestige, money takes on the mystifying form of individual persons. The exchange of gift and counter-gift is concealed by the greatness of whoever is doing the giving. It follows from this that debt is not a freely consented relation between individuals. Rather, debt is ontological, constitutive of the obligation to give.

The second logic is that which dominates today – the logic of equivalence, as was explained at some length in Chapter 1. Money establishes social value through equivalence. The exchange of equivalents presupposes the existence of a homogeneous space of commensurability, within which social acts are objects evaluated by a common standard of measurement. This homogenisation process is at the origin of the fetishism exposed by Karl Marx in which social relations take the form of relations between things.

7   Stéphane Breton, 'Monnaie et économies des personnes', introduction to special issue of *L'Homme*, no. 162, 'Question de monnaie', April–June 2002.

THE PRIMACY OF ETHICAL CONFIDENCE AND THE LEGITIMACY OF MONEY

At the end of Chapter 1, we defined the three hierarchically organised forms of confidence that exist in market societies. These are: methodical (or routine) confidence in the reciprocity of private debt contracts; hierarchical confidence in the authority of the institution that issues money (today, the central bank); and the ethical confidence through which citizens recognise the cohesive power of the monetary order as a whole. Max Weber, conversely, aptly noted the way in which the self-referentiality of the market in fact eroded social cohesion. For Weber, this process took the form of the 'disenchantment of the world'. The instrumentalisation of money goes hand-in-hand with the unleashing of individual desires for liquidity. The modern collective value able to challenge this is the *political autonomy of the nation*, conferred on what becomes a *national currency*.

Within the payment system, hierarchical confidence is founded on the central bank's superior position in relation to the settlement of banking debts. Commercial banks are subordinate to the central bank because they collectively benefit from its guarantee that it will preserve the payment system from the risk of a chain of failed settlements. This is the origin of what is called the function of the lender of last resort. This function is a collective insurance, which is of greater benefit to the banks than the other actors in the economy. In return, the banks are obliged to insure their clients' individual deposits up to a legal maximum. In this way, hierarchical confidence completes and, during phases of financial tension, supplants methodical confidence.

On the register of private debts, the essential dimension of methodical confidence is that it offers security. This form of confidence results from the repetition of the acts which bring exchanges to their proper conclusion, and which bring private debts to settlement. Methodical confidence emerges within market practices on account of the repeated realisation of business relations between the same partners. It operates in various different ways: in the mutual respect of agreements, in the group mentality that facilitates loss-sharing and collective support in situations of vulnerability, and in the acceptance of regulation that limits risk exposure (position limits and margin calls on the markets). In short, in all of the practices that go against the liberal *doxa* of transparency and maximum competition. Such practices are based on the same logic: that of confidence in the objectivated rule, which conceals the authority that enunciates this rule. The objectivation of the rule puts it out of reach, creating the perception that it is a natural reality. Methodical confidence thus relies on the regularity of transactions and can be characterised in terms of a loss of distrust that stems from the repetition of acts and relations which can be assumed to be secure. This form of confidence is purely procedural; it does not entail any moral attitude with regard to others.

In the modern world, our highest moral values invoke the integrity and wellbeing of the human person. This promotion of human rights has combined with the autonomisation of the market economy, for better or worse. For, within the logic of the market, the human person has no ontological foundation. Rather, she is conceived as a projection of her own becoming, in her pursuit of a constantly-deferred future happiness. The disenchantment of modern societies flows from this. The pursuit of wellbeing is an 'ought' that is internalised in individual reason; it is therefore an ethical attitude. But the projected liberation of the subject is threatened by uncertainty over the future. This enslaves the subject to a self-referential logic, by way of the frenzied search for liquidity. An ethical confidence founded on the supremacy of human life can avoid this abyss of self-referentiality by affirming the primacy of the struggle to keep death at bay. Today, we face the threat that climate change will produce a civilisational collapse at some undefined future point. Recognising as much could be the basis for an ethical conscience that is able to block the markets' rush toward the abyss over the coming decades. The archaic and the modern unite at this unmentionable blind spot. If we are to go further in our understanding of ethical confidence, we must now turn to the links between money's legitimacy and forms of sovereignty.

THE PRINCIPLE OF SOVEREIGNTY AND THE LEGITIMACY OF MONEY

How can we bring this conceptualisation of confidence to bear on the representation of monetary sovereignty? Over the long course of history, various different forms of sovereignty have existed. But the sovereign's position within the 'social whole' has always represented that of a radical caesura between mortality and immortality. These forms of sovereignty have included: the holy as consubstantial with nature; the ancestral; the divinely transcendent; the absolute monarchy based on divine right; the symbolism of the homeland that unites a people; and the constitutional order of the nation. In any case, what produces institutions endowed with the powers to regulate society is the fact that society is something other than the aggregate of its members (society is neither a sum of individuals nor a system of relations between individuals). And money is the most eminent of these institutions.

The great transformation of human societies, in the leap from the logic of the sacred to the logic of equivalence, arises as we become more distant from the sacred (Figure 2.1). This process represents the autonomisation of the political and of civil society. Its material basis is the building of cities, from Sumer onwards; it achieves its formal representation through the invention of writing and numbers. According to David Graeber, a movement of concentrated human settlement in Mesopotamia after 2500 BC gave rise to slavery, the foundation of the market.[8] Since its origin, the market has oozed violence. Slavery is the ultimate violence. Indeed, slavery strips human relations of all ethics. As Marx shows, wage labour was not so different in this regard, when it lacked the social rights later established in reaction to the violence of the market. For the capitalist, the choice between slavery and wage labour is merely a question of cost and profit. Besides, Western multinational companies still opt for slavery in numerous developing countries; can we really call forced child labour by any other name? In Sumerian times, the movement towards sedentarisation, through urbanisation and the regrouping of populations, encouraged the development of the state, which concentrated military force for the purposes of waging war. This took place concurrently with the development of market commodities, which included women's bodies.

Of course, such market practices are not consistent with the theory of pure economics. Pure economics stands at a distant from market practices and their excesses. But these latter can be interpreted in terms of monetary economies. Only the power of an ethically

---

8   David Graeber, *Debt: The First 5,000 Years*, Brooklyn: Melville House, 2011.

enlightened state can contain these excesses; we will study the conditions under which democracy can produce such an ethics in Part II.

Through the institution of the political after the 'great transformation', and the division of labour that flows from it, sovereignty becomes a separate authority that dominates society. It stands in contrast to the multiplicity of social activities, yet reunites them through the logic of abstraction. Sovereignty, understood in this sense, delimits space ('us' versus 'others'), defends borders, establishes standards of measurement, identifies subjects, and counts objects on the basis of an institutionally established unit of account. The logic of equivalence is inherent to the political.

Services to the collective do not disappear, but change in nature. They take the form of tax obligations to the state (or tribute payments in empires), in return for the state's obligations towards its 'subjects': in other words, its expenditure on their protection. Money is the medium for the payments that make up social debt. The circulation of wealth becomes a double movement: a movement towards the centre of sovereign power, and away from it. Social differentiations take the corresponding form of large-scale classification, a process which is itself subject to monetary evaluation. Thus, in the Roman census, everything was valued according to a single standard, and everything from wealth to prestige and honour became commensurable and thus possible to exchange. Statuses were no longer anything but wealth gaps, established by way of a simplifying measure: the monetary unit.[9]

Money appears as the great identifier of wealth, for all wealth is only valuable by way of its capacity to transform into liquidity. But in an order in which politics is separate from and exercises power over society because it can invoke the will of the people, in what sense can money be declared sovereign? We will deal with the relations between the different forms of money across history, and across the transformations in such political systems, in Part II. But to conclude this first part, we must examine the meaning of ethical confidence in money a little further. What are the relations between the monetary order and

9   On this point, see the contribution by Jean Andreau, 'Cens, évaluation et monnaie dans l'Antiquité romaine', in Aglietta and Orléan (eds), *La monnaie souveraine*, pp. 213–50.

Figure 2.1

The autonomisation of the political

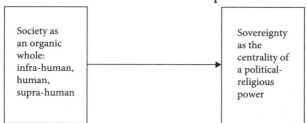

the political order in contemporary democratic societies? Is confidence in money politically produced?

First of all, we might note the homology that exists between political logic and monetary logic. Both logics define and guarantee standards: in the monetary order there is a single standard of value, while in the political order there are various standards of measurement. These logics differentiate the positions of individuals in society. In the monetary order, these positions are identified in the terms of the distribution of wealth; in the political order, they are identified in terms of the codification of knowledge through qualifications. These logics delimit the spaces of sovereignty: the space in which means of payment corresponding to the same liquidity circulate; the territorial space in which a monopoly of legitimate violence reigns; and the juridical space that determines who is part of the collective and who is excluded from it.

More fundamentally, the monetary order and the political order contribute to one and the same goal: that of social cohesion. In the former case, social cohesion implies the acceptance of monetary rules by the subjects of market exchange; for the latter, it implies citizens' adherence to the law. Let us hypothesise that in the contemporary world, the degree of social cohesion depends on the extent to which three goals are realised by monetary institutions and political authorities: namely, *stability*, *fairness* and *growth*. In order to achieve these goals, these entities must collaborate under the auspices of a single principle of sovereignty: that of the constitutional order. This detailed organisation of such relations between the political and monetary order is displayed in Figure 2.2.

The constitutional order incorporates and formalises the values that enable the members of a community to recognise one another as citizens of the same nation. The constitutional order feeds on symbols, which – through images, celebrations and commemorations, and more generally in the structures of human experience (language, religion, politics, mythology, art, law, political and legal institutions, and so on) – renew the mode of belonging that we call a people's culture. This culture sinks deep roots in history. The constitution formalises this reservoir of collective values in principles and norms that citizens accept *qua* members of a people that has instituted these same values and norms. This is the principle of sovereignty.

The constitutional order establishes the authority of the state as a public power, and the status of the central bank as a public institution that makes up part of the sovereign order. The debt of the central bank thus becomes the unanimously accepted superior liquidity. Because of this mutual dependence on the principle of sovereignty, the state and central bank are organically linked, even if public powers are organised so as to guarantee the legal independence of the central bank. The central bank's missions are inscribed within the aims of the nation, for which the state is responsible. The state guarantees the central bank's capital, and the central bank guarantees the predominance of public debt as a vertical debt – indeed, as the counterparty to collective wealth. This leads the central bank, quite legitimately, to remove public debt from the market in stress situations, where the liquidity-obsessed financial markets are no longer capable of producing differentiated evaluations of the different types of debts. A non-defaulting sovereign state's public debt is sheltered from default because the state has the ultimate capacity to monetise its debt. This is the *sine qua non* condition of sovereignty.

The state is, after all, the guarantee of the nation's cohesion over time, for it supplies the collective capital that provides public services. Public debt is honoured in the flow of taxes, whose legitimacy depends on the recognition of the common good. In a nation in which the state is not defaulting, the public debt results from an inter-generational transfer whereby the state takes on debts in order to provide public services, and thus to finance them through taxes deferred over time.

Figure 2.2
The sources of confidence in money in democratic societies

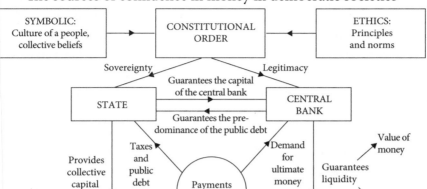

Public debt is the pivot of the payment system. This is because it is the most secure means of access to ultimate liquidity, through the deferral of settlement balances over time. There is thus a marked hierarchy in the forms of confidence in money described above. Ethical confidence is derived from the legitimacy of the central bank, conferred on it by the constitutional order. Hierarchical confidence, acting as the pivot of the payment system, is consolidated by the organic links between the state and the central bank. These links are themselves informed by the common aims of stability, fairness and growth. It is this institutional bedrock, and this alone – not any supposed intrinsic efficiency – that establishes the methodical confidence internal to finance.

Box 2.1
Teaching money

Money is an enigma, including for economists. The abundance of recent publications on money shows that the definition that is today common in the economics textbooks is not a satisfactory one if we are to understand money it in all its complexity. According to this definition, money was invented alongside the development of exchange in order to bypass the constraints of barter and to facilitate the rise of markets. Yet historical scholarship teaches us that the origin of money in fact goes much further back; money preceded and shaped the social order of exchange. The standard definition upholds a purely economistic vision of money, reducing it to three functions: that of a unit of account, an intermediary of exchange, and a reserve of value. Yet money is more than just an economic instrument. A study of money deserves to be enriched by insights from the human and social sciences more broadly. An institutionalist approach to money invites us to go beyond the economistic approach, taking the following eight points as a foundation:

Breaking with the Fables of Barter
Money is not a human invention designed to solve the problems of barter. It is not simply an intermediary of exchange developed to reconcile doubly coinciding needs. Money precedes the market. It stands logically prior to market relations, as a more fundamental social bond.

The word 'barter' is coloured by great semantic confusion. One common use of the word has nothing at all to do with market exchange. We use it to refer to mutual aid, or reciprocal exchanges of goods and services between people who know each other, and who are often linked by way of family, friendship or vicinity. This is a sort of informal exchange of gifts, which is of no concern for a theory of the market economy. We also encounter, however, the idea of a barter society: that is, a society of individuals who do not know each others' needs and desires, but who nevertheless develop a system of entirely decentralised exchanges able to realise the desires of all, through barter alone. Anthropologists tell us that no such society has ever been discovered. Barter cannot possibly be a principle of coordination for market societies. A third usage of the term 'barter' is with reference to market economies in which money already exists as a mode of coordinating exchange. Here, barter is a monetary exchange whose means of transaction are neither the official currency nor means of payment that can be converted into the official currency according to well-defined rules. In reality, this refers to exchanges in a fragmented monetary system, which accepts plural means of payment uncoordinated by formal convertibility with some superior means of settlement.

Money: A Relation of Belonging to a 'Social Whole'

Before it is an economic instrument, money is a social relation. It is an institution that perennially links the individual to society as a whole. Money institutes the relationship between the individual and the collective. It highlights the life debt borne by all members of a society towards the 'social whole'. This can mean either an inherited debt, in societies without a state, or a citizenship debt, in societies that do have a state.

The Increasing Dematerialisation of Monetary Supports

When we consider money as a unitary phenomenon across history, we can see that its different forms have evolved over time, in a process of increasing dematerialisation. This has not, however, changed money's deeper, underlying nature as a signifier of belonging to a social order or community. Traditional monies and what we might call 'paeleomonies', which were long supported by essential or ornamental goods, were first replaced by metal monies issued by sovereigns, and then by paper money. After that came scriptural money, recorded in the accounts of the banks, and then electronic and virtual currencies. These important monetary innovations succeed in inspiring confidence among their users, despite their increasing disconnection from any material basis. Confidence is thus at the heart of the monetary process.

Confidence, Legitimacy, Sovereignty

Money, as an institution, relies on the confidence of those who use it. It must be legitimate in their eyes. The sovereign, or the state, can play an active role in the institutional establishment of money, imposing its use (and taxing it) through the fiscal process. When the sovereign authority decrees that only unit of account X can be used to settle compulsory debts, agents are forced to procure this unit of account, encouraging its circulation. Hence, the fact that only one unit of account is legal tender constitutes the bedrock of monetary circulation. John Maynard Keynes himself foresaw this in the first pages of his *Treatise on Money* in 1930. Money operates like language: it renders values and debts commensurable by implementing an invariable standard of measurement. But the violence of the fiscal and legal process is not enough, for even when economic agents are compelled to use the official unit of account to settle their taxes and duties, they may consider it illegitimate. That is what happens, for example, in economies that are dollarised or subject to hyperinflation, when the national currency no longer inspires confidence and economic agents prefer some alternative currency or monetary sign.

The Hierarchy of the Three Forms of Confidence

We can identify three forms of confidence in market societies. Methodical or routine confidence relies on the repetition over time of actions that assure the realisation of exchange and the settling of debts on proper terms. This confidence is complemented by hierarchical confidence, which corresponds to the central bank or monetary authority's capacity to preserve the stability of the banking system and to guarantee the continuity of the payment system. Finally, ethical confidence concerns the cohesion and legitimacy of the values and principles at the basis of a sovereign society's constitutional monetary order. If one of these three pillars of confidence is eroded, the whole edifice can break apart or even collapse altogether. This means monetary crisis, which very often leads to political crisis.

Constitutional Order

Building confidence in money is a matter of essential importance. But such confidence always remains fragile and complex. Confidence cannot simply be decreed. To understand how it operates, we need to return to our initial hypothesis: that money institutes a relationship of social belonging. This relationship is established on the basis of the confidence that individuals place in a sovereign institution to unite them and guarantee the values, principles and norms of their community. It is confidence, therefore, that renders money an effective reality. Money draws its origins and strength from a community of cultural symbols and values. These are given juridical form, and the force of law, by the political and constitutional order. Confidence is more easily granted when a system of production is able to efficiently and fairly supply and share out the goods and services for which money will serve as counterparty.

Minting, the Creation of Money and Liquidity

The integrity of the payment system that structures the market is based on the articulation of three principles. The first principle is the existence of a common unit of account that allows wealth and debt to be evaluated. The second is the presence of a money-creation rule that organises access to means of payment. This rule differs across different payment systems. In modern economies, money appears in the credit operations that banks grant for the purposes of financing production. It is worth noting the exclusive character of the banking function: banks have the power to create money *ex nihilo*, which is to say in the absence of any prior resources or reserves. This power to create money is not unlimited, however. It is subject to both the need to obtain repayment from the borrower (hence the importance of evaluating borrower risk) and to the prudential regulation that imposes boundaries on banking practices. The third principle is that of the settlement of balances. In banking economies, money – created through the intermediary of credit operations – circulates by way of payment symbols which bear the mark of different banks. Banks accumulate debts to one another, whose overall sum is equal to the function of the exchanges between the different banks' clients. Provision must be made for the possibility of clearing the interbank balances so that this tangle of operations can be resolved. Indeed, it is vital to be able to turn to an instrument through which all debt relations can be evaluated and resolved. For this to be the case, there must exist a unique, unanimously accepted form of ultimate liquidity. Today, the supply of this liquidity is the exclusive prerogative of the central banks. The payment system is thus, necessarily, a hierarchically organised one.

Money and the Commons
Money is a common good. If it is deprived of this primary function, or if it is appropriated only by certain actors, the constitutional monetary order will be compromised and society will be rendered more fragile. Today, bank money has been diverted from its principal object: financing the real economy. According to studies by Philip Turner and the Bank for International Settlements, only 15 percent of banking credits serve to finance investment. In Europe, the euro no longer succeeds in incarnating a common project or any shared prosperity, due to its incompleteness and to the austerity policies associated with it. It is no surprise, then, that we are seeing the emergence of localised currency initiatives seeking to reappropriate money as a common good and reattach it to the ethical and community principles shared by its users. Here we can take the example of carbon currency. In connecting money to the major challenge of the energy transition, carbon currency constitutes a different, more global means of rehabilitating money in a way that enables it to serve the common good.

Part II

The Historical Trajectories of Money

In Part I, we saw that money is a total social phenomenon. This has been true throughout history. Wherever anthropologists have been able to discern something that we could call an economy, money existed. Money is universal and transhistorical. This would seem to make the description of its evolutions an impossible task. Can we produce a global history of money? No doubt we could, but this would be a collective and multi-disciplinary project. Of course, this is not the ambition of Part II, nor indeed of the parts that follow. Rather, Part II aims to use the tools of political economy to gain a deeper understanding of the fundamental concepts defined in Part I, whose relations make up the title of this book: namely, the relations between money and debt, and those between money and sovereignty.

In exploring these concepts, we will take as our foundation the theoretical elaboration developed in Part I, which presented money as the foundation of value. Here we can also invoke the authority of Frank Hahn, one of the most renowned theorists of money working within the naturalist theory of value. Hahn argued that the gap in the theory of value lies in its inability to account for the universal and enduring character of the phenomenon of money.[1] Part I echoed this critique and offered an alternative theory of value based on money. Part II seeks to show that this theory also provides us with a basis for the analysis of money's historical trajectories. Investigating this very

1   Frank Hahn, *Money and Inflation*, Oxford: Basil Blackwell, 1982.

long history may, additionally, enable us to find some bearings for the future. Is there a way of understanding money's metamorphoses that will also allow us to grasp the emerging forms of monetary creation? Which methodology should be adopted in order to do so?

STEERING CLEAR OF FORMAL MODELS OF HISTORY

The theorists of global history identify three key tendencies to avoid: the creation of ideal types, historical determinism, and institutionalism.[2] The first leads to the description of a multiplication process across history in which everything is unique, every development is contingent, and diversity can be explained through cultural factors alone. Conversely, historical determinism postulates that all existence and all transformation have a hidden rationality; nothing could have happened other than what has indeed happened. Institutionalism, finally, makes institutions the main generators of change and the sole means by which to understand the workings of history.

It is worth acknowledging that no formal model can be the be-all and end-all of our understanding of a phenomenon. The best thing to do is to adopt an evolutionary postulate. Starting out from our theoretical presuppositions regarding our field of investigation – in this case meaning the organisation of money – we can thus identify its tendencies. Avoiding any kind of normative drift, such as that evident in the equilibrium model of pure economics, we must accept that money's formal rules are inseparable from the social practices through which these rules are realised. These practices have varied significantly across history. Recognising this allows us to steer clear of the reflexively Western orientation formalised by the English liberal school from the seventeenth century onwards, the notion of a natural order that gave rise to the theory of equilibrium. Its historical success in the age of the gold standard was not, in fact, the end of history.

We have already outlined three postulates that will guide our historical investigation: (1) money resembles a language, the language

2 See the introduction to Philippe Beaujard, Laurent Berger and Philippe Norel (eds), *Histoire globale, mondialisations et capitalisme*, Paris: La Découverte, 2009.

of accounting; (2) money is a system, the payment system, which links it to technology; and (3) money is overseen by a principle of sovereignty that confers on it a common legitimacy within the space of sovereignty under consideration. Based on these conclusions, we can make three hypotheses, which will direct our course through the development of money across the extended *longue durée*. These hypotheses regard:

- The advancement of abstraction, according to the principles of monetary creation;
- Technological innovations in payment systems;
- Changes in the forms of confidence in money, in relation to the evolution of sovereignty.

Over the next two chapters, we will explore the foundations and historical trajectories of these interrelations. The first chapter works through a very long history, stretching from the foundation of agrarian states to the monetary order of the gold standard. We will not deal with stateless societies. In Chapter 2, we saw that the principle of equivalence that unifies a space of commensurability is not established in such societies. The use of money is instead differentiated according to personal status, and the intergenerational bond (life debt) responds to a principle of descent that stratifies societies into communities of belonging. It follows that the very meaning of history is not the same here as in societies where the autonomisation of sovereignty has set the sacred at a distance from material civilisation, in Braudel's sense. The subsequent chapter will deal with the upheavals of the twentieth century and the emergence of new forms of money.

But great historical transformations do not proceed without crises; indeed, it is precisely through crises that such changes occur. Monetary crises are particularly important moments in revealing the real nature of money, and especially its links with sovereignty. In this regard, we can turn to the collective work edited by Bruno Théret, *La Monnaie dévoilée par ses crises* ('Money Unveiled by its Crises').[3] Taking this same perspective, this two-volume work addresses a large number of

---

3 Théret (ed.), *La monnaie dévoilée par ses crises*.

monetary crises in both the distant past and our own contemporary era. In Part II, we will signal only those crises that precipitated major transformations in the trajectory of money. The logic of monetary crises and the regulations implemented across the different eras to keep them at bay – what we call monetary policies – will instead be studied in Part III. Finally, the trajectories of money cross both space and time. The interdependencies that are established by the rise of debts transcend the spaces of sovereignty through the generalised market universe called capitalism. They set these spaces in communication, often in a conflictual and uncertain manner. These interdependencies across capital markets, whose dynamic Fernand Braudel called 'the time of the world',[4] pose the enigmatic question of international money. Indeed, all money is founded on a principle of sovereignty, yet there exists no universal sovereignty. In Part II we will encounter the question of international money, before we deal with it more specifically in Part IV.

---

4 Fernand Braudel, *La dynamique du capitalisme*, Paris: Arthaud, 1985.

3

From Ancient Empires to the Gold Standard

The Foundation of Centralised Sovereignty:
Money and the State in the Agrarian Empires

At the end of the Neolithic period (4000–3000 BC), the population in Egypt and Mesopotamia became more densely settled, in a fertile space reduced in size by unfavourable climate change. The result of this change was desertification, outside of narrow strips of territory between the Tigris and the Euphrates, as well as along the Nile plain. According to Graeber, numerous nomadic populations came from the countryside to settle in these territories.[1] Wars broke out in the struggle to appropriate land. Groups centralised their resources for the purposes of war, giving rise to the form of organisation known as the state. Wars between states persisted up until sovereignty was unified in the form of the empire.

Centralised political sovereignty was manifest in the unification and codification of social belonging in both writing and in law (in Sumer from 3550–3000 BC, and in the Old Kingdom of Egypt from 3000–2700 BC). It seems that the principle of a socially valid measurement based on equivalence, as well as the invention of accounting – which was itself linked to the codification of property – were created

---

1   Graeber, *Debt*.

in these same eras. *The relationship of social belonging known as value was institutionally established.*[2] *Nowhere did it come from previously constituted markets.* However, it did allow for markets to flourish, thus conforming to the monetary theory of value. The private developed in the interstices of the public, on the basis of the public system of valorisation. Contrary to the assumptions of many economists ignorant of history – and thus of the scientific method in the social sciences – it was not the public realm, of which money was a part, that took form amid the incompleteness of market relations.

The first known units of account were the *shekel* in Mesopotamia and the *shat* in Egypt. These units of account were present in Mesopotamia as early as 3000 BC, on tablets covered in inscriptions allowing for accounting. They signalled the power of the central administration (the Palace). The accounting registers were kept by the top dignitaries in the Palace. They determined the rural communities' tax contributions and the redistribution carried out in name of the prestige of the empire. In the first chapter, we showed that the unit of account designates money as a numerical language of value. Legitimated by sovereignty, this language creates shared significations of belonging to society.

A sexagesimal numerical system was adopted in both empires. In Egypt, where gold was abundant, the *shat* was equivalent to 7.5 grams of fine gold. The multiple of the *shat* was the *deben* (90 grams of fine gold = 12 *shats*).[3] In the New Kingdom (1550–1230 BC), silver made its appearance as a monetary standard, while gold was reserved for exchange between kingdoms. A new unit appeared under the nineteenth dynasty, the *kite* (around a tenth of a *deben*). The *deben* and its subdivisions were perhaps also used as means of exchange. The price of goods indicates labour's very high value: a day of slave labour (in producing textiles) = 2 *shats* = a quarter of the value of a cow. So, we have some idea of the relations of exchange. Yet we know nothing of the fluctuations in the cost of living, since the papyri of these distant epochs were not conserved.

2   Jean-Jacques Glassner, *La Mésopotamie*, Paris: Les Belles Lettres, 2002.
3   François Daumas, *La civilisation de l'Égypte pharaonique*, Paris: Arthaud, 1987.

THE DEVELOPMENT OF EXCHANGE AND PAYMENT SYSTEMS

In first-millennium Egypt, silver bars and rings of 1 *deben* and 1 *kite* were used as means of payment. The use of silver rings as means of transaction – together with strips of copper – appeared as early as the New Kingdom. We can presume that this diversification was itself the counterpart of the diversification of exchanges now taking in ever wider and less wealthy strata of society. Payment was made with these pieces of metal – or rings made with these metals – which had to be weighed with each transaction. Indeed, before the Ptolemaic era, there was no monetary stamp on these metals to define their legal value.[4]

Morris Silver estimates that stamped silver metal guaranteed by the authorities may have been in circulation in Mesopotamia as early as the eighteenth century BC.[5] All the same, it remains doubtful that there existed struck and stamped precious metal up till the first millennium. Georges Le Rider indicates that in the neo-Babylonian and neo-Assyrian periods (609–539 BC and 704–612 BC, respectively), crude metals cut up into ingot-pieces served as means of payment in private transactions.[6] Silver was the primary metal used for money and copper secondarily so. As we have seen, gold – which was only in abundance in Egypt – served only for official exchange between empires.

Only cut-silver ingots have been found in sealed bags. The deposits in which we found these treasures would have been hoarded by rich Palace dignitaries. The existence of these pieces of metal, lacking a sovereign stamp, indicates that the creation of money – that is, the cutting of silver ingots – had multiple origins. These included the Palace, of course, but also the temples, and perhaps merchants as well. Indeed, from the beginning of the second millennium BC, tablets indicate that sealed bags of silver functioned as means of payment – but

4   Bernadette Menu, 'La monnaie des Égyptiens de l'époque Pharaonique', in Alain Testard (ed.), *Aux origines de la monnaie*, Paris: Éditions Errance, 2001, pp. 73–108.
5   Morris Silver, *Economic Structures of Antiquity*, Westport: Greenwood Press, 1995.
6   Georges Le Rider, *La naissance de la monnaie: Pratiques monétaires de l'Orient ancien*, Paris: PUF, 2001.

they do not mention this silver having been minted. Silver rings have been discovered that served as means of payment for lower-value transactions. But texts from the Akkadian Empire do not refer to hall-marks; the rings were weighed during the transaction. According to Jean-Jacques Glassner and other archaeologists, these means of payment have been discovered in the Ur royal tombs, and date back to as early as the middle of the third millennium BC.

In this intriguing arrangement, neither the weight nor the fineness of the means of exchange were authenticated *a priori* by hallmarks attesting to the existence of monetary standards. The only issuers could have been people close to the Emperor, respected temples, reputed merchants involved in the Assyrian trading circles of Cappadocia, or, in the seventh and sixth centuries BC, in the trade between empires, intermediated by the Phoenicians.

Beyond means of payment, from the beginning of the second millennium, Assyrian merchants in Cappadocia developed credit. Merchant guilds were institutions made up of family businesses. Clay tablets demonstrate the existence of credit, attesting to the practice of loans on interest and the use of bearer instruments.[7]

A BRIEF INCURSION INTO CHINESE ANTIQUITY

The Chinese tradition seems to have been very different. François Thierry refers to the existence of 'primitive' monies that took the form of spades, without any inscription.[8] These date back to the distant Shang era. Different monies appeared in the late seventh and early sixth centuries BC, in the Spring and Autumn period. These monies were issued by the sovereigns of the Warring States or by merchants. Contrary to the traditions of Egypt and Western Asia, the Chinese money issued in the Yellow River states was, from its first appearance, a fiduciary money. *Its purchasing power in an exchange was not linked to the weight value of the coins themselves.* That is why China was the first country in the world to be able to issue notes.

---

7   Klaas Roelof Veenhof, 'Modern features in Old Assyrian trade', *Journal of the Economic and Social History of the Orient*, vol. 40, no. 4, 1997, pp. 336–66.
8   François Thierry, 'Sur les spécificités fondamentales de la monnaie chinoise', in Testard (ed.), *Aux origines de la monnaie*, pp. 108–44.

The oldest coins (from 2700 BC) had no inscription of any kind. Then came coins vested with symbolic figures: first of all, the dragon – the figure of imperial dignity, fertility and creative energy. Yet inscriptions with the emperor's effigy, bearing the name of the reign and the year of minting, appeared only in 633 BC.[9] Coins became standardised as flat circles with holes that allowed them to be strung together by ligatures.

The Invention of Minting in Lydia

There is controversy over the exact date of the first minted coin bearing the sovereign's mark, though not over its location. Such coins first appeared in Sardis, capital of Lydia, Asia Minor, on the eastern shore of the Aegean Sea. The last two kings of Lydia, Alyattes (610–560 BC) and Croesus (560–546 BC) were responsible for this.[10] Coins were stamped in electrum (a natural gold-silver alloy), in an ore carried along by the river Pactolus. They bore one to three marks on the reverse, according to their weight and the metrological group to which they belonged. This money was *dokima*, meaning that it was legal tender. It was forbidden to weigh it and to verify its quality. It was thus a fiduciary money. Its legal tender applied not only in Lydia but also in all the Milesian cities subject to the influence of the Lydian kingdom. Thus the Lydo-Milesian monetary standard was established. As for the date of its appearance, the dominant opinion among archaeologists places this at around 580–575 BC, under the reign of Alyattes. At any rate, it was prior to the first Greek monies, which appeared around 550 BC.

MINTED MONEY AND THE ADVANCE OF ABSTRACTION

Of all the innovations in human history, minted money represented one of the most formidable. On one of their faces, coins were diverse: an abundance of monetary types was represented by all kinds of mythological symbols. But what they had in common were the marks

9   W. S. Ament, 'The Ancient Coinage of China', *The American Journal of Archaeology and of the History of the Fine Arts*, vol. 4, no. 3, 1888, pp. 284–90.

10   Olivier Picard, 'Les origines du monnayage en Grèce', *L'Histoire*, no. 6, 1978, pp. 13–20.

that they bore on the other side, which authenticated a numerical measure completely detached from the coins' weight. This established a set of purely quantitative relations between coins, which we call value ratios. Such ratios were decreed by the sovereign and stamped on the coins at the minting workshop, the public institution that minted money from the metals it was supplied.

These coins, as monetary signs certified by the sovereign, are defined by their anonymous circulation and their universal acceptability. From its very origin, the invention of legal tender represented a mutation of the political, for it enabled monetary reform. Disconnecting coins' nominal value from the weight and quality of the metals themselves enabled the sovereign to adjust the ratios between coins, since money remains *dokima* – that is, unanimously accepted by its users. It is evident that from its origins, the art of monetary policy has been an art of confidence.[11] In separating the sign (the quantum of value inscribed on the coin) from the thing signified (the weight and the fineness of the minted metal), *dokima* money transforms value into a purely social logic. The hierarchical confidence in the sovereign power allows for the reduction of the weight of metal contained in a coin, even while conserving its nominal value. A monetary reform could thus instantly change the value of debts.

The first known monetary reform was carried out by Hippias in Athens in 527 BC.[12] Seeking to increase the city's resources during its war with the Persian Empire, Hippias withdrew all legal money, reduced the official price of the metal supplied to the minting workshop, ordered a new type of money to be minted, and put new coins into circulation. This was the first stage of what would become a long-term practice, leading to what we will later call the 'hyperbola of money'. From this point onward monetary reform became a powerful tool of the state, just as it remains today.

According to Plutarch, however, it was Solon who carried out the first monetary reform. This was in Athens before the end of the sixth century BC, in an effort to alleviate the poor peasants' debts to the

11   Jean-Michel Servet, *Nomismata: État et origines de la monnaie*, Lyon: Presses Universitaires de Lyon, 1984.

12   Moses I. Finley, *Économie antique*, Paris: Éditions de Minuit, 1975.

landowners. According to Plutarch's account, Solon reduced the value of these debts by 30 percent by devaluating the drachma by this same proportion. The weight of silver worth seventy drachmae before the reform was worth one hundred afterwards. As compared to Hippias's reform – whose objective revolved around war – Solon's reform underlined the redistributive and social role of monetary policy. It was exactly the opposite of the postulate of neutrality that prevails in pure economics. If we follow Aristotle's reading, the establishment of *dokima* money allowed the social bond to be re-established, and this enabled the social crisis in archaic Greece's rural communities to be overcome. It was this reform that brought the Hellenic world into the era of the free trading cities that created democracy.[13]

Minting money also represented a direct tool of fiscal policy, by way of seigniorage. From its very origins, the invention of *dokima* money was linked to the transformation of political sovereignty. The kingdoms of Asia Minor and the Hellenistic cities were states with small territories, poor in agricultural resources and surrounded by great empires. In minting money, the sovereigns of Lydia sought to resolve both a political and a fiscal problem. While these states could not draw on any major tribute from agriculture, they had to bear an increasingly heavy military expenditure in order to preserve their independence from the threat of the Achaemenid Persian Empire. The monopoly on issuing money reinforced the kingdom's collective identity and centralised its capacity to acquire resources to finance the mercenaries called on to defend the kingdom, thanks to seigniorage. As we described in our accounting analysis in the first chapter (Table 1.2), the minting workshop collected a fiscal debt for state accounts among those buying money in exchange for metal. The state became the counterparty of all those who held money, on whom it imposed a tax levy. Beyond those who sought metal, the other contributors were merchant intermediaries of foreign trade. When they received money in crude metals or foreign monies, they had to convert it into legal tender in order to spend it in the kingdom itself. Seigniorage thus represented the primacy of legal tender over crude metal within the political space where it was established.

13   Louis Gernet, *Anthropologie de la Grèce antique*, Paris: Gallimard, 1968.

DIGRESSION ON MINTING IN THE ACHAEMENID PERSIAN EMPIRE

In 546 BC, Croesus was defeated by the Persian emperor Cyrus. The Achaemenid Empire imposed its authority over all of Asia Minor, as well as threatening Greece. The first Persian emperors after the conquest of Lydia were Cyrus (546–530 BC), Cambyse (530–522 BC), and most importantly Darius (522–486 BC). The Persian Empire was divided into two areas – the East and the West – separated by the Euphrates. In the East, there was no change in monetary practices. When Western monies arrived in the East, they were treated as bits of metal to be checked and weighed. The Persians thus respected that the communities they conquered would retain autonomy with respect to their internal affairs, including their local monies. In the Western part of the Empire, Darius played a crucial role in the history of money, carrying out the first royal mintage since the one inherited from Croesus. He created the gold *daric* and the silver *shekel*. The gold *daric* circulated across the whole Empire; the silver *shekel* remained a provincial money. The coins bore the image of the crowned king represented as an archer; four categories of coins corresponded to different representations of the archer-king.

This was a two-metal system. The Persians chose a fixed gold–silver ratio of 13/3 to 1, unlike in Egypt's twentieth dynasty (in the 1200s BC), where it was worth 2 to 1! The Persian ratio remained fixed for over two hundred years, while in Greece the relation between gold and silver fluctuated. This stability was doubtless the consequence of the relatively separate circulation of the *daric* and the *shekel*, which meant that monetary conversions were of little significance.

In the Persian Empire, as in a lot of empires that have succeeded one another throughout history, sovereignty was all-embracing. It left a lot of autonomy to the administrations of the collectivities that the Empire ruled over.[14] To this administrative decentralisation corresponded relatively autonomous monetary spaces. This relative segmentation was an effective mode of regulation, allowing empires to last for several centuries.

---

14 See the fundamentally important study, Jane Burbank and Frederick Cooper, *Empires in World History: Power and the Politics of Difference*, Princeton: Princeton University Press, 2010.

The *daric* was accepted very widely, not only in the immense Persian Empire but also outside of it. Its weight and quality were superior to those of other gold coins in the Mediterranean world. Its prestige was that of the Great King. Indeed, numismatists have found *darics* far and wide: in public treasuries in Asia Minor, in sanctuaries in Greek and Sicilian cities, and in private treasuries. Darics served as the vehicle for the Great King's gifts, guaranteeing him the allegiance of statesmen under his influence as well as foreign ambassadors. If the political function of money was dominant here, merchants also had an advantage when they carried out 'international' transactions in a money recognised as being of high value. In a sense, the *daric* was the first key currency in the sense that the US dollar is today.

Grandeur and Decline of the Hellenistic System

We cannot emphasise enough the importance to human societies of fiduciary money objectivated in the means of exchange. Hierarchical confidence – the belief in a social form of sovereignty deposited in the state – is tested and experienced in exchange, in the unconditional acceptance of minted money.

The invention of minting had enormous political implications. The most important of these, in the long term, was the advance of abstraction, through which the state united society by settling the social debt. The monopoly on issuing money reinforced the society's collective identity. The contradiction between the arbitrary power of the sovereign over money and the legitimacy of this power as acting in the name of the common good has traversed the history of Western civilisation. According to the theory of confidence presented in Chapter 2, the monetary order is closely linked to the political order; through this link, the hierarchical confidence in the state is subordinated to ethical confidence. On the contrary, monetary disorder always and everywhere equates to social and political disorder. In Athens of the fifth century BC, the great century of Pericles, and its decadence in the Peloponnesian War, provide a marvellous illustration of this proposition.

The city-states of ancient Greece struck different types of monies. The type of money was defined by the unit of account and by the number of hallmarks, which determined the value of the coin (subdivisions of the standard). In their rivalry with the Persian Empire, from 477 BC onwards, the Greek cities formed an alliance, the Delian League, through which most of the Greek cities rallied to Athens's political and monetary system. Unlike the Persians, who had allowed the subordinated local authorities to retain much autonomy, Athens's imperialism tended to centralise.[15] Athens imposed its standard measures on its subordinate allies. A monetary union was established on the basis of a silver-gold standard. Silver was the preponderant metal for money, thanks to the Laurion mines owned by Athens. The monetary pivot was the famous silver *tetradrachm* (which was 99 percent pure silver), imprinted with the emblem of the Pallas Athena owl, the City's protector. Athenian currency was *dokimon* – that is, legal tender – in all the League's cities.

Moreover, throughout the Mediterranean Basin, the silver *tetradrachm* circulated as an international trading money, in competition with the gold *daric*. *Money was a constituent part of the political system*. Its guarantee was not market exchange, but the law. In Athens's political constitution, money was the institution of the rule of law that guaranteed the uniformity of exchange relations among citizens. Thanks to the confidence the city inspired, it was able to undertake monetary reforms. After all, the rate fixed by law was accepted by its citizens. It was the city's political solidity that established support for the official mint, for merchants always had the possibility of comparing the official value of coins with the commercial value of the metal that they contained.

The uniformity of minting made it possible to levy customs taxes and to conduct controls on merchants. It seems that in fifth century BC Athens, a 5 percent tax was levied on minting. Added to this was the foreign exchange gain that resulted from the conversion into cash of all the metal accumulated through foreign trade. The exchange rates were set by the city magistrates, who determined the rate at which the city should accept foreign coins. Thus, Athenian money became the permanent regulation mechanism for a deficitary foreign

---

15   Olivier Picard, *Guerre et Économies dans l'Alliance Athénienne, 490–322 av. J.C.*, Paris: SEDES, 2008.

trade balance, whose counterparty was the tribute that the other cities paid to Athens.

Exchange rates thus had multiple highly developed functions. They simultaneously provided means of payment for merchants, the basis for one-way transfers and the vehicle for transfers of private wealth. Finally, they arbitrated between the diverse range of monetary types and metals in circulation. In short, the Athenian system was no less extensive than the eurozone, both in terms of its organisation of a monetary space with a single currency, and the international role that was thereby granted to money. But Athens, of course, had the enormous advantage of open political leadership. Nonetheless, the Athenian system was not immunised against what we have called (at the end of Chapter 1) the ambivalence of money. While the monetary order facilitates the rise of an international financial and commercial capitalism, it is corroded by the destructive force of a desire lacking in wealth. This contradiction preoccupied Aristotle to the highest degree.

ARISTOTLE'S THEORY AND THE TEST OF THE PELOPONNESIAN WAR

Aristotle was much preoccupied with the ambivalence of money. In his view, the social bond that money maintained was under threat from the private monopolisation of monetary wealth. The name Aristotle gave to the dark side of money – the insatiable accumulation of private hoards – was 'chrematism'.[16] As he argued, money was and had to be pure law. Chrematism perverted the authority of this law by unleashing the evil of private greed in opposition to the public good. According to Aristotle, the city was a web of reciprocal solidarities. Mutual exchange was the basic link in this web, and must not become a means of monopolisation that sets the citizens against one another. Yet the financing of maritime trade encouraged loan operations. The operations were sometimes secret, in the effort to avoid tax, allowing these loans to be sources of private monetary enrichment.

For Aristotle, the role of a universal standard of value was to evaluate each form of service at its 'just price' – in other words, to evaluate each citizen's contribution to the public good. Only the 'just price' protected social cohesion. It was necessary, therefore, to oppose any

---

16   Aristotle, *Nichomachean Ethics*, IV, 1119b.

market perturbation of this just price, for the reciprocal debt between citizens and the city was not to be fixed by the wandering course of the markets, but by politics. The political was to lead civil life; this meant that any arbitrary power was to be avoided. Here we can make out the very distant echo of the Freiburg School's ordoliberalism. Sovereignty stands over everything, for it is sovereignty that inspires the law, which must remain in conformity with the principles that founded the city.

In the political order, *dokima* money was inextricably bound to the public finances. In critical moments of waning political authority, the excess of state debts could lead to monetary reforms that were not universally accepted, for they damaged influential private interests. The city's political order would thus deteriorate and cause interlinked financial and monetary crises. In the ancient world, monetary difficulties could result from prolonged and exceptional military spending, military defeats and the loss of the territories from which metallic resources were extracted, as well as civil wars within the cities themselves. All of these situations could lead to a shortage of metal relative to the state's needs. But as long as the confidence in the state was not undermined, this did not lead to a self-referential monetary crisis – that is to say, a crisis sustained by individuals' simple quest to preserve their private wealth. All the same, pure monetary crises were possible under the influence of chrematism. Such crises caused shortages of liquidity on account of the cumulative monopolisation of liquidity as private wealth.

The great Athenian crisis of the late fifth century BC was caused by the long Peloponnesian War (431–404 BC), a war for hegemony that put the sovereignty of Athens in question.[17] The war opposed the oligarchic political regimes led by Sparta (and allied to Persia) to the democratic regimes of the Delian League, led by Athens. The first phase of the war, from 431 to 421 BC, was marked by attrition, as the two parties exhausted one another's resources. After some respite, the war resumed with the Athenian expedition against Syracuse between

---

17 Catherine Grandjean has studied the Athenian monetary crisis. Catherine Grandjean, 'Guerre et crise de la monnaie en Grèce ancienne à la fin du Ve siècle av. J.-C.', in Théret (ed.), *La Monnaie dévoilée par ses crises*, vol. I, pp. 85–102.

415 and 413 BC, which ended in failure. This failure began the final phase of the war, lasting from 413 until 404 BC, which concluded with Athens's final defeat after the Spartan forces occupied Attica, resulting in the loss of the Laurion mines and a maritime blockade, which cut off the grain route. The defeat in Syracuse weakened the Delian League. Athens was forced to mobilise its reserves through three extraordinary tax levies. The allies objected to paying the tribute. Seeking to deal with the silver shortage that had resulted from the loss of the Laurion mines, Athens decided to mobilise the gold offerings at the Acropolis in order to import grain and strategically important materials. Thanks to this mobilisation, between 411 and 407 BC the city got its house back in order.

But the decisive defeat was the elimination of Athens's fleet in 406 BC. In combination with fiscal pressures, this defeat broke the city's political unity. The landowners sought to make peace with the Spartan leader Lysander and to establish an oligarchic regime. The monetary crisis partly accounted for these political dissensions. After minted silver disappeared as a result of hoarding, it became necessary to mint bronze coins and try to have them accepted like the silver *tetradrachms*.[18] Implemented under constraint, this reform combined with a shortage of foodstuffs set off a rise in prices that in turn undermined confidence.

The Athenian democracy had to capitulate in March 404 BC allowing the opposition to mount a coup backed by Lysander. This was the era of the Thirty Tyrants, established under Spartan supervision and protected by a garrison that occupied Athens. This was a regime of terror, and it abolished the democratic institutions. Yet its exactions were so terrible that they set off an insurrectionary movement. The Thirty were rapidly chased out of power, opening the way to the resolution of the political crisis. The restoration of Athenian democracy allowed the city to pursue a deft diplomatic strategy that played on the divergences between Sparta and the Persians. The Athenians managed to overturn the alliance system. Allying with the

---

18 Martin Jessop Price, 'Early Greek bronze coinage', in Colin M. Kraay and G. Kenneth Jenkins (eds), *Essays in Greek Coinage, Presented to Stanley Robinson*, Oxford: Clarendon Press, 1968.

Persians, they were able to take back the Laurion mines and finance the resumption of the war in 394. By 377, Athens had recovered enough to be able to establish the second Delian League, a century after the first and a half-century after the outbreak of the Peloponnesian War.

Integrating bronze money would have represented an opportunity to develop the monetary system. Instead, however, a deflationist choice prevailed, as the bronze coins were demonetised and withdrawn from circulation. Fortunately, economic recovery was sufficiently rapid and prevented any long-term crisis in public debt – albeit not in the debts of peasants, artisans and small traders. The conservatism at the source of the city's sovereignty made its triumphant return, restoring the unity of the citizenry. As for the innovation of bronze money, it would reappear much later in Macedonia under Philip II, and then under Alexander III – known as Alexander the Great. After the conquest of Babylon in 331 BC, it spread throughout the whole Hellenistic empire, including Ptolemaic Greece. It would subsequently become a pillar of the Roman Republic's three-metal system: gold, silver and bronze.

Political Conflicts and Indebtedness in the Roman Republic
Confidence in money is essential to the construction of the state, standing separate from the particular interests of merchants. For such confidence to exist, the perception of money must become systemic: it must express a common sense of belonging linked to the state in question. This feeling cannot simply be taken for given, for there is a dialectical relationship between confidence and lack of confidence.

In Rome, the monetary system was hierarchical. Its pivot was the unit of account, borne by the minted coin. In the third century BC, in the era of the Punic Wars, this was the bronze *as*; under the Republic, the bronze *sesterce* (equal to 2.5 *asses*); under the Empire, the silver *sesterce* or its multiple, the *denarius* (equal to 4 *sesterces*).

In an era in which precious metals were scarce, the official monetary hierarchy could be challenged by the users of the coins. Users revalued and devalued certain coins, entering into conflict with the monetary authorities. Compromises were achieved through monetary reforms in which the authorities withdrew certain coins from circulation, carried out recasting, or even changed the unit of account. In 64 AD, Nero lowered the weight of the *aureus* from 1/42 *libra* (7.8 grams) of gold to 1/45 *libra* (7.4 grams) and the weight of the *denarius* from 1/84 *libra* (3.86 grams) to 1/96 *libra* (3.38 grams). In addition, he reduced the fineness of the silver coin from 98 to 93 percent fine silver. This reform enabled the multiplication of silver coins. Fears of a shortage of money allowed these new coins to be accepted in spite of the decrease in the coins' metal value. For, indeed, previous episodes had shown that a lack of money seriously disturbed everyday payments and even caused financial crises, because they prevented debts from being settled.[19]

THE FINANCIAL CRISIS IN THE SECOND PUNIC WAR (218–201 BC)
This episode was recounted by Titus Livius (Livy).[20] At the beginning of the war the monetary standard was the libral bronze *as*. By 217 BC it had become semi-libral. There came a rapid succession of devaluations, leading to the oncial *as* (1/12 *libra*) in 211 BC. These devaluations were prompted by enormous military expenditure, as Hannibal threatened Rome's very existence. The budget deficit surpassed three million *sesterces*. This was a case study for public debt crises resulting from wars – crises that would multiply throughout European history. To deal with it, the city of Rome borrowed private silver and suspended a number of payments, creating a forced debt that reverberated on creditors. The city also took exceptional measures, including leasing public buildings and warships, requisitioning Roman citizens' private wealth, and selling assets in the public domain. As the city was in danger, there was a frenzy of precious metal lending. These sums were reimbursed in three stages after the war, the third time through land concessions.

A triumvirate of magistrates was created in 214 BC to manage the state's debt and credit accounts, and then to register the repayments.

---

19 Jean Andreau has studied the crises and monetary reforms across the whole Roman period in comparative historical perspective. See Jean Andreau, 'Crises financières et monétaires dans l'Antiquité romaine entre le IIIe siècle avant J.- C. et le IIIe siècle après J.- C', in Théret (ed.), *La Monnaie dévoilée par ses crises*, vol. I, pp. 103–29.
20 Titus Livius (Livy), *History of Rome*, Book 27.

The climate changed from 207 BC onwards, after the victory over Hasdrubal in the Battle of the Metaurus, and private business recovered, allowing tax receipts to get back in order. Even though the war would drag on for six more years, state finances improved and the authorities could proceed with repayments.

CONFLICTS BETWEEN CREDITORS AND DEBTORS DURING
THE POLITICAL CRISES OF THE FIRST CENTURY BC

Financial transactions were governed by the rules of private law. But Roman laws did not apply to allies [*socii*] – meaning non-Roman citizens in Italy – and this was notably the case for the regulation of loans on interest. This made it possible to circumvent Roman law, since there was no office registering private contracts. Such loopholes encouraged excessive risk-taking, dubious transactions and over-indebtedness; hence the recurrence of private debt crises. Even though these were private debt crises, they demanded state intervention, for they had the potential to disrupt payment systems. Here we find an illustration of the close relations between debts, finality of payment and liquidity, as discussed in Chapter 1.

The state had at its disposal a panoply of exceptional and temporary measures to get a grip on debt crises. The use of these depended on political choices. The extreme scenario involved doing nothing: that is, refusing any debt adjustment and repressing any disturbances. This is what Cicero chose to do in 63 BC. Leaving aside that disastrous policy, it was possible to deploy adjustment strategies. These were every bit as good as contemporary techniques. It was possible to reduce excessive indebtedness by restructuring payment deadlines, thereby diminishing the amounts outstanding or the interest paid; to organise the sale, under public control, of parts of the debtors' assets; and to direct public funds into donations or zero- or low-interest loans in order to inject liquidity into the economy.[21]

These mechanisms did not, therefore, imply monetary reforms, but nor did they rule out this possibility (indeed, such reforms took place in 91 and 81 BC). In most crises, the public authorities chose to put more money into circulation. In doing so, they implemented a

---

21   Andreau, 'Crises financières et monétaires dans l'Antiquité romaine'.

policy of what is called 'expanding the balance sheet' (quantitative easing, or QE). In light of this, the cries of bloody murder coming from the neutrality-of-money purists in our own time, in opposition to the sheer 'nerve' of the central banks, appears rather comical.

Indeed, the worst crisis was that of the 'Catilinarian conspiracy', between 64 and 62 BC, in which Cicero refused to take any measures to manage over-indebtedness. Cicero was consul in 63 BC, at the heart of the crisis. At the July 64 BC elections, he had dramatised the crisis to extreme proportions in order to mobilise public opinion. Catiline stood against Cicero for the consulship in 63 BC. Addressing his partisans during his campaign, Catiline emphasised the contrast between their poverty and indebtedness and the wealth of the ruling oligarchy, who benefited from state emoluments. He supported passing a bill in the Senate to clear the debts. In the crisis of 86 BC, three quarters of the debts had been wiped, and in 64 BC, sections of the Roman *plebs* were very heavily indebted.

Cicero became consul in 63 BC on a political programme very hostile to debt reduction. Catiline was again beaten at the 62 BC elections for the consulship, and together with his partisans – rallying both plebeians and young people from the élite – he turned to violent action. In October 62 BC, Cicero implemented a state of emergency, giving exceptional powers to the consuls. On both sides, troops were mobilised for civil war. The acute indebtedness coupled with the threat of civil war put a freeze on payments. Money disappeared due to hoarding, reflecting the pursuit of absolute liquidity. Cicero banned the export of precious metals. Ultimately, Catiline and his partisans were defeated and massacred by the regular army in Tuscany in January 62 BC.

The interesting lesson for us today is that, in the 'Catilinarian conspiracy', indebtedness was able to prompt an insurrectionary movement. There was a unification of the interests of rural and urban plebeian debtors, as well as of young élite debtors. For the acquisition of elevated political positions was very expensive, which resulted in extreme inequality between generations. Indebted senators had to sell a greater or lesser share of their estate (land, slaves, buildings, precious objects) to reimburse their creditors. The massive sales caused deflation.

THE LOGIC OF MONEY IN THE DECADENT ROMAN REPUBLIC

The Roman Republic had become a society of inheritors.[22] It was also a political society, because only politics allowed access to social recognition. In order to become a senator, it was necessary to inherit a substantial estate. Whoever lost this estate was excluded from the élite. There was a confrontation, then, between a plutocratic logic based only on money and an aristocratic principle founded on heredity. Such a society made upward mobility impossible, and it inevitably slid towards sclerosis.

There were two logics governing access to money: money was gained or lost in private business, or it was guaranteed by the state in exchange for services rendered by a patrician family over the generations. Thus, the pureblood patrician Catiline believed that the state owed it to him to guarantee his estate, and he treated Cicero as a usurper. The state would thus have had to guarantee a form of political regulation between two categories of social values. But, caught in the hurly-burly of conflicts of interest, it was incapable of doing so. The Emperor, as the emanation of a higher sovereignty than that of the Republic, would later implement this regulation.

As for the close relationship between indebtedness and the deflationary monetary crises of the first century BC, it was hoarding that caused payment crises. It was the frenzied quest for liquidity that destroyed liquidity. Of course, this dynamic – so feared by Aristotle – was all the deadlier the more rigid the money supply was, on account of the monetary policy conducted by the creditors in power. An echo, indeed, of Greece's contemporary crisis in relation to the eurozone!

In 49 to 47 BC, civil war broke out between Caesar and Pompey, following fresh tensions between debtors and creditors. The price of land fell and cash disappeared. But Caesar did not act as Cicero had in the same position. He had assets evaluated at their prewar value so that debtors could pay their debts without being dispossessed. Moreover, he abolished part of the debts, and prohibited the holding of more than 60,000 *sesterces* in cash. Finally, he requisitioned the

---

22   Paul Veyne, *Le pain et le cirque. Sociologie historique d'un pluralisme politique*, Paris: Seuil, 1976. See this excellent book for an analysis of Roman society and the functioning of its republican oligarchy.

Senate and the sanctuaries' treasuries and had gold and silver money minted. This was a very wise policy that nevertheless did not manage to prevent profound social disorder.

THE ROMAN EMPIRE: FROM PEAK TO DECLINE

The Roman Empire defined a centralised and unified principle of sovereignty. This had drastic consequences for its monetary regime: *the Roman Empire did not have debts, and foreign monies were unknown there*. In these conditions, violent financial crises disappeared. Moreover, the first century AD was an era of stability and growth for the Empire. From the second century onwards, however, there emerged slow and long-term monetary depreciation crises.[23]

The principal cause of these was the Empire's expansion. The costs of pacifying conquered regions and of defending distended and increasingly remote borders were high: increased expenditure had to be made on the military, on logistics and on the development of conquered land. This expenditure exceeded the tributes drawn from the newly conquered areas. The scarcity of slaves made farming less productive. There was a clear deterioration of public finances around the 190s AD under the emperor Commodus, by which time Rome was fighting defensive wars. The deterioration of the public finances brought about irreversible monetary depreciation. The fineness of the *denarius* fell from 95 percent to 65 percent fine metal. Prices in *denarii* doubled, but prices in bronze *sesterces* or in the *aureus* – which had not been devalued – remained constant. In 215 AD, the emperor Caracalla introduced the *antoninianus*, a 5 gram coin of less than 50 percent fine silver. Stable up till 238, this new money was then devalued in stages, in both weight and fineness. It replaced the silver *denarius*, which stopped being struck after 250 and disappeared totally in 274 AD.

Initially, the *antoninianus* was exclusively struck in mints at the margins of the Empire, and circulated only in those provinces where it was needed to finance military operations. Hence, the Empire's

---

23   Jean-Michel Carrié, 'Les crises monétaires de l'Empire romain tardif', in Théret (ed.), *La Monnaie dévoilée par ses crises*, vol. I, Paris: Éditions de l'EHESS, 2000, pp. 131–69.

monetary circulation became segmented. Its aim was to increase the money in circulation – but, given the worsening situation of the public finances, it was impossible to do this without impoverishing the metal content of money. The monetary hierarchy established by Augustus – gold, silver and bronze – was maintained up till around 250 AD.[24] Until 258, gold and silver minting were depreciated in tandem in order to maintain the 25/1 ratio. Subsequently, however, the collapse of the *antoninianus* prompted the disintegration of the monetary hierarchy. In 274, the emperor Aurelius carried out a monetary reform which prompted the great Roman inflation crisis. We will study this inflation in the third part of this book, devoted to monetary crises.

It is interesting to note the astonishing stability in prices between 215 and 274. It seems that consciousness of the devaluation of money came slowly, as long as the monetary hierarchy between the different metals was respected. Moreover, the segmentation of circulation between old and new coins put a brake on the declining confidence at the heart of the Empire.

THE MONETARY INVENTIONS OF THE MIDDLE AGES

After the fall of the Roman Empire in the fifth century AD, the monetary economy in the West declined steeply, continuing a process that had begun during the great Roman inflation of the fourth century. The collapse in sovereignty was accompanied by distrust around any minting of money. The high Middle Ages saw a regression to rudimentary forms of exchange that used ingots and old Roman coins, exchanged according to their weight. The social space of value fragmented, the return to weight-based measurement revealing this loss of ethical confidence. The disappearance of the urban economy and the destruction of communications routes brought about the disappearance of the market economy, aside from snippets of immediate exchange here and there. Dispersed across vast spaces surrendered to nature and traversed by armed bands of plunderers (the *bagaudae*) from the old

24   Jean-Pierre Callu, *La politique monétaire des empereurs romains de 238 à 311*, Paris: De Boccard, 1969.

Roman garrisons, the monasteries became the only depositaries of the Late Empire's monetary heritage. As long as social belonging was defined by ethnic criteria, the mints were confined to the monasteries. These workshops were dispersed and lacked mechanisms for quality control or for regulating exchange rates.

The Difficult Re-establishment of Sovereignty

The Church, therefore, represented the continuation of what the Late Empire had bequeathed at the levels of both sovereignty and money. But the advent of the Frankish kings brought the preponderance of clan forms of government, in which belonging was defined by ethnic criteria. Certainly, the Frankish kings continued to apply Roman fiscal principles, and real estate transactions were still priced in metallic money (the *sou*). But this form of money concerned no one other than the Merovingian landowning aristocracy.

THE ABORTIVE RESTORATION OF IMPERIAL SOVEREIGNTY AND THE ESTABLISHMENT OF AN OVERLAPPING HIERARCHY IN THE YEAR 1000

The relations between the Frankish kings and the Church were hardly restful. Beginning with Charles Martel, the Frankish kings picked up the habit of confiscating ecclesiastical properties, the selling of which financed their armies. Negotiations began with the Church to restore the confiscated properties. With difficulty, an agreement regarding their distribution was achieved. This was the *fief model*, as a social bond and emblem of sovereignty. The feudal lords held onto the confiscated Church lands, but they paid a financial contribution to the Church in recognition of its *eminent* ownership.[25]

It is clear how important the invention of a new principle of sovereignty was for the whole ensemble of social relations. For several centuries, the Church and the monarchical states were bound together by the principle of *overlapping hierarchical sovereignty*.[26] Overlapping hierarchy was not particular to the Christian West alone. We find it in

---

25 Georges Duby, *Guerriers et Paysans*, Paris: Gallimard, 1973.
26 Louis Dumont is one of the eminent theorists of this phenomenon. Dumont contrasts the principles of sovereignty in hierarchically organised societies and those where market individualism reigns. See Louis Dumont, *Essais sur l'individualisme*, Paris: Seuil, 1983.

imperial societies across Eurasia, over several centuries. The king is sovereign at the level of temporal affairs; the Church is sovereign at the level of the sacred. The two modes of sovereignty overlap under the eminent preponderance of the Church.

The overlapping hierarchy in the principle of sovereignty entailed an overlapping hierarchy in the forms of confidence. Ethical confidence proceeded from God's commandments, taught by the Church. Hierarchical confidence proceeded from the authority of the state. The moral precepts of Christendom inspired the law and guided the sovereign's conduct. At least, this was supposed to be the case. The symbol of the king's allegiance to the Church was the coronation, which made the king the intercessor of the divine order within the social order. In return, the king committed to protect the Holy See. This was the birth of what was called the Christian West, starting with Pepin in 760. In 800, Charlemagne received the imperial crown and restored social order by putting an end to centuries of discord among the clans and reanimating commercial exchange. The sovereign decreed his monopoly on the creation of the markets, from which he drew tax receipts. A guilds code was drafted.

But the Carolingian restoration, which had sought to re-establish the Roman Empire, was a failure. The Carolingians had reinstated the state monopoly on minting, giving monetary form to the hierarchy of the social body. Minting the gold *sou* was an exclusive prerogative of the emperor, while minting silver monies was delegated to the lords. Yet the Carolingian Empire fragmented well before the year 1000. The fiefs became autonomous again. In the ninth and tenth centuries, the space in which money circulated shrank, while rivalries among feudal lords degenerated into the ravages of perpetual wars. Only the distant trade with the Byzantine and Muslim empires continued to be conducted in gold money.

The Church was the only institution equipped with the moral authority to remove violence from political rivalries. It was the Church, then, that established the political foundations for a reanimation of monetary circulation, by way of reforms that institutionalised the principle of overlapping hierarchical sovereignty. First of all, it managed to impose God's truce on the warring barons and to structure social time by establishing a liturgical calendar. From this foundation, the Pope then promulgated the Gregorian reform, which was fundamental to Europe's destiny. Through the ban on selling ecclesiastical dignities, the sacred was placed outside the bounds of the market. The canon law was erected, stipulating that abbeys, princes, lords and free towns must pay the *cens* to the Papacy.

It was the payment of fees that revived money circulation. Since the Church was organising a supra-territorial network of pontifical finances but did not itself create any money, it used taxpayers' local monies. This was the impetus for the development of exchange markets. The pontifical exchanges mutated into merchant bankers, draining the tax on the Church's immense land property, across Europe and back to Rome.[27] The Holy See thus concentrated resources that were then redirected into monetary circuits via its expenses as it sought to re-establish its authority over holy sites. This meant enormous financial flows between Rome and all Europe. Guild codes were introduced, the franchises granted to towns were promulgated, and fairs were organised. The network of fair towns, extending across the whole space of Christendom, was the fertile soil in which capitalism took root, starting with the beginning of the Crusades at the end of the eleventh century.

This new conceptualisation of sovereignty marked a profound break with antiquity. Politics was no longer the primordial source of social status and the principle of legitimation of conduct. Christianity established the conception of the human being in God's image, whose purpose in earthly life was individual salvation. This spiritual purpose was legitimated by the Church, not by politics. Corresponding to this, Christianity made slavery immoral and valorised the labour contract between free individuals. The ethical foundations of the double separation constitutive of what would become capitalism were elaborated by the Church, and they received juridical form in canon law. The encounter, over the course of the centuries, between the aspiration to salvation and what Max Weber called 'the spirit of capitalism' opened the way to the private financial innovations of the Middle Ages.

27 Claude Dupuy, 'De la monnaie publique à la monnaie privée au bas Moyen Âge', *Genèses*, no. 8, 1992, pp. 25–59.

Over centuries, the king of France would practise a pact of alliance with his people, for the coronation established him as a ruler by divine right. The king's individual person was, in a sense, double: on the one hand, he was a mortal human person while on the other, he was the sovereignty expressed in the hereditary line of royal succession. 'The king is dead, long live the king!' From the eleventh century, finance played a crucial role in the affirmation of royal power. The alliance with the Church was strengthened through the Crusades, the first of which was launched in 1095. The Crusades considerably increased the financial needs of lords and kings. The wars to impose the centralisation of royal power over the feudal lords also fuelled the public authorities' insatiable thirst. Financial coordination from one end of Europe to the other became the prerogative of the Italian merchant bankers who created the network of fair towns.

The monetary innovations of the late Middle Ages marked a great leap towards abstraction in the institutionalisation of money, and thus a great leap in the regulation of value. Of the two great monetary innovations, one was public – the introduction of abstract units of account – and the other private – the invention of the bill of exchange. The articulation of these two elements constituted the dualist international monetary system, which regulated the first phase of capitalism's rise, up until the discovery of silver deposits in Potosí, Peru, during the sixteenth century.

The Creation and Rise of the Dualist System in the Thirteenth to Fifteenth Centuries

Despite the development of deposit money – which we will examine later – Europe's economies were highly dependent on metallic monies for retail payments and the settling of debts. Yet precious metals were being drained from Europe in order to finance the structurally deficitary trade balance with the East. The cost of the Crusades was even larger. The European mines did not produce enough to cover the metals transferred out of Europe as well as the losses from the continual wars between Europe's monarchs. The shortage peaked at the end of the fourteenth century, ushering in the great deflation of the fifteenth century: the rise in the price of precious metals, the fall in that of commodities, and the devaluation of common coins through the depreciation of their metal content.

The sometimes latent, sometimes acute shortage of precious metals prompted monetary innovations from Europe's monarchs, each of whom sought to assert their sovereignty over the others while preserving their stock of cash. This was the invention of abstract units of account – that is, ones separated from any basis in metal – in which debts were priced. The most renowned were the *livre tournois* in France, the pound sterling in England, and the *maravedí* in Spain. After this invention, metal monies were priced in units of account that were the pivots of the European monarchies' monetary systems. These systems thus became dualist, with abstract units of account and metallic means of payment. Thus, in 1266, upon his return from the Third Crusade – where he had been taken prisoner and released in exchange for an enormous ransom – Louis IX struck the gold *écu* and the silver *gros*. Through his sovereign power, he fixed the value of the coins in the *livre tournois* in which the debts were expressed. No number was written on the coins. Louis IX thus offered his successors the opportunity to decree monetary mutations without having to remodel the weights or the fineness of the coins in circulation.

The purchasing power of money could increase overall without its structure being altered, as long – of course – as prices did not increase to the point of cancelling out the gains from this change. When the king decided that the gold *écu* should be increased by 20 percent (and the *livre tournois* reduced), the whole constellation of coins realigned itself according to the new definition of the unit of account.

Over several centuries, monetary mutations were the instrument of royal policies that consisted of (most of the time) devaluing or (in exceptional cases) raising the value of the unit of account, according to the financial interests of the state, which was both debtor and creditor.[28] In France, the dualist system lasted up until the Revolution. This policy was effective in a context of deflation. Amid the deflation

---

28   Marc Bloch, 'Mutations monétaires dans l'ancienne France', *Annales ESC*, vol. 8, 1953, pp. 145–58.

of the fifteenth century, it met with the approval of both the merchant guilds and the general population. It enabled boosted expenditure by injecting means of payment with greater purchasing power to buy goods. This made it possible to keep the price of commodities up, putting a brake on deflationary forces. Conversely, in the sixteenth century with the arrival of mintable metals from the Americas, the depreciation of the money of account amplified the inflationary effects of the abundance of money. The devaluation of the *livre tournois* revealed the contradiction between the regulation of money and the state's financial needs, becoming the grounds of acute social conflicts.

THE DUALIST SYSTEM IN THE GREAT HYPERBOLE
OF MONETARY ABSTRACTION

The dualist system is a mode of monetary organisation that has lasted for five centuries in France and four and a half in England. It is inscribed in the multi-century progression of monetary abstraction. This trajectory results in the irreversible and generalised devaluation of units of account in terms of the weight of the money minted, ultimately leading – in the twentieth century – to the unit of account's complete independence from metal. The unit of account prices itself. It is the liabilities-side unit of the institution that issues it. It is exclusively fiduciary.

We will aim, first of all, to ascertain whether this trajectory follows a quantitative law of development. Then, we will evoke the major qualitative stages in the abstraction of money. These stages demonstrate that the social invention of money was above all an act of sovereign power, and that this invention was a process composed of alternating phases of intense change and stability. Thanks to the information gathered on coins, which allows us to measure precisely their fineness and weight in gold or silver, it is possible to calculate the weight of fine gold whose price is equivalent to the unit of account in which coins are priced, also taking account of the gold-to-silver ratio when the unit of account is defined in silver. In the case of inconvertibility, by way of convention we suppose that the metal content of the unit of account is the inverse of the price of a kilo of fine gold on the free market.

Table 3.1 summarises Cailleux's synthesis of studies of money by historians.[29] It suggests that the depreciation of units of account over two and a half thousand years is faster than exponential depreciation. The rate of depreciation grows over time. Cailleux shows that it is possible to adjust to these data an exponential-hyperbolic law of the type $p = \frac{a}{b - e^{at}}$ where p is the price of gold and t is time.

This law is intriguing, because according to this law the price of gold and its rate of increase tend towards infinity in a finite time. However, this is not a regular process. That means that the parameters of this function estimated across the past do not allow us to calculate the future date of the destruction of the money economy! Indeed, the eras of accelerated depreciation are interrupted by eras of monetary stability. Order and disorder seem to follow one after the other. The eras of order stop the monetary bubble's expansion and push back the end date. Nonetheless, the monetary crises that we will study in the third part of this volume, degenerating into hyperinflation, teach us that monies can be destroyed in local contexts, and thus that monetary sovereignty is mortal.

Among the well-known stages of stabilisation, we could cite first of all the one that took place under Caesar, who carried out a reform on the basis of the gold standard by creating the *aureus*. This stability lasted for over two centuries, since under Nero the depreciation of the *aureus* was only 10 percent and in 215, under Caracalla, only 20 percent. But as we saw above, the economic crisis of the third century was accompanied by rapid monetary degradation, with a fall in the money economy in the provinces and a contraction in trade across the Roman world. The reforms by Diocletian and Constantine, who we will study in relation to the great Roman inflation, sought to re-establish the monetary unity of the Empire which was by then beginning to fragment. But this stabilisation was short-lived. The shortage of metals and the disaggregation of the Western Empire brought about a territorial carve-up of Western Europe during the early Middle Ages. Thus, the apparent stability of the *solidus* (ancestor of the *sou*) was the stability of a unit of account that no longer circulated – the symbol of a remote sovereignty that faded over time.

29 P. Cailleux, *Revue de Synthèse*, no. 99–100, 1980.

Table 3.1

From antiquity to Charlemagne, and from Charlemagne to the franc[30]

Era	Unit of account (1)	Fine gold content (mg)	Price per kg of fine gold (franc equivalent) (2)
Croesus (560 BC)	*Libra* (by weight)	450,000	0.022
Sulla (87 BC)	20 *as*, libral	218,800	0.046
Caesar (45 BC)	20 *aureus*	162,700	0.061
Augustus (0)	20 *aureus*	156,000	0.064
Nero (52 AD)	20 *aureus*	145,000	0.069
Diocletian (295 AD)	20 *aureus*	109,000	0.092
Constantine (312 AD)	20 *solidus*	90,000	0.111
Salic law (620 AD)	20 *solidus*	76,000	0.132
Charlemagne (805 AD)	*Livre*	24,000	0.42
Louis IX (1266)	*Livre tournois*	8,270	1.20
Philip IV (1311)	*Livre tournois*	4,200	2.38
Louis XI (1480)	*Livre tournois*	2,040	4.90
Henri IV (1600)	*Livre tournois*	1,080	9.26
Louis XIII (1640)	*Livre tournois*	621	16.1
Louis XIV (1700)	*Livre tournois*	400	25.0
Louis XVI (1789)	*Livre tournois*	300	33.3
Bonaparte (1803)	*Franc*	290	34.2
Poincaré (1928)	*Franc*	58.9	170
Daladier (1938)	*Franc*	24.75	404
Pinay (1958)	*Franc*	1.88	5,320
D'Estaing (1972)	*Centime*	1.08	9,290
Barre (1979)	*Centime*	0.23	43,000

(1) The nominal correspondence between units of account is:
   20 *aurens* ~ 20 *solidus* ~ 1 *livre*
   1 *livre tournois* ~ 1 *franc* = 100 *centimes*

(2) The nominal continuity of the franc was broken in 1960 with the creation of the *nouveau franc* (equal to 100 old *francs*), which became the *franc* in 1963.

As we saw earlier, from Louis IX to Louis XVI, monetary mutations were a key instrument of royal policies. Such policies involved devaluing or revaluing the unit of account according to the balance of the state's interests as a public debtor or fiscal creditor. This system made possible much faster devaluations than had existed in antiquity.

---

30   Source: Ibid, p. 253.

Even within the dualist system, the devaluations of the unit of account varied significantly in intensity depending on the mode of sovereignty in play, and the way that it conditioned ethical confidence. The French monarchy was absolute and based on divine right. This provided the state with greater freedom in financial matters, encouraging the instrumental use of money.[31] In England, on the other hand, the political power of merchants and private financiers expressed itself through Parliament, from the promulgation of the Magna Carta in 1215 onwards. Devaluation virtually ended with the reign of Elizabeth I (Table 3.2). Contrasting England and France brings into view the decisive role of ethical confidence, which restricted the state's capacity to use monetary policy in a purely instrumental way. Money had to be universally accepted for it to establish itself as the norm of value. However, historians have observed a change in the perception of monetary mutations around the end of the fifteenth century. Up until then, such mutations had been defined in relation to the money of account, which was considered as the centre of the monetary system. But beyond that point, these mutations were priced in reference to metal monies and thus identified as devaluations of the unit of account. At the same time, distrust in the *livre tournois* arose during periods of serious instability. This resulted in attempts to replace it with alternative points of reference, such as private units of account, in spite of the royal ban. What was the reason for this major reversal of trust in the *livre tournois*?

THE RISE AND FALL OF THE DUALIST SYSTEM

The weakening of the unit of account enabled the progressive strengthening of the coins in circulation. When the royal authorities decided that the gold *ecu* had risen by 20 percent, the whole constellation of coins would align with the new definition of the money of account, according to the coins' relative values. However, the relative values of the coins also posed the problem of the bad money driving out the good, on account of the distortion between the coins' declared values and the prices at which metals were traded. This 'law' was formulated by the philosopher Nicolas Oresmes in the fourteenth century – that is to say, two centuries before it was stated by the financier Thomas

31   Bloch, 'Mutations monétaires dans l'ancienne France'.

Gresham, to whom this law is attributed! However, the abstraction of the unit of account enabled the dissociation of the general problem of the adequation of the money supply to the kingdom's needs, on the one hand, and that of the structure of the means of payment, on the other.[32]

Table 3.2
Five centuries of monetary mutation in England

France				England		
Reigns and dates of measure	Mg of fine gold in the *livre tournois*	residual value of *livre tournois* (% of initial value)	Reign	Mg of fine gold in the pound sterling	Residual value of pound sterling (% of initial value)
Louis IX (1266)	8,270	100	Edward I (1278)	20,500	100
Philippe le Bel (1311)	4,200	50.7	Edward III (1350)	17,400	84.8
Louis XI (1480)	2,040	24.6	Edward VII (1489)	15,470	75.5
Henri IV (1600)	1,080	13.1	Henry VIII (1535)	9,200	44.9
Louis XIII (1640)	621	7.5	Elizabeth I (1560)	7,750	37.8

Source: *Cailleux*, Revue de Synthèse, *p. 254.*

The alternation between periods of monetary depreciation and stability can probably be located in the *longue durée* cycles that have punctuated Europe's history since 1000 AD. Long phases of economic prosperity, price rises and abundance of money follow phases of scarcity, falling prices and shortages of means of payments. After the eventual failure of the Crusades, the fourteenth and fifteenth centuries corresponded to an era of terrible deflation, aggravated by profound and enduring social ills (climate cooling, the demographic crisis caused by the Black Death of 1348–9, and the Hundred Years' War). The devaluation of money was the sole means of fighting against inflation. Moreover, certain monarchs' temporary initiatives to restore the value of the unit of account encountered resistance from both the guilds and the general population. On the other hand, in the sixteenth

---

32 Jean-Gabriel Thomas, *Inflation et nouvel ordre monétaire*, Paris: PUF, 1977.

century, with the arrival of mintable metals from the Americas, the depreciation of the money of account amplified the inflationary effects of the abundance of money. So, the economist and philosopher Jean Bodin and the lord and economist Jean de Malestroit, who had argued about the causes of inflation, were both right. Jean Bodin, a partisan of the quantitative theory of money, had blamed inflation on the massive amounts of silver arriving from Potosí, which were made into money in Seville before flowing across Europe. The lord De Malestroit, a member of the king's council, had reasoned in terms of the old dualist system, which still survived. He emphasised the role of the devaluations of the *livre tournois*. Indeed, these devaluations had become the stakes of sharp social conflicts.

After Columbus's conquest of the New World in 1492, silver flooded into Spain. It was monetised in Seville, before flowing across Europe (Table 3.3). Monetary circulation swelled enormously, feeding powerful inflation. The resulting financial disorders combined with the enormous social transformations of the so-called Renaissance era. To understand these events properly, it is worth comparing the dualist system to the contemporary system of fiduciary money, in which the money of account and the means of payment are merged. Today, when the unit of account depreciates, creditors in nominal value and those who hold liquidity are in the same losing camp. In the dualist system, creditors and hoarders were in opposite camps. The purchasing power of credit had diminished in terms of its metal equivalent, whereas coins' purchasing power increased as long as the rise in prices did not catch up with the rate of transformation. As private credit – the source of the rise of capitalism – developed, distrust towards the money of account was a barrier to the productive use of savings. This is why monarchs carried out monetary mutations from time to time in order to push the value of the *livre tournois* back up again. These were attempts to restore confidence in the unit of account. But these sporadic efforts were no more than expedients. The dynamism of private business required durable means of stabilisation – a transformation of the monetary system. The fact that this transformation took place in England far sooner than in France is not unrelated to England's preponderance in the classical age.

Table 3.3

Global production of precious metals and their import into Seville (mean for each period, in tonnes)

Periods	Global production (1)		Arrivals in Seville (2)		2/1 as %	
	gold	silver	gold	silver	gold	silver
1495–1544	330	475	60	265	18	8
1550–1600	380	17,890	95	7,125	25	40
Growth (% rate)	15	410	62	2,618		

Source: Vilar, Or et monnaie dans l'histoire.

The Revolution in Payment Technology

In antiquity, the invention of hallmarked money enabled the extension of market exchange. The causal relation between money and the development of trade was exactly the opposite of what the economists' fables tell us. Hallmarked money did not result from the spontaneous extension of exchange. It flowed from the sovereign mint, which was behind the general acceptance of money as a social abstraction. Metal was promoted as a means of payment by way of the sign printed upon it. It conferred the status of a commodity on objects, through the exchange prompted by its common acceptance. Exchange determines economic value; prior utility-value does not determine exchange. Throughout antiquity, this social abstraction did not go further than the sovereign hallmark printed on the metal. Without any purely ideal unit of account, there was no possibility of scriptural money, and thus no banks, nor transfers by signature. The high points of monetary transformation in this era were relations between changes in the monetary system and the invention of forms of payment. By this yardstick, the thirteenth century is without parallel. The bill of exchange invented in this century represented nothing less than the invention of capitalism.

The bill of exchange was a private monetary invention set in circulation by Italian merchant bankers in the thirteenth century. The Crusades made it necessary for monarchs and the Papacy to transfer means of payment from one end of Europe to the other – amounts that were considerable for the time. The kings' efforts to establish their supremacy within the national space had dislocated feudalism, prompted the irreversible decline of the great abbeys, and visibly weakened papal authority. The resumption of trade flows towards the Near East prompted the rise of the merchant cities, many of which had achieved political independence from the feudal lords.

In properly monetary terms, autonomous private monies, as distinct from the non-transferable private debts that existed under the Roman Republic, were only possible if they could be expressed in abstract units of account. In Roman law, debts were personal engagements. They could not be assimilated to monetary symbols, allowing others to acquit their engagements. It was the establishment of the dualist system that made it possible to transfer debts. The unit of account became separate from the sovereign monetary mark, making it possible for merchant communities to create abstract units of account, at the same time that the bill of exchange acquired a certain autonomy from metallic means of payment.

MERCHANT BANKERS AND THE BILL OF EXCHANGE

The bill of exchange is a monetary instrument that originated in thirteenth-century Genoa. It made a lightning-fast advance in the fourteenth century with the development of long-distance trade.[33] In the fifteenth century, it became the private means of international payment across Europe. The bill of exchange was well suited to intra-European trade, which needed disposable funds in different places. Over three centuries, it overcame the separation of public monetary spaces by creating a homogeneous private banking network at the European level. The bill of exchange was thus the vehicle for the first era of global capitalist finance, linking separate monetary spaces via international capital flows.

The bill of exchange amalgamated different spaces, times and units of account. It combined credit and coinless exchange. For exchange by letter supplies money in site A in exchange for a document (the letter), which generates a money payment in site B upon the presentation of the document. It is thus a contract for the exchange of a present money for an absent money. The exchange is also the conversion of one unit

33 Raymond De Roover, *L'Évolution de la lettre de change, XIV–XVIIIe siècles*, Paris: Armand Colin, 1953.

of account into another money of account. Finally, exchange by bills is indissolubly an act of issuing credit. The time separating the issuing of the bill from its presentation is the time of *usance*. Thus, four economic agents are linked together by the bill of exchange. In site A, the *creditor* hands over a sum of (metallic) money A to a *buyer* (or drawer), who gives him a bill of exchange in return. The drawer draws the bill on an economic agent of his choice (the *payer*, or drawee) who is his correspondent in site B. Finally, the *beneficiary* receives the creditor's bill by courier. He hands it over to the payer who accepts it after having verified it against the payment of the sum stipulated in the currency used by the beneficiary. The creditor and beneficiaries might be any kind of economic agent, from traders to pontifical agents. The intermediaries (the buyer and payer) are bankers who make up part of a correspondent banking network whose members are linked by the mutual confidence that is nourished by the repetition of credit contracts over time. That is to say, they are linked by methodical confidence (Figure 3.1).

The bill of exchange thus expresses a relation inverse to that of the banking money that developed from the eighteenth century onwards. As a payment order, the bill of exchange was directly addressed to the person charged with executing the payment. In principle, it was not a negotiable instrument of credit. It would become such an instrument through its circulation among the international community of merchants. When the bill of exchange became accepted as proof of a prior obligation – first in practice, and then in law – it became itself a financial instrument. It acquired this juridical status only at the end of the fifteenth century.

Since the payment stipulated by the bill of exchange had to be realised in a monetary space other than the payer's own, it represented an instrument of exchange between bankers. The bill of exchange was thus linked to long-distance trade, and it enabled the latter's expansion. When trade was sufficiently intensive and diversified, trading companies had funds available in certain centres and payments to make in others. It was from this situation that the relations of correspondence between bankers originated. When the interdependence thus established became multilateral, problems arose for the clearing of bills of exchange. Merchant bankers' organisation of this clearing was a means of freeing themselves, as much as possible, from having

Figure 3.1

Principle of the bill of exchange

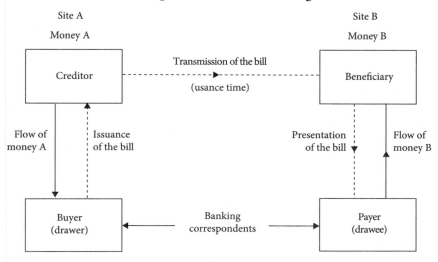

to settle in metallic money, and hence from the whim of the official mutations decreed by kings. Corporations of merchant bankers invented private units of account for the purposes of clearing bills of exchange, so that they could evaluate the bills accepted for clearing and calculate net positions. When the relations of correspondence were not sufficiently dense and stable from place to place, clearing only took place periodically. It was conducted through the network of fair towns. This was the first form of international money market that evaluated bills of exchange of different qualities; made conversions between these payment instruments when they were made out in different units of account; practised arbitrage; and enacted the deferral over time (until the next fair) of net clearing balances or their settlement in metallic monies.

THE ORGANISATION OF BILLS OF EXCHANGE AND
THE RISE OF INTERNATIONAL FINANCE

Exchange through bills was a strongly structured means of organisation. There were sites of exchange which functioned all year round as well as trade fairs that were open during certain periods. The monies used in this exchange could overlap with territorial units of account, or they could be specific units of account derived from agreements between bankers with a common interest in freeing themselves of the

government-decreed mutations. Such was the case of the money dominant at the central fair in Lyon, an *écu de marc* defined in gold coinage.
The crucial point, and the reason for the endurance of the bill of
exchange system, was the following: *it guaranteed the systematic enrichment of the merchant bankers who were its intermediaries*. Profits were
made in the back-and-forth resulting from the issuing of bills by clients,
in both directions. It was structural, because it was anchored in the
superiority of the certain (the *Res du change*) over the uncertain (the
Pretium). The profit was systematic, because the superiority of the *Res*
over the *Pretium* was inscribed in the networks of exchange. It varied
according to the financial conditions that determined the scarcity or
abundance of money in different centres. But it was always positive.[34]

It remains to be understood why arbitrage did not cancel out profit,
and why it could be systematic without being a high-risk activity. The
reason is to be found in the articulation of exchange by notes and
exchange by coins, of private practices and official rules. The systematic
difference in the price of exchange by notes – the difference that bankers
exploited – was based on the seigniorage included in the legal tender of
coins. The legal tender of a coin in the country in which it was minted
was always higher than the trade value of the metal that it contained.
Conversely, in outside territories, foreign coins circulated at their trade
value. Thus, each coin was overvalued relative to the others in the territory in which it was minted. If we call the rate calculated on the basis of
the coins' legal tender the 'par of exchange', then the bankers' systematic
profit came from the systematic difference between the price of exchange
by notes and the par of exchange – a difference owing to the distortion
produced by seigniorage (see Box 3.1).

The Structural Crisis of the Dualist System and the Transformations of Capitalism

From the monetary and financial point of view, we adhere entirely to
Fernand Braudel's conclusion in his fundamental set of works,

---

34 For a detailed demonstration of a systematic profit on exchange for intermediaries, see Marie-Thérèse Boyer-Xambeu, Ghislain Deleplace and Lucien
Gillard, *Monnaie privée et pouvoir des princes*, Paris: Presses de Sciences Po, 1986,
pp. 179–84.

Civilization and Capitalism.[35] Capitalism was born in Europe between the thirteenth and sixteenth centuries. Its first phase was entirely international; it was a financial and commercial capitalism. The network of bills of exchange between the autonomous cities of Italy (Genoa, Florence, Venice) and Northern Europe (Antwerp, Amsterdam and the Hanseatic ports) was the dominant means of financial circulation. One route spread across France, with Lyon as the main financial centre. Another route snaked past this one, connecting the lands of the Holy Roman Empire (Milan, Bavaria, the Rhenish cities). The finance needed for distant trade, for the Crusades, and for the wars waged by monarchs to unite territories into nations and subject the feudal lords to their power all strengthened the power of the great private financial families.

Box 3.1
The structural enrichment of market bankers

Let's consider the two great trade hubs of Lyon and Genoa.

In Lyon, 1 *sol tournois* = a Genoa *sous*.

In Genoa, 1 *sol tournois* = a' Genoa *sous*, where $a' < a$.

This results from the fact that

In Lyon, 1 écu de mars = m Genoa *sous*

In Genoa, 1 écu de mars = n Genoa *sous*, where $m > n$

In Lyon, 1 écu de mars = p sols *tournois*

In Genoa, 1 écu de mars = q sols *tournois*, where $p < q$

So we get $a = m/p$ in Lyon $> a' = n/q$ in Genoa. So the merchant-banker's profit from the back and forth between Lyon and Genoa is $(m-n)/n$ in écus *de mars* in Genoa, or $(q-p)/p$ in *sols tournois*. Added to this structural enrichment are variations in the exchange/par rate in the dynamic of international trade.

---

35   Fernand Braudel, *Civilization and Capitalism, 15th–18th Centuries*, 3 vols, London: Harper and Row, 1979.

The power of private finance was radically different to the sovereign power of monarchs. Certainly, financial power was based on hierarchal confidence in the common good, which was in turn provided by the public space of value instituted by the official monetary rule. But finance broke from this rule, and circumvented it, by expanding a network of debts that escaped the public authorities' control and regulated itself through methodical confidence. We have shown how these two components of money were articulated up until the sources of mintable metals changed in the second half of the sixteenth century. It is necessary, then, to understand why this system entered into structural crisis.

When the silver supplies from Potosí poured into Spain and then into Europe, inflation replaced deflation. Undertaken at the initiative of the monarchs, the devaluation of monies of account amplified the inflationary effects of the abundance of money. The mutations in the units of account met with the hostility of the merchant guilds, on account of the redistributive effects they involved. These forms of redistribution had become harmful to capitalism's own development. This was because the mutations set the lenders, whose credits were made out in the unit of account, against the hoarders, whose coffers were in metallic money. When mutations devalued the unit of account, the hoarders were favoured and not the lenders. In consequence, as private credit developed, the distrust towards the money of account – a distrust aroused by transformations taking place amid a context of inflation – was a barrier to the productive mobilisation of savings.[36]

From the second half of the sixteenth century onwards, monarchs sought to consolidate nation-states by structuring capitalism along territorial lines. For the technical inventions of the Renaissance had now opened up the era of manufacturing capitalism, which would produce a form of wealth capable of overturning the former social equilibrium. *The foundation of wealth became accumulation in production through the subordination of labour, replacing its previous base in real estate wealth and the financial wealth that flowed from the intermediation of exchange.*

---

36   Thomas, *Inflation et nouvel ordre monétaire.*

Yet the form of capital accumulation linked to industrial enterprise was very different from the old forms. It was necessary to invest capital in the long term, in illiquid forms, and to concentrate considerable masses of savings. When the state became a manufacturer or sponsor of manufacturing companies, it had to fight against the sterile hoarding of wealth, against the sterilisation of the land and the capture of land rents by the aristocracy, and against permanent monetary instability. It had to encourage the rise of a bourgeois class. The manufacturing state needed a unified national money – it thus needed to abolish dualism, to prohibit the circulation of foreign coins, to establish a bank whose mission was to stabilise exchange, and to attract precious metals by adopting a mercantilist doctrine.

This upheaval destroyed the power of the Italian merchant bankers through the bankruptcy of the Spanish Habsburgs in 1627, in turn causing the bankruptcy of the Genoese bankers in 1631. More fundamentally, it brought the end of the international Christian order which had regulated capitalist Europe. It brought terrible political crises, pivoting on the discordance between the principle of overlapping sovereignty that linked the Church to the state, on the one hand, and the national sovereignty able to open up the space of capital accumulation to the emerging manufacturing bourgeoisie (allowing it to mobilise the potential of the nascent scientific rationality) on the other.

The Bank of Amsterdam was created in the United Provinces in 1609, during the Dutch war for independence from Spain.[37] Only after a century of political convulsions, monetary disorders, and economic ravages resulting from violent revolutions, would the pacifying revolution be carried out by the House of Orange in 1689, which offered the English throne to William III. The House of Orange promulgated a Bill of Rights which codified the relations between King, Parliament and people, and established parliamentary control over tax-raising. In the last decade of the seventeenth century, the English economy rapidly deteriorated: the public spending to finance the Great Alliance's war against Louis XIV's hegemonic ambitions (1689–97) was

---

37   Lucien Gillard, *La Banque d'Amsterdam et le florin européen au temps de la République néerlandaise* (1610–1820), Paris: Éditions de l'EHESS, 2005.

accompanied by soaring agricultural prices and contracting imports. The crisis in the public finances combined with a monetary crisis.

War in Europe had changed in scale. State spending tripled and the public debt hit 35 percent of national income. The state's needs had developed to the degree that short-term financing by goldsmiths became totally inadequate. After a fruitless attempt to raise a long-term loan in 1693, on 27 July 1694 Parliament voted to found an establishment of a new type, the Bank of England. This took the juridical form of a company of 1,300 people, members of the new and rising bourgeois class, who had collectively underwritten equities of a value of £1.2 million. All of the capital was loaned to the state. The counterparty was Parliament's right to oversee the public finances. The absolute monarchy became a constitutional monarchy.

The monetary crisis of the 1690s was extremely violent. It was not only economic and financial in nature, but also – and above all – ideological. The crisis was a clash of two monetary doctrines. We will study it in detail in Part III. The public debate over the solution assumed a dramatic dimension: one side argued for the recasting of all metal coins and for deflation in order to push up the coins' metal content, putting an end to the generalised lack of confidence. The other side argued that the pound sterling should be devalued in order to prolong the dualist system.

The arguments of the two protagonists in this confrontation, the philosopher John Locke and the Secretary to the Treasury William Lowndes, expressed the interests of the social classes now in conflict. Lowndes was supported by the conservative interests of the landowning aristocracy and the goldsmiths, the Tories; together, these groups represented the old order of financial capitalism. The Whigs, who represented the interests of the rising bourgeoisie, asked Locke to refute Lowndes's arguments.[38] In 1695, Locke published a book in which he went far beyond the immediate problem of the monetary reform and introduced a new concept in the political sphere: the natural monetary order. From behind the concept of a natural standard

---

38   Ludovic Desmedt, 'Les fondements monétaires de la révolution financière anglaise: le tournant de 1696', in Théret (ed.), *La Monnaie dévoilée par ses crises*, vol. I, pp. 311–38.

allowing the orderly development of market exchange, there emerged the whole theory of objective value. Monetary disorders were interpreted as imbalances owing to bad coinage. It was thus necessary to recast the coins in order to adjust them to the natural standard, and to accept the deflationary adjustment of prices. From the perspective of monetary doctrine, the debate around the crisis advanced the idea that if money were freed from royal authority, it would conform to the natural order. This was a transformation in the very bases of sovereignty. According to Locke, political power should be based on majority consent; it should not bear any reference to the sacred. Money's value thus arose from the tacit agreement that it should be recognised as valuable. This perspective conforms to the theoretical definition of money we proposed in Part I: 'Money is the institution through which society gives back to each of its members what it judges each of them to have given to it'. The sovereign's role is, from this point of view, to guarantee this logic of social validation, which incorporates individuals into society by preserving the monetary standard.

One of history's tricks is the fact that measures taken to resolve some urgent problem can produce turning points that alter the course of history, and consequences that no contemporaneous government had even imagined. In putting the monetary system on the gold standard by demonetising silver, the Recoinage Act of 20 November 1695 opened up a new era, bringing about the golden age of capitalism.

FROM REFORM IN ENGLAND TO THE INTERNATIONAL GOLD STANDARD

The first part of this book showed that the legitimacy of money – grounding its permanent and generalised acceptability – depends on the bedrock of confidence that emanates from the principle of sovereignty. Above, we studied a principle of sovereignty that we called the order of Christendom. Yet the economic and social transformations initiated in the Netherlands in the seventeenth century, and irreversibly pushed forward by the English Revolution, implied the radical transformation of this principle. These were, indeed, transformations of the way in which the world was conceived. The old alliance of the monarchy and the aristocracy, forged under the auspices of the sovereignty of divine right, was giving way to a new form of sovereignty, able to politically advance the conception of a natural order. The Enlightenment sapped belief in the overlapping hierarchy of the sacred and the profane, instead defining the moral and juridical bases of the principle of citizenship. The French Revolution accelerated history by driving forward the development of the nation-state.

What is the foundation of the nation-state's sovereignty? What consequences does this have for the monetary order? The British conception of the natural order and the French conception of the general will have, for a long time, been in conflict. Moreover, in the nineteenth century, American exceptionalism entered into the political game – albeit in the absence of a monetary system compatible with the rise of capitalism in the United States.

We should ask, first of all, then: what are the ideal types of sovereignty of the nation-state? And what monies are aligned with these respective forms of sovereignty? This leads us to the advent of a new monetary institution, the central bank. We will emphasise the Americans' delay in this regard, and trace it back to conflicts over sovereignty in the United States. Finally, we will see how inter-state relations evolved towards a monetary order characteristic of the classical age of capitalism; the gold standard.

The Principles of Sovereignty in a Society of Citizens

What is the foundation of sovereignty? In Chapter 2, we argued that sovereignty is founded on the postulate that while a society's members are mortal, the society itself is immortal. This ontological opposition between morality and immortality is the source of a collective belief that unites a society's members. In ancient societies as in Christendom, the erection of a principle of unity and a political authority that governed social relations was expressed through the preponderance of the Sacred. A divine Law conferred its legitimacy upon the bearer of political authority.

From the Renaissance to the Enlightenment, a revolution in conceptions about the world saw the abandonment of belief in divine law. Denying the divine law and destroying absolute power posed political philosophy with a considerable problem. Sovereignty became self-referential, because the people decreed the law which each of its members had to obey. The idea of the nation was built atop this symbolic void. The principle that now imposed itself was democracy, meaning popular sovereignty. The people takes the position of the One faced with the multiplicity of social bonds; and it is the people that is now destined to maintain the cohesion of these bonds.

Democracy means that 'The people has power over . . .' Over what? Over itself. The people commands the people. Such is the form of the self-referential. The belief that founds the collective remains empty. It is up to political philosophy to fill in the void. We already anticipated the solution to this problem in Chapter 2: the constitutional order. The people assembles itself through the election of a constituent assembly. This is not an assembly that votes on and declares laws. It is one that institutes the formal principles governing the organisation of public powers, determines leaders' responsibilities, and sets up institutional barriers to forbid the proliferation of arbitrary power. The logic whereby the people projects itself above itself, in order to appear united in the Constituent Assembly, is a logic of *self-transcendence*. This is the process that we already observed in Chapter 1, with the coordination by the future through the market. Nonetheless, this unity of the people does not directly result from the procedure that produces the collective decision. This procedure is the majoritarian rule that does not in itself prevent the dictatorship of the majority over the minority. This procedural logic undermines the unifying principle that is inherent to self-transcendence. The people meeting in the Constituent Assembly has to project itself beyond itself in a more fundamental way. The constitutional order must incorporate counter-powers in order to prevent majority rule from degenerating into majority dictatorship. Of course, this involves the independence of the judicial order and of the media's power to inform the public. Yet that is only a formal solution. We need a lot more than that. We need an ethical foundation that articulates the common good – the condition of living together – and inspires the formal principles of the constitutional order. This foundation alone can guarantee that confidence in money will endure. And since this ethical foundation is rooted in the cultures of peoples, it does not provide just one solution; hence the plurality of the principles of sovereignty with which various democratic societies identify. Indeed, this is why – as we will see in Part IV – European integration is impossible, at least for the moment.

UNITARY SOVEREIGNTY: THE NATURAL
ORDER VERSUS THE GENERAL WILL

English political philosophy has produced two conceptions of the democratic order, articulated by Thomas Hobbes and John Locke respectively. According to Hobbes, society is threatened by a war of all against all. It is necessary to keep death at bay by means of a foundational pact through which the people confers its unity onto the state. The state is the Leviathan which is delegated an absolute power, capable of containing the destructive forces of generalised violence.

Hobbes's conception of the state did not succeed in imposing itself, for the 'state of nature' which it presupposed conflicted with the concept of natural order at the foundation of the emerging liberalism. Locke rejected Hobbes's model on account of the risk it contained of a drift towards tyranny. For Locke, the 'state of nature' was instead a state in which individuals were equal, reasonable and free. Together with reason, there existed moral norms. Indeed, reason stood above rationality. Where rationality was nothing more than the calculation of interest, reason was the recognition of a responsibility with regard to the 'social whole'. But this state of nature was spoilt by the desire for the private and exclusive appropriation of common resources. This was only exacerbated by the desire for money: property set individuals against one another, secreting inequality and conflict. The liberal state was indeed the product of a self-transcendence. Property-owning individuals united among themselves by delegating a principle of a sovereignty to the liberal state, identified with the protection of property rights. And property rights, in turn, were the source of the law.

This political tradition, oriented towards the achievement of the 'natural order', would be continued by David Hume and Adam Smith. Given that the principle of property was founded in nature, the liberal state was open to the world market. It promoted a doctrine of free trade, opposed to mercantilism – indeed, this latter was ultimately defeated in the United Kingdom with the laws of 1844. But the Lockean conception of the property-owning individual has an additional aspect: the moral norm enjoins us to work and to save in order to achieve individual salvation. Divinity still exists, but it exists outside of this world. It takes refuge in individual conduct, to which it dictates some obligation. The sovereignty of the individual is not, therefore, the sovereignty of the people.

Jean-Jacques Rousseau differentiated himself radically from natural law, rejecting the hypothesis that human individuals were moral beings born into a state of nature. But neither did he subscribe to Hobbes's solution according to which the sovereign state becomes the substitute for the people. Rousseau regarded human development as an evolutionary process: an extended anthropogenesis that advances through the structuring language. For Rousseau, the invention of the symbols and institutions that govern meanings lie at the foundation of all societies. This collective framework for reasoning makes possible the formation of ethical norms. From here, Rousseau arrives at the concept of the general will, as a principle of sovereignty distinct from that of both Hobbes and Locke.[39] But Rousseau did not solve the problem of how the will of the people was to be expressed in democratic institutions. It would be the task of the French Revolution to transpose the will of the people into the terms of national sovereignty: here, it is the nation that provides unity, for it embodies the people in the Constituent Assembly. The constitutional order is, then, a national order. The sovereignty of the people is condensed in the republican principle.

The Germanic tradition provides another solution, running from Johann Gottlieb Fichte to ordoliberalism. This solution is the founding principle of the Federal Republic of Germany. In his 1807 *Addresses to the German Nation*, Fichte is faithful to Rousseau when he suggests that sovereignty is anchored in the immortality of the people.[40] For Fichte, the people is a collective that transmits an ethic across the generations. This ethic expresses the general will which, being the source of the law, imposes itself on the state. In a sense, we here again the overlapping hierarchy so dear to Louis Dumont, even after the removal of all reference to the sacred. The nation expresses the general will as an ethical-symbolic entity; state power, in turn, is a political power existing in order to realise the ethical norm.

---

39 Gérard Mairet, *Le Principe de souveraineté. Histoires et fondements du pouvoir moderne*, Paris: Gallimard, 1997.
40 Johann Gottlieb Fichte, *The Closed Commercial State*, New York: SUNY, 2012.

Despite his theoretical advance, Fichte did not inspire the political unification of the German nation. This unification would take place more than sixty years after the *Addresses to the German Nation*, in the form of the centralised Wilhelmine Empire which Prussia unified in 1871 through armed force and Bismarck's will. The empire developed steadily up until World War One. The drama prompted by this cataclysm left a shattered Germany to become the prey of a charismatic form of sovereignty in the person of Hitler, based on state totalitarianism. This was a plunge to the bottom of the apocalyptic abyss, where the nation's soul is lost. The historian Johannes Willms gives an admirable account of what he calls 'the German sickness', shedding light on the values that the German people bears up until the present day.[41] For indeed, this is a case of a people united by a culture, as according to Fichte, rather than that of a nation homogenised by the general will that results from an elective process, in the manner of the French nation.[42]

It was amid this wreckage that the Freiburg School, bringing together philosophers, political scientists, economists and jurists, rethought the ethical bases of national sovereignty for the postwar period. The doctrine that resulted was ordoliberalism. It was a child of the 1930s. Nourished by cultural values rooted in communitarianism, it was on this foundation that this current of thought sought to build a political system for the post-Nazi period; its primary aim was to prevent a return to totalitarianism. Ordoliberalism aimed to establish a juridical-political order capable of reconciling the communitarian values of the German middle classes with economic liberalism, which was conceived as a barrier to the subsumption of these values by totalitarianism. As Fabrice Pesin and Christophe Strassel remind us, the political adoption of ordoliberal principles took place thanks to Ludwig Erhard, who secured their acceptance by the Christian-Democratic Union.[43] Erhard's long career as a statesman – first as

---

41   Johannes Willms, *La Maladie allemande. Une brève histoire du présent*, Paris: Gallimard, 2005.

42   Michel Aglietta and Thomas Brand, *Un New Deal pour l'Europe*, Paris: Odile Jacob, 2013.

43   Fabrice Pesin and Christophe Strassel, *Le Modèle allemand en question*, Paris: Economica, 2006.

Finance Minister in Adenauer's government, then as Chancellor – made ordoliberal ideology the immutable doctrine of German economic policy. Ordoliberalism establishes an indissoluble link between political institutions and economic organisation. It is as foreign to the Keynesian mixed economy as it is to Thatcherite-Reaganite ultra-liberalism, which proclaims the all-powerful character of the market and the need for the state to retreat back to its most minimal sovereign functions. In ordoliberalism, before anything else there is 'order', codifying the moral aspirations of the German middle class in the rules of law. These juridical laws, which were institutionally established in the Basic Law of 1948, give form to sovereignty and stand above state power. They continue to impose themselves, no matter what the changes in the parliamentary majority. They could only be changed through a transformation of the society's most entrenched moral values. It follows from this that the notion of the constitutional state has a much stronger meaning in Germany than in other countries.

The juridical order stands in the way of any arbitrary power, whether this emerges from a political capture of the state by the majority or from groups of private agents, monopolies, cartels or lobbies. But in no sense does the state play a minimal economic role. Ordoliberalism has a pessimistic perspective on market self-regulation. It rejects the postulate according to which pure and perfect competition is a natural state that the economy tends towards if it is not blocked by 'legal restrictions'. On the contrary, juridical rule must guide both interactions between the state and the market – in order to impede the distortions caused by discretionary interventions – and endogenous market forces, whose spontaneous interplay would ineluctably lead to the constitution of dominant powers. It follows from this that the state should intervene in market mechanisms only in order to avoid distortions in the price system. But through its economic policies it must inscribe its action in the institutional framework of the market. This action must be entrusted to independent authorities, so that it does not risk drifting towards arbitrary power. Thus, ordoliberalism institutes a genuine economic constitution whose keystone is money. Money is the cement of the nation because it establishes the most general bond of confidence. It preserves savers' interests, the conservation of assets, and the autonomy of regional states, which are themselves responsible for policies which support small and medium businesses. What follows from this is that the stability of money is a constituent element of the social order, more fundamental even than the political.

THE AMERICAN CHALLENGE TO INDIVISIBLE SOVEREIGNTY: FEDERAL SOVEREIGNTY

The elaboration of a principle of sovereignty in the United States cannot be detached from the conditions under which an irregular set of federated territories tore itself from the colonial yoke through the War of Independence. Of course, every nation is born of war. But what is interesting about the American war is that it did not result from a consciousness of collective belonging that then sought to provide itself with institutions endowing it with political power. Instead, it was unleashed by an English monetary bill in 1764, the Currency Act, which prohibited the issuing of parallel currencies at legal value, and instead forced the payment of taxes in pounds sterling. Benjamin Franklin showed how harmful the act was, paralysing trade and alienating the American colonies from the British crown. Franklin believed that separation from the metropolis was inevitable. The revolution was launched. In 1774, the Continental Congress demanded the withdrawal of the Currency Act and other intolerable laws. But the preponderant goal was the political revolution. Once this was achieved, Congress adopted the dollar as the official currency, on 6 July 1785. The Constitution drawn up in 1786 defined a tripartite authority: a bicameral legislature, an executive incarnated by the president of the Union, and a Supreme Court. In 1787, a constitutional convention in Philadelphia established the Union's power of taxation, allowing a reabsorption of the Continental Dollars issued during the war and received in tax payments. The convention forbade the states to issue their own debt, and announced a clause that made gold and silver coins the only legal tender for debt payment.

This was indeed an act of sovereignty, for it established the power of taxation. But one crucial problem persisted. Should the outstanding securities inherited from the war be financed by issuing new devalued bonds, or at their face value? The states had very varied financial situations. Lacking financial systems, the farming states were unable to bear a debt at its full metal value. Not mutualising the war debts would have run the risk of a monetary (and hence a political) fragmentation of the Union. There were sharp disagreements in Congress. The debate set two camps in opposition: the partisans of political federalism, on the one hand, and those who stood for a confederation of states, on the other. The latter violently opposed the transfer of the debt to the federal government. They did not lack reasons for opposing it: if such a transfer were to take place, the speculators who had bought debt securities from investors in difficulty would be reimbursed; certain states would have a greater burden relieved than others; and the central authority would be strengthened, to the detriment of Congress and the states. The most vehement advocate for this current of thought was James Madison, who spoke for the Southern states. Madison feared that the centralisation of the debt would put the states under the thumb of a distant and irresponsible power. Beyond that, he argued that mutualisation would force the virtuous states to come to the aid of impecunious ones, and that this would threaten the young Republic.

The federalists wanted to remove the states' right to issue money, and instead to establish a uniform minting process. For them, the unity of money went hand-in-hand with the unity of public debts. Uniform conditions for recognising debts would lie at the foundation of the federal state. Alexander Hamilton vaunted the efficiency of a unified securities market, and added that the states had issued their debts in a common cause: the fight for independence.[44]

In 1790, soon after he was named Secretary of the Treasury, Alexander Hamilton proposed to centralise states' debts by issuing new bonds supported by credible fiscal receipts. He argued that the formation of a national debt would attract investors and constitute a strong social bond for the Union.[45] Hamilton succeeded by making a

---

44 Hamilton also understood the close link between money and the public finances in tax payments and the repayment of the public debt. He thought that a uniform monetary standard following a two-metal system was the social link that would unite the country's citizens.

45 Robert E. Wright, *One Nation Under Debt: Hamilton, Jefferson, and the History of What We Owe*, New York: McGraw-Hill, 2008.

concession on where the federal capital should be located. It was moved from New York to the banks of the Potomac, and to a new city called Washington, in order to distance it from the financial powers of New York and Boston. The debt was centralised and financed by federal taxation. Connected to this was Hamilton's proposal for the creation of a national bank, the Bank of the United States, in which those who held government securities could become shareholders. This proposal met with heavy criticism, which confirmed the depth of the North–South rivalry. The bill that resolved to create the Bank was nonetheless adopted in 1791, under a twenty-year charter. Finally, through the Coinage Act of 1792, Congress anchored the dollar in a two-metal system.[46] A non-provincial, non-land banking system had been put in place.

What does this experience tell us about the formation of principles of sovereignty? This formation was evidently an evolutionary process, in which there were explicit contradictions, debated in structures which ultimately allowed for their overcoming. The collective that had emerged from the war was now transformed and institutionalised. Indeed, the resolutions arrived at through these discussions helped to establish the power of the state. Budgetary unification constituted a federal state superior to the federated states, and it was recognised as superior because it increased the power and effectiveness of citizens' activity across the whole territory. Here we see again the crucial importance of the status of public debt as a vertical debt, which Chapter 2 demonstrated to be constitutive of sovereignty.

According to Alexis de Tocqueville, it was civil equality that had driven people to take up arms against colonial oppression, and which thus constituted the original unity of the American people. This civil equality asserted a principle of justice that is still present in the contemporary world, as in the elaborations of Rawls. This principle goes far beyond the property rights constitutive of the natural order. The evolutionary character of the US Constitution, whose amendments are institutional codifications of the social developments that have traversed the country, is itself the trace of a series of political struggles that sought to deepen the principle of civic equality.

46 The mint was established in the US capital of the time, Philadelphia.

The Transformations of Finance: From the
Principle of Banking to the Central Bank

All of the techniques of international finance were invented between the thirteenth and sixteenth centuries. Yet, as Braudel emphasised, the basic economic relations – the exchanges of everyday life – have barely changed. Capitalism was born as a European phenomenon when private debts became transferable debts; it extended across the globe in the sixteenth century, long before it deepened as it took hold of the economic activities within the various nations. For that to be possible, individuals had to become citizens, through the transformation of the principles of sovereignty. The political always precedes the economic. As Marx noted, primitive accumulation preceded the Industrial Revolution by several centuries. The Industrial Revolution presupposed a monetary revolution which resulted from the transformation of sovereignty. In Britain, this monetary revolution – marked by the creation of the Bank of England – itself preceded the Industrial Revolution by nearly a century. The intermediary phase was that of manufacturing capitalism.

The monetary revolution has two aspects. On the one hand, it involves the abolition of the dualist system and the stabilisation of the unit of account on the basis of metal. On the other hand, it involves the transformation of payment systems on the basis of the banking principle.

BANKING MONEY, THE LAW OF REFLUX AND
MULTILATERAL COMPENSATION SYSTEMS

The Netherlands was the pioneer of explorations in the banking principle, with the creation of the Bank of Amsterdam in 1609. This followed an acute monetary crisis prompted by the Dutch war of independence from Spain. This war undermined confidence in the then-prevalent Spanish currency to such a degree that there was a return to payments in weights of metal. In proliferating metallic means of payment of uncertain relative values, this monetary chaos brought profits to money changers, but not to producers and savers.

Seeking to prevent the money changers' largely fraudulent enrichment, in 1609 Amsterdam decided to ban private money changing in the city. With the authorisation of the States General in The Hague, a municipal decree centralised money changing in the hands of a single operator, the Bank of Amsterdam. This benefited from a municipal guarantee on the deposited funds, and an exclusive prerogative for foreign exchange. Foreign transactions had to be paid through transfers between accounts held at the bank. The mission of the Bank of Amsterdam was to stabilise the exchanges between the new money, the *florin*, and foreign monies. But the money war with Spain continued, now between the Northern provinces and the Southern provinces that were under Spanish control. This caused a cascade of devaluations. In 1619, the Orange-Nassau dynasty took power in the North and subsequently resumed the war against Spain. The government standardised money creation across both parts of the territory, but the board of the Bank of Amsterdam refused to endorse this. The latter considered the coins from the Southern provinces as foreign specie, to be valued at the rate of non-minted metals. There were two units of account, then, in an upside-down situation in which the official currency was less coveted than an unofficial one. The *banco florin* had a bank money premium of around 5 percent over the official *florin*. Despite the enormous mass of metal in its coffers, the Bank of Amsterdam was able to use its advantages to maintain a symmetrical regulation of the relative value of the units of account. On the one hand, making a deposit for foreign transactions implied having an account with the bank, in return for the guarantee that the funds deposited there were inviolable. On the other hand, as had been known since the invention of the bill of exchange, transaction costs for account payments were much lower than for transfers of metals. Since the Bank was considered totally able to reimburse deposits, the *banco florin* was at the centre of the European payment system throughout the seventeenth century. This owed also to its political autonomy, which was finally destroyed only in the upheavals of the American War of Independence and then the French Revolution. By that point, however, the Bank of England had already become the agent of a financial revolution becoming preeminent over Europe.

The originality of the Bank of England was that it was not a deposit bank. Unlike for the Bank of Amsterdam, the coverage for the notes issued was very low (3 percent in the beginning). These notes, the counterparty to its loans to the state, replaced bills of exchange and became national and international means of payment for the bank's customers. They were not legal tender until 1833. But the securities issued by the bank, bringing interest on the public debt, became legal tender for all payments to the government from 1697 onwards. The Bank of England had established the banking principle. The credit it supplied to the private sector was self-referential. Its credibility was based exclusively on confidence in the political institutions, emerging from the new foundation of sovereignty and the notion of the nation's enrichment. Indeed, as a state bank, the Bank of England benefited from the parliamentary control of the public finances that accompanied the establishment of a constitutional monarchy. The imbrication of the political, the monetary and the economic was complete.

It was not until the eighteenth century in England that it became possible to fully grasp the efficacy of harmonising the principle of monetary convertibility with the banking principle of risk distribution. The adequation of the two is expressed in the *law of reflux*. Each issuance of *real bills* – meaning credits bearing signatures to certify that they finance the sale of existing goods – will be reimbursed in a given timespan. The money issued in return for these credits flows back toward the issuer and is thus destroyed in the reimbursement of the credit. Banks therefore bear minimal risks in issuing notes or deposits in return for their credits, over and above their cash reserves, if these credits are indeed *real bills*. Banknotes circulate as means of payment. Notes and deposits are convertible, on demand, in the metallic cash that is the base money. If the bank logic functions in its pure state (*Free Banking*), then the quantity of base money is not controlled by the monetary authority. The government contents itself with defining the unit of account, by declaring an official price for a weight of metal that it has chosen as the basis for coinage. Convertibility is the rule whereby bank monies are validated. The law of reflux is the process through which convertibility limits the issuing of competing bank monies. It simultaneously economises on coins and verifies the quality of notes.

The theoretical difficulty here does not reside in the assertion of the law of reflux. Rather, it lies in the attempt to understand the characteristics proper to the banking principle within finance. These characteristics mean that the law of reflux is fulfilled in the centralisation of the relations between interbanking correspondents within multilateral clearing systems.[47]

Banks are institutions that offer non-tradable credits combined with the provision of payment services. They invest in specific information whose quality cannot be evaluated by depositors. This asymmetric information structure, linked to network effects in the payment system, implies that the most effective relationship is for deposits to be valued at par in units of account, and hence convertible at par into the base currency. This relationship expanded greatly in the second half of the nineteenth century, when deposits became transferable via cheques. Payments by cheque transfer deposits from one bank to another and create interbank positions. The law of reflux is the process whereby these positions are cleared and settled between banks.

If the daily bilateral balance between two banks – that resulting from the balance of the cheques collected between them – had to be settled in cash, then the law of reflux would be highly restrictive. The need for liquid reserves to satisfy this law would pose obstacles to the expansion of bank credit. This is why banks found it advantageous to enter into cooperative arrangements in order to economise on specie. These arrangements produced a leap forward for payments technology through the organisation of clearing houses. The multilateral clearing of the interbank positions on the clearing house's books, with the settlement of net balances, is the matrix in which basis payments are centralised. We formulated this matrix in Chapter 1. It brings into relief the ambivalence of money, as a collective structure whose coherence derives from the cooperation between competitors. While this cooperation is to the common advantage, it cannot be taken for granted. After all, the solidarity of the banks

---

47   One, only partial, interpretation of the law of reflux is the theory of real bills. This stipulates that in order for means of payment to be acceptable, banks should issue them only against commercial bills which can easily be verified to be safe collateral. If that is the case, then the money does indeed return to the issuer for destruction. But that means that the loans have been made on the basis of public information and that they can just as well take the form of tradable securities. Thus, at most, the real bills doctrine explains the existence of financial intermediaries issuing acknowledgements of debt whose value depends on that of the assets held by the intermediaries. It does not in any way explain the historical role of banks in the development of capitalism.

constrained by the law of reflux can draw them all into bankruptcy even if just one of them fails. Such is the systemic risk associated with the centralisation of payments. This contradiction was resolved through the formation of a hierarchical structure with the central bank as its pivot, set up as the banks' bank. Nonetheless, the so-called Free Banking school claims that the principle of reflux does suffice, on condition that it is understood as self-regulation within bank clearing houses when there exists a metallic money into which bank monies are convertible at par, and banks accept that these monies are not convertible within these clearing houses.[48] The monetary entity on whose books interbank credits and debts are cleared is the banks' bank, among the community of banks who accept the system's rules. The American experience shows that Free Banking can be a solution within financial communities, but not for vast and hetero-geneous monetary spaces like large states. The small and dispersed banks of agricultural states were in distress in moments of metal-money shortages. They had to come to terms with more or less severe discounts of their notes against the dollar, and underwent numerous bankruptcies.

FREE BANKING: PAYMENTS SYSTEMS WITH BANK MONIES CONVERTIBLE INTO AN OFFICIAL METALLIC MONEY

Gold, or a gold-silver two-metal system, lends its substance to the unit of account. This money is also the ultimate means of settlement. The means of payment are bank monies, or debts issued by banks on them-selves that take the form of notes or deposits from which cheques can be drawn. As indicated above, the idea of Free Banking is to identify the law of reflux with the old theory of real bills. If all bank credits are by definition debts backed up by absolutely safe guarantees, then the reflux will always operate correctly, either through deposits being returned to the issuer bank or through interbank clearing. But this is sophistry, for any bank credit is uncertain when it is issued. The *ex post* monetary constraint of the convertibility of bank monies does not guarantee that credits will be real bills *ex ante*.

---

48 George A. Selgin, *The Theory of Free Banking*, London: Rowman and Littlefield, 1988.

The law of reflux only works when a centralised mechanism for clearing and settling credits and debts between banks exists, in a money accepted by all banks. What happens when there is not enough metal money: when it is hoarded or unequally distributed? What happens when there is no institution capable of issuing a level of debt high enough to settle the other debts? The American experience is telling in this regard. Under the constraint imposed by the law of reflux, it created the equivalent of a pseudo-central bank between the financial communities that had intensive interbank relations. However, this ignored the banks in the rest of the country.

The adoption of Free Banking was the result of Andrew Jackson's presidency between 1829 and 1837.[49] Twice, in 1832 and in 1836, Jackson vetoed the renewal of the charter of the Second Bank of the United States. Elected on a programme hostile to the East Coast financial powers and supported by the farmers of the West, Jackson represented a populist democracy. The Free Banking era extended from the Free Banking Act passed by the New York State assembly in 1838 to the National Bank Act of 1863. The principles of Free Banking were as follows. Banks could issue notes and deposits without any restriction. These had to be convertible, however, even if there was only partial collateral in gold and silver.[50] It was assumed that monetary regulation would be endogenous through the law of reflux in deposits, allowing the destruction of money at its site of issue. It would be completed through the interbank clearing mechanism.[51] The law of reflux is insufficient in periods of stress in which the banks lack metal reserves: this results in runs on these banks' deposits, and panic spreading through the networks of correspondent banks. The system can only be viable on condition that it creates clearing houses that fulfil the role of

49 Andrew Jackson was the seventh US president. Himself a wealthy slaveowner, he instigated the creation of the Democratic Party. He vetoed the renewal of the second US bank's charter, thus beginning the period of free banking.

50 Formally, the monetary system was bimetallic. Yet the 1834 Coinage Act increased the gold–silver ratio from 14:1 to 16:1, which meant devaluing the dollar/gold coins by 6 percent. Moreover, in the free banking period, marked by recurrent monetary droughts, foreign specie like Spanish dollars was accepted as legal tender. Murray Rothbard, *The Mystery of Banking*, Auburn: Mises Institute, 2007.

51 Laurent Le Maux, 'The Banking School and the Law of Reflux in General', *History of Political Economy*, vol. 44, no. 4, 2012, pp. 595–618.

a lender of last resort during liquidity crises. To this end, the clearing house must regulate the banks that are members of the system. So, Free Banking is viable only if it transforms into its opposite: into a system organised hierarchically around a superior bank capable of injecting a means of interbank payments that is acceptable in all circumstances.

This system functioned in a few states. In agricultural states, interbank debts and credits remained bilateral between banks which had fragile bases of deposits, given that they were all dependent on farming activity. Because each bank issued its own notes, liquidity shortages made it impossible to maintain convertibility between them at par. Recessions forced these banks to discount their notes, and there were waves of bankruptcies. This added to the cash shortages during the annual agricultural cycle. The most efficient system was established in New England, where the Suffolk Bank created in 1818 took the role of a clearing house. By granting overdrafts to the banks that accepted its supervision, the Suffolk Bank created interbank liquidity *ex nihilo*, which safeguarded the convertibility of notes even during banking crises. The other famous system was the New York Clearing House Association (NYCHA) created in 1853. This dealt with banking panics by issuing Clearing House Loan Certificates, which were successfully used during the terrible banking crisis of 1857.[52]

Exacerbating tensions between the economic interests of the Northeastern industrial and financial states and those of the Southern and Western states, the 1857 crisis sowed the seeds of the Civil War.

THE NEED FOR A HIERARCHICALLY ORGANISED BANKING
SYSTEM, AND THE ADVENT OF CENTRAL BANKS

A clearing house is, then, a centralised organisation which introduces collective rationality into payment systems. But clearing houses were not content to be merely mechanisms that economised on specie and reduced the costs of collecting cheques. They also issued settlement certificates on behalf of their members who deposited reserves with

52   Laurent Le Maux, 'Le prêt en dernier ressort. Les chambres de compensation aux États-Unis durant le XIXe siècle', *Annales, Histoire et Sciences Sociales*, vol. 56, no. 6, 2001, pp. 1223–51.

them. In times of crisis, and particularly when convertibility was suspended, the clearing houses in the United States acted as central banks: transferring their certificates was equivalent to settlement among their members. The higher quality of settlement money that resulted gave the clearing houses hierarchical authority over their members. In order to preserve the integrity of payments among the commercial bank clubs of which they were the centre, the clearing houses guaranteed the irrevocability of payments, but on condition that the banks abide by the restrictive obligations that they imposed.

Our analysis here deepens the approach we took in Chapter 1, where we introduced the payment system as an object of theory. Irrevocability guarantees that a collected cheque is a final payment for its beneficiary, even if the account on which it has been drawn has insufficient funds or if the payer's bank does not have sufficient means of settlement available. Irrevocability means that the beneficiary's account is credited immediately. Payment is guaranteed against the payer's bank defaulting. In order for this guarantee to function, the members of a clearing and settlement system must collectively agree to cover the liquidity risk when any one of them is unable to settle its net position with the clearing house at the end of the day. The clearing houses therefore assumed very strict regulatory powers: conditions of access to banks; capital requirements; reserve ratios; loss-sharing agreements; committees of experts at the clearing houses monitoring members' financial situations; and penalties for irregularities, which could go as far as exclusion.

Irrevocability is, therefore, the principle that allows us to conceive of the payment system as a network in which everything is interrelated. Thanks to this principle, payments mediated by banks supplanted the earlier forms. A century of banks taking over monetary economies gave shape to national payment systems, putting an end to the fragmentation of means of payment. But here we clearly see the limit of the theory of Free Banking. Interbank relations, the scaffolding of the market economy, called for centralisation. Indeed, the need for cooperation that was required in order to put the principle of irrevocability to work demands a centralisation that transcends the capacities of the competing banks, unless they are to subordinate their autonomy to the common rules of interbank settlement. The limits of private cooperation were overcome through the primacy of central banks. Whatever its origin and legal status, the central bank imposed itself in the payment system as the banks' bank. In different eras and in different countries, the legal status of the central bank was aligned with the logical need for finality in the payment system, which in turn enabled it to be the operator of value in the monetary system in question.[53]

Indeed, a truncated collective rationality tends to be ineffective when it comes to public goods. The United States example in the second half of the nineteenth century demonstrates this clearly. In the same period, the Bank of England was asserting its preponderance at the summit of the banking hierarchy. The monetary system of convertibility was thus strengthened, because liquidity crises could be overcome without having to suspend it. On the contrary, in times of crisis, private clearing houses preserved only their members' internal payments. Excluding the other banks, they aggravated the crisis for the peripheral banks whose debt positions had to be settled in cash. Thus, the American payments system became even more vulnerable with the use of scriptural money up until the Panic of 1907. Notwithstanding the regional clearing houses circulating their certificates, withdrawals by depositors demanding their conversion into gold extended across the whole country. From the US example it is possible to grasp, the essential innovation that gave the principle of irrevocability the necessary scope to unify a national payment system – in other words, that of a central bank capable of providing an elastic supply of a single, unanimously accepted means of payment and of assuming the responsibility of lender of last resort. In Part III, we will show how decisive this function is for containing the devastating effects of the financial crises that characterise market finance. We will also see how the role of central banks in times of financial crisis is linked to monetary regulation in 'normal' times.

The International Gold Standard

In this chapter, we have identified capitalism's monetary institutions in the classical era and shed light on their logic. While the major

53   Michel Aglietta, 'Genèse des banques centrales et légitimité de la monnaie', *Annales, Économies, Sociétés, Civilisations*, no. 3, May–June, Librairie Armand Colin, 1992, pp. 675–98.

European nations exhibited different principles of sovereignty, British preponderance meant that it was the property-owning individual that reigned in international exchange. This was the great expansion of the first globalisation of finance, and its apogee in the Belle Époque. We will study the regulation of this international monetary system in Part IV. Here it will suffice to relate it to what has gone before.

The international gold standard defined an unwritten monetary constitution, founded on the ethical legitimacy of a capitalism that became global in the last third of the nineteenth century. The under-estimation, or even outright ignorance, of the oppositions between Anglo-Saxon liberalism, the French nation-state, and the German and Russian empires ought to have sounded the alarm for the latent conflicts in the international sphere. But the Anglo-Saxon philosophers of the Belle Époque, just like Francis Fukuyama after the fall of the Berlin Wall, were quick to extol the end of history. They believed themselves to be carrying forth universal values, and that it was their mission to introduce them around the world. And what better vehicle for, indeed, this than finance?

The pound sterling's longstanding gold convertibility sanctioned its preponderance as a key currency. Nonetheless, the gold standard was not a monetary union of the type of the Delian League or the eurozone, where there are compulsory limits on monetary sovereignty. A sovereign currency still had the capacity to suspend or repudiate the common rule that it had signed up to. So, in order to sustain states' interest in maintaining convertibility, the international system had to provide sufficient advantages to the influential parties in the various countries.

These advantages were found in the international payment system, whose universal means of payment was the bill of exchange in pounds sterling. These liquid claims on British banks by foreign banks were universally considered equivalent to gold, which freed the British banks from having to maintain high gold collateral relative to their liquid engagements. The beauty of the gold standard was that when it was balanced (albeit not during crises) it could function without actual payments in gold.

Ethical confidence was conveyed by contemporaries' talk of a 'free monetary order' and 'sound money'. This confidence expressed the belief that the rule of convertibility had not been manipulated and that the par of exchange – the ratio of official parities in metal money – was a natural relation. The gold standard seemed to fulfil the Germanic conception of the sovereignty of the human person, in a moral rule which the philosopher Georg Simmel expressed as follows: 'It is in money that the modem spirit finds its most perfect expression'. This corresponded directly to the sovereignty of the liberal state. Respecting convertibility was a categorical imperative that stood, in principle, above the internal objectives of economic policy.

At the end of the nineteenth century, gold money symbolised a bourgeois civilisation that exalted liberty and property. The essential social bond was the contract between free individuals, supposed to reconcile personal interest with the common good. Personal responsibility was the principle underlying contractual compliance. The law constituted society's frame of reference for the punishment of breaches. Financial security was guaranteed by the convertibility of money, founded on the continuity of private engagements. This is why the intangible convertibility into gold was, morally speaking, a categorical imperative. It signified the unbreakable confidence that preserving the value of private contracts was more important than the collective preferences that states could have achieved through an instrumental use of money. In the foundations of democratic sovereignty, common belief in the 'natural order' was doubtless a more powerful cement than the symbolic fetishism of gold. Because ethical confidence predominated over hierarchical confidence, monetary policies conformed to the formal structure of the international order. The monetary adjustments implied by this structure could thus take place unhindered, and constitute a stable international monetary regime.

But this comforting image represented only the surface of the world economy, reflecting the imaginary of international finance (what else is new?). As we shall see in Part III, this supposedly charmed period was in fact rocked by financial crises, as is the case whenever globalisation is on the advance. Moreover, as Braudel emphasises, the social changes produced by the industrial revolutions gave rise to forces that did not identify with the figure of the property-owning individual, nor the conception of the 'natural order'. This undermined the supposed universalism of this form of sovereignty. The rise of nation-states whose sovereignty was foreign to that of the liberal state (Germany, Russia, and later Japan) presented a threat to the continued existence of the monetary order. Already there were internal cracks in the Russian Empire, as well as colonial competition (in Lenin's terms, an inter-imperialist competition) between the German Empire and the already-established French and British colonial empires. Through the interplay of alliance systems, these factors combined to unleash the cataclysm that brought an explosive end to the golden age of capitalism.

4

The Upheavals of the Twentieth Century

World War One irreversibly altered the course of world history. If the reader has grasped the essential message of Chapter 3, she will have understood that the great monetary innovations in history have accompanied transformations in the principles of sovereignty governing societies. Money is a non-natural, non-individual foundation of value, and it is thus inherently political. Unsurprisingly, this common thread through the history of money also provides the key to interpreting the enormous changes in money over the twentieth century.

World War One laid waste to the idea that the natural order was the foundation of sovereignty, and therefore also to the international gold standard order. The attempt to restore this order once its moral bases had definitively disappeared was a prominent cause of the economic and financial crisis that led to the Great Depression of the 1930s, as well as the rise of totalitarian states which led to World War Two.

Among all those tendencies that shook up the social order in the twentieth century, the most important emerged from within capitalism. These included the development of the salariat, the expansion of social struggles for recognition, and – after World War Two – the advent of institutions, based on the sovereignty of nation-states, which regulated *labour societies*. The advent of labour societies transformed social debt and money in parallel. Social debt encouraged the promotion of an entirely new idea at the political level: namely, the idea of *social progress*. Money definitively cut all links with its basis in metal, becoming entirely fiduciary. This was a giant leap towards monetary abstraction.

As a universal demand, social progress inscribes itself in the United Nations' problematic of human rights. As a demand for equality, it is a lever for disrupting global power relations. Nonetheless, in the twentieth century, the political game of social progress remained confined to the Western world, and most importantly Europe, where redistributive policies were developed in the wake of World War Two. These policies accompanied transformations in income distribution, although these did not go so far as to upset the forms of property within the enterprise. It is for this reason that this first, truncated era of social progress – a society of redistribution but not participation (for example, France's *Trente Glorieuses* or 'golden age') – entered into crisis, as income growth became detached from productivity gains. This crisis was carried forth by money, in the form of a generalised inflation.

The manner in which this crisis was resolved produced a historic aberration: the resurgence of liberal ideology. This could no longer claim to express the sovereignty of the property-owning individual, so instead it claimed to embody the sovereignty of the human person. What followed was an extraordinary ideological swindle, by way of the claim that the new era of globalised finance was in fact serving to eradicate poverty and reduce global inequality. Of course, the systemic financial crisis has put an end to these illusions. It has left lasting destruction, however, in terms of a drastic fall in growth and massively increased inequalities.

At the beginning of the new millennium, the world has entered into a crisis of extraordinary scope and duration. This is simultaneously a financial, social and environmental crisis. It is, therefore, a crisis in human development, which demands a profound rethinking of the question of social progress. Such a reconsideration is necessary if we are to grasp the full environmental and societal dimension of this question. Today this question is expressed in terms of sustainable development and the 'quality' of growth. Advancing along this path radically relativises the market's place in economic relations, and implies a refoundation of the principle of sovereignty on altogether new grounds. This demands that we take into account citizens' profound lack of interest for the breathless political ideas forged in the eighteenth century – ideas to which the Western world is still living by.

We are not attempting to predict what principles of sovereignty will take hold, or, therefore, the forms of political organisation that will be established in the future. Rather, we will take the same approach that we have pursued thus far, albeit inside out. New forms of money are emerging. Does this signify the continuation of past developments in payment technology? Or can we see within these new forms the seeds of social binds that will strengthen citizens' control over economic activity? If monetary forms are developing on the direct initiative of citizens themselves, how will the unity of money express itself – and according to which principles of sovereignty?

SOCIAL DEBT AND NATIONAL CURRENCY

Capitalism's most fundamental tendency consists in its elimination of other modes of production through the development of wage labour. This process took on new dimensions in the twentieth century. In the latter half of the twentieth century, capitalist nations were transformed from bourgeois societies into labour societies. This followed decades of convulsions, in which nations identifying with contradictory principles of sovereignty clashed in merciless wars.

Labour society completely transforms the debt system that constitutes the matrix of social relations. In consequence, it radically transforms the monetary rules that prevailed under the gold standard. In the classical era, the predominant debts were private debts. In labour societies, the predominant debts are instead social debts. These result from the need to protect workers without jobs who are deprived of their means of existence. This is why the welfare state has become a principal institution of social cohesion.

The welfare state brings together the rules of social legislation, of unions that represent employees' and employers' collective interests, and of negotiation procedures and collective bargaining. It is thus an essentially political institution, and as a result it differs from one nation to another. Thus, Anglo-Saxon social liberalism, Scandinavian social democracy, German ordoliberalism and French social corporatism constitute varieties of capitalism that differ in terms of their respective income distribution and production of public goods. But what all of them have in common is an enormous rise in social debt, in the form of state debt and (or) social security agencies, depending on how they are financed.

National Currencies, Economic Policies and Hierarchical Payment Systems

In nations in which social debt is preponderant, monetary rules and the forms of confidence in money are radically transformed in relation to the form they take in bourgeois societies where wage-earners are not in the majority, where citizenship is the citizenship of the property owner, and where community and family solidarities are largely responsible for social protection. In labour societies, money is completely nationalised, in the sense that national economic policies take precedence over any other form of legitimacy. Price measurement no longer rests on a universal standard of value provided by gold convertibility, but rather on a national standard.

The first change, therefore, concerns the monetary unit, which has made a leap into abstraction. This change is the disappearance of gold convertibility in the domestic use of money. What is the national currency unit? It is no longer the equivalent of a weight in gold. Rather, it is the name (the dollar, the pound sterling, the euro, and so on) given to a unit of the issuing central bank's liabilities. It is, therefore, *purely self-referential.* The measure of value conforms entirely to the principle of a pure social bond.

To cut the ties of convertibility with a metallic substance is to give up on believing in the 'natural' value of money, so dear as this notion was to Locke. It is to assert the autonomy of the social world from ideal economic laws, which are imaginary. It is to admit that social rules – and monetary rules first among them – are entirely man-made and instituted by society without any transcendent point of reference. The religion of gold – the symbolism of precious metals, which did so much to bolster ethical confidence – has totally disappeared. That era of human history has now been left behind. Money's legitimacy is purely political. Its foundation lies in democratic deliberation. Hierarchical confidence thus plays the essential role. It is expressed in economic policy, in which monetary policy participates. Ethical confidence has not disappeared, for morality itself now belongs to the secular order. Ethical confidence bases itself on the principles of democratic legitimacy to which we referred in Chapter 3, at least in those nations that identify with this mode of sovereignty. Money is legitimate if the policies that governments implement, by means of the capacity for debt granted by money, do not pursue merely arbitrary or partisan goals.

To conform to the collective norms that prevail in democratic nations, and thus to allow money to enjoy ethical confidence, economic policy must respect three principles: a *guarantee principle* that maintains the stability of finance and of money's purchasing power; a *growth principle* that preserves sustainable full employment (potential growth); and a *principle of justice* that establishes an acceptable level, relative to the nation concerned, of income redistribution, of risks, and of access to credit.

THE PAYMENT HIERARCHY IN NATIONAL MONETARY SYSTEMS

National payment systems are networks of interlocking networks. The central bank is their pivot, because the liabilities that it issues are the ultimate means of settling interbank balances. The superior liquidity of central bank money is consistent with the definition of the unit of account in fiduciary monetary systems. The unit of account is the unit for measuring the liabilities that the central bank allows to be accepted as money. Contrary to what 'legal restrictions' theorists tell us, this mode of organisation results from the development of the logic of banking, and not from the state imposing a rule. We already saw this in Chapter 3. Conversely, the monopoly conferred on the central bank to issue notes is indeed a legal restriction. But the hierarchy of monetary signs in fiduciary systems does not, as a logical necessity, mean the direct holding of the money issued by the central bank in the form of notes. From the perspective of the logic of payments, and of the stability of payment systems, a cashless mode of national monetary organisation is perfectly possible. Whether citizens would accept it is quite another matter. Here we again encounter the question of ethical confidence.

The characteristics of the various means of retail payments are summarised in Table 4.1. We can note that the characteristics of

Table 4.1
Instruments of retail payments

Monetary characteristics	Notes and coins	Scriptural money	Electronic money
The logic of circulation, and the medium for the payment	Decentralised, mechanical, anonymous (physical transfer).

Perpetual (except insofar as it wears out). Sovereign mark. Counted. | Centralised, arithmetical and personalised, (transfer of book entries).

Ephemeral (cheque). Acceptance by signature. | Centralised by interconnection. Electronic, personalised.

Ephemeral (electronically direted). Card or e-wallet guaranteed by issuer. |
| Information associated with payment | Memory dispersed and extinguished with each transaction.

The circulation of notes is equivalent to settlement. | The cheque is a voucher. Memory stored in movement between accounts.

Irrevocability means that payments can be guaranteed. But payer solvency is not monitored in real time. | The card is a certified voucher: signature by PIN.

With smart cards, payer solvency is monitored in real time |
| Liquidity and security | The means of payment is liquid.

Low security (vulnerable to theft) | Dissociated from the means of payment (cheques/≠accounts).

Protected (except signature theft). Collective security (lender of last resort) against bank insolvency. | Card provides account identification.

Protected by PIN. Collective security through lender of last resort. |

scriptural money and electronic money are similar in nature: both involve the centralisation of payments and the personalisation of the means of payment, which implies a mode of organisation that has fixed costs and growing yields. Electronic money is able to win out over scriptural money because of its greater technical efficiency (the reduction of value dates), because of the greater wealth of information it can convey, and due to the greater security of user identification it offers. So, we might imagine that in future electronic money could entirely replace scriptural money. The characteristics of coins and notes are the opposite to those of means of payment reliant on organised networks: coins and notes represent decentralisation as against centralisation, anonymity as against identification, a self-supporting as against a deposited liquidity, and a sovereign mark as against a private signature. Certainly, the electronic wallet does incorporate some of the traits of fiduciary money. Between two charging dates it does itself bear liquidity, because the payments that it realises are not individually relayed back to the bank account. So these payments are decentralised to a certain degree. But it is not anonymous, and the record of past payments is not erased with each transaction. It remains attached to a bank account and is debited in order to charge the wallet. It has to be guaranteed by the issuer bank. It does not, therefore, bear an absolute liquidity. Rather, it depends on the security provided by the hierarchical organisation of payments, which is itself reliant on the central bank.

Electronic transfers have revolutionised large-value payments over the last thirty years. The interconnection between computers, the extraordinary increase in their capacities to store and process information, and the breakthroughs in remote transmission techniques, have enormously increased the payment flows acting as the counterparties to financial transactions. Large-value payments comprise three categories: interbank funds transfer systems, systems for settling transactions in financial equities and derivatives products, and multi-currency payment systems. These make up large-value payments, as opposed to the low-value (retail) payments considered in Table 4.1. Large-value payments constitute the key sites of systemic risk, because their flows totalise the errors of judgement and the hazards that affect economic exchange as a whole. More precisely, large-value payments concentrate those risks that bear a heightened possibility of transforming into systemic risk. *A contrario*, large-value payment systems are liquid when they can transport large amounts rapidly (time-value) and securely (guaranteed final settlement). This liquidity in the broad sense is threatened by the combination of several types of risks.

Credit risk arises when payment orders that have already been transmitted are used to make other payments before the former have been settled. These risks are aggravated by time pressures. In particular, the risks arising from interbank positions during a day can be incurred on extremely high debts. Liquidity risk in the narrow sense arises when the payment branch and the delivery branch for an economic or financial object become dissociated. When the counterparty has been delivered and the payment has still not taken place, there is a pure liquidity risk. In the interconnection of payments, the liquidity risks induced by this dissociation take two forms: time to settlement and desynchronisation of settlement (or a Herstatt risk, in multi-currency payments).

Secure payment depends on the organisation which takes on these risks in order to guarantee final settlement. This presupposes that payment orders are irrevocable for the beneficiaries, as we have already mentioned. The subsequent settlement by the central agent must also be unconditional. In payment systems in which the central agent is a private institution, this unconditionality cannot be established since the agent cannot create, *ex nihilo* and in potentially unlimited amounts, the unconditionally accepted ultimate means of settlement. That is why there has to be a hierarchy of payment systems, with net balances from private systems feeding into the higher system (or systems) that settle accounts on the ledgers of central banks.

Rising risk levels have led European countries' monetary authorities to develop at least one large-value interbank payment system per country. These latter must be capable of processing multi-currency transactions, and they must also be both irrevocable and unconditional, in order to contain systemic risk. These higher-security systems, which take in the central bank operations executing monetary policy, have been interconnected via the TARGET 1 and then TARGET 2 systems since the launching of the monetary union. In order to increase security even further, these privileged systems make use of the most advanced information technology. This allows them to switch from end-of-day net settlement to continuous gross settlement.

From the origins of interbank clearing, each bank's net balances on the clearing house's books were calculated and settled at the end of each day. Central banks took on the liquidity risk on settlement. In order to avoid having to bear the inherent credit risks, the central banks established strict regulations. These included loss-sharing agreements between members, guarantees to the central bank in order to collateralise its credit lines, and limits on daily overdrafts.

In guaranteed gross settlement procedures, interbank payments are presented in real time and accepted after it has been verified that the payer can procure the necessary liquidity. For the central agent in the system, the credit risk can disappear entirely. But, when payments are rejected on account of insufficient immediate liquidity, a payment freeze can spread from one agent to the next. In order to prevent this, banks must have available abundant liquidity. This can be provided by the central bank thanks to reliable computer programmes that optimise the order of payments in a queue instead of delaying them, and thanks to intraday advances against very high-quality paper collateral.

The point to take from this tendency towards the centralisation of payments is the difficult choice between the efficient execution of payments, on the one hand, and the stability of the systems that organise these payments, on the other. Inventing a greater variety of private means of payment does not itself undermine the influence of central banks. On the contrary, it strengthens it. After all, the complexity of payments, swelling volumes and shorter time intervals all increase systemic risk. Private arrangements are incapable of imposing control over systemic risk, because such risk threatens the very foundation of confidence in money: namely, the definition of the unit of account in an unconditionally accepted monetary sign. That is why the integrity of payment systems goes far beyond questions of a merely technical nature. It makes up part of the regulation of the economy by money, via finance.

ARE RECENT DEVELOPMENTS IN VIRTUAL MONIES
A THREAT TO MONETARY STABILITY?

If one believes certain writers who are rather too keen on science fiction, electronic money would appear to be introducing such radical innovations that the anchoring of money in sovereignty is going to disappear. In this reading, the generalisation of electronic exchanges of assets and debts could realise the dream of pure economics: a globalised, intertemporal system of equilibrium prices. Yet nothing could be further from a reasonable evaluation of this phenomenon.

In Chapter 3 we showed that the proliferation of private monetary innovations is inherent to the history of capitalism. We have seen above that these first-generation electronic payments, looped back into banks, do not present any characteristics novel enough to concern the integrity of money. The fact that payments are irrevocable is the condition of their finality, and thus of the realisation of value. And the fact that the clearing-settlement system is looped into the central bank ensures that they remain irrevocable.

But what about the arrival of second generation means of payment, which is to say, ones operating on open retail or wholesale networks? Open networks are a product of the Internet revolution. Their main innovation is the provision of payment services and payment execution in chains that do not directly involve banks. Indeed, electronic wallets can be stored on computer hard disks, so that a transfer of value between two economic agents, A and B, can be realised through electronic transfer *e* without involving A and B's bank accounts with their banks *a* and *b*.[1] Contrary to what is often claimed, these transactions are not equivalent to cash. The transaction costs are, of course, much lower if transaction volumes are high. But these transactions require an electronic apparatus, with the possibility of counterparty recording, in contrast to the absolute anonymity of banknotes. Yet the need for absolute liquidity itself makes up part of the confidence in money in decentralised transaction mechanisms. That is above all why electronic transfers have the capacity to replace paper-based scriptural money. What would be threatened would be deposits with financial intermediaries.

Let us assume an online issuer of means of electronic transfers (for example, Google, Alibaba, Microsoft, and so on). Through its networks, it supplies electronic means of payment *e*. The accounts of individuals with the issuer's recording system are market commitments and assets. They produce continual flows of payments. A payment from agent X to agent Y is a sale of financial assets on a computer, or a pre-programmed commitment, a pre-programmed investment that Y makes on his online portfolio. The intermediary is

1   Charles Goldfinger, 'Intangible economy and electronic money', in OECD (ed.), *The Future of Money*, Paris: OECD Publications, 2000, pp. 87–122.

an online platform that handles the accounts of the economic agents. This intermediary guarantees the values of the assets to be transferred. It is the guarantor of a computerised settlements system, but it is not a bank, in that it does not make loans or issue its own debts. However, doing the job of a financial intermediary involves a lot more than arranging networks to connect different actors, however effective these may be. It also requires specialised information and a specific expertise for selecting assets and distinguishing good projects from bad.[2] That is to say, the informational asymmetries that result from the act of credit cannot be eliminated by transfer technologies. This is why the Internet giants will very likely be uninterested in becoming financial intermediaries. If they were to become such, what would define them as banks would be the combination of a capacity for intermediation and a payments network. They would then be regulated *as banks* in their banking activities.

In this book, we have shown that money is a social system founded on sovereignty. The contemporary nature of this sovereignty confers a general, permanent acceptability on the legal tender within a given country. This is why electronic transfers cannot acquire the same characteristics as fiduciary money. It is possible that future developments in electronic transfers will lead to transformations in the principles of sovereignty. In Chapter 3, we showed that such transformations have taken place throughout history. But there has to be a form of sovereignty to guarantee a base of fiduciary money. This base may be rather modest in quantity relative to the total means of payment held. But it must always be strictly positive; this suffices for the central bank to be able to control nominal interest rates.[3]

If electronic money mechanisms do not threaten the conduct of monetary policy, what do they mean for financial stability? Virtual monies like bitcoin are particularly unstable. The main question is how they interact with the monetary space that is anchored in the official money. Are there exchange flows between virtual monies and

---

2   Charles Goodhart, 'Can Central Banking Survive the IT Revolution?', Special Paper, Financial Markets Group, London: London School of Economics, 2000.

3   Michael Woodford, 'Monetary Policy in a world without cash', *International Finance*, vol. 3, no. 2, 2000, pp. 229–60.

bank deposits or notes? If there are, do these flows work in just one direction, or in both? Bitcoins pose a problem because they are an open-loop, bi-directional virtual money.

We should not confuse electronic money for virtual money. In the electronic transfer mechanisms considered above, the link between the official money and the electronic money is preserved. This latter has a basis in legal tender, in that the funds stored on computers are expressed in the official unit of account. But in virtual money mechanisms like bitcoin, the unit of account is itself virtual. This poses a serious problem when the virtual money operates on a bi-directional open loop: it becomes a tool of speculation by way of its entirely self-referential exchange rates. If there is any control over the exchange rate, it can only come from the issuer. And if this issuer is opaque and unknown, then extreme uncertainty will result.

So, what should central banks do, faced with the vagaries of speculation, if the virtual money can also be used to buy real goods and services? If the virtual money is created through a pre-existing conversion of money, and if the inverse exchange destroys the virtual money, then no money has been created. Can the conversion of central bank money into a virtual money have an impact on the speed of money's circulation to the degree that it would significantly reduce the central bank's balance sheet? In order to handle this risk, if it did materialise, central banks would have to impose compulsory minimal reserve rations on virtual monies. And what about the rebound effect that virtual monies have on the real economy? Leaving aside the risk of fraud, such an effect would result from the impact that unexpected fluctuations in the quantity of central bank money could have on Bank of International Settlements (BIS) interest rates.[4]

The rebound effect of virtual money above all concerns financial stability, by way of the fluctuations in its exchange rate. The exchange rate's self-referential character is entrenched by the lack of any settlement of virtual monies in bank or central bank money, and thus the lack of a lender of last resort. Yet, when asset transactions are settled in virtual monies whose exchange rates fluctuate widely, risks can

4   Bank of International Settlements (BIS), *Innovations in Retail Payments, Report of the Working Group on Innovations in Retail Payments*, May 2012, bis.org.

become systemic. For the irrevocability of payments is not guaranteed.[5] If the transaction flows in both directions took on such dimensions as to render them seriously liable to activate these risks, central banks would have to keep watch over these arrangements and apply the security rules of the payment system to them.

FROM THE INFLATIONARY GROWTH POLICIES UNDER
ADMINISTERED FINANCE TO THE LOW-INFLATION
POLICIES UNDER LIBERALISED FINANCE

The transformations of finance have not only transformed the instruments of monetary control. They have also profoundly altered the key institution of monetary sovereignty, by ripening the ideological and political conditions that have underpinned central bank independence.

Table 4.2. contrasts the regulatory consequences of administered and liberalised finance respectively. It is clear that the cyclical phenomena of the capitalist economy are not regulated in the same way. Administered finance has rigid interest rates. It is the inflation rate that fluctuates and regulates tensions on the markets of goods and credit. In particular, inflation reduces the value of debt. Inflation favours growth, so long as it does not imperil money's purchasing power to the degree that it is negatively perceived by the population. This was true in the Europe of the postwar 'golden age'. But this form of monetary regulation is vulnerable to an acceleration of inflation when economic agents lose confidence in the 'truth' of nominal values, and multiply their indexation formulas in the effort to preserve their share of the national income. In liberalised finance, on the other hand, inflation is stationary, so it is not sensitive to the cycle of economic activity. Rather, the nominal interest rate is flexible. This introduces vulnerabilities into the value of debts. It follows that the stability of money's purchasing power has as its corollary the instability of the credit on which the economic cycle depends. Financial crises replace spurts of inflation as symptoms of the difficulties of controlling the dynamic of capitalism through money.

---

5   European Central Bank (ECB), *Virtual Currency Schemes*, October 2012. www.ecb.europa.eu/pub/pdf/other/virtualcurrencyschemes201210en.pdf.

Table 4.2
Monetary regimes and financial structures

Administered finance (1950–1982)	Liberalised finance (1983–2007)
Rigid nominal interest rate: pivot is the bank base rate. The nominal rate reflects variations in inflation only with some inertia.	Flexible nominal interest rate: pivot is the obligatory rate. The nominal rate anticipates the central bank reaction to inflation.
Negative correlation between real rate and inflation. Debts are devalued by inflation: inflation-based monetary regime. The business cycle is regulated by variations in inflation.	**Positive correlation between nominal rate and inflation.** Debt quality depends on asset price fluctuations: monetary regime based on low, stable inflation. Economic cycle is regulated by asset price bubbles.

In hierarchical financial systems, the central bank is the institution on which confidence depends. Table 4.2 illustrates that these systems are buffeted by forces that serve to undermine them: namely, the variability of inflation, or financial instability. In Part III we will examine the deeper reasons for the contrast between these two monetary regimes. What they do have in common, however, is their mutual break with metal convertibility, which radically transforms the manner in which hierarchical confidence is legitimised.

The objectives of monetary policy express the balance of power in a given society. Finance, however, conveys a distorted image of this balance of power. The predominant influences comprise very different levels of political responsibility: the higher social purposes of nations, the financial structures that transmit economic imbalances, and the relations between the state and the central bank.

Two monetary doctrines were established after World War Two, in the context of administered financial systems. The differences between them would continue to be evident even within the context of liberalised finance. On the one hand is the Anglo-Saxon, Keynesian macroeconomic regulation (excepting the short 'monetarist' period of the 1980s). On the other is German ordoliberalism (Table 4.3).

Table 4.3
Contemporary monetary doctrines

	Anglo-Saxon Keynesianism	German ordoliberalism
Dominant principle	Growth (full employment) Justice (welfare state)	Stability guaranteed by civic rules Social-market economy
Assumptions regarding social cohesion	Finance is chronically unstable because capitalism is traversed by social conflicts that the markets are unable to regulate.	The market system is able to regulate the economy, on condition that it is structured by an order of public rules that will protect civil society from any arbitrary power.
The central bank's stance	Need for a policy mix: joint macroeconomic regulation by the public finances and by money. Constrained discretion policy.	Money has to be protected from political influence. Central bank is pre-committed to a monetary rule incorporated into the bargaining between social partners.
Impact of liberalised financial structures	Financial instability on account of the lever effect of indebtedness and asset speculation. Risk management.	Strengthen prudential rules and monitor risky conduct. No monetary effect so long as inflation is unaffected.

THE RISING POWER OF THE CENTRAL BANKS

The great inflation of the 1970s traumatised savers and prompted financial innovations that opened the way to the liberalisation of finance. This inflation also drove sharp critiques of monetary policy. Ethical confidence was shaken, because the balance between the principles of monetary stability, growth, and justice was upset. The dramatic about-turn in US monetary policy in October 1979 reflected a will to break out of inflation, at any cost. It showed that the population was prepared to grant increased weight to the principle of guaranteeing monetary stability. The change in the criterion of confidence was accompanied by the reorientation or reform of certain countries' institutions. The idea arose that in a universe that had become unmoored from metal convertibility, there needed to be some form of self-limitation on the power to issue money, in order to anchor confidence in the future development of money's purchasing power. For this to be achieved, it was necessary to establish and preserve the independence of the central banks.

The central bank's independence guarantees it an external position on the basis of which it can exercise the monetary sovereignty of which it is the depository. It is this independence that makes the central bank appear as an impartial mediator between the opposing interests of society. Central bank independence does not postulate any particular form of political action. It establishes an attitude of constrained discretion, and draws on a variety of monetary doctrines in order to guide its action. In a world in which the belief in a natural order has disappeared, confidence in the stability of money results from a game of coordination among different expectations. This game has no univocal solution, but multiple equilibriums. This does not mean, however, that it leads to mere indeterminacy.

After all, it is in the nature of collective standards, as conventions, that users adhere to them only with great inertia. Such is the case for the value of money.[6] Only when faced with repeated and consistent indications to the contrary will agents let go of the idea that money's purchasing power remains stable. When they do give up on this view, this leads to confusion about the meaning of the price movements they can observe, and suspicion when it comes to anticipating how prices will evolve in the future. The uncertainty leads to an anxious search for the surest support for liquidity.

It is, therefore, up to monetary policy to fix the point around which agents implicitly coordinate their expectations. This means providing a framework that eliminates all balances outside of a range indicated by the central bank. This framework attaches itself to a renewed monetary doctrine: flexible inflation targeting.[7] This means placing

6   Through econometrics, Anton Brender and Florence Pisani show the great inertia in expectations of inflation. See their *Les Taux d'Intérêt. Approche Empirique*, Paris: Economica, 1997.

7   An expression introduced by Ben Bernanke and Frederic Mishkin. See their 'Inflation targeting: A new framework for monetary policy?', *Journal of Economic Perspectives*, vol. 11, no 2, 1997, pp. 97–116.

monetary policy's short-term discretionary actions under the constraint of medium-term rules, thus assuring price stability. This stability is defined as a range of viable future inflation rates, within the scope of which the central bank's actions enjoy the confidence of economic actors.

Nonetheless, if central bank independence gives weight to the principle of guaranteeing the unit of account's statistical value, this cannot be its exclusive concern. The growth principle is threatened by financial instability and wiped out in financial crises. Moreover, the principle of justice has been destroyed, with social inequalities widening over more than three decades. The central bank thus has a dual responsibility: to prevent inflation corrupting the measure of values, and to prevent financial instability, which unleashes costly crises. The central bank's course of action in times of financial insta-bility is inspired by the doctrine of the lender of last resort.[8] This doctrine took form in the nineteenth century, the same time that the central bank was established as the banks' bank in order to prevent banking panics. Such panics result from rushes on deposits, out of fear that the banks lack liquidity. They also stem from the paralysis of the interbank market, on account of banks' reticence to circulate liquidity. *The central bank lends 'in the last resort' when it supplies banks on the money market with potentially unlimited sums of its own money, on conditions which it decides in a sovereign manner.* This action goes beyond the market logic of the exchange of credits; it is taken in order to contain systemic risk. It is ambiguous because it can itself feed incautious bank behaviour, insofar as it provides a collective insurance to banks that they can themselves anticipate. That is why the central bank has to keep its intentions unpredictable

---

8   The doctrine of the lender of last resort was first formulated by Bagehot, the *Economist* columnist, after the terrible financial crisis of 1866. This crisis was aggra-vated by the attitude of the Bank of England. As a competitor to the banks, it refused to lend to the financial institutions that were in trouble. Bagehot showed that in financial crises, the majority of financial institutions were solvent but illiquid. It was the shortage of liquidity that transformed localised financial difficulties into a general crisis. The Bank of England needed to act as a banks' bank; it needed to lend to the solvent but illiquid banks. It should have lent non-predetermined amounts taken from the higher liquidity it created at a penalising rate, against a collateral provided by borrowers and evaluated at pre-crisis levels.

and concern itself only with overall financial stability and not the fate of this or that particular financial institution. Yet in the global financial crisis of 2008, banks guilty of failing to respect the most basic rules of risk, or even of gross fraud, were saved without distinction and without condition, demonstrating that these principles were not being applied.

THE CHALLENGES OF SUSTAINABLE DEVELOPMENT
AND NEW FORMS OF MONEY

The world is caught in a three-dimensional crisis: an economic-financial crisis, a sociopolitical crisis, and a climate and environmental crisis. The dimensions of this crisis are interrelated. The first dimension is the enduring fall in growth rates, accompanied by a permanent rise in the total (public and private) debt relative to GDP in practically all countries, since the 2008 financial crisis. The second dimension of the crisis pivots on the first, by way of insufficient demand, rising income inequality, the financial strangulation of social systems, endemic underemployment, and the failure of education in promoting upward social mobility. Poverty traps deepen, and for many parts of society the prospect of improved living conditions is ever more distant. Citizens' distrust for political discourse grows in tandem with governments' inability to redefine social progress or indicate a way forward. Environmental degradation deepens social inequalities, and casts doubt over the immortality of democratic civilisation. This threat to the planet, linked to the climate imbalance, puts into question the viability of current forms of political sovereignty. This concern is all the more significant given that formal democracy provided no defensive fortification for the governments that proved powerless, under the blows of finance, to get a grip on the disorders of the 1990s and 2000s that led to the crisis. The worst expressions of this took place in the European Union, a confederation of nations incapable of agreeing on how to share out sovereignty. Yet it is indispensable that they do so, if the countries of the EU are to accept a minimal dose of institutionalised cooperation.

Nonetheless, outside of the inner circle of the established political institutions, the problems of inclusive and sustainable growth and sustainable development have forcefully pushed their way into public debate. That has been evident for a number of years. Sustainable growth is a new form of growth that incorporates ecological constraints while pursuing social equity. Its theoretical framework is that of inter-generational social wellbeing. A path for development is sustainable if this wellbeing does not decline across the generations. The impor-tance of this debate is in the radical challenge it presents to the ultra-neoliberal drift in economic theory over the last forty years, which has made possible the hegemony of finance over politics. For fundamental reasons, neoliberal economic theory cannot accommodate the perspective of sustainable development.

A Principle of Social Justice Is the Foundation of a New Principle of Sovereignty

Social wellbeing is not the aggregation of individual preferences. Indeed, Kenneth Arrow's impossibility theorem shows that it is impos-sible for any social choice process in a democratic society to aggregate heterogeneous individual preferences according to an incontestable idea of social wellbeing. It follows from this that any attempt to eradi-cate poverty and reduce inequalities must proceed the other way around, taking a criterion of social justice as its starting point. The utilitarian foundations of orthodox economic theory cannot provide this criterion; they even explicitly reject it. Indeed, we should define equality in such a way that interpersonal comparisons are possible not only through the calculation of empirical indicators, but also at the level of the principles that legitimise state decisions. Representative democracy offers no help here, either, because the rule of majoritari-anism – a rule that is purely procedural, and not substantial – cannot establish a just form of social redistribution. Majoritarianism under-values common goods, including nature, and crushes the interests of politically underrepresented minorities, just as the market excludes those who do not have access to money.

Only an ethical principle allows us to transcend the aporias in which liberal-democratic societies are today embroiled. There is a dramatic deterioration of common goods at the social level – where democracy is caught in the clutches of business – and at the environ-mental level, from the local to the planetary scale. Faced with these threats, the human collectives of the twenty-first century will, or will not, be ethical. We thus need to reinvest in the resources of political philosophy in order to drive transformations of sovereignty, in the sense of direct citizen involvement in state choices. In this domain, the Rawlsian principle of social justice is of fundamental importance.[9]

In defining justice as fairness, John Rawls offers a solution to the social-contract problem posed by Rousseau. In setting fairness at the heart of justice, Rawls sweeps away Jeremy Bentham's utilitarian theory. Human beings have moral faculties that define the meaning of the common good. It follows from this that reason is a human aptitude of a higher order than rationality, for reason offers the freedom to use 'public reasoning' in social evaluation. This is not only a formal freedom. It can only be exercised through access to primary goods, and if the principle of justice-as-fairness is respected, then no one can be denied these goods.

Primary goods establish the real freedom by which yardstick we should measure inequalities. Such goods are the material, educational and institutional resources at the basis of individual opportunities. They make up an ensemble that extends far beyond income alone. They include the quality of public health, primary education, basic freedom, as well as the absence of barriers (especially money and cronyism) to the powers and prerogatives attached to social functions and environmental goods. It follows from this that the only just inequalities are those that improve the situation of the most disadvantaged in terms of accessing primary goods.

These principles do not allow us to form an ordered classification of public policies from the perspective of fairness, nor to define an optimum of wellbeing, which is intrinsically out of reach. But they define the terms of a comparative approach, on which basis we can declare certain social situations unjust and reach agreement on shared ideals of justice. If development is to be inclusive, such agreements are obligatory.

Because it has a truncated view of labour and postulates a separation between labour and capital, economic theory that takes

---

9   John Rawls, *Justice as Fairness: A Restatement*, Cambridge, MA: Belknap Press, 2001.

individuals as its foundation is indifferent to the divisions between such individuals' situations. For it automatically assumes that these divisions are based on merit, in that they result exclusively from individual choices. According to this view, the market pricing system determines the most efficient allocation of resources by taking these choices into account.

If, on the contrary, we consider equality and freedom to be inseparable in the production of the common good, then we again find that Rousseau's social contract contradicts Locke. Inequality has a societal dimension, completely external to individualist conceptions of it. For Pierre Rosanvallon, the intersecting dimensions of the societal crisis that we are now living through proceed from the crisis of individualism. What follows from this is that sovereignty has to be reconstructed on the basis of *reciprocity* and the *common*.[10] Reciprocity signifies equal involvement in the polis. This is, indeed, an ethical notion, because reciprocity is a requirement for real equality in the use of authority. It thus provides a civic space on the basis of which a citizen sovereignty can be constructed. The notion of the common indicates what the sovereignty of the people could look like. It is at work in the organisation of urban space, in public debate that generates collective solutions to problems of spatial segregation and ecosystem degradation. These public choices can reorient money's own trajectories towards sustainable development.

We can thus understand this latest rupture in the long transformations of sovereignty explored in this part of the book. The sacred order that founded imperial sovereignties, in a political power interceding between Heaven and Earth, was transformed by Christendom. It evolved into an overlapping hierarchy, because the Church constituted itself as an institution autonomous from politics. The intellectual revolution that accompanied the great discoveries of the Renaissance destroyed divine transcendence and instituted the individual as the foundation of a democratic principle. We have seen that this democratic principle unfolded in different ways, concurrently with the separation of the political space into nation-states. We are living through a crisis of the aggravated individualism that results from

10   Pierre Rosanvallon, *La Société des Égaux*, Paris: Seuil, 2011.

society's enchantment by finance. It is necessary to exorcise this perverse deformation of individualism, reflected in the exaltation of 'letting the market decide', and instead recognise the meaning of the common. More than ever, individuals need to be able to act. This demands that they break out of the chains of individualism and rediscover reciprocity and the power of collective action.[11]

FROM THE PRINCIPLE OF JUSTICE-AS-FAIRNESS TO THE PRACTICE OF PUBLIC REASONING

Intergenerational social wellbeing is not just a matter of private consumption. It also includes public services – themselves producers of primary goods, and heavy consumers of intangible capital – and the environmental services derived from natural capital. This first dimension of the integration of the economic and the social invalidates the deluge of economic models claiming to study the pathways of sustainable growth by maximising the intertemporal consumption of a representative agent! For the irrepressible rise in inequality and the denigration of public goods through the domination of finance are essential characteristics of the unsustainable development of our economies.

The productive resources of societies guided by the criterion of justice-as-fairness should account for all those forms of social capital that are determinants of wellbeing. These determinants should be the object of a generalised accounting of nations' wealth. In Chapter 1 we showed that the measure of value resides in the monetary accounting of wealth. Pursuing inclusive and sustainable growth demands the generalisation of a principle of value that far transcends market valorisation. This must lead to an accounting revolution, and thus to an extension of the realm of money, as a language of numbers, to an accounting system that is at the same time national and private, and which includes human and intangible resources, as well as natural resources, as forms of capital.

11   There is a growing literature on the commons. We might note the following works: B. Coriat (ed.), *Le Retour des communs. La crise de l'idéologie propriétaire*, Paris: Les Liens qui libèrent, 2015; P. Dardot and C. Laval, *Communs. Essai sur la Révolution au XXIe siècle*, Paris: La Découverte, 2014; T. Negri and M. Hardt, *Commonwealth*, Cambridge, MA: Belknap Press of Harvard University Press, 2010.

Criticisms of the inclusive-wealth approach confuse prices with market prices. A price is a shared value resulting from a social contract whose significance depends on the size of the whole set of participants involved in the agreement. When this agreement escapes market organisation – because it concerns public assets, goods held in common, or relations that are external to the market – it nonetheless has a social value. For resources have been consumed, goods have been produced (the cutting of a given quantity of greenhouse gases is a good that has been produced), and services have been supplied (the depollution of a river, or the recycling of waste, is a service that has been supplied). These social values are the product of political processes in the broadest sense, which is to say, of reasoned public debates between stakeholders that bring together collective competences. Their elaboration represents a deepening of democracy, in accordance with the principle of justice-as-fairness. Estimating these kinds of prices implies a common conception of wellbeing and a shared understanding of the social and natural processes that bring about these social values. It also requires quantified information on these processes, allowing hypotheses to be elaborated regarding the possibility of substituting these different types of capital for one another.

Such a deepening of valorisation practices is indispensable if we are to organise a decentralised productive base oriented towards sustainable growth. This would also have major consequences for corporate governance. The bearers of competences whose productivity is realised through complementarity and cooperation are stakeholders in the product. They are, therefore, participants in the company's strategies for contributing to social wellbeing. Moreover, the enterprise's economic boundaries no longer coincide with the legal codification of the private company, in the presence of externalities. It follows that the enterprise must be recognised as an autonomous body, whose partners contribute different types of capitals. Through its board, which is its political organ, the enterprise defines its social interest – its common. In this way, the principle of sovereignty can be inscribed at the heart of civil society. Sets of companies that form industrial systems become stakeholders in collective partnerships, which make collective decisions in order to produce common goods.

These shared valorisation practices must overcome two additional distortions, each corresponding to different situations that the market is unable to correct. In the first place, the market underproduces goods and services that provide positive externalities – in other words, the social yield is superior to the private yield. In the second place, the market overproduces goods and services that combine to produce negative externalities – in other words, the private cost is lower than the social cost. A collective agreement on social value is the prerequisite for the provision and calibration of economic policy instruments appropriate to closing this gap and incentivising enterprises to work for sustainable growth. This way of organising interdependencies, which transcends and completes market relations, is particularly relevant when it comes to the interrelations between the economy and the environment.

Biodiversity and climate change are the two great environmental fields that appear as public goods and are, therefore, impossible to substitute for forms of capital produced according to market-based incentives. Nonetheless, the problems they pose for sustainable development policies are very different.

Climate change is a global, measurable phenomenon. Even so, the accumulated body of scientific research shows that the composition of the atmosphere can be linked to rising temperatures, and the damage that results can be analysed, even if it cannot be quantified in precise terms. A precautionary principle could allow for an agreement on the limit to acceptable temperature rises. Policies can be defined on the basis of a valorisation of carbon; investments can be deployed in order to counter the rise in greenhouse gas emissions, and financial instruments can be put to work as part of the recognised tools of economic policy.

Of course, biodiversity is also a public good from the perspective of the services provided by ecosystems. But it also defies analysis, on account of its heterogeneity and its dependence on specific contexts. More than a single public good, biodiversity encompasses sets of public goods that partially overlap and can also conflict with one another. While some forms of biodiversity are renewable, this is not the case for others; while some are local, others extend to a global scale. It follows that territories become the pertinent spaces for the exercise of sovereignty as the pursuit of the public good.

The Territorial Level and the Potential for Local and Complementary Monies

The territorial level is the privileged site for the pursuit of justice-as-fairness. Territories structured by urban organisation are the sites of cooperation *par excellence*. Indeed, towns are increasingly productive locations, on account of the effects of agglomeration, network externalities and information-intensive activities. But they are also the sources of social costs and forms of discrimination and exclusion, on account of the sprawl effects driven by real estate prices. From this, there result factors for social dislocation: congestion, time wasted, physical and mental attrition and pollution. These are all negative externalities, bringing an enormous loss of wellbeing. That is why a change in the urban economic model, inducing a change in our lifestyles, is a vehicle for inclusion and sustainability.

THE POTENTIAL OF LOCAL COMPLEMENTARY CURRENCIES

Since the late 1990s, there has been a significant development of local complementary currencies. This has deepened the social ties established by citizen efforts at territorial regeneration. As of 2013, we can list more than 4,000 local complementary currencies in over fifty countries, and their development has sharply accelerated since 2008. These monies are defined by specific units of account, developed at the initiative of groups of actors (private citizens, associations, cooperatives, enterprises, local collectives, foundations, and so on) who come together through a network or delimited territory. They serve to account for and to settle the exchanges between citizens, consumers, service providers and businesses. These complementary monetary systems are highly diversified (they include time-currencies, time banks, local commercial monies, and netting agreements between companies). Their forms vary according to the circulation technologies used, from paper money to scriptural or electronic money (including payment by SMS or smart cards).

These are monetary interventions produced by the sovereignty of the common, which is imbricated in the wider sovereignty of the nation-state. Depending on the concrete example in question, these interventions seek to fulfil three objectives. Local complementary currencies seek to support economic dynamism anchored in the local territory. They seek to establish new production and consumption practices that respect the environment, by encouraging production which conserves ecosystems, low-pollution transport, clean energies and reduced waste output. These mechanisms are an expression both of relations among humans and relations between humans and nature. In both cases, these are relations guided by values of solidarity, reciprocity, proximity, mutual aid and the fight against discrimination, by reintroducing into the circuits of exchange those previously excluded populations. For the collectives driving these initiatives, the goal is to transform the use of money by reinforcing its role as a social medium. It does this by increasing its speed of circulation and discouraging its accumulation through private appropriation. This means fighting against the ambivalence of money. For such local complementary currencies, money is perceived as a common good in the service of the collective. It is not seen as a means of personal enrichment. In this sense, it is quite the opposite of virtual currencies and their purposes. In complementary monetary systems, money appears as something consistent with its essence as a public good: a principle of forming and realising value that conforms to a social ethic.

Finally, local and complementary currencies seek to encourage civil society participation in managing the city's political administration. Indeed, these monetary initiatives fight for the transformation of individual behaviours, through the emergence of a collective consciousness that grasps the current challenges that capitalist societies face. This form of involvement differs from the delegation of responsibility characteristic of formal democracy, which separates citizens from the political spaces in which power is exercised. This indicates, therefore, the beginning of a transformation of the principle of sovereignty. This is a question of considerable importance, because here the individual citizen takes an active position, and her citizenship expresses itself through her belonging to a political community organised in a given territory. Thus, the real democracy of an active citizenry has the power to transform formal democracy by engaging local political elites in territorially-based sustainable development projects. Complementary local currencies are a financing and payment vehicle for the economic exchanges to which these projects give rise.[12] This promotes new relationships with the political, as well as novel modes of action, allowing individuals to act in view of common wellbeing and empowerment. All this requires that we construct the rudiments of a participatory democracy, taking its place within a logic of social and solidaristic economics and sustainable development.

These new forms of money thus represent means of cooperation between citizens, enterprises and public authorities in the social spaces most favourable to transforming the growth regime and thus driving away the perils of our current century.

LOCAL CURRENCIES AND BITCOIN: OPPOSED MONETARY LOGICS

A parallel is often made between local and complementary currencies and bitcoin. These two categories of monetary innovation, characteristic of the early twenty-first century, both question the relationship between money and sovereignty and express the will of their users to regain control of money. In the case of bitcoin, this takes place virtually and in a network, whereas for local and complementary currencies it takes place at the local territorial level. On the model of numerous other crypto-monies, bitcoin has clashed with the traditional conception of money, as something unitary, sovereign, territorial and centralised. But it is mistaken to compare it with local and complementary currencies. Far from it: bitcoin is instead a 'local complementary anti-currency'.[13]

Bitcoin is nothing but a disembodied monetary instrument. It is a private monetary innovation, detached from any notion of the public good, and disconnected from any sovereign authority that might guarantee its liquidity and perennial endurance. Bitcoin maintains the illusion of a virtual community through the networks of those who promote it and exchange knowledge about it. But it is not supported by any hierarchically organised banking system overseen by a central bank, or by a

12 Jean-Philipe Magnen and Christophe Fourel, *D'autres monnaies pour une nouvelle prospérité*, Report by the Mission d'études sur les monnaies locales complémentaires et les systèmes d'échanges locaux, 2015.

13 Denis Dupré, Jean-François Ponsot and Jean-Michel Servet, 'Le bitcoin, une tragédie du marché', Report by the Mission d'études sur les monnaies locales complémentaires et les systemes d'échanges locaux, 2015, pp. 18–22.

clearing system that would allow the lasting sustainability of payments to be guaranteed. It is completely decentralised. So, it cannot guarantee the liquidity necessary to the requirements of the economic circuit through which goods and services are produced, by way of advances that finance the real economy. When economic activities drop off, bitcoin cannot provide public stimulus measures. By definition, the distribution of bitcoin is highly unequal: it favours those who had it first (early adopters), to the detriment of the latest users. The hyper-volatility in its price means that it is a monetary instrument little-conducive to fixing expectations and making payments permanent.

Contrary to the idea that it could provide a solution to the problems posed by the international monetary regime, bitcoin cannot fulfil the functions of a global public good. Fixed in advance, the supply of bitcoin cannot respond to the global need for liquidity. Its highly speculative character does not work in favour of stabilising the international monetary system. Holding such currency is all the riskier given that there is no guarantee that it can be converted into 'official' money by the public authorities. While the protocol for validating transactions is itself highly secured, the same is not necessarily true of bitcoin storage. The anonymity of bitcoin transactions (or at least, the difficulty in tracing operations) is a godsend for cyber-criminality and money laundering. If we take a look at the crypto-anarchist and libertarian ideas that inspire bitcoin, we see that it seduces users through the illusion that they are taking ownership over money and ridding themselves of what they consider to be the harmful interventions of the actors charged with controlling it (states, central banks and other banks).

Bitcoin thus reveals its true nature as a money that is anonymous, anti-sovereignty, anti-bank, anti-state and – therefore – anti-commons. This is quite unlike local currencies. Given their social character and the fact that they complement legal tender, local currencies in fact strengthen the sovereignty of the commons at a territorial level, without necessarily entering into contradiction with the sovereignty of legal tender. Of course, their development does express a challenge to the existing symbolic order of money: the citizens interested in these currencies deem the official currency to no longer embody collective wellbeing, the banks to no longer serve the real economy, and even money to be no more than a pure instrument of speculation. In taking recourse to citizens' currencies, these agents seek to take back owner-ship of money and to associate it with new values attached to sustain-able development and collective action. To some extent, they do contribute to laying the foundations for a new monetary regime.

Nonetheless, if bitcoin is nothing but a speculative avatar of the ideology of a world without institutions, the payments technology that it supports does concern banks. In Chapter 1 we showed that the finality of payments is the pivot of the monetary system, as a process that realises value through exchange. The clearing and settlement that permits this finality is realised on the basis of the banks' position on the clearing house accounts kept by the central bank. The central clearing house holds the general ledger of payments. Taking inspira-tion from the technology that underpins bitcoin, the big banks have begun to explore the possibility of a structure that organises clearing and settlement anonymously through a computer network (a block-chain) that records, validates and updates transactions in real time. The blockchain is charged with showing who possesses what amount of money on any given date.

Certainly, the banks' idea is not to extend the decentralised settle-ment system to just anyone, but rather to keep it within a banking club. Such a banking club could be able to establish a clearing and settlement system without any central bank, with the aid of cryptogra-phy. The banks are currently investing in this because they think that this mode of real-time clearing and settlement could dramatically reduce transaction costs and transaction times (the time separating the recording of payment orders from the final verification of the payment). Some have projected that this could save as much as $20 billion a year.

But this is still far in the future. The banks will have to overcome huge obstacles to prove that the technology is safe and robust. The change of scale presents a formidable challenge. Bitcoin technology limited the quantity of money created to very small amounts. How can it be adapted to the gigantic sums involved in the transactions of globalised finance? If we know that final liquidity is inherent to the very concept of money, and it is not plugged into the settlement of debts, then how can the supply of money be determined? How would the system be regulated to limit the inflationist effect of the flow of payments accepted in the blockchain? Many questions will need to be resolved before entirely private clearing and settlement systems can produce the public good that is money.

DO COMPLEMENTARY LOCAL CURRENCIES THREATEN THE OFFICIAL MONETARY SYSTEM?

When civil society actors create local and complementary currencies, they are seeking common mediums that benefit communities. Their intention is not, however, to break away from the official currency. Indeed, complementary monetary systems normally borrow their symbolic and practical frame of reference from the official monetary system. This serves the creation, acceptance and regulation of these currencies. But it is also useful if they are to operate functionally within local markets.[14] The rules for the issuing and regulation of these currencies reveal as much. One can lay one's hands on the local currency by exchanging it for the official currency. This exchange takes place at parity with the official currency. This is not a legally established ratio of equivalence, but it is practically useful in that it gives the market participants proper bearings for comparing prices. The majority of local trading currencies build up reserve funds in the official currency, collected when the participants who want to acquire sums in the local currency convert the one for the other. These reserve funds are deposited in accounts at either conventional financial institutions, or else cooperative or ethical ones.

Because the local currency's purchasing power is backed up by that of the official currency, there is no specific risk of inflation from uncontrolled issuance. The local currency is issued for an equivalent deposit in the official currency. This is a substitution, which does not result in any overall (net) creation of money. The advantage of local currencies is that they encourage the circulation of money. In the case of mutual-credit currencies (time banks and clearing houses) the possibilities of an overdraft in local currency are very limited. Debits by some correspond to credits by others. So there is no risk of

---

14   Pepita Ould Ahmed, 'Can a community currency be independent to the state money? A case study of the credito in Argentina (1995–2008)', *Environment and Planning A*, vol. 42, no. 6, 2010, pp. 1346–464.

inflation. There are a few systems that represent exceptions (the WIR system in Switzerland, or community development banks) in that they offer credits for investment, provided in the official currency. The risks, here, are no different to any issuance of bank money.

These mechanisms are tied to the official monetary system, so there is no need for the monetary authority to provide specific regulation in order for them to be properly structured. Their development benefits from a collective learning process, which draws lessons from past experiences that posed problems of fraud and inflation. Such was the case of the local currency initiatives taken in Argentina.[15]

Beyond Local Currencies: The Monetary Financing of the Energy Transition

Taking action against global warming and emerging from economic stagnation are the two urgent tasks of our time. The public authorities – especially in Europe – are addressing these as if they were totally separate problems. And up until now, they have failed on both counts. On the one hand, the International Panel on Climate Change (IPCC)'s mean projection tells us that the world is on course for a 4°C rise in temperatures by the end of the century, and there is a non-negligible possibility of an extreme risk of around 6°C. On the other hand, the long-term growth slowdown in the advanced countries, so-called secular stagnation, persists thanks to the dramatic weakening of productive investment. According to the International Monetary Fund, at the end of 2014 aggregate productive investment in the advanced countries, measured in terms of real value, was 25 percent below the level it would have reached if the tendency prior to the 2008 crisis had continued.[16] This anaemic capital accumulation is accompanied by very weak inflation, a drastic collapse in the price of raw materials, and a generalised rise in indebtedness, which has gripped the entire world. Central banks are the only public authorities to have taken reactive measures, but this cannot compensate for the

15   Ibid.
16   IMF, *World Economic Outlook*, Chapter 3, 'Where are we headed? Perspectives on potential output', and Chapter 4 'Private investment: What's the holdup?'

negligence of the political authorities, particularly in Europe. The central banks' 'non-conventional' policies, involving the massive creation of liquidity by buying mostly public equities on the secondary markets, have only had very limited success in the attempt to revive effective demand and kickstart growth. This is because the process of transmitting monetary policy through the purchase of pre-existing financial assets does not directly create any new income. It has only an indirect and uncertain effect on the behaviour of private actors, coming as it does after the trauma of the crisis. And even this is vulnerable to serious losses along the way.

The problem that economies are facing is of a different order altogether than it would be if it was just a matter of coming out of a recession in a short-term cycle. Systemic financial crises engender long periods of stagnation because they herald deep changes in growth regimes, so-called industrial revolutions. These revolutions bring forth waves of 'secular' innovations that shake up existing ways of living and drive major political and institutional changes. Table 4.4 presents a synopsis of the great secular innovations. These revolutions also concern energy and information and transport networks. That is why they have the capacity to extend across all activities, and to remodel whole economies.

Table 4.4
Secular innovations

Type of innovation	Emergence	Spread	Adjustment crisis	Maturity	Total period
Steam engine, textiles	1762–1774	1794–1834	1834–1845	1844–1861	1762–1861
Rail and steel	1831–1847	1847–1888	1888–1895	1896–1917	1831–1917
Mass production	1882–1908	1908–1937	1937–1949	1950–1973	1882–1973
Information and communication	1961–1981	1981–2000	2000–2013	2013–?	1961–?
Environment	1972–2015	2015–?	?	?	1972–?

Sources: *Joseph A. Schumpeter*, Business Cycles, *New York: McGraw-Hill, 1939*; *David S. Landes*, The Unbound Prometheus: Technological Change and Industrial Development in Western Europe from 1750 to the Present, 1969, *Cambridge: Cambridge University Press; Michel Aglietta*, Régulation et crises du capitalisme, *Calmann-Lévy, 1976. These latter two revolutions are the author's own estimates.*

These industrial revolutions have a fundamental impact on money and finance. At the same time, transformations in monetary systems forge the means of regulating them. Thus, the great rail revolution involved both massive and long-term investment. These investments could only be financed by state engagement and public guarantees, as well as an extension of the banking principle to large-scale branch banking and a huge expansion of bond markets, which itself owed to the legal recognition of limited companies. The systemic risks that stemmed from these new forms of indebtedness led to the promotion of central banks as the banks' banks.

The mass production brought about through Taylorism and the massive rise in individual car ownership in the third industrial revolution resulted in the emergence and then blossoming of 'labour societies' in the second half of the twentieth century. This followed in the wake of terrible worldwide financial and political crises. In labour societies, finance was regulated in order to facilitate the investment in production. The rise in real incomes was indexed to productivity gains, and social protection systems were developed. This resulted in the greatest expansion of industrial capital in history.

In its opening phase, the wave of IT innovations essentially encouraged finance and the services associated with it. Industrial companies were financialised and their objectives and modes of governance were subjected to the so-called 'shareholder value' principle. The result was spectacular: a fall in growth and in productive investment, a deceleration of productivity gains, stagnation in real median primary wages, and enterprise growth coming through external means. This increased the concentration of capital ownership and offered elite managers gigantic windfalls, camouflaged as salary benefits. Finally, and most importantly, this meant that profits were monopolised by financial intermediaries and the services associated with them (which is to say, all manner of consultancy firms and law offices).

The planetary challenge of the new industrial revolution – both the second phase of IT innovation and the energy transition necessary to meet the threats of climate change – consists in placing finance at the service of the economy. Finance must be deployed in the interests of a massive new wave of productive investment at the global level. The principle guiding this new age in societies' development must be the *promotion of the commons*. This principle unfolds from the local level – accompanied by the local currency innovations mentioned above – to the global level. For the warming climate is a global public good. Between these two levels, we must also take into account the interdependence between ecosystems and economies of different spatial scales.

Thus far, this interdependence has been an externality which capitalism has shamelessly exploited, without recognising its value. If we are to extend the principle of value beyond the market economy, under the sovereignty of the commons, then this requires a fresh transformation of monetary systems and their articulation with finance. The climate emergency is the window of opportunity to launch this new great transformation.

The lack of value placed on the transition to low-carbon economies and the lack of finance for this transition represents a double failure of market logic. This transition could restructure our perspectives on the future and revive the incentives to invest. We still need political measures to establish a social value for carbon, thus orienting investment towards the objective of sustainable growth in those countries where political priorities are evolving. What also remains to be done is to redefine financial intermediation, and to do so in connection with the development of the role of money as a principle of value realisation. We should recognise that fighting greenhouse gases through fresh productive investment has a universal social value, whose monetary expression is differentiated across the various sovereign countries. Doing this would open up the opportunity to transform the financial securities and credits issued in order to finance such investment into carbon assets. This could proceed via the purchase of these securities and the repurchase of these credits by the central bank, in its bank refinancing operation. *This is a question of a monetary recognition of the commons, on which basis we could overcome environmental externalities.*

Innovative productive investment – whether related to new sources of energy, mass transit infrastructure, or means of improving energy efficiency – encounters obstacles that do not only owe to the lack of a reference carbon price that would enable the selection of the most efficient technologies. When the theorists of pure economics assert that this is indeed the stumbling block, they presuppose unlimited access to a perfectly efficient finance. We saw in Part I how untenable this hypothesis really is, and the historical analysis of this part has further confirmed this. Low-carbon investment is immersed in a both ecological and technological uncertainty, yet it is itself long term, with income flows staggered across time and with costs concentrated on the initial phase. In the current conditions of secular stagnation, characterised by a mass of idle savings and a low level of productive investment, organising a financial intermediation that could reallocate these savings with the aid of public guarantees for private risk-taking would mean retrieving a form of financial organisation that allowed the historical development of public transport. It is bewildering that we no longer know how to finance public and private investment, when we did a hundred and fifty years ago.

If, instead of buying securities on the secondary market, which creates no new income, the central banks bought assets that were the counterparty to new real investment, this acquisition would be directly linked to the income growth produced. This balance-sheet expansion policy could be plugged into a low-carbon investment programme directed at cutting carbon. Indeed, governments could set this latter objective according to the commitments made in an international agreement. This would create an impulse to investment, which would in turn allow us to set in motion a growth process that began to transform the production structure in the direction of a low-carbon economy.

A MONETARY PLAN TO FINANCE INVESTMENT IN THE ENERGY TRANSITION

The foundation of this plan is a public guarantee for a new category of assets. This category would be based on cutting greenhouse gases, measured in carbon. This guarantee would allow the central banks to refinance credits to companies engaged in low-carbon investment, certified *ex post* by independent certification agencies. The companies making this investment would obtain carbon certificates for the amounts certified. Their monetary value would be the quantity of carbon saved multiplied by the social value of carbon as established by the public authorities. Companies would then pay back their credits with these certificates. The lender banks who collected these certified credits could then exchange them at the central bank, which would transform them into carbon assets by taking them off the assets side of its balance sheet. The counterparty to this would be a creation of monetary reserves for the banks.

For such a mechanism to function, two kinds of engagement by public authorities would be necessary. They would have to both guarantee the reduction of a predetermined quantity of carbon over a given period (for example, five years) and establish the social value of carbon. This notional value (which is not a market price) recognises the social cost of the damage that climate change causes, as well as the social advantages of economic activities that reduce this damage. We would have to create an appropriate financial mechanism on this basis. Its pivot would be an independent certifying body that defined the typology of low-carbon plans and the methodologies for evaluating reduced emissions, depending on the technologies involved, the economic sectors and the timescale of the projects. This body would supervise decentralised agencies who would do the evaluation work on the ground.[17]

Establishing a social value for carbon (SVC) plays a critical role here. This compensates for the disadvantageous effect that the discount rate poses to long-term investments by allocating them a flow of certified value that grows over time. It protects against any risk that excessive amounts of money will be created, because the money is created *ex post* on certified investment, whose aggregate volume cannot exceed the amount defined in advance by the government guarantee. Finally, it prevents any carbon bubble, because the SVC is not a market price. Rather, the SVC's evolution is fixed in relation to the government's objective. The SVC is an innovation greatly superior to the introduction of a market price for carbon, for it applies to new investments and encourages innovators, without directly devaluing already-established capital, as a high market price for carbon would. This is not a price that judges the social value of the damage and the social

17   Michel Aglietta, Étienne Espagne and Baptiste Perrissin Fabert, 'Une proposition pour financer l'investissement bas carbone en Europe', *France stratégie. Note d'analyse*, no. 24, 2015.

cost of spending on cutting carbon. Such values are totally uncertain in the long term, since there is no certainty over how greenhouse gas emissions, temperature shifts and the resulting economic damage will interact. Rather, this price is the marginal cost of cutting a predetermined amount of emissions. There is much less uncertainty over the value to choose for this.

On such a basis, the financial mechanism could work as follows. The banks that have financed enterprises recuperate the certified investment through the repayment of credits. The credits are grouped into categories according to criteria defined by the body that supervises the certification process. Pools of certified credit are established, bought from the banks by public financial bodies for the purposes of securitisation. Categories of securitised bonds are issued as a counterparty, whose junior tranches these bodies themselves hold onto. The other tranches are sold to institutional investors. A market for securitised carbon bonds is formed. The central bank can purchase these bonds on the same conditions as it purchases public debt titles. It can do this according to its monetary policy objectives. It could also intervene on this market in such a way that the bonds' price does not diverge from the SVC.

This mechanism could thus simultaneously both mobilise bank credit and redirect long-term savings towards low-carbon investments. This would continue the historical path of relations between monetary innovations and the transformations of societies. In our current century, this signifies a mutual adaptation between the evolution of the forms of money and the establishment of the sovereignty of the commons.

Part III

Crises and Monetary Regulation

As we have seen in Part II, money's historical trajectory can be likened to a long river whose flow has been far from tranquil. There have been gigantic systemic changes, with social transformations causing (and being caused by) political upheavals. The enduring element has been money itself, as a system that defines and realises economic value. But the permanence of this social logic is not automatic. History is traversed by monetary crises. These crises are both recurrent and singular. How can we keep monetary crises at bay? How can we prevent them from threatening the endurance of our societies? As we saw in Part II, this is not always possible. Some monetary crises blow apart the order of sovereignty on which the monetary system is based. Others, conversely, lead to monetary reforms that change the rules and modes of regulation but also re-establish confidence in the principle of sovereignty on which the existing monetary order is founded. What guidelines can we follow in order to understand crises across the breadth of time and the diversity of monetary societies?

MONETARY CRISES: CRISES OF CONFIDENCE?

Money is the operator of value, which is a social relationship of belonging. Part I showed that the institutional architecture underlying this role engenders three hierarchically ordered levels of confidence: the ethical, the hierarchical and the methodical. The operator of these levels is the payment system, which itself functions according to three rules: evaluation on the basis of the unit of account, the circulation of debts, and finality of payment through the settlement of debts. Confidence is reproduced as a result of the effectiveness and solidity of the rules for the social validation of transactions.

The payment system reflects the tensions and dysfunctions that run through society and transmit themselves to the debt structure. They introduce fragilities regarding the finality of payment in this structure, because they create doubts as to the solvency of debts deferred over time. The possibility of these doubts transforming into a generalised crisis of confidence presents a *systemic risk*.[1] This term designates the generalised failure of financial markets and intermediaries to coordinate the behaviour of those who demand means of financing and those who ring-fence their savings. Systemic risk is the risk of the emergence of conditions in which individual agents' attempts to improve their financial situations worsen the overall situation of all agents. The materialisation of this risk in a systemic crisis paralyses the monetary channels through which the mobilisation of available savings takes place. Such a mobilisation depends on confidence. The scale and extent of a crisis thus depend on the level of confidence that is damaged or, indeed, destroyed.

Methodical confidence is founded on practice. It results from the repetition of the acts that bring exchanges to their proper conclusion, and debts to settlement. This confidence is methodical because it reproduces itself through routine or calculation. It can accommodate itself to foreseeable variations in the monetary flows of receipts and expenses, on condition that the extent and the sequential ordering of these variations are consistent with past experience. So, it is the first line of defence. It absorbs the asset price fluctuations that produce

---

1 Systemic risk is the domino effect whereby the financial fragilities that build up during the expansive phase of a financial crisis spread and rebound across the system. These fragilities owe to the rapid development of indebtedness and the rise in the price of financial assets, which lead to bubbles of speculation. When the bubble bursts, the debts appear excessive to some actors. This provokes a drying-up of liquidity among financial intermediaries, on account of the counterparty risks that spread through the spider's web of reciprocal debts. The interbank financing market becomes paralysed. Another route through which it spreads is the fire sale of financial securities by indebted actors who need to honour urgent repayment deadlines. This provokes a fall in equities prices, which spreads from market to market.

transfers of wealth limited enough as to not put into question the legitimacy of the sovereign monetary institution.

When there are large-scale shocks, or a series of upheavals whose force increases with momentum, we can no longer use the same bearings to analyse the quality of debt. The result is confusion in the circulation of debts, and confusion about the possibility of settling them. If the policy of the institution that issues the ultimate liquidity does not manage to restore these bearings, then more confusion will follow. This triggers strategic interactions that result in a polarisation of the quest for liquidity. Methodical confidence enters into crisis and unleashes a contagious and thus polarised quest for liquidity. This means an overvaluation of hierarchical confidence. Here, it is important that the monetary authority is capable of mastering this obsessive demand for its own debts. Only then can it avoid a paralysis of the financial system, if creditors no longer agree to bear any other form of debt than this authority's own.

Hierarchical confidence concerns the authorities that have the power to change monetary rules. When these authorities are confronted with an extraordinary demand for liquidity in relation to the usual requirements of monetary circulation, doubts arise: do these authorities have the means to satisfy demand? Have they understood why this is happening? Do they have political will? This latter question depends on creditors' and debtors' respective political influence, but also on state interests. If there is a public debt and it deteriorates as the crisis develops, will the state be inclined to monetise its debt, to an extent that arouses its creditors' concerns? Or has it already done so? If these questions persist and spread, hierarchical confidence can itself be undermined. That is especially true if the state takes advantage of its superior position to take political actions that are judged arbitrary or partisan.

This, indeed, is the reason why political power must be backed up by an uncontested principle of sovereignty, meaning a representation of collective values in which the society's members identify the sources of their 'togetherness'. Politics adapts itself to this representation, reinforcing its legitimacy, and thus maintains the ethical confidence without which hierarchical confidence would enter into crisis. *When ethical confidence is shaken, the official currency ceases to be* dokima – *not*

188 CRISES AND MONETARY REGULATION

simply legal, but legitimate. When the currency is not considered to be legitimate, the agents who use it lose confidence in the established ultimate liquidity, and feverishly search for another basis for wealth that is better able to protect their assets. This search is a hazardous one. It brings the crisis to its climax. The space within which value is measured loses its homogeneity, as each actor seeks to assert her own unit of account over the others.[2] The coherence of prices is destroyed, and economic time disappears. There is no longer the opportunity to embark on new projects, nor the time to take initiatives. All that counts is the immediate, feverish search for some means of protecting existing assets. The results of this search end up polarising around some new shared belief, whose grounding is often external to the former monetary space; often, this means a foreign currency, which becomes the new unit of measurement. Hence, mimicry is the general logic in play in extreme monetary crises, at the critical moment in which the official currency is rejected. We will go on to show how the collective rejection of the national currency climaxed in the German hyperinflation of 1923.

We can thus outline a correspondence between the forms of confidence and the rules that constitute money as the system of coordinating market exchanges.

Forms of confidence	Rules of systems of payments
Methodical	Circulation of debts, transfer of risks
Hierarchical	Clearing and settlement
Ethical	Preservation of the unit of account

THE TOPOLOGY OF MONETARY CRISES: CENTRALISATION AND FRAGMENTATION

Money is the pivot of a system of debts, in which it is itself the highest debt. Confidence in money demands that the hierarchy of debts be respected. That is why the issuer of the ultimate debt must impose a constraint to ensure that the other debts are settled. This is necessary

2   André Bejin, 'Crises des valeurs, crises des mesures', *Communications*, no. 25, 1976.

in order to contain the potential rivalry between debtors and creditors.

Crisis symptoms appear when the system of debts is not organised in a proper hierarchy. In this situation, the legitimate deferral of debts over time, and their ultimate settlement, are no longer taken for granted. This awakens the latent conflicts of interest between creditors and debtors. In this context, two opposed situations are possible. In the first situation, the debtors are subject to excessive constraints in terms of repayment or the costs of their credit. This threatens their solvency for global reasons, independent of their choices of projects. In the second situation, the debtors are financed in such a way that the renewal of the debts is assured by the automatic creation of money. Such a situation effectively frees debtors from the constraint to settle their debts, whatever their quality. This unduly protects debtors and thus deprives creditors of their rights to capital. From these two situations there flow two structural dysfunctions in the payment system, corresponding to two types of monetary crises.

The first of these is fragmentation. Money is so scarce that debt settlement becomes paralysed, resulting in a spread of bankruptcies and a collapse in asset prices. Actors' preference for holding onto liquidity aggravates the situation by increasing the shortage of money. This is a deflationary crisis, to which metal-based systems were particularly vulnerable. The recasting of coins, the minting of the basest metals and the transformation of units of account were the public policies implemented in response to these perils, albeit without managing fully to get rid of them.

The second form of structural dysfunction is extreme centralisation. The hierarchy of debts is undermined by confusion between the different levels. The evaluation of the quality of debts is blurred, because the central bank automatically refinances debts whose deadlines cannot be honoured. What results is excessive issuing of money, with the increase in liquidity destroying the compulsion to settle. Savers feel that their wealth is being threatened, and in the attempt to preserve it they search for substitutes for money. As they run away from money, an inflationary spiral develops that raises doubts over the long-term integrity of the unit of account. As a consequence, the conservation and transmission of assets are impaired by the collapse of confidence in liquidity. This is an inflationary crisis, which can degenerate into hyperinflation. This unleashes a situation of strategic interdependence, as actors seek an alternative form of liquidity outside of the official monetary system. Ethical confidence, and thus money's legitimacy, must be re-established through a monetary reform that also implies a change of political regime, or even a refoundation of the principle of sovereignty. Monetary systems with a self-referential fiduciary unit of account are vulnerable to this type of crisis in a context of acute political conflict resulting from the unsustainable burden of public debts.

This theoretical framework provides a set of parameters for interpreting monetary crises, building on the observations of the first two parts. Seeking to delve deeper into such processes, Chapter 5 examines the types of crises that have punctuated history. It does so by setting these crises in relation to the main stages of monetary innovation and the associated principles of sovereignty, as were already highlighted in Part II. Here we will not deal with capitalism's global financial crises, from 1873–96 to 1929–38, and the one that began in 2008, which directly concern international financial and monetary relations. We will deal with these in Part IV.

Chapter 6 investigates monetary regulation in capitalist societies in greater detail, from the classical age to the era of labour societies. In so doing, it also addresses the contemporary problems posed by the great transformation that is sustainable development.

5
Monetary Crises in History

Following the path set out in Part II, this chapter examines episodes of crisis in the metal-based systems of antiquity, the dualist systems from the Middle Ages to the eighteenth century, the gold standard era, the inflationary periods of the twentieth century, and finally the return to deflationary crises heralded by the great financial crisis that began in 2007.

CRISES IN THE METAL-BASED SYSTEMS OF ANTIQUITY

In Part II we showed that minted – and thus legally established – metallic money is inextricably bound to the public finances. In the critical moments of weakened political authority, monetary crises were closely linked to crises in the state's finances. In the Greek cities, monetary difficulties owed to prolonged exceptional military spending, to military defeats that resulted in a loss of territories from which metal ores were extracted (as with Athens in 413 BC after the defeat at Syracuse), or else to civil wars within the cities. Monetary crises were above all the consequence of financial or budgetary crises. Nonetheless, there were sometimes also purely monetary crises, which is to say self-referential crises. These were triggered by the contagious demand for money resulting from the fear of liquidity shortages. During the Peloponnesian war, all of these factors interacted. In Athens, the shortage of silver-money forced the city's government to mint bronze coins. This alloy of copper, tin and lead was not a precious metal; in fact, at the end of the fifth century BC, the bronze/silver ratio was of the order of 100:1. The bronze money was minted with the same type as the *tetradrachmas* that had disappeared from circulation. The fundamental point is that citizens had strong enough confidence in the Athenian democracy for them to accept the bronze coins during the war, despite the price rises resulting from this injection of base-metal money.

Bronze money also appeared in the territories of Athens's enemies in this period, in Corinth and Syracuse. It improved monetary circulation by replacing miniscule silver coins that had proved impractical.

In the Roman Republic, as we saw in Chapter 3, the government rapidly devalued the libral bronze *as*, which had been the monetary standard at the beginning of the Second Punic War. But this was not enough. The state had to borrow private money, suspend payments, use public assets as a guarantee for loans, and requisition wealth in addition.

The crises of the first century BC were different. These were private debt crises that caused payment freezes as money disappeared due to the fear of civil war. Roman society had indeed become very unequal in a number of ways. The increasing concentration of wealth that resulted from military conquest had created enormous inequalities between the people (the plebs) and the landowning and political aristocracy. There were also intergenerational inequalities among the patricians, because access to the higher public functions (including Senate elections) was extremely expensive. Finally, this plutocratic society was divided over the question of the legitimacy of different forms of enrichment – between the *parvenus*, who had been able to buy their lofty social positions because of their business success, and the heirs, who considered that their forebears' past services to the state entitled them to perpetual annuities. Following these episodes came a payment crisis, a product of hoarding, which itself owed to the extreme rivalry between debtors and creditors. This crisis resulted in deflation, amplifying the debts' real value even further, with devastating effects. The state took expedient measures, abolishing part of the debt, requisitioning the sanctuaries' coffers in order to mint money, and banning the holding of liquidity above a maximum level.[1]

The Great Inflation Crisis in the Late Roman Empire

At the end of the second century AD, the deterioration of public finances forced a reduction in the fineness of coins. The fine metal purity of some of the coins that already existed was reduced, and subsequently, in 215, the emperor Caracalla introduced a new silver coin, the *antoninianus*. His aim was to increase the mass of money in circulation. Up until 258, the depreciation of monies compared to their metal content was regulated, such that the hierarchy of value ratios in Rome's three-metal structure was respected. This was sufficient to preserve relative stability in the prices of goods. Subsequently, the depreciation of the *antoninianus* accelerated, triggering the disintegration of the monetary hierarchy.

In 274, the emperor Aurelian undertook a monetary reform which, although posed as a return to order, in fact served to precipitate the crisis. Aurelian decided to re-establish the *antoninianus* at the same gold-to-silver ratio that had existed before 258, even though the coin hardly contained any silver anymore. The market re-established the 'real' value of this coin through a huge nominal inflation in the price of goods. Thus, between 274 and 295, prices in Egypt multiplied forty-eight-fold. *The situation was as if economic agents had rejected the official unit of account and chosen to fix prices to gold.* Indeed, market prices and the price of gold in silver *denarii* increased in tandem. This was a case of a collective lack of confidence in the legitimacy of the monetary rules, and thus a crisis of ethical confidence.

In 296, the emperor Diocletian embarked upon a new monetary reform in an effort to restore confidence. He formally re-established the three-metal hierarchy. He minted the *solidus* (forerunner of the *sou*), a 5.4 gram gold coin, reconstituted the silver *denarius*, and completed the set with base-metal coins called *billons*. But the gold was immediately hoarded. The silver *denarius* was caught up in this same trend, and in 301 it stopped being minted. Only the *billon*

---

1   Andreau, 'Crises financières et monétaires dans l'Antiquité romaine'.

remained in circulation, and its dizzying depreciation accelerated, aggravating the inflationary crisis under Constantine. This was a vicious cycle:

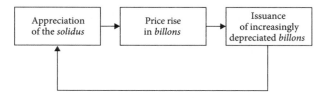

Prices multiplied six-fold between 330 and 348, and fifty-fold between 348 and 354. In total, over a fifty-seven-year period, nominal inflation rose from 1 to 1,000 for silver coins, and from 60,000 to 22.5 million for a pound of gold. The rise in the value of a pound of gold in Egyptian *denarii* was the following: 1,125 in 179; 3,000 in 191; 50,000 in 280; 1,400,000 in 319 and 3,300,000,000 in 400.

How did Rome break out of this spiral of inflation? The solution came in several phases. Diocletian introduced a more effective fiscal system to collect taxes. The military situation at the margins of the Empire improved, helping Rome to control its military spending. Finally, and most importantly, in converting to Christianity and prom-ulgating it as the Empire's official religion, Constantine transformed the principle of sovereignty.[2] This had considerable consequences for money. The emperor confiscated the treasuries of the pagan temples which, alongside the extraction of new gold deposits, enabled him to reconstitute a monetary system on the basis of gold. The *solidus* became the official unit of account. To ensure that gold remained in circulation, he decreed that fiscal debts be paid in gold. In conse-quence, between 346 and 388 there was a twenty-fold increase in the circulation of gold money.

Thus, through a long process, the imperial state managed to rein-stitute a system of currency issuance able to restore hierarchical confi-dence. It could only do so after having taken account of the private behaviours that implicitly made gold the price benchmark for evaluat-ing the depreciation of *billons*. It was the change of political

2   Callu, *La politique monétaire des empereurs romains de 238 à 311.*

sovereignty that allowed an effective monetary reform, and not the other way around.

MONETARY AND FINANCIAL CRISES IN DUALIST SYSTEMS

The crises in antiquity brought to light the virulent disruptive effects of money's ambivalent character. This ambivalence resides in the tension between money's two inextricably linked aspects: on the one hand, the social cohesion that comes from the obligation of settlement, and on the other hand, the private power to accumulate money. Money's ambivalent character develops over time in the form of a structure of credits and debts. Within this structure, a mutual dependency and rivalry develops between creditors and debtors. When rivalry prevails, the payment system can be disrupted. We can then speak of a financial crisis with monetary effects. As this dysfunction worsens, it creates wider dangers, putting into question the settlement of debts. This can lead to a general undermining of confidence in money, or even to the destruction of the monetary system. This is a monetary crisis in the proper sense.

The Roman crises of the first century BC were financial crises with monetary effects, which could be solved within the established monetary system by implementing exceptional and temporary political measures. The crisis in the Late Empire, on the other hand, was a monetary crisis in the proper sense, whose solution demanded the restoration of the hierarchical confidence that had been destroyed. In the dualist systems of the thirteenth century onwards, states disposed of a powerful means of altering the value of debts by changing the abstract units of account that they had created. This tool of monetary policy proved its effectiveness in the fourteenth century, which was marked by a permanent shortage of precious metals lasting up until the Spanish conquest of the Americas.

The deflationary crisis came to a head in the second half of the fourteenth century, after the Black Death of 1348–49, which wiped out two-fifths of Europe's population. This demographic catastrophe was accompanied by an era of climate cooling and the Hundred Years' War, both of which devastated agriculture. In this gloomy era, the only way of fighting against deflation was to devalue the money of account.

The monarchies that embarked on this course of action met with the assent of the merchant guilds and the wider population. Conversely, any attempt at revaluation came up against general opposition.

The Abundance and Scarcity of Money

The dynamism of private finance was linked to the long-distance trade to which it committed its funds. For this very reason, periods of 'easy' money (abundance) and 'tight' money (scarcity) alternated according to the comings and goings of shipping fleets at Europe's ports. We can take the example of the circulation of capital between the Venetian traders and the Florentine bankers of the fifteenth century. At the moment the ships set off, there was maximum scarcity in Venice; specie was rare and bills of exchange were issued on Florence in order to finance the commissioning of the ships and the constitution of their cargoes. The excess supply of bills of exchange pushed down their prices. Consequently, the *florin* appreciated in relation to the Venetian *ducat*. Conversely, when the fleet returned – if it had not been wrecked in a storm or intercepted by pirates – the merchandise arriving from the Orient flowed into Venice and then spread across Europe. The trade hubs of Northern Europe in turn drew bills of exchange on Venice, to remit the exchange value of the commodities that they had purchased. The Venetian debtors could settle their debts to their Florentine creditors, and the *ducat* recovered relative to the *florin*. Moreover, the exchange rates camouflaged the interest that had been collected. Since the Florentines were structurally creditors of Venice, they received a camouflaged interest on their loans. According to the political and financial journalist Paul Einzig, this interest was of the order of 8 to 12 percent.[3] Bills of exchange on debt titles issued in Venice were settled in Florence, and this brought interest payments for the Florentine bankers.

These cyclical variations took place between two free cities with continuous business relations. These relations gave rise to significant volumes of bills of exchange that were cleared over time, which also saved on the use of metal specie. More complex were the relations between private financiers and monarchies. The latter carried out

---

3   P. Einzig, *The History of Foreign Exchange*, London: Macmillan, 1970.

mutations in the unit of account and manipulated the metal parities of minted coins in order to attract precious metals or stop them from haemorrhaging elsewhere.

Indeed, the monarchs' monetary policies were far from transparent. They sought to prevent metal being exported and to limit the circulation of foreign specie on their territory. They obliged the holders of foreign currency to hand it in to the mint so that it could be recast and struck with a metal content that would allow for substantial seigniorage. The intensity of these controls depended on how easy or tight the relative supply of specie was from one country to the next. Thus, in the mid-fourteenth century, traders could perceive how the scarcity or abundance of metal specie in different locations influenced scriptural exchange rates, via the intermediary of metal points. Yet these rates were highly variable, for they depended on the greater or lesser restrictions on the export of specie, and financiers' expectations of future monetary mutations.

We can now consider the contradictory effects that a prolonged period of monetary scarcity had on a given realm. The political authorities tightened the restrictions on exporting metal and increased the seigniorage on the recasting of imported foreign coins. The metal's market value thus increased relative to its official purchase price at the mint. This widened the gap determining the metal export point. But domestic hoarding produced one first leak in the system, frustrating the authorities' intentions. At the same time, when specie was scarce, the scriptural exchange rate for the local unit of account depreciated. Metal shortages thus led to the issuing of more bills of exchange. Given that the export of bills was less restricted than the export of specie, the scriptural exchange rate depreciated by more than the difference on the metal's market value. When the scriptural exchange rate fell substantially below the metal export point, there was an advantage in paying in specie in another country to such a degree that leaks developed in the controls. The export of metal combined with domestic hoarding to contract the available supply of means of payment. The government would then have to decree a devaluation of the unit of account, in order to incentivise hoarders to put their money back into circulation, and traders to begin importing foreign specie again.

The result of this process was that changes in the unit of account were a crude and brutal yet indispensable means of regulating the supply of money in this first era of capitalism.[4] They had the disadvantage of exacerbating the conflicts between the nations that were taking form at this point. Thus, in the sixteenth century, the kings of France sought to resist the depreciation of the *livre tournois* relative to the *maravedí* (the Spanish monetary unit) by making it more difficult to transport precious metals from Spain to the Netherlands. They did this by implementing controls of varying intensity. The ban on remittances caused a rise in the price of debts issued in Antwerp and Amsterdam, a depreciation of the Spanish scriptural exchange rate, and finally a devaluation of the *maravedí*. Mutations of units of account thus bore all the characteristics of modern competitive revaluations or devaluations. The objective here was not to export unemployment or inflation; it was to attract precious metals. But the transformations that ensued rewarded hoarders and increased the risk premiums camouflaged by the scriptural exchange rates for credit. As we saw in Chapter 3, when capitalism began to implant itself territorially, such transformations became an obstacle to its development.

In the sixteenth century, the fleets arriving in Seville with Potosí silver led to an abundance of specie in Spain. The abundance of metal reduced seigniorage, prompting a fall in the price of bills of exchange on all foreign trade centres. Spain profited, however, as it imported masses of commodities financed by foreign metal exports. The result was a rise in the price of bills of exchange, and metal shortages in Spain . . . until the next cargo of silver arrived.

Thus, the movement of metal along the intra-European trade routes brought Spain a structural trade deficit and a similarly structural trade surplus in Northern Europe. Bills of exchange headed in the opposite direction, towards Spain, to finance the imports necessary for the fleet's next departure. Financial crises grafted themselves onto this alternating monetary circulation. Such crises were unleashed by capital losses owing to the hazards of navigation, piracy and wars, but also to state embargoes on metal and the unanticipated mutations of the units of account. For two centuries, the merchant bankers of

---

4 Bloch, 'Mutations monétaires dans l'ancienne France'.

Italy managed to maintain exchange networks by centralising the issuance and remittances of bills of exchange. They were able to do this thanks to the periodic clearing that took place through the circuit of fair towns. But the rising tensions from 1570 onwards swept away the monetary arrangements that had prevailed during the Middle Ages.

The Structural Crisis of the Dualist System

Attempting to eradicate the inflation that had been exacerbated by the wars for the French throne (also called the Wars of Religion), the ordinances of 1577 abolished the dualist system, bringing about the re-emergence of a metallist conception of money. The *écu d'or au soleil* became the unit of account in which all accounts had to be defined. The silver *franc* bore an engraving with its denomination. The rate of equivalence was 1 *écu* to 3 *francs*, thus respecting the two metals' respective values. The value in *écus* was engraved on all coins. The implicit link with the *livre tournois* was maintained. Indeed, the rates of equivalence were: 1 *franc* to 20 *sous* (20 *livres tournois*), and thus 1 *écu* to 60 *sous*. This ratio represented a weakening of the *écu* relative to the previous rates, the result of an implicit 10 percent rise in the *livre tournois*. This was, therefore, an openly deflationist policy. The quantitative theory of money generated the expectation that all prices would fall in proportion. The French monetary system became bimetallic, with a gold to silver ratio of between 111:3 and 111:2. Exchange was strictly regulated. There was a ban on all foreign coins whose legal value and quality were not respected, which had to be melted down and repurchased at their metal weight. Only ten foreign coins were allowed to circulate.

Yet this attempt to homogenise accounting did not succeed. In the merchants' bookkeeping, an *écu de compte* overlapped with the *écu soleil* coin, and the former gradually lost value. There was such confusion that a dualism insinuated itself into the system anew, albeit under the single name *écu*. Traders reacted quickly in the attempt to recoup their losses in metal *écus* with the profits that resulted from the rise in nominal prices. In the 1580s, the 'wars of religion' intensified. Deflation in France worsened, faced with the combination of the Beggars' Revolt, bankruptcy in Spain, and the decadence of Antwerp. The result was a major financial and trade crisis. Moreover, the 1577 reform destroyed the structural enrichment of the merchant bankers who acted as intermediaries of exchange through their use of bills (see Chapter 3).

The conditions were there for a money war, which would drain off foreign specie. The market rates in France were 10 to 15 percent higher than the price at which the Hôtel des Monnaies purchased metal. There had hitherto been a hierarchical system of price differentials between metal coins at the various trading hubs which regulated exchange by bills. This system was now destroyed. The disappearance of Italian coins forced out the Italian merchant bankers. Exchange by bills drifted away from any reference point in foreign exchange parity. Lyon's central role in financial flows disappeared. The surviving exchange by bills now circumvented France, and was centred on Bizansone, in the territory of the German Holy Roman Empire.

The main factors behind the crisis were deeper, however. As was seen in Chapter 3, the dominant tendency at the time was the implantation of finance within the spaces of national sovereignty that had begun to establish themselves. Far removed from the merchant bankers whose wealth was founded on long-term trade and arbitrage on exchange rates, there now appeared national financiers whose wealth was based on tax farming, in exchange for financing the public debt. The development of annuities and the political influence of these financiers, within a framework of national sovereignty, would become the motor of a new financial capitalism.

The 1577 monetary reform did not manage to construct a monetary system that could support this transformation of finance. This was because national sovereignty was not yet consolidated. A long period of monetary convulsions would follow in France, as well as in England. Meanwhile, Spain would irredeemably decline, on the ruins of the Spanish arm of the Habsburg Empire.

MONETARY SUCCESSES AND FAILURES DURING THE ADVENT OF THE NATION-STATE

For centuries Europe was shaken by wars of religion, from the Catholic Counter-Reformation and the decline of the Habsburg Empire, all the way up until the Vienna Congress of 1815, which finally codified the concert of European nations. Throughout this period, the continent had been caught up in political convulsions that led to the formation of nation-states. This painful gestation process produced almost continual wars that set European powers against one another.

We have already seen in Chapter 3 that the Dutch war for independence from Spain established a powerful merchant nation in the Netherlands. As was demonstrated, this national liberation from the yoke of empire produced a highly significant monetary innovation through the creation of the Bank of Amsterdam. We will not dwell further on this point here. The civil wars and aborted revolutions in England over the greater part of the seventeenth century had, by 1688, produced a dynastic change that definitively shifted the European alliance system. In the wake of this refoundation of sovereignty, England pursued a constant policy of seeking a balance among the powers on the continent. We have already seen how it provided itself with the means to achieve this through the *creation of the Bank of England and the introduction of the gold standard.*

This did not take place without difficulty, nor did it lack for international consequences. The first lesson of this experience is that the conquest of national sovereignty went hand-in-hand with the centralisation of money in the hands of the state. When the national currency sought to impose itself against foreign influence, dangerous rivalry emerged among monarchs who each attempted to draw precious metals towards their own states, to the disadvantage of the others. Trade and financial rivalries were all the more powerful on account of the enormous public finance problems that resulted from war. The dual objectives of creating a single currency and financing the state throughout frequent episodes of conflict led to monetary crises. These crises took the form of metal shortages and the massive depreciation of coins. The monetary confusion was at its height in England up until the end of the seventeenth century, and in France up until 1726.

CRISES AND MONETARY REFORM IN ENGLAND

Seventeenth-century England was a land of economic disorder and political revolution. The circulation of money was disastrous. Coins were trimmed, worn down and insufficient in volume; metal deposits continually leaked abroad. The public finances deteriorated; it was uncertain whether the public debt was solvent; and the search for new means of finance was very difficult. The clash between the Crown and the goldsmiths – which is to say, private financiers – was exacerbated in the final decade of the seventeenth century. This owed to the demands of financing the Grand Alliance's war against France, fought to contain Louis XIV's bid for hegemony.

At the beginning of the 1690s, the fragmentation of money was at its peak. As we saw in Chapter 3, the crucial monetary reforms of this period were able to take place only in the wake of a political upheaval that transformed the power relations among the ruling classes. The disappearance of the Stuarts with the flight of King James II made it possible to abolish the absolute monarchy. The Orange dynasty brought with it a constitutional order based on the King, the Parliament and the people (the Bill of Rights). This legitimised Parliament's control over tax-raising.

Yet the monetary system was fragmented. The unit of account was represented by the pound sterling and its subdivisions (shillings and pence). The means of payment were bimetallic. The price of silver was fixed by the state, while the price of gold fluctuated freely. This revealed the state of monetary tensions. Foreign specie, mostly from the Netherlands, circulated alongside domestic specie. The deterioration of monetary circulation was apparent in the fact that most coins were either trimmed or worn out by use, leading to a confusion between 'true' and 'false' money. Counterfeiters were tolerated because they helped to reduce the shortage of coins. But transaction costs were prohibitively high, because it was necessary to specify which money was being used to settle each transaction. Fixing commodity prices thus depended on a problematic negotiation concerning the money used. Better-quality coins were hoarded or exported. The famous private search for money, which theorists assumed would bring about a single means of payment as a point around which actors would converge, led nowhere. In total, on the eve of the 1693 reform, there were 11 million trimmed or counterfeit coins out of the 13.5 million coins in circulation. Since 1650, ten million coins had disappeared. There were 3 to 5 million gold coins and foreign coins, with a value estimated at £1 million.

The goldsmiths were organised in the guilds of London's Lombard Street. This latter had prospered over the seventeenth century, through a diversification of the goldsmiths' activities, which now included metal transactions, coin exchanges, loans and deposits, and discounting. Their notes circulated among the merchants of London, each backed up in a long chain. As the merchants made ever-more deposits with the goldsmiths, the latter became the favoured creditor of the Crown itself. But there was little confidence underpinning the goldsmiths' relations with the authorities. In a sense, the goldsmiths had an ambivalent role. They encouraged circulation by agreeing to issue credit to the state. But they also weakened circulation, because they exported the best quality specie. For its part, the Crown had twice proven its arbitrary character. In 1640, when backed into a corner, Charles I took the authoritarian move of seizing the specie deposited at the Tower of London, amounting to £120,000. This prompted merchants to increase their deposits with the goldsmiths. But permanent wars continued to intensify the state's need for finance. In 1672, the Crown was forced to declare a 'stop on the exchequer', meaning an interruption of its debt repayments. This had unfavourable repercussions on the goldsmiths' notes, which were the counterparties of discounted public debt titles.

These two events clearly demonstrated that the arbitrariness of the public authorities had made it impossible to establish a national debt. The merchant classes refused to lend to the state as long as they were denied any control over its finances. Yet unless there was a public debt that was accepted as an expression of the national unit, there could be no sovereignty to ground confidence in money. The crisis of sovereignty reached its climax in 1688, when the Whigs and Tories made an exceptional alliance in order to foment a revolution to depose James II, whose hostility to Parliament had prevented any dialogue. It was after James II's flight that the political parties called on William III of the House of Orange to take the English throne. The new sovereign, a Protestant and enemy of Louis XIV, threw himself into the War of the Grand Alliance. This coalition brought England into common cause with the Netherlands. The conflict now changed in scale, as the state's annual spending tripled from £2 to £6 million. Such costs could not be sustained by the goldsmiths; their short-term financing was totally inadequate to these demands.

Thanks to the establishment of the new sovereign, it had become possible to levy a loan by mobilising the nation's savings on a large scale. This took place in three stages from 1693 to 1694, through the tontine, the lottery and, most importantly, the creation of a banking establishment of a new type, the Bank of England, whose characteristics we defined in Chapter 3.

The transformation of capitalism in England was truly a textbook case for the theory of money that considers it as a fundamental social relation underpinned by sovereignty. This transformation inaugurated the classical age, propelling the nation along the path of the manufacturing and industrial revolutions. The national unity established due to a transformed principle of sovereignty sealed a social pact through which the state attached itself to the nation. This unity was validated financially through the transformation of the public debt due to the creation of the Bank of England under private law (a society of 1,300 individuals, making a subscription of £1.2 million). So much was confidence in money linked to the public debt, that it took a financial solution to open the way to monetary reform. *The gold standard could be established because the Bank of England had been created as a state bank.*

What remains to be mentioned is the final deflationary crisis: the gigantic social cost of the monetary reform. From 1689 onwards, the economy rapidly deteriorated, through war spending, bad harvests and soaring agricultural prices. As the monetary system lay in tatters, there was both the large-scale export of metal and a rush on commodities. Economic activity was paralysed. From 1693, distrust towards silver-money was at its height. The gold guinea appreciated by 40 percent in two years. In 1695, the exchange by bills of the pound sterling in Amsterdam depreciated by 12 percent. Something had to be done to re-establish order.

In Chapter 3 we presented the doctrinal and practical debates on the choice between recasting and devaluation, debates which were themselves expressions of divergent class interests. It was William III that tipped the balance. As a partisan of the intangibility of the monetary standard, the King supported Locke. The Recoinage Act was decreed by Parliament on 22 November 1695.[5] The reform favoured the rich, the state's creditors and landowners, but had malign effects for debtors and the most destitute. The citizens who were able to bring their trimmed coins to the Tower of London within a five-month window – either as tax payments or as advances to the state – could benefit from having their money accepted at face value. The less wealthy had to get rid of their coins at the rates offered by the gold-smiths. The recasting lasted until 1699, and caused a terrible monetary drought. The contraction in the stock of money was enormous: a stock of coins at a nominal value of £15 million was replaced by £9.5 million worth of new coins. From summer 1696 onwards, deflation swept across the country. The interest rate climbed to 20 percent in the second half of the year, while commodity prices fell by 30 percent. Rioting broke out across the whole country. It has been estimated that the total cost of the reform reached some £2.7 million, £1 million of which the poorest had to bear. The disappearance of silver coins continued, effectively putting the monetary system on the path towards the gold standard.

A Fresh Failure for Monetary Reform in France: Law's System
From 1688 until 1715, France was almost continuously at war, except for a short period between the Ryswick peace in 1697 and the onset of the War of the Spanish Succession in 1701. These wars engulfed France's resources. The conflict between land wealth and merchant wealth, unfolding under the surface of the absolute monarchy, under-mined the French economy. This was an endemic financial crisis, fed by high public indebtedness, very low tax incomes, a very onerous annuities system (with an actuarial interest rate of over 5 percent) a chronic shortage of cash, and interest rates of close to 20 percent on money lending.

The tax system preserved its feudal mould. Indirect taxes were farmed. Direct taxation through capitation, raised in 1689 in order to finance the war, was based on individual status, stratified into twenty-two classes! The insufficiency of tax receipts relative to the costs of the war made it impossible for the amount of interest that was being paid

5   Desmedt, 'Les fondements monétaires de la révolution financière anglaise'.

to be soaked up by the primary surplus. The public debt was thus heading along an unsustainable course; expedient measures had to be taken. There was an attempt to gather resources through monetary manipulation: the king had the power to change the legal price of coins without parliamentary control, nor any possibility of being challenged before the courts. In 1690, the state sought to increase its seigniorage on coins. The Hôtel des Monnaies withdrew the coins in circulation and minted new coins at a value in *livres tournois* at x level higher than the coins' former value. It set them in circulation at the price $y < x$ and kept $x - y$ per unit of silver weight, which it transferred to the state. Seigniorage would supposedly decrease consistently over time, until it reached the level of the *livre tournois*'s old metal value. But these operations had to be repeated on a systematic basis. The result was that the depreciation of the *livre tournois* accelerated during the wars, and through the failure of Law's system. In total, per unit of weight in silver, the value of the *livre tournois* depreciated by 55 percent between December 1688 and June 1726.

Inspired by real bills theory and the Scottish free banking experience, John Law argued that the solution to France's financial problems was to issue paper money backed up by the capital of the producer classes. This would allow the interest rate paid on public debt to be pushed down to 2 percent, instead of 5 percent for the payment of annuities guaranteed by land wealth. The 2 percent rate would stimulate agricultural and industrial production, creating revenue that would in turn generate tax receipts, which would help to guarantee the solvency of the debt.

Law thus had a very modern approach to economics. He wanted to introduce the logic of capitalism in France, based on providing credit through money creation. *Money creation had to be based on expected future wealth, and no longer on the past wealth accumulated in precious metals.* Seeking to realise this visionary project, with the Prince Regent's agreement, Law created a bank that issued convertible notes. This was the first time that a bank in France had issued paper-money defined in *livres tournois*. Tax collectors had to accept the notes at their legal value, thus allowing the banknotes to circulate at parity. At the outset, in 1717, there was sufficient confidence to allow 40 to 50 million *livres*' worth of notes to be issued per year. The bank engaged in 'classic' practices: discounting, currency exchange, depositing and account management. An initial error, however, was the nationalisation of the bank in December 1718, which converted it into a royal bank.

Law based the second pillar of his system on a trading company designed to build trade with Louisiana. The shares in the trading company, like those in the bank itself, were payable in state notes. Law's company developed through the merger and acquisition of the Compagnie du Sénégal and the Compagnie des Indes, as well as by securing a monopoly on tobacco.

The company changed in character in July 1719, after it bought the right to manage minting and became the sole tax collector. It was at this point that Law created his 'system'. He proposed to buy up the whole national debt by issuing shares in the company. These would be paid for by those holding state annuities. This was supposed to allow the state to pay an interest rate of only 3 percent on a perpetual loan. The variable part of tax revenues and the company's alternative sources of income would serve to pay the dividends to shareholders.

The viability of Law's plan depended on stock prices remaining stable at a level that brought a dividend with a 2 percent yield, so that the rentiers would end up with a total 5 percent yield (3 percent from the interest paid by the state and 2 percent in dividends). Regulating the system in this way relied on maintaining consistent ratios between the prices of coins, banknotes and shares.

Law in fact sought to remove coins from circulation by making bills the only means of payment. He encouraged the payment of bills of exchange in notes, as well as the circulation of notes on foreign markets. He thus sought to uphold the share prices, so that the public debt could be converted at the desired rate. But, at the beginning of 1720, these share prices began to slide. Law was forced to monetise the public debt by issuing money. The rapid growth in the mass of money between March and May 1720 was accompanied by signs of a loss of confidence in bills. The exchange rates in London and Amsterdam depreciated.

The return to coins demonstrated this loss of confidence. This shift was all the stronger because of Law's own efforts to reduce the mass of money by buying back the bills. But this expedient measure failed, and the bank had to give up on buying back the bills at parity. This effectively put an end to their convertibility. In August 1720, the bills were demonetised and the freedom to make out contracts in gold and silver and to circulate coins was re-established. The company's commitment to take charge of the public debt could no longer be maintained, and Law had to leave France in December 1720.

How should we interpret the failure of this 'system'? Law wanted to absorb the conversion of the public debt in order to reduce the influence of the financiers, who had long profited from the state's financial needs. They had been able to do this because of the state's own inability to borrow on a capital market. Law wanted to implant on French soil the securities markets that existed in Amsterdam and London in order to channel the savings of the active classes. In concentrating monetary and fiscal functions, he sought to make the king's interests compatible with those of his creditors, at the same time as getting rid of the incentive towards monetary manipulation.

Law's system failed because of the unviability of the underlying macroeconomic regime. The targeted discount rate of 2 percent was too ambitious. Given the income that the company could reasonably anticipate, the share price could only be maintained with an interest rate of at least the 3 percent achieved in the United Provinces, and a growth rate of 1 percent that no European country was able to maintain on an ongoing basis prior to the Industrial Revolution. Thus, at their peak, the shares were highly overvalued.

This economic explanation, however, does not get to the heart of the matter. France's profound contradictions could not be overcome without a radical change of sovereignty. A social structure based on fixed orders and the conservative mentality of France's ruling classes could not permit any overall transformation of the system's rules, short of a revolution.

Law was unable to achieve such a transformation because the support for his policy relied on the confidence of the Prince Regent alone. The policy was confronted with the speculation typical of deteriorating dualist systems. England and the Netherlands had only been able to overcome this situation by re-establishing sovereignty on a basis that was able to advance the interests of the new capitalist bourgeoisie. The financiers' ruinous and sterile speculation stood opposed to the convertibility of notes via exchange and the price of metal coins. In combatting the financiers, Law was forced to take recourse to the very methods he sought to abolish: monetary manipulations to ensure that the bills were accepted, issuing notes against government counterparties rather than general economic activity, and too many yields that were too low to avoid the hostility of the financiers and aristocrats, who had maintained their full political influence. Monetary stability was re-established in 1726, but France had only just begun to lose ground economically.

FINANCIAL CRISES AND CENTRAL BANKS IN THE CLASSIC AGE OF CAPITALISM: THE ADVENT OF THE LENDER OF LAST RESORT

We have shown above that repeated public debt crises and monetary instability were closely linked to the formation of nation-states. The reform in England provided a stability that lasted across the greater part of the eighteenth century. But the Napoleonic wars brought a return to major instability, severely testing the monetary system that had been established between 1694 and 1699.

At the beginning of the 1790s, the repercussions of the French Revolution were destroying the balance of power in Europe. For England, this balance was itself the most important of all public goods. War spending resumed at a level far higher than it had been a century previously. The shortage of gold reappeared, but not the disorders of the seventeenth century. Indeed, the Bank of England had had time to establish its authority and occupied the central place in the monetary system. Its notes were widely accepted. Thus, the government undertook a monetary innovation. It suspended gold convertibility in 1797, hoping that confidence in the Bank of England's notes would be maintained. The Bank would be able to feed liquidity into the system of payments, thus avoiding the monetary strangulation of the past. It was probable that confidence could be preserved, because gold convertibility had existed for a century and the Bank of England's authority was well established. Moreover, the population would be able to understand why convertibility had been suspended, for it was motivated by England's participation in a coalition against France. This period of non-convertibility would last until 1821, transforming the Bank of England's responsibilities.

This new role, which would later be called the 'lender of last resort', was noted by Henry Thornton as early as 1802.[6] Thornton emphasised the Bank of England's responsibility to provide liquidity to healthy banks in a period of banking panic. His advice, however, was not followed. In the period between 1790 and 1866, England suffered eight years of panic.[7]

Even with the return to political order in Europe after the Vienna Congress of 1815, there remained very high levels of public debt and major economic disruption. England's public debt level reached 260 percent of GDP. In these circumstances, the return to gold convertibility again raised the spectre of deflation. Only in 1821 did the government decide to re-establish convertibility. England had an advantage in making an adjustment towards sustainable levels of public debts. At the end of the eighteenth century it had embarked upon the Industrial Revolution, and thus enjoyed comparative advantages in profiting from the revival of trade in Europe. Up until 1848, it was able to limit deflation to low, albeit persistent, rates. It took no less than forty years to bring the public debt back down to 100 percent of GDP.

From the 1840s onwards, the business cycles of industrial capitalism set the rhythm of financial crises. Each turnaround in the business cycle after its peak degenerated into a financial crisis. These panics were triggered by the collapse of some important financial institution, precipitating the demand for gold conversion in all banks. Constrained by convertibility, the Bank of England sought to protect its own reserves, in turn worsening the panic. When it did decide to intervene, it was far too late to avoid a cascade of bank collapses. In 1844, Peel's Bank Charter Act separated the Bank of England into two departments. The issuing department which created banknotes had to respect the limited gold coverage, thus stiffening the supply of

---

6   Henry Thornton, *An Enquiry into the Nature and Effects of the Paper Credit of Great Britain*, introduction by Friedrich August von Hayek, London: Allen & Unwin, 1939.

7   Michael D. Bordo, 'The Lender of Last Resort: Alternative Views and Historical Experience', *Federal Reserve Bank of Richmond Economic Review*, January–February 1990.

liquidity. At the same time, the Act strengthened the Bank's powers by banning commercial banks from issuing banknotes. This reform thus hardened the constraints on issuing notes, at the same time as it generalised the Bank of England's monopoly on issuing notes from London to the whole country. The banking department exercised banking functions, constrained by liquid liabilities that it was unable to expand during moments of tension on the money market. This reform represented the ideological victory of quantitative theory (the Currency School), which took the issuance of bank money to be the cause of inflation. The result was to make panics considerably more intense. The climax came with the financial crisis of 1866. It was in observing this crisis that Walter Bagehot (1873) formulated his famous doctrine of the lender of last resort.[8]

The crisis broke out in May 1866 with the collapse of the Overend Gurney Company. This episode was the endpoint of a crisis that had developed out of financial positions weakened by a collapse in global cotton prices, dating back to 1864. But this collapse was ignored, because it took place at a moment when credit was strongly expanding through speculation. The London rediscounting houses were very liberal in accepting paper notes. Amid this atmosphere of euphoria, in July 1865 the Overend Gurney Company chose to transform into a limited company quoted on the Stock Exchange. This fuelled speculation to the point that by October the capital gains on the company's shares had reached 100 percent. The craze for all shares on the market was exacerbated, as companies outbid each other in handing out dividends. Short buying pushed up interest rates on the money markets. The Bank of England was in thrall to the market. Given the financial distress among its clients who sought to invest on the money market, the Bank was losing reserves on account of the demand to convert its notes. It took the fatal decision to raise its discount rate from 3 percent to 7 percent. The resulting financial distress took hold of the discounting houses, and ended up also taking over the clearing banks. Suffocated by the shortage of liquidity, speculation died away until May 1866, with the final crash.

8   Walter Bagehot, *Lombard Street: A Description of the Money Market*, London: H.S. King, 1873.

Bagehot and the Doctrine of the Lender of Last Resort

In the crisis of 1866 as in previous crises, there was great indecision. How could the effects of the panic be relieved? Did responsibility lie with the Treasury, or with the Bank of England? Was it necessary to suspend the limits on discounting capacity that the 1844 Bank Act had imposed on the Bank? When, and to whom, should loans be made – to the well-established securities houses, or to whomever had an acceptable level of collateral? Indeed, what kind of collateral is acceptable in a time of crisis? Was it possible to promise to increase the money supply without restriction?

This multi-faceted debate resumed at periodic intervals, without any definitive conclusions being drawn either among the Bank's leaders in the City, or within the government itself. Yet the volume and complexity of financial activity continued to develop as industrial capitalism boomed. The interlinking of financial engagements and the influence of international connections made financial crises ever more painful. More losses had to be borne, and their consequences were more uncertain. The Bank's decisions weighed increasingly heavily on the financial system. For this reason, there was mounting practical experience of negative externalities in crisis situations. This was also the reason why Bagehot's formulation regarding the experience of the 1866 crisis fell on fertile ground. What was later recognised as the classic doctrine of the 'lender of last resort' in fact represented the formulation of a collective rationality. This doctrine was a set of principles designed to guide the Bank's conduct in the face of exceptional situations. It was generally accepted because the most influential financiers had perceived that it was indeed in their interest to help competitors in distress, for the collapse of these competitors would have a rebound effect. *The danger to be fought was, above all, contagion.* To this end, it was necessary to have a source of liquidity that was external to the money markets, which also acted independently enough not to be the hostage of its beneficiaries.

If we want to understand the rationality of the lender of last resort, we need to make a conceptual distinction between the overall stability of the financial system and the fate of particular institutions. That is to say, we first of all need to abandon the hypothesis of a pure and efficient market.[9] To act as the lender of last resort is to conduct an operation that goes beyond the rules of competition. Indeed, it is to suspend the constraint of settlement obligations, which is the fundamental rule ensuring the stability of the payment system.[10] *To act as the lender of last resort is to suspend the logic of the market economy for the purposes of preserving and perpetuating that same economy.* This involves a violation of the logic of the market, since private engagements are suspended by a sovereign decision and not deferred in time by contractual means. At the same time, the market is perpetuated, because this suspension preserves other private engagements that are healthy but cannot be honoured on account of the external repercussions of those other failed engagements. This intervention involves a certain moral hazard, for it unbinds social cost from private cost. This is why Bagehot achieved a *tour de force* in providing a doctrine that applies to what are necessarily exceptional situations.

The general principles of Bagehot's doctrine are as follows. The loan of last resort must not have lasting consequences that could endanger the monetary order, which is to say, which could threaten the unshakeable confidence in the gold convertibility of the bills issued by the Bank of England in normal times. The financial assistance provided by the Bank must anticipate the liquidity crisis, and it must also be temporary. It must be provided out of the sole concern of maintaining the overall stability of the financial system. This excludes aid for financial institutions that have already gone to the wall, which must be sold to new owners and recapitalised.

These principles give rise to specific directives for action. Their implementation demands a proper interpretation of each particular situation, and appropriate judgement. Stifling panic requires lending to all sound borrowers, without any limit of quantity, and regardless of whether or not they are bankers. The borrowers' quality is defined by the quality of the collateral they are able to put up, acceptable collateral being any kind of security that would be considered good quality in normal times. The Bank must accept these at their pre-crisis values,

---

9   Gillian Garcia and Elizabeth Plantz, *The Federal Reserve: Lender of Last Resort*, Cambridge, MA: Ballinger Press, 1988.

10   Aglietta, 'Genèse des banques centrales et légitimité de la monnaie'.

so that sound debtors are not penalised by the general fall in the price of financial assets that have become illiquid on account of the systemic crisis. Moreover, the loan of last resort should be accorded at penalty rates in order to discourage borrowers from taking recourse to such loans when other sources of liquidity are still available to them. This penalty rate is also justified by the risk the Bank is taking, in that it has to cover the potential losses inherent to accepting collaterals at their pre-crisis values. The last recommendation concerns credibility. Assuring public confidence while containing moral hazard demands that the Bank announce its principles in advance and then strictly abide by them.

The Bank did this very effectively. In striking contrast to what happened in the United States – a country which did not at that time have any central bank – in the United Kingdom the major financial crises of 1878, 1890 and 1907 did not degenerate into generalised panics. The rescue of Baring Brothers in 1890 was telling in this regard. This was a situation masterfully handled by the Bank of England, enlightened by Bagehot's principles. The firm was in financial distress in November 1890 after the default of its bankers' acceptances on Argentina.[11] When Baring's true financial situation became public, the Bank of England feared that the panic would spread. But it had low gold reserves, and increasing its prime rate in order to rebuild these reserves was inopportune in this context. After contact with the Chancellor of the Exchequer, the Bank of England arranged a loan in order to strengthen its reserves, granted by the Bank of France. It formed a board of experts composed of Bank of England directors and City financiers in order to evaluate the amount of Argentinian securities on the market. After the experts concluded that Baring was solvent in the long term, on condition that it was provided £8 to £9 million in liquidity, the Bank discounted the bills of exchange presented by Baring. The Bank's governor secured the chancellor's agreement that the government would share the losses on Baring paper that the Bank was going to discount. Armed with this agreement, the governor met with the owners of eleven private

---

11   Charles P. Kindleberger, *Manias, Panics and Crashes*, New York: Basic Books, 1978.

banks, with the aim of persuading them to contribute to a guarantee fund that would cover Baring's commitments. He also secured the Russian State Bank's agreement that it would not withdraw the £2.4 million deposited with Baring. In total, a fund of £7.5 million pounds was constituted, and this was subsequently brought up to £10 million. This impressed public opinion and allowed the restructuring of the firm without triggering a panic. On 25 November 1890, a new Baring Brothers and Co. firm was constituted, with £1 million of capital.

The American Exception and the Difficult Creation of the Federal Reserve System in 1913

From 1838 to 1863 the United States remained under the free banking regime. This system was not, however, sufficient for the North's financial needs during the American Civil War. In 1862, therefore, Congress passed the Legal Tender Act, which authorised the federal government to issue non-convertible paper money, greenbacks, for a total of $450 million. In 1863, it voted through the National Bank Act. By the end of the war, greenbacks had depreciated by over 50 percent of their face value. This was expressed in the premium on gold, which was now being hoarded.

The National Bank Act defined the conditions upon which commercial banks could issue national notes. These bills could be converted for legal metallic money and greenbacks up until 1879. Banks that wanted to issue national notes – notes issued by banks that had received a national charter – had to buy public securities (federal treasury bonds) and deposit them at the Treasury on the ledger of the Controller of the Currency. This latter agency was created within the Treasury in order to supervise the quantity of money issued by banks who had chosen national bank status. Before 1900, the securities deposited had to be 90 percent of the value of the notes issued, and 100 percent after that point.

The National Bank Act established an unprecedented set of monetary rules. The national banks authorised by the Controller of the Currency could only issue notes against an obligatory prior deposit. There was a $300 million ceiling for the total value of notes issued. Discounting was forbidden. In agricultural regions, where the need for notes varied seasonally, these rigid rules caused seasonal monetary cycles accompanied by recurrent shortages of money.

The supply of banknotes was thus almost totally dependent on deposits of state bonds. As the price of these securities rose, it became more expensive for the banks to issue notes. Given that there was no bank discounting mechanism, the issuance of notes was not adjusted to demand, but rather varied according to the price of public debt. This disconnection between the issuance of money and the seasonal agricultural cycle intensified the monetary conflict between the states of the West and the Midwest, who demanded elastic banking credit, and the financial interests of the East, who emphasised the need for sound money. After winning the war and establishing themselves in power, the Republicans were entirely won over to the cause of the now-booming industrial capitalism. In an age of transcontinental railways, the Republicans wanted to promote heavy industry, oil exploration and steelmaking. They considered it necessary to reduce the war debt in order to channel savings towards the accumulation of industrial capital.

Seeking to re-establish confidence in money, the Republican majority in Congress decided to redeem greenbacks at face value, with the 1875 Resumption Act. Greenbacks remained a fiat money until 1879. But monetary deflation would bring down the premium on gold, to the point of cancelling it out completely. This came about through the gradual withdrawal of greenbacks, which was only compensated at 80 percent through an issuance of national notes (notes issued by the banks according to the rules of the National Bank Act). On 31 May 1878, the premium on gold was cancelled. From then onwards, the total value of greenbacks was definitively frozen at $346 million. Issuing new ones was forbidden. The confidence in the expectation that greenbacks would eventually be withdrawn altogether enabled gold convertibility to be established on 1 January 1879. The Resumption Act thus resulted in a prolonged contraction in the money supply. Together with the advances in productivity that resulted from the industrial boom, the Act initiated a long period of deflation in the final quarter of the nineteenth century (1873–95).

This long-term deflation was marked by two terrible financial crises, in 1873 and in 1893 respectively. In autumn of 1873, there

The interbank interest rate rose

developed an extreme shortage of gold reserves. Forced into dire straits and lacking direct connections with clearing institutions in the main financial centres, the banks of the US interior withdrew their deposits on a massive scale from the banks of New York. The latter drew on their greenback reserves. The interbank interest rate rose from 4.5 percent in August to 61 percent in September. The stock market slumped by 20 percent. Faced with an urgent situation, Congress was obliged to put $26 million into circulation in greenbacks, pushing the interest rate back down to 5.5 percent in January 1874.

At the beginning of 1893, it was again a string of bankruptcies in the banks of the US interior that triggered the crisis. By April, the federal Treasury's metal reserves had fallen to $100 million. Added to that was a monetary controversy. The 1873 Coinage Act had put an end to minting silver. On the recommendation of a House commission, an 1878 law authorised the issuance of legal-tender certificates in silver, in order to mitigate the insufficiency of metal reserves in times of crisis.[12] But this did not re-establish bimetallism. The quarrel over silver resumed in 1892 and reached its climax in the 1896 election campaign.[13] Concerned by the erosion of metal reserves, foreign investors sought to withdraw their gold assets. Gold reserves contracted by some $45 million, with the result that, in June 1893, a banking crisis broke out in New York. John P. Morgan, pope of the city's bankers, had to go to London to negotiate a gold loan, so that he would in turn be able to loan $65 million to the Treasury. This would allow the value of reserves to be pushed above the minimum level of

12   The Bland–Allison Act of 1878 re-established the free minting of silver and ordered the federal government to buy a value of between 2 and 4 million ingots of silver at market price and mint them as silver dollars.

13   The influxes of silver in the 1890s pushed down the value of silver in the minting of coins. There were two camps in the political conflict. On the one hand stood the agrarian interests gathered in the Greenback Party. With the country mired in a long period of deflation, this camp wanted to preserve bimetallism in order to drive an inflation that would allow farmers to repay their debts more easily. On the other hand were the Eastern financial interests, who called for sound money and the establishment of the gold standard. The height of the controversy was the famous speech by the Greenback Party candidate William Jennings Bryan, in which he declared, 'you shall not crucify mankind upon a cross of gold'.

$100 million. Due to his success, the United States overcame the monetary crisis. The return to growth and the resurgence of prices allowed for the official establishment of the gold standard in 1900.

The issuance of national notes did not, however, put an end to the nagging problem of the inelasticity of the money supply, or the incapacity of the supply of ultimate liquidity to adapt to the varying needs expressed by the variations in monetary demand across the economic cycle. The population's fear of money shortages provoked rushes on notes, which dried up the banks' reserves. Given the strength of demand, the banks also held national notes in reserve, rather than demand their repayment in metal. This latent shortage drove the circulation of substitutes for money, in the form of negotiable cheques. This was, indeed, the invention of a parallel money: payable to the bearer, these cheques were used by companies to pay their employees.

The National Bank Act failed in its attempt to put an end to the fragmentation of the American banking system. The Act stipulated that the bills issued by the national banks had to be exchanged at parity, but it was not accompanied by any federal clearing and settlement system. For this reason, the fragmentation of the banks spread beyond the East Coast. The financial situation was to worsen still further, threatening the financial centres themselves.

It was the 1907 crisis that made the banks' fragility intolerable. By October, it had come to destabilise New York finance. Private securities markets had developed with the industrial boom. A new category of financial intermediaries drove a craze among those who wanted to invest their savings. This was the trust company: a sort of unregulated savings bank. Trust companies had grown considerably in both size and number in the great wave of expansion during the early years of the twentieth century. On 21 October, the Knickerbocker Trust Company was unable to honour the deadlines of its engagements with banks on the New York market.[14] This prompted a bank run on its deposits and the suspension of its payments. This financial firm was

---

14 For a study of the trusts' role in the 1907 crisis, see John R. Moen and Ellis W. Tallman, 'Clearinghouse membership and deposit contraction during the panic of 1907', *Journal of Economic History*, vol. 60, no. 1, 2000, pp. 145–63.

not a member of the New York Clearing House (NYCHA) because, like most other trusts, it had refused to accept the latter's conditions. It was thus unable to make use of the clearing house's emergency aid. On 24 October, the contagion spread to all trusts and banks. The demand for interbank liquidity exploded. The bank refinancing rate (call loan rate) jumped to 100 percent. The NYCHA issued loan certificates to its members in large amounts. But a major run on deposits in the banks of the interior set off a chain of bankruptcies, prompting an enormous contraction of liquidity. Once again, the metal reserves proved dramatically insufficient. John P. Morgan had to get back on the boat to London, cap in hand, to negotiate a fresh gold loan . . .

This time the trauma was enormous. By the beginning of the twentieth century, the United States had established itself as the world's leading industrial power. Yet the extreme fragility of its banking system made it a monetary and financial dwarf. It was absolutely necessary to create a mechanism capable of issuing an elastic supply of liquidity, able to meet demand during banking crises. This had to be a national mechanism, able to cover all banks and financial intermediaries who handled economic actors' supposedly liquid savings. Moreover, financial dependence on London was humiliating for a country that aspired to global supremacy. Something had to be done! That is why the Aldrich–Vreeland Act of 30 May 1908 designated a bipartisan National Monetary Commission, entrusted with the mission of proposing a system that could respond to the following questions: What degree of centralisation should be adopted? Was the priority a single central bank with regional branches, or a federation of regional banks?[15]

Despite this common objective, the original sin of US independence – the contradictory aspirations of states' autonomy and the federal unity of the nation, haunting American domestic political life to this day – tore through the National Monetary Commission.[16]

15   Laurent Le Maux and Laurence Scialom, 'Antagonismes monétaires et constitution d'une banque centrale aux États-Unis', in Théret (ed.), *La monnaie dévoilée par ses crises*, pp. 339–68.
16   For an analysis of the conflict between these doctrines see Elmus Wicker, *The Great Debate on Banking Reform: Nelson Aldrich and the Origins of the Fed*, Columbus, OH: Ohio State University Press, 2005.

What resulted were two proposals: one from the Republicans, one from the Democrats. The Republican project, proposed by Aldrich, was highly decentralised. It advocated the formation of a National Reserve Association, which would issue money in response to the demand for notes, in return for the re-discounting of commercial bills at face value. This would be an institution ruled by private law and directed by its member banks. The country's reserves would be centralised and participation in the system would be universal, including the trusts. The Democrats proposed a Federal Reserve System: semi-autonomous federal reserve banks (in twelve districts, in order to avoid coinciding with the federated states themselves) that would be supervised by a Federal Reserve Board. This latter would be a public institution. Each federal reserve bank would have a capital of its own, underwritten by the member banks. They could issue money by re-discounting commercial paper; they could also conduct open market operations and fix the discount rate. The federal reserve banks would hold the member-banks' compulsory reserves and operate clearing in their respective district. The Democrat project won the day, thanks to the Democratic victory in the 1912 elections. The Federal Reserve Act was passed and then signed into law by the US president on 23 December 1913.

TWENTIETH-CENTURY HYPERINFLATION CRISES

Hyperinflation is an extreme phenomenon that leads to the destruction of the official currency. It can only be halted by monetary reform that establishes new rules and, in doing so, re-establishes the sovereignty of the state. Money only disappears when it can no longer be used to make payments, when its power to purchase goods is reduced to zero. Hyperinflation is the process whereby this phenomenon takes place locally, in the monetary system of some particular nation.

The logic of hyperinflation

As we have emphasised, all monetary systems are subject to money's ambivalent character. Liquidity is both the pivot of the payment system and an object of unlimited private desire. This contradiction is overcome through the hierarchical confidence that restrains the desire for the immediate appropriation of liquid wealth. A monetary crisis is a situation in which this confidence is broken.

In order to understand how this can happen, it is worth remembering that a system of monetary rules determines a structure of interest rates according to which the circulation of private credits is oriented. This system regulates the intensity of payment obligations and influences the selection process whereby assets are devalued. Crises change the conditions under which debts and credits circulate over time.

As we have seen, these crises are polarised into two types. One corresponds to a *fragmented monetary system*, in which the ultimate liquidity becomes so scarce that it disappears. These are deflationary crises, where the settlement of debts becomes a problem. We have encountered numerous such cases in the historical episodes examined above, marked by the scarcity of minted metal. The other type of crises corresponds to a situation in which the *monetary system is centralised in the extreme*, and all debts are validated by the creation of money. It thus becomes impossible to distinguish between different asset qualities. The foundation of hyperinflation, in this case, is the centralisation and automatic reproduction of all the failures engendered by an unstable debt structure.

Indeed, systematic monetisation centralises risks and losses. In doing so, it avoids revealing these risks and losses to the agents who are forced to bear them. The financial structure is no less unviable for that, but instead of this unviability being expressed through the devaluation of insolvent assets, it is concentrated on the ambivalence of money itself. Automatic monetisation undermines the conservation of wealth in the form of liquidity. Instead of infinitely extending the agents' prospective horizon (as we might believe, if we forgot that debts circulate with the objective of being settled so as to allow the private appropriation of assets), systematic monetisation destroys this horizon. The immediate conservation of wealth becomes the only concern. It is as if accounting in the official unit of account had lost all meaning. Private actors throw themselves into a feverish search for any means of conserving their wealth. They do this in different ways, depending on their position in the economic system.

One strategy is internal indexation. Rather than express prices in the common unit of account, the suppliers of goods and services seek to validate prices indexed to the costs that they have seen during their past transactions as buyers. Yet in a hyper-centralised monetary system, the conditions are the same for everyone. The suppliers are thus frustrated by costs rising to levels higher than they had calculated. They revise their evaluations by indexing their prices to the cost rises that they anticipate. But they find themselves faced with the same problem; prices continue to rise faster than they expected, since others have done the same thing as them. A self-perpetuating spiral thus develops, through which prices as a whole rise higher and higher. What is crucial is that this price movement loses any link with the real conditions of production. It becomes simultaneously cause and effect of a spiral that accelerates at an ever-greater rate.

A second strategy, if the country is not totally shut down, is to seek some external reference point for value. A foreign currency – that is, a fully-functioning one – is an ideal refuge for whoever wants to avoid their liquidity melting away. Standing above the fray of internal indexations, a foreign currency can become the focal point for actors' expectations, as long as it is available on a freely accessible exchange market. The interplay of internal indexations is thus replaced by a single indexation, which looks to the substitute unit of account provided by the foreign currency. The more generalised the indexation of domestic prices to the foreign currency's exchange rate, and the more widespread the loss of confidence in the official currency, the more the value of the national currency will fall in relation to the foreign currency, tending towards zero.

If the conditions for accessing foreign currencies are not realised, and the inflationary spiral becomes widespread, it is possible that economic actors will seek out real goods, which they choose as a kind of substitute currency. These are goods that play the role of the foreign currency, but which remain multiple and thus differentiated. In this configuration, we end up with a pathological differentiation of the monetary space. Transactions become fragmented according to the use of particular substitute currencies in different territories or between different groups of exchanging parties. That is how cigarette currency came to be used in Germany after the collapse of the Third

Reich, when sovereignty had fallen to nothing and the Allies were occupying its territory.

For those who are interested in mathematic formalisations, Box 5.1 below models these two processes: internal indexation, on the one hand, and indexation to a foreign currency, on the other. In both processes, the inflationary dynamic becomes totally autonomous of the economic 'fundamentals'. Contrary to what monetarism claims, inflation is not a reflection of the increased quantity of money in circulation. The rise in prices is not proportional to the rise in the quantity of money. On the contrary, the 'real' mass of money – the nominal mass of money divided by the general level of prices – tends towards zero. Monetary expansion is a catalyst that can help to set the self-referential logic of indexation in motion. This catalyst is what casts doubt on the permanence of monetary rules, and thus undermines confidence in money. But once this phase of indexation is underway, it no longer depends on monetary expansion. This phase leads to the destruction of the unit of account, because it expresses a loss of confidence in the established monetary sovereignty. However, it has many other potential catalysts: the loss of control over the public finances, an (either civil or international) war that turns out badly for the powers-that-be, or the intensification of social antagonism. In any of these cases, the self-referential logic gives rise to hyperinflation. In this sense, Milton Friedman's claim that inflation is always and everywhere a monetary phenomenon – in the quantitativist sense of the relation between money and inflation – is a falsehood. The self-sustaining logic of hyperinflation means that inflation will accelerate indefinitely unless it is stopped by a radical monetary reform. It has no link with any kind of fundamental cause.

Following this same theoretical schema, let us now discuss some of the famous episodes of hyperinflation: Germany in 1922–23, China in 1947–48 and the Latin American hyperinflation of the 1980s.

The German Hyperinflation of 1922–23
After World War One, metal convertibility disappeared more or less quickly in the belligerent countries, depending on the degree of damage they had sustained. The worst-affected country was Germany, which was subjected to the Treaty of Versailles's absurd tribute payments

('reparations').[17] Added to the massive destruction resulting from the war and the amputation of both its colonies and part of its own territory, these payments would destroy Wilhelmine society, excite civil war and unleash hyperinflation.[18] As we indicated in our theoretical discussion above, German hyperinflation developed through two phases.

Box 5.1
A self-sustaining inflationary logic

From expectation to adaptation
The real demand for money is a decreasing function of the expectation of inflation:

$$\log \left(\frac{M}{p}\right)_t = -\alpha \pi_t^a$$

Expected inflation is revised upward when inflation observed is higher than expected inflation:

$$\frac{d\pi^a}{dt} = \beta \left(\frac{d \log p}{dt} - \pi^a \right)$$

Differentiation of the demand for money:

$$-\frac{1}{\alpha} \left(\frac{d \log M}{dt} - \frac{d \log P}{dt} \right) = \frac{d\pi^a}{dt}$$

Using the equation for the revision of expected inflation, we get

$$\beta(\log P - \log M) = \frac{d \log M}{dt} - (1 - \alpha\beta) \frac{d \log P}{dt})$$

$$\frac{\partial}{\partial P} \left(\frac{d \log P}{dt} \right) = \frac{-\beta}{1 - \alpha\beta} \left(\frac{1}{P} \right)$$

---

17   John Maynard Keynes, *The Economic Consequences of the Peace*, New York: Harcourt, Brace and Howe, 1920.

18   German hyperinflation has been the object of countless analyses. For a synthesis using the conception of money adopted in the present volume, see André Orléan, 'Crise de souveraineté et crise monétaire: l'hyperinflation allemande des années 1920', in Théret (ed.), *La monnaie dévoilée par ses crises*, vol. II, pp. 177–220.

There is a phase shift as we move from an inflation fed by growth in money supply (in a monetarist system), when it is < 1, and a self-referential inflation driven by the logic of expectations alone, when it is > 1.

Expectations for inflation form on the exchange market: $\pi_t^a = \log \hat{e}_t - \log e_t$ where e_t is the spot exchange rate and $\hat{e}_t$ is the expectation of the future exchange rate. Expectations on the exchange market are guided by a focal point $\bar{e}_t$ with the effect that

$$\log \hat{e}_t = E_t \log e_{t+1} = a + \beta \log \bar{e}_t$$

The demand for money is

$$\log \left(\frac{M}{p}\right)_t = -\alpha \pi_t^a = -\alpha(\log \hat{e}_t - \log e_t) = -\alpha(\beta \log e_t - \log e_t + a)$$

And to differentiate the demand for money:

$$-\frac{1}{\alpha}\left(\frac{d\,LogM}{dt} - \frac{d\,LogP}{dt}\right) = \frac{d\pi^a}{dt} = \beta\,\frac{d\log e_t}{dt} - \frac{d\log e_t}{dt}$$

In a hyperinflationary process, nominal developments are much greater than real variations. We can overlook these latter and focus on relative purchasing power parity (PPP):

$$\frac{d\log P}{dt} = \frac{d\log e}{dt}$$

It is the exchange market that guides the revision of expectations for inflation. From this we deduce the inflation dynamic:

$$\frac{d\,LogP}{dt} = \frac{1}{1+\alpha}\,\frac{d\,LogM}{dt} + \frac{\alpha\beta}{1+\alpha}\,\frac{d\log e_t}{dt}$$

Depending on whether $\beta < 1+1/\alpha$ or $\beta > 1+1/\alpha$ we find two different inflationary regimes: one is directed by monetary expansion, and the other is self-referential.

The first phase ran from 1920 to the summer of 1922. This period can be broken down into sub-periods, each of which was characterised by a political event that altered confidence in money (Table 5.1). After the sharply accelerating inflation that followed the Treaty of Versailles, a right-wing government established in power through a putsch attempted a classic deflationary policy. But the appreciation of the *mark* relative to the dollar was a lot stronger than the fall in domestic prices. The loss of competitiveness worsened the state of Germany's foreign accounts, making it clear to everyone that the reparations could not be honoured. The question of 'Who is going to pay?' became the beating heart of the social struggle, because the reparations were compounded with Germany's own domestic public debt. Inflation and the depreciation of the *Reichsmark* began their mutual spiral.

Speculation on the *Reichsmark* led to it being overvalued, which stimulated both production and inflation. Monetary expansion brought negative real interest rates, a strong demand for credit, and an erosion of real wages. At issue in this phase was an increase in the overall quantity of money, which led to a 'classic' case of financial instability. Euphoric forecasts of the advance of German companies' sales on world markets led to excessively extended investment. Securities prices plunged, rendering balance sheets illiquid.

From June 1922 – a month marked by the murder of the industrialist Walter Rathenau – until June 1923, substitute currencies were used by enterprises and municipalities to pay their employees and provide aid to the unemployed. This was not enough to stop extreme food shortages. Summer 1922 was the crucial moment of transformation of the financial structure. Commercial bills were transferred *en masse* to the central bank. Commercial banks became pure transmission belts between companies and the central bank. Private debts were systematically refinanced. The monetary system became entirely centralised. The real interest rate plunged to extreme negative levels, while the fiscal coverage for public spending collapsed. A generalised indexation was underway, fed by the spiralling wage and price rises.

The real value of deposits collapsed and the private money market disappeared. Industry concentrated itself vertically in order to economise on monetary means of payment and bought up banks in order to have direct access to Reichsbank refinancing. At this stage, the *Reichsmark* began to be replaced in bank balance sheets by the dollar. On the assets side, the banks bought up currency as a consequence of speculation on the exchange markets. On the liabilities side, they received foreign currency loans from banks abroad, especially American ones. Speculation ballooned and centred on the dollar, which became the unit of account for those economic agents linked to international trade. The dollar became the ultimate liquidity, the capital-commodity *par excellence*. For economic agents without direct foreign links, the crisis of the money of account was expressed in 'accounting innovations'. There was a pursuit of social recognition for heterogeneous forms of private accounting that were supposedly of 'constant value'.

The purely endogenous, self-referential phase of hyperinflation began in June 1923. This would destroy the currency. In November 1923, the quantity of central money expressed in real value only represented 1.6 percent of its 1914 level, at the moment war was declared. In August 1923, the government attempted a final manoeuvre by issuing a new *goldmark* debt, made out in small denominations. But the notes were immediately hoarded. The state thus itself helped to organise the disappearance of the *mark*. During this last phase, any economic agent who could not index her income to anticipated future price rises was instantly ruined. Monetary expansion thus eroded confidence in ultimate liquidity. This led to an erosion of money's reserve function, to the point that it was completely destroyed.

The final stage of hyperinflation was realised through the transformation of payment circuits and the disappearance of the *Reichsmark* as a means of circulation. From the summer of 1923 onwards, there was total monetary chaos. There circulated a heteroclite variety of monetary signs of uncertain purchasing power. *The monetary crisis had reached its final stage, because it had now become a crisis of state sovereignty.* The concerns of big business integrated vertically. Local exchange circuits used substitutes for money, without any rules to regulate conversions between them. This brought monetary anarchy. A division developed between the towns and the countryside, resulting in a retention of agricultural produce from the market. The consequence was a collapse in economic activity. *Nominal hyperinfla-tion is also real hyperdeflation.* This totally contradicts the quantitative theory of money and the supposed neutrality of money in relation to the real economy.

How does hyperinflation stop? The blaze is so vast that it only ceases when the flames have nothing left to consume. The fact that the domestic public debt was made out in *Reichsmarks* meant that it was reduced to almost zero. This removed one of the crucial battlegrounds of the social conflict. The generalised and instantaneous indexation of all prices and incomes prevented supplementary real benefits from being drawn. There was no longer any economic horizon, and no value bequeathed from the past. There was only the present moment, and the telescoping between anticipated inflation and the inflation that had already taken place. Ultimately, power shifted decisively in favour of the industrial bourgeoisie, which allowed a political solution to be imposed.

Table 5.1
The seven phases of German inflation

Phases	Wholesale prices (% monthly variation)	Dollar (% monthly variation in paper marks)*
August 1914–November 1918 (armistice)	1.7	1.1
November 1918–July 1919 (Treaty of Versailles)	4.7	9.2
July 1919–February 1920 (right-wing putsch forces SPD out of government)	25.4	31.0
February 1920–May 1921 (London's ultimatum)	− 1.7	− 4.0
May 1921–June 1922 (assassination of Rathenau)	14.0	13.5
June 1922–June 1923 (explosion of inflation)	60.0	62.8
June 1923–November 1923 (end of hyperinflation)	3,171	2,783

The dollar's value had been 4.2 *goldmarks. Source: table based on Aglietta and Orléan la violence de la monnaie,* pp. 188–9. *Data drawn from C. Bresciani-Turroni 1937.*

Finding a way out of the crisis presupposed the rebuilding of a hierarchically organised monetary system. This would be based on a new, unifying unit of account that could become the focus of collective confidence and enable new issuance rules to be established. This was a political process. Indeed, monetary reform can only succeed if it brings together a sufficient range of interests to secure political supremacy.

In the domestic sphere, a new central bank was established, the Rentenbank, which began to issue a new currency, the *rentenmark*. The Rentenbank was the product of an alliance between agrarian, industrial and financial interests. Those who held *rentenmarks* were granted a conversion guarantee in annuity titles made out in *goldmarks*, which received a 5 percent rate of interest. Of course, if realised *en masse*, this conversion would prove illusory. The guarantee could only catalyse confidence if the conversion did not in fact take place! In fact, the *rentenmark* immediately stabilised, and stable it remained. The decisive factor was the change in the rules for issuing money, as the Rentenbank was forbidden to finance the state. But this extreme prohibition was only possible thanks to an international solution.

This solution would have dramatic consequences later on, during the Great Depression. It re-established monetary regulation and made the central bank a means of reinserting German capitalism into international relations. The two pillars of the monetary system, the public debt and the central bank, now came under foreign control. In 1924, the dollar debt for reparations was restructured through the Dawes Plan. The central bank acquired legal autonomy from the government and was placed under international supervision. The domestic public finances were subordinated to monetary administration. In truth, the *rentenmark*, which was supposedly guaranteed by the ensemble of real estate property, was in fact guaranteed by foreign capital. This owed to the influx of American loans, which allowed the German banks to rebuild their liabilities.

One thing remains constant. All monetary systems are built on sovereignty. In the case of Germany, sovereignty was very fragile because it had largely been transferred abroad. Hitler would make this a powerful means of propaganda as he built the Nazi party. Let us examine, now, how another hyperinflation process was eradicated by a radical change of sovereignty.

The Chinese Hyperinflation of 1947–48

In 1945, the Chinese war of liberation from Japan came to an end. This war had seen an alliance of circumstance between the Kuomintang, led by Chiang Kai-shek, and the Communist forces led by Mao Zedong, but the civil war was now reignited. The Kuomintang's sovereignty was largely illusory. The economic situation was catastrophic: savings had dried up, the countryside was in revolt, and taxes were impossible to collect, or else siphoned off by the collectors themselves.

There was a systematic monetisation of the public deficit in order to pay civil servants and soldiers and to finance spending on the civil war. Speculation on gold and the dollar ran riot. Foreign banks and property owners liquidated their assets, converting them into dollars and transferring them to Hong Kong. Those who earned their incomes from the public deficit did the same. In these conditions, the central bank could not put a halt to either the rise in gold prices or the rise in dollar prices, which were strongly correlated on account of the double speculation. In April 1948, the government attempted a monetary reform to re-establish the currency on the basis of gold: one gold yuan was exchanged for three million of the former monetary unit. The government forced the private holders of precious metals and foreign currency to exchange it for the new monetary unit. It was thus able to rebuild its reserves of gold, silver and foreign currency, covering the attempt to put a lid on prices. But as the civil war turned against the government, the deficit reached 75 percent of public spending. Because the use of gold in private exchange was forbidden, in November 1948 there was an outbreak of speculation on raw materials. This indicated that the population had rejected the new monetary units; the government was itself forced to pay its expenses in dollars. By May 1949, as the Communist forces made their decisive advance, the gold yuan was no longer worth anything.

It was the radical change of sovereignty that enabled monetary reform to be realised. The Communist government issued a new currency in each area it conquered. It allowed the old currency to be converted at a set rate, up to a certain date. After that, it would no longer be worth anything. Monetary unification took place through the merger of the issuing bodies in each area, thus forming the central bank of the People's Republic of China. The latter bought up the regional currencies at a strict parity. The unification was accomplished through the declaration of the People's Republic on 1 October 1949.

The Communist government forbade the use of gold and foreign currencies as units of account or means of payment, and violently repressed the black market. But it allowed the free holding of such assets, even as it offered very favourable conversion rates to those who did want to exchange them. Inflation and the budget deficit could only be brought down gradually, for it was necessary to organise the upkeep of millions of functionaries and soldiers who had come across from the former regime. The government created a real-value savings certificate in order to put a freeze on liquidity. It was defined by a basket of 3 kilos of rice, 750 grams of flour, 1.3 metres of cotton and 8 kilograms of coal. This basket was re-evaluated in the money of account every ten days.

These savings certificates were a massive success. The result was a contraction of the money supply in circulation, which slowed inflation and allowed it to cease completely by March 1950. From that moment onwards, control was established over the public finances. At the end of 1950, the budget was balanced. At the same time, the banking system was totally centralised under the control of the political authorities: there was a single source of credit, a single clearing centre, and direct supervision of all transactions in scriptural money.

The Latin American Inflation of the 1970s–90s

Between the 1970s and the late 1990s, the economies of Latin America experienced numerous monetary and financial setbacks: debt crises, exchange crises, banking crises, but also hyperinflationary crises. Late-1980s Peru, Bolivia and Nicaragua were the most acute cases, with five-figure rates of inflation. The examples of Chile, Brazil and Argentina deserve particular attention, for they best underline the importance of the conflict over redistribution from which hyperinflationary tendencies develop, as well as their self-referential character. Firms' market power, companies' and workers' real wage targets, as well as unions' power to negotiate, were essential factors in determining what repercussions would result from the rise in the costs anticipated by the suppliers of goods and services, which lay at the origin of the hyperinflationary spiral.[19] Here we find an old and well-known set of circumstances, which had already been highlighted by Michal Kalecki and Joan Robinson: hyperinflation is the consequence of a violent conflict over resources, the presence of an indexation mechanism and the sudden abandonment of the national currency in favour of a substitute.[20]

Inflation in Chile began to accelerate in 1973. This took place in the final year of Allende's presidency, before Pinochet's military coup. The public deficit, including its companies' deficit, only grew with the sharp rise in wages and social security costs, controlled prices, the rapid decline in productivity and the disorganisation of the channels of trade. The deficit was financed by increasingly large advances from the central bank. Speculation ran riot on anything that stood outside of state control, from foreign currencies to real estate and luxury goods. Here, hyperinflation did not reach the level of the complete destruction of the currency. Instead, it was the establishment of the dictatorship that bloodily suppressed the social conflict. Without doubt, however, in the final months of the Allende presidency, inflation had entered into the self-referential phase. The cost of living index had increased a hundred-fold in four years, while the real money stock lost 70 percent of its value in two years. The monetary advances to the state multiplied more than a hundred-fold in four years. Private credit then took up the slack.

After the coup d'état, there was both a restructuring of the public debt and a collapse in workers' and peasants' real incomes. The macroeconomic effect was drastic. 1975 was a year of depression: there was a 13 percent fall in GDP, a 30 percent fall in industrial production and year-on-year inflation at 375 percent. The axis of the fascist government's economic policy, inspired by the Chicago Boys, was the reprivatisation of the financial system and the liquidation of state-owned production. Up until July 1975, the banks remained trapped in a tight

---

19   For a recent analysis of hyperinflation in Argentina see Jonathan Marie, 'Hyperinflation argentine de 1989: une interprétation post-keynésienne', *Revue de la régulation*, vol. 15, no. 1, 2014.

20   Michal Kalecki, 'A model of hyperinflation', *Manchester School of Economics and Social Studies*, vol. 30, 1962; Joan Robinson, 'The Theory of Distribution', in her *Collected Economic Papers*, vol. II, Oxford: Basil Blackwell, 1960.

regulatory straitjacket. This allowed free reign for financial innovations. There was an upsurge in financial companies who lent to rich households and invested funds in very short-term securities at very high interest rates.

This was the moment that radically changed the property structure. Those who were able to borrow in foreign currency centralised financial power in their own hands. Financial intermediaries took control of the banks. The new property titles gained rapidly in value, while debts to the state lost value just as quickly, because they were indexed to a consumer price index that was kept artificially low by price controls. Nonetheless, the essential lever of the property transfer was the international credit attracted by Chile's high interest rates and the rapid rise in the value of the new property titles. Private indebtedness assumed an increasingly important place in the country's foreign debt, rising from 16 percent of the latter in 1974 to 41 percent in 1979.

Having played their role in the transition, the financial companies' position now declined. The banks became the centre of financial power. The gap between the rates that Chilean banks paid on euro-credits and the very high domestic interest rates left an enormous margin for intermediation, and all the more so given that the massive influx of capital stabilised the peso. The banks' clients were public enterprises, who were in fact forced to be clients to these banks on account of the state's refusal to finance them either through the budget or the central bank. These companies above all belonged to international financial groups.

Nonetheless, the most important thing was not this intermediary function, but rather the credit that the banks procured for themselves from abroad, in an inverse transformation. The banks obtained medium-term eurocredits and lent to very-short term, speculative financial operations. This was a self-sustaining process, because the incoming capital overvalued the peso, creating an external current deficit which required the influx of fresh capital. The risk of borrowing in foreign currency rose ever higher. It was for this reason that the turnaround of US monetary policy in October 1979, which would provoke a global recession and a catastrophic fall in raw materials prices, necessarily brought a devastating devaluation of the peso.

The recession caused by the US monetary policy reversal brought an oil shock, which, combined with prohibitive international interest rates, drove fresh crises in all raw-materials producer countries. Mexico initiated the chain of crises in Latin America in August 1982. Brazil experienced sharp inflation across the 1980s, to which a series of monetary plans were unable to put a stop. Four-figure hyperinflation appeared in 1989, and only came to an end after the activation of the Real plan launched on 1 July 1994. Beyond the fight against hyperinflation, the Real plan included a vast programme of structural reforms. In fact, the measures against inflation had been activated already in 1993 with the Immediate Action Programme (PAI) formulated by Economy Minister Fernando Henrique Cardoso. This stabilisation programme included four different aspects: 1) a rigorous budget consolidation policy; 2) the introduction of a new unit of account, the URV (Unidade Real de Valor), which eased the path towards deindexation and the subsequent establishment of a new stable currency, the *real*; 3) interest rate rises; 4) exchange rate controls and the liberalisation of import prices.

The monetary reform was based on a consideration of the inertial character of inflation and the implicit acceptance that hyperinflation was a self-referential process. According to those who promoted this reform, the hyperinflationary spiral had been fed by the day-to-day revision of prices on the basis of the exchange rate and developments in domestic price indices. Given that contracts were adjusted according to different indices and not in a synchronised manner, there was always an imbalance in relative prices and, as a result, strong inflationary pressure. It was thus necessary first to put a stop to the conflict over redistribution, fed by the series of price and wage indexations that concerned ever shorter periods.

A single index was adopted in order to break the circularity effect. The whole economy was indexed to the new unit of account, the URV, an index whose value in *cruzeiros* was determined day-by-day according to the exchange rate. Concretely, all prices were defined in URV and in *cruzeiros*, but only these latter could be used in payments. In July 1994, the bimonetary schema gave way to the new currency, the *real*, which met with rapid success. The first month of the *real* saw only 4 percent inflation.

If this monetary mechanism constituted the bedrock of monetary stabilisation, it is also worth emphasising the role that other measures played. The powerful rise in interest rates encouraged the massive influx of foreign capital, and in particular the repatriation of capital that Brazilian oligarchies had previously held abroad. The resulting appreciation of the new currency's exchange rate was largely supported by the government, for two reasons. On the one hand, it exerted a downward pressure on the price of imported goods, thus helping to limit imported inflation. On the other hand, it blocked self-referential anticipations on exchange rates, which had until that point been accustomed to a perpetual depreciation of Brazilian currency. Another reason for the Real plan's effectiveness was the continuing will to ground the reform on consensual and participatory bases. The Real plan was subject to prior consultation across the whole range of socio-economic actors. Its implementation did not occasion any price freeze, any confiscation of goods or savings or any break of existing contracts. Despite its downsides, the Real plan succeeded in putting an end to the mounting hyperinflation.

Two other countries distinguished themselves through the radical strategies they took to break out of spiralling hyperinflation: Argentina and Ecuador. These two countries each took recourse to foreign anchoring (a 'hard peg') in order to escape the monetary chaos. Argentina had experienced numerous crises of confidence in money. All had originated from the difficulty of establishing a lasting compromise on income distribution, in the political paralysis emerging from a succession of fragile political coalitions, and repeated monetary reforms adopted abruptly and in a poorly concerted fashion.[21] Seeking to avoid such pitfalls, in 1991 Argentina adopted a simple and credible monetary reform through the convertibility law. Its main objective was to make each new peso issued strictly equivalent to a dollar. The currency board regime established a monetary regulation that guaranteed convertibility at parity, with dollar reserves totally covering the

21   On this point, see Jaimes Marques-Pereira, 'Crecimiento, conflicto distributivo y soberanía monetaria en Argentina', in Rober Boyer and Julio Neffa (eds), *Salida de crisis y estrategias alternativas de desarrollo, la experiencia argentina*, Buenos Aires: Miño y Dávila, 2007, pp. 177–207.

monetary base. In order to undergird the credibility of this rule, the convertibility law was written into the Constitution. This strategy proved successful: within a few months, there was a decline in hyper-inflationary tensions.

The second case was yet more extreme. In 2000, Ecuador simply chose to abandon its national currency and to introduce a total dollar-isation of its economy. This decision was motivated by the Ecuadorian authorities' incapacity to restore confidence in the currency after a grave financial crisis and the onset of hyperinflation, which set the country on course towards devastating political instability. This choice is an interesting one for an analysis of the relationship between money and sovereignty: ultimately, for the Ecuadorian government, dollari-sation consisted in attempting to reconquer the political sovereignty that had been lost internally by abandoning the last attributes of monetary sovereignty, and thus abandoning external political sover-eignty. This apparently paradoxical strategy went beyond simply pegging the currency to some external referent of value. Unlike in the case of the Argentinian currency board, here the national currency disappeared, and the realm of legitimacy and confidence was instead transferred to the dollar.

While it met with a certain degree of resistance – notably from indigenous populations – the transition to dollarisation in Ecuador was rapidly accepted by the population. This owed to its effectiveness in neutralising the hyperinflationary process, and again in pinning anticipations to solid bases. But as in the Argentinian case, this effec-tiveness in combatting inflation brought significant constraints. Where both the currency board and dollarisation are concerned, the growth dynamic remains dependent on net capital entries, and the central bank is unable to assume its usual prerogatives: it is not able to take any significant action regarding interest rates, and its function as a lender of last resort is also limited, weakening the banking system.[22]

---

22   See Jean-François Ponsot, 'Currency boards', in Louis-Philippe Rochon and Sergio Rossi (eds), *The Encyclopedia of Central Banking*, Cheltenham: Edward Elgar Publishing Limited, pp. 130–2; Jean-François Ponsot, 'Dollarisation et banque centrale en Équateur', in Elsa Lafaye de Michaux, Eric Mulot and Pépita Ould Ahmed (eds), *Institutions et développement. La fabrique institutionnelle et politique des trajec-toires de développement*, Rennes: Presses universitaires de Rennes, 2007, pp. 233–58.

The end of the currency board in Argentina came with the catastrophic crisis of 2001. This illustrated the long-term dangers of a radical strategy attempting to block self-referential hyperinflation by using a hard peg.

THE LIBERALISATION OF FINANCE AND THE RESURGENCE OF POWERFUL FINANCIAL CRISES IN THE LAST THREE DECADES OF THE TWENTIETH CENTURY

The contemporary globalisation of finance has been accompanied by a great variety of financial crises, affecting the banks, asset markets and foreign exchange in both developed countries and emerging ones. This book's objective is not to provide a complete review of these crises, as the IMF has done with all its great means of investigation. Here we attempt instead to pick out the elements common to their logic, with a particular focus on the role of money.

Financial crises, and especially banking crises, have led to enormously costly public interventions. The IMF has calculated that, across thirty-four countries and over a thirty-year period (1970–2000), the budgetary cost was an average of 12.8 percent for the developed countries and 14.3 percent for emerging countries. There are also extreme cases. The Asian crisis cost 50 percent of Indonesia's GDP, 34 percent of Thailand's and 27 per cent of South Korea's. As for the crises in Latin America, in 1982 the cost was 42 percent for Chile and 22 percent for Uruguay.

Of course, the costs relative to GDP are lower in developed countries: 3.2 percent of US GDP in 1981–82, but 8 percent in Sweden and 15 percent in Finland in 1991. Contagion played a major role in most crises: such was the case of the EMS exchange crisis (1992–3), the bond crisis (1994), and the stock market crisis (2001–02) in the developed countries; but so, too, in emerging countries and countries in transition, from the Asian crisis (1997–98), to the Mexican (1994–95) and Russian (1998) crises.

Crises in Developed Countries

Banks always play a crucial role in propagating crises, even when they are not at their origin. In stock market crises, the contagion results from worries over market liquidity after an initial fall in prices. Thus, on 19 October 1987, the Wall Street market fell 22.6 percent under the weight of sales orders concerning some 600 million securities. The collapse rebounded on the Chicago futures market, producing a mass of margin calls. For the stock market to continue to function, arbitrageurs – securities firms – had to advance enormous credits to their clients to enable them to maintain their positions. Thus, as the market opened on 20 October, there was extreme tension over liquidity. Kidder Peabody and Goldman Sachs had to advance $1.5 billion in two hours! Here we can grasp the crucial role of these market markers. They themselves need enormous amounts of liquidity in order to finance their counterparty positions for the avalanche of sales orders, such that a floor price can be found. This is an essential precondition if speculators are to be able to act as buyers again.

But the commercial banks were worried by the financial fragility of the market marker firms, and were thus reticent about lending to them. The securities settlement system was endangered by the possibility that one of these firms would collapse. The Fed's last resort intervention was decisive for stabilising the market, as it encouraged the banks to lend $7.7 billion to the market markers on 20 and 21 October.

The Stock Exchange was not the only market vulnerable to the drying-up of liquidity. The global bond markets collapse in 1994 was a spectacular case of international contagion across markets. In turn, this crisis precipitated the Mexican crisis. It began with an unanticipated tightening of US monetary policy in February 1994, catching the market on the back foot. Indeed, at the end of 1993, the opinion on the market was that the rates were going to fall. It was this expectation that drove institutional investors to take long positions. These positions were financed by short-term credits. Since short-term loans were the debt levers that financed the acquisition of long-term securities, there was a massive exposure to rate risks, owing to the discordant maturity dates on the US bond markets. When the Fed raised its policy rate, investors hurried to close their positions in order not to have to renew their debts at higher rates, and to avoid extra margin calls. The result was a massive sale of bonds that raised long rates by 300 base points in a few weeks. Once again, this phenomenon resulted from a deterioration of market liquidity on account of the capital losses that followed the price rebound. The markets' international interconnections played an essential role in propagating the crisis. *The proliferation of risk-management tools created more fragile markets.* There was a multiplication of derivatives markets, some of which were weak links on account of their lack of liquidity and concentrated arbitrageurs. Risk propagates itself by transferring across different segments of the market. From this we can deduce a certain reticence towards providing liquidity in stress situations, above all in over-the-counter markets without clearing mechanisms and without a central settlements agent. *Abundant macroeconomic liquidity can thus coexist with insufficient market liquidity, on account of informational asymmetries and counterparty risks.*

Banking crises are the most serious crises because they strike at the heart of the monetary system's functioning. They show how insufficient the law of reflux is in ensuring this system's stability. Contagion leads to three categories of banking crises. The original crises are panics produced by the conversion of deposits into cash. These should normally be averted by way of deposit insurance. However, in numerous recent cases we have seen that this did not happen, from the run on deposits at Northern Rock in September 2008 to the much more recent eurozone banking crises in Cyprus and Greece. A second type of crisis results from settlement failures in interbank payments. In principle, these should also be avoided, if all systems operated through gross settlement in the money of a central bank that also plays the role of clearing house. But it is far from the case that all settlement systems obey such a schema, especially when it comes to settlements on financial securities and derivatives products. The third, and most important, type of crisis results from the deteriorating quality of bank credits. This rebounds on banks' intersecting engagements and since these engagements constitute a system, it becomes impossible to distinguish sound banks from fragile ones. The banks become reticent to continue opening up lines of credit to one another.

That is how the international interbank market froze in mid-August 2007, thus obliging the central banks to mount a coordinated last-resort intervention. But the interbank market did not truly recover, and its paralysis became much more serious in September 2008 after the collapse of Lehman Brothers.

The deregulation of finance in the 1980s initiated the transition to market finance. This further weakened the banks in all countries.

Indeed, the enormous boom in securities transactions was financed by debt levers provided by bank credit, which repeatedly proved excessive. Errors in appreciating asset price movements translated into massive undervaluations of credit risk, insufficient reserves, inadequate own funds, and distorted maturities. This resulted in improper exposure to the variations in short-term rates. In sum, the management of the bankers was calamitous.

It was through such practices that dodgy credit accumulated during the US real estate boom from 1987 onwards. The rise in short-term rates in 1989 triggered the banking crisis. Restructuring took a long time, and required a new law, the FDICIA (Federal Deposit Insurance Corporation Improvement Act), adopted in 1991. The Act's objective was to strengthen the legitimacy of the banks' supervisory body in forcing the banks to manage their risks properly. The essential idea was the obligation placed on the supervisory body to take pre-emptive corrective action, and thus to detect which banks were fragile and force them to increase their own funds, or else restructure them before they fell into bankruptcy. This mechanism proved effective in restructuring and closing regional banks by limiting their losses in the acute crisis of autumn 2008. Yet it did not apply either to investment banks or to bank conglomerates with the status of bank holding companies.

In the 1980s, bank crises originating in real estate were not limited to the United States alone. The Scandinavian countries provide a case study of the explosive cocktail of financial liberalisation and the asset price cycle. All banks became more fragile as they exposed their balance sheets to much more risk than they had previously. Thus, in Sweden, government bonds passed from 25 percent of total bank assets in 1983 to 11 percent in 1992, and credits to the private sector from 46 percent to 60 percent. The increase was concentrated in the real estate sector, and financed by borrowing on the money markets. The banks' fate thus depended entirely on real estate speculation and the marginal cost of monetary resources. The hardening of monetary policy and the reverse in real estate speculation prompted a thunderous crisis. It took large-scale government intervention, at a prohibitive social cost, to avoid a total disintegration of the financial system.

The Scandinavian and American cases saw violent banking crises, but also a rapid return to order. In France and Japan, by contrast, the rot took hold more gradually. In both countries, the public authorities' complicity with bankrupt financial interests was motivated by opposition to change. At the beginning of the crises, the authorities' guiding approach was to do nothing and hope that a favourable turnaround in the financial situation would soak up the losses (forbearance). This was the opposite of the attitude that motivated the FDICIA.

Crises in Emerging Countries

Most crises in emerging countries are of a dual nature, closely binding together exchange and the banks. When these countries benefit from macroeconomic stabilisation, and possibly also competitiveness policies, they experience a strong appreciation of their exchange rates. This owes to capital inflows out of proportion to the size, and especially the depth, of their financial markets. This appreciation brings a current account deficit and a dollar indebtedness, making the resident economic agents vulnerable to both credit and exchange risks. When short-term indebtedness in foreign currency exceeds the country's foreign exchange reserves, the interest rates on its external debt climb. The sovereign risk deteriorates more than that of private agents, bringing a deterioration of the country's risk rating. When a loss of confidence takes hold, speculation on foreign exchange can break out at any moment. This brings an abrupt withdrawal of short-term foreign capital, precipitating a banking crisis, which in return aggravates speculation on exchange.

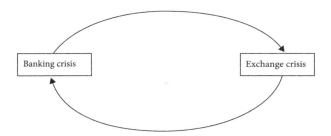

We see, in these cases, the circular schema typical of self-sustaining crises. The banks are indebted in foreign currency and lend in the national currency, as ballooning credit drives them to lend to agents who do not have income in foreign currency. Such was the case of the financing of real estate speculation (Thailand in 1997), of the state (the Mexican *tesobonos* in 1994, and Russian GKO in 1998), of the private sector (Argentina in 2001) and industrial companies that overinvest (Korea in 1997).

The proliferation of these crises, concentrated in a short period of time, illustrated the contagion between the emerging countries. This can develop through a mechanical transmission (spillover) by way of the interdependence of trade and finance. It can also result from psychological transmission (pure contagion) as the weakening confidence in national currencies spreads. Finally, it can result from the dynamic hedging of the portfolios of the international investors who detach themselves from emerging countries simultaneously. This is especially the case when they hold synthetic products (Exchange Traded Funds, or ETF), built on indices that combine financial assets from an array of emerging countries. The result is a rise in the correlation of asset yields across several countries. The macroeconomic effect of exchange crises in countries with debts in dollars and incomes in national currencies plays out on the balance sheets of both banks and non-banking actors. The debt liabilities to asset values ratio is a function of the exchange rate. If the country is on a floating exchange rate, the anticipated depreciation of the currency's exchange rate will be self-fulfilling. The rise in the foreign exchange rate swells indebtedness and weakens the balance-sheet structure. This increases risk premiums and thus increases the short-term cost of renewing the debt. The result is a fall in capital's profitability, weakened investment and a sharp brake on growth, or even a recession if the balance sheets worsen significantly. If the country has fixed exchange rates, this same anticipated depreciation of exchange rates will bring a fall in the foreign exchange reserves of the country respecting this constraint. If this country is to preserve this constraint without exhausting its reserves, it must increase the interest rate through a restrictive monetary policy. At the same time, it has to hope that this will put an end to capital flight. But the rise in interest rates brings a sharp fall in the country's asset values and increases the cost of debt. The balance-sheet structure continues to deteriorate, placing fresh pressure on exchange. As a result, there is a further draining away of reserves, until the point that the country is forced to float its currency, and thus to enter into the logic of floating exchanges.

This phenomenon has recurred on numerous occasions. The initial trigger depends on the initial source of indebtedness. The financial fragility comes from public indebtedness coupled with a persistent balance of payments deficit in the countries with weak domestic savings. The financing of the deficit relies on inflows of capital in dollars, leaving the banks' balance sheets vulnerable. Public indebtedness was responsible for the crises in Mexico in 1995, in Brazil in 1999, in Argentina in 2002 and in Russia in 1998. In Asian countries with high savings and strong growth, financial fragility came from massive capital inflows, attracted by the yields on investments. These capital inflows favoured the expansion of credit in the private sector, and encouraged real estate speculation bubbles. This was especially true of Thailand and Indonesia. The crisis that broke out in Thailand in July 1997 spread across the emerging Asian countries that had got rid of controls on the inflows of international capital. From September to December it became generalised, striking developed countries like South Korea and Hong Kong. The crisis was so intense, and its capacity to spread so dangerous, that it drove the US Federal Reserve to conduct a loan of last resort operation to help out South Korea. Each time the exchange rate collapsed on account of a self-fulfilling anticipation that reserves were going to be exhausted. Crises became more and more harmful to development, demanding long-term support for growth rates. This was the reason why, at the turn of the millennium, Asian and Latin American countries made major changes in their monetary and financial policies, moving to become export countries that accumulated foreign exchange reserves as a protection against future financial shocks.

6

Monetary Regulation Under Capitalism

Monetary doctrine only slowly recognised the idea of a central bank serving as a bank for banks. As we saw in the last chapter, this idea did not originally stem from the needs of what would, in the twentieth century, be called monetary policy. Rather, it derived from an assessment of the devastating financial crises of the mid-nineteenth century. In other words, the central bank was first able to establish its central position in the monetary system on account of its role as a lender of last resort.

The recognition of the central bank's position was not self-evident in a monetary system founded on metallic convertibility, whether the gold standard or a bimetallic standard. What the financial centres challenged was simply the prospect that banks that had been created to manage the public debt, and not regulate money, could hold some higher status. Nonetheless, the financial crises of 1847, 1856 and 1866 were so serious that gold convertibility had to be *de facto* suspended, even though no legal dispositions existed to legitimise this suspension *de jure*. The financial community had to recognise that the law of reflux did not function all by itself, and that private clearing mechanisms alone were not sufficient. When convertibility was suspended, banking debts had to be settled in another form of debt – one which would *ipso facto* be hierarchically superior. It became apparent, ultimately, that the existence of a debt issued for the purposes of settling all the other debts was the necessary condition for the integrity of the payments system. This makes up part of the set of rules that constitute the payment system, as set out in Chapter 1.

Nonetheless, Bagehot's doctrine of a 'lender of last resort' did not address the Bank of England's full range of social responsibilities. Its role as a settlement agent in the payment system made its discount rate the crucial variable in the money market. Yet this did not itself indicate how its Bank rate ought to be handled. The central bank cannot effectively play its role during crisis situations if it is not at the centre of the payment system during normal times. That is the foundation of what we call monetary policy. But the monetary order calls on different monetary doctrines in different circumstances. The question of which doctrine is appropriate depends on whether the legitimacy of the central bank's hierarchical position rests on the rule of convertibility, or whether it establishes and maintains itself in monetary systems based on a purely fiduciary ultimate liquidity. We will thus consider each of these two configurations in turn. First, however, we need properly to understand why the central bank is in a position to fulfil such a unique mission.

CENTRAL BANK RATIONALITY

What is the rationality of the central bank? Where does it get the information that allows it to fulfil its duties? The central bank's missions include guaranteeing settlements and preventing systematic failure, but also controlling the supply of means of payment, defining prudential rules for the banks, and oversight to make sure that the banks are respecting these rules. The centralisation of payments was established with the invention of scriptural money, alongside bank deposit accounts. Scriptural money is a private signature that circulates under a bankers' mark. This payment technology detaches the instrument (the cheque or debit card) from liquidity (the deposit registered in the account). It follows from this that the flow of payments can be disrupted by the risk of default and by the limited area in which signatures circulate. When central banks organise centralised clearing/settlement systems, this confers a uniform quality upon the means of payment used within the national community. This, indeed, is the reason why doubts over a bank's capacity to honour settlements of its debtor positions tend to transform into a systemic risk. This is because such doubts damage depositors' confidence in the inter-convertibility of bank monies, thus casting suspicion over the quality of all banks' signatures. That is why the central bank has to concern itself with the security of payment systems as a whole. *It manages the national community's most general public good.*

Correlated to this is the fact that the organisation of centralised payment systems gives central banks the means of information and practical experience to set in motion a logic of pragmatism. That is no guarantee of how effective their actions will be. But it does preserve them from the dogmatic arbitrariness preached by ayatollahs of market efficiency. The central banks have understood that the monetary base – the quantity of money that they issue on the liabilities side of their balance sheets – must respond flexibly to the variations in economic agents' needs, and thus respond to all the uncertainties that affect economies. This is only true, of course, in countries where the central bank operates at the heart of already-developed banking systems. It is from such systems that the central bank is able to elaborate a detailed understanding of the state of financial tensions.

When scriptural money is used, the basic information contained in each payment becomes arithmetical, personalised and recorded in the bank accounts of each of the counterparties to the transaction. That is why the payment system is the mediator of the passage between the microeconomic and macroeconomic levels. Each bank's positions relative to other banks are calculated in the end of day balance on the ledger of the interbank clearing house. In these positions, we find a summary of the payment flows that have passed through the economy, whatever their counterparties were. Banks can belong to multiple clearing systems (for small retail payments, for large financial transactions between residents, for transactions on securities and derivatives products, or for transactions between residents and non-residents). But the balances to be settled on final positions must discharge onto the central bank's books, if they are to be settled in the currency that acts as the ultimate means of settlement. So it is in these books that we see the kinds of financial tensions that the banks encounter. In order to honour their settlement obligations, they must supply themselves with the central money. They do this by drawing on their own reserve accounts, borrowing funds from other banks that are in surplus on the interbank market, repurchasing negotiable financial assets, and making use of the discount window opened up by the central bank.

All these processes directly plug the central bank into supplying liquidity to the banking system as a whole. That is why the central bank can closely relate the day-to-day conduct of monetary policy to the state of the financial tensions expressed by the payment system. It can also learn how to read the situations of banks that are in difficulty, how to judge the possibility that tensions will develop into a systemic risk, and how to decide whether it should grant a loan of last resort. There are multiple aspects to the central banker's craft, and there is no artificial barrier between preventing systemic risk and the conduct of monetary policy.[1]

This leads us to a very important theoretical conclusion. In a monetary economy, the central bank has information that other agents do not have regarding the overall state of the economy. This is because payments provide the central bank with a set of information that the market is not itself able to produce. Such information is extracted from the webs of interlocking payments that are calculated in the central clearing process. This invalidates the hypothesis that money is neutral. After all, the central bank can use this information to take action leading to economic conditions in which social wellbeing is improved – conditions which would not be achievable if it did not take this action. This thus justifies the possibility of taking discretionary actions which have real effects. Of course, these effects will only favour overall economic stability if the collective rationality that the central bank promotes is continually enriched with a practical knowledge, drawn from its presence on the capital markets.[2] As we saw in

---

1   Ralph George Hawtrey, *The Art of Central Banking*, London: Longmans Green, 1932.

2   The information that central banks draw from their central role in the payment system and their presence on the capital markets has to be organised in statistical information systems. The central banks have done much to develop such systems. They allow for analyses on the basis of which banks decide how they will conduct their monetary policies. On this question, see the contributions in the collective volume Olivier Feiertag (ed.), *Mesurer la monnaie. Banques centrales et construction de l'autorité monétaire (XIX–XXe siècle)*, Paris: Albin Michel, 2005.

Chapter 5, the Bank of England developed this knowledge as it came to learn its function as a lender of last resort. We will now examine how it converted this knowledge in its monetary policy.

Monetary Regulation in the Classical Era

Once the Bank of England's role as the settlement agent in payment systems had been established, its rediscount (Bank) rate became the pivot of the money market. The development of the London financial markets and the implantation of foreign banks in the City from 1850 onwards considerably increased the international influence exercised by the Bank rate. But in the 1850s, the Bank of England was not yet the bank for banks. It was still competing with other financial intermediaries in London. Of course, it was recognised that the Bank had particular responsibilities in managing state finances. This role had considerably helped to strengthen its prestige in the City. Nonetheless, the fact that the Bank was concerned with its own profits conflicted with its incipient collective responsibilities.[3] The Bank's administrators followed the competition in order to limit their own risks. Prudence was necessary, considering the three tasks that the Bank had to fulfil: guaranteeing the gold convertibility of its notes, within the straitjacket of the 1844 Peel Act; satisfying the state's financial needs; and preserving its shareholders' incomes. The Bank had little room for manoeuvre in these missions, for its free reserves (those that were not frozen up in cover for banknotes) were very low relative to its liquid commitments towards both resident and non-resident agents.

For decades, the Bank remained aligned to the money market rate in order to preserve its own profits. It did not take any stabilising action. On the contrary, when the demand for credit began to balloon during upturns in the business cycle, the Bank kept its rate low in order to maintain its own market share, when it should instead have tightened monetary conditions by raising its discount rate early enough to interrupt speculation. When the crisis broke out and it lost gold reserves, it abruptly increased its rate. This ended up strangling

3   R. S. Sayers, *Central Banking after Bagehot*, Oxford: Oxford University Press, 1987.

liquidity and precipitated bank collapses. Today we would say that it was enacting a pro-cyclical policy, due to incentives stemming from the non-recognition of its central position.

After Bagehot's doctrine became official, its logical complement was that the Bank should come to learn its collective responsibilities in the day-to-day operations of the money market. The 1873 crisis was the opportunity to put Bagehot's doctrine into practice. But this was not the crisis of a usual business cycle. Rather, it introduced a long phase of deflation that extended across capitalist economies as a whole. Not only did credit become rarer, but new types of branched commercial banks appeared, thanks to the new status of joint stock companies. Because these banks were branched, they were also more creditworthy. They confined the Bank of England to a marginal part of the credit market. On the other hand, the sterling bill of exchange had become the universal financial instrument for financing international commerce. Short-term capital movements thus became highly sensitive to the monetary rate in the City. The structural changes in finance thus obliged the Bank to organise its missions in a hierarchical order and to find permanent means of controlling the money market. Given that the Bank of England had no legal means of forcing commercial banks to maintain minimum reserves, it had to invent the art of central banking. This was a perfect example of how an evolutionary model can allow us to understand the emergence of a collective rationality, taking the markets' own dynamic as our point of departure.

In 1878, the Bank decided to deal with financial intermediaries by way of an official rate that would be set higher than the market rate, at the Bank's own discretion. The discount rate became the upper limit among all money market rates. As the Bank borrowed on the market in order to siphon off liquidity, it prevented the market rate from evolving independently of its own rate. The latter became flexible in relation to the Bank's gold reserves, as well as to the indications that the settlement of interbank positions provided regarding short-term tensions on the money market. It was then up to the banks to understand the significance of the information that the Bank was communicating to the market through the variations in its policy rate. The banks' responses became sharper in both timing and extent. As their roles became more clearly differentiated, a shared practical knowledge developed in the City.[4]

The Bank refined its communications technologies in order to strengthen the transmission of its decisions to the market. Truly emblematic of its power was the fact that the official rate was formally announced by the board at precisely 11 a.m. each Thursday. In the classical era, none of the monetary policy objectives that we usually ascribe today to central banks ever got a mention. The Bank did not seek to shape economic activity or to stabilise prices (inflation varied over the business cycle) and nor was it concerned by instabilities in the balance of payments. It had only one categorical imperative: to guarantee the gold convertibility of its own notes. This rule averted strategic conflicts between the Bank and the government, and preserved the independence of the former. But in no sense did this imperative set money management on automatic pilot, as monetarist dogma claims. The rule had to be interpreted in the face of each situation on the monetary market. Only then could the board decide on the policy interest rate.

It had to be decided each week whether or not the free gold reserves were sufficient for the purposes of anticipating short-term movements. The latter included both the domestic and foreign drain on reserves. The governor watched not only the ratio of free reserves to liabilities but also the absolute volume of reserves. Given the very narrow margins within which the Bank operated, it also took a view of the absolute critical minimum. Anticipated seasonal drain could also have an influence on the Bank's rate. This was also true of external fluctuations, and notably those coming from the US economy. This latter was very sensitive to the rhythms of agriculture and was unable to produce a flexible liquidity supply. This resulted in strong seasonal gold demand in London, which the Bank's administrators had to anticipate.

The central bank's power over gold movements was thus essentially monetary in character and exercised on account of short-term international capital movements. The elasticity of these movements

---

4   R. S. Sayers, *The Bank of England 1891–1914*, Cambridge: Cambridge University Press, 1976.

depended on the power of the leverage effect that variations in the Bank's official rate had on the money market's rate. When the Bank wanted to reduce the availability of funds, it siphoned off the liquidity that served the London discounting houses in financing the purchase of international equities. In order to achieve this, the Bank itself acted as a borrower of the funds that would otherwise have been loaned on the money market. Usually the Bank's rate varied within the 3–5 percent band, where it could be taken for granted that it would have a weak effect on credit conditions. That changed with the 1907 crisis, which forced the Bank to raise its rate to 7 percent. From 1906 onwards, the transformation of the financial system forced the Bank to adapt its methods. It turned to borrowing directly from the clearing banks, which had now become big commercial banks following their absorption of the regional banks. An oligopolistic discounting market developed, guided by the Bank of England. This structure would endure for most of the remainder of the twentieth century.

So long as the London money market condensed the state of worldwide financial tensions, the Bank of England's actions could have an acute effect on the global conjuncture. Non-residents took out short-term loans in London, because the bill of exchange in pounds sterling was the universal means of payment for international trade. Non-residents also held liquid balances in English banks, because this enabled them to benefit from these banks' international credit. The Bank of England therefore acted as a lever on all short-term rates internationally, intervening among the clearing banks and the discounting houses on the London interbank market.[5]

It is worth highlighting the full subtlety of the Bank of England's macroeconomic regulation role. Ballooning international credit increased the stocks to be financed more quickly than it increased sales. Discounting houses were increasingly called upon to discount the credit bills that were issued in international trade and accepted by the banks. The discounting houses thus themselves had to borrow

5   Harold Van B. Cleveland, 'The international monetary system in the interwar period', in Benjamin M. Rowland (ed.), *Balance of Power or Hegemony: The Interwar Monetary System*, Lehrman Institute, New York: New York University Press, 1976.

liquidity. The pressure that international trade bills exerted on interest rates rebounded on the London interbank market rate. When the banks hurried to rediscount, the gap between the market interest rate and the Bank's official rate fell. This was one first indicator of financial tension. If the Bank rediscounted a growing volume of eligible bills at a single rate, then it had to issue an increasing quantity of money as a counterparty. This caused an increase in the ratio of outstanding liabilities to free gold holdings in the issuing department. This was the second and most important indicator of tension. The Bank decided to increase its rate in order to re-establish the desired ratio. The degree of rate increase was based on its past experience. This increase had an immediate effect on the rate used by the discounting houses, and very soon had repercussions for the financing of international trade. Simultaneously, disposable liquidity around the world flowed into the London money market, for it was attracted there by the higher rate of remuneration. This short-term capital movement tended to cause appreciation in the pound sterling, which in turn sparked reaction from the central banks of the countries linked to the gold standard. Interest rates thus evolved in concert around the world, under the direction of the Bank of England (as shown by Barry Eichengreen).[6]

The national monetary regulation of fiduciary money

When we studied money's historical trajectories, we observed that the upheavals of the two world wars and the Great Depression of the 1930s led to the nationalisation of money, and control over money being entrusted to the state. The thirty years preceding World War Two saw the advent of labour societies; the thirty years following the war saw such societies thrive. This period overhauled the state's role in the economy. Organised social groups were tied to multiple institutional engagements. These latter both proved indispensable to social cohesion and influenced income formation. The capitalism that bloomed within national spaces in the growth era was an organised capitalism.

In the period following World War Two, Europe was at the cutting edge of developing a labour society. This was because the

---

6   Barry Eichengreen, *The Gold Standard in Theory and History*, London: Routledge, 1985.

principle of sovereignty had been transformed. In continental Europe, the pre-war ruling classes had been discredited by their collusion with the monstrosity of Nazism. In France in particular, new elites and political ideas had emerged from the Conseil national de la Résistance. In Germany, ordoliberalism was presented as the political doctrine that could rebuild a society that had been reduced to ruins. The European ideal rapidly appeared not only as a means of putting an end to wars on the continent, but also of promoting a new and dynamic principle that could cohere labour societies. And this principle was social progress. Two institutions of social mediation were charged with putting this principle into practice: collective bargaining over wages, and redistribution via the state budget. There was a wide political consensus, across party divides, in favour of the notion of social progress and the legitimacy of the institutions tasked with promoting it. Collective bargaining over wages played a decisive role in this regard, aligning progress in real wages to productivity advances at the macroeconomic level, and moreover imposed limits on inequalities, within the terms of a stable wage structure in the major branches of industry. This encouraged regular and self-sustaining long-term growth, stimulated by booming mass consumption, urbanisation and the expansion of the economically active population.

These transformations had drastic effects on money, both in theory and in practice. In the nineteenth century, the possibility of using monetary policy to orient economic development towards social ends had been unthinkable. But this was now widely recognised. The very notion of monetary policy – that is, a strategy for guiding money's influence on the economy – is a collective rationality radically distinct from that of the Bank of England under the gold standard.

The peg established by defining the unit of account in gold expressed an unbreakable confidence in the validity of nominal values, and thus in the contracts sealed on the basis of these values. The implication of gold convertibility was that the society as a whole had committed to preserving the nominal value of private contracts between individual property-owners. This was a norm inherent to the natural-order principle of sovereignty, held to be superior to the goals that governments might otherwise achieve by manipulating money. This ethical attitude towards convertibility – by Max Weber's account, an attitude characteristic of the spirit of capitalism – was a collective belief that protected the central bank from political influences.

The abolition of the gold standard poses the problem of the legitimacy of monetary signs. The unit of account is nothing other than the name given to the numerical unit of the central bank's liabilities. The central bank becomes the focus of the contradictory forces that shape money's purchasing power. Even if the central bank is not directly exposed, it is nonetheless implicated on account of its relationship with the state, which judges inflation while also being subject to it. This poses the problem of how money is to be controlled. This control was realised in different ways in different countries, for sovereignties had themselves become national. Various structural factors influenced choices over monetary regulation: the existence or otherwise of developed public debt titles markets; the degree of protection of the banking system, and thus its solidity faced with the risk of insolvency; the predominance of intermediated financing or recourse to capital markets; the extent and tightness of exchange controls; and the explicit regulation of interest rates by the authorities, as well as their implicit regulation by the banking oligopoly.

These were nationally separate systems of limited openness. Within these systems, monetary policy was a backup for an economic policy seeking firstly to achieve full employment, and secondly to stabilise the balance of payments. Price stability was only considered in relative terms: for the most open countries it had to be made competitive with inflation in other countries, while for the largest countries – first of all the United States – it was considered in terms of arbitrating between inflation and underemployment. Monetary regulation was divided between two poles, or two regimes that could be combined in different ways. One of them, mostly prevalent in the Anglo-Saxon countries, acted on the structure of interest rates by directly influencing the price of the liquidities that the central bank made available to the economy. The other, mostly prevalent in continental Europe, acted on the availability of banking credit, by either directly overseeing or else tightly delimiting the margins of their amount of liquid resources (Table 6.1).

Table 6.1
Money anchorage regimes

Type of anchor	Control of ultimate liquidity	
	By price	By quantity
Foreign currency	Metal or currency base. Convertibility (Bank of England under the gold standard).	Exogenous fiduciary base. Quantitative rule. (Bundesbank 1970s–1990s)
Domestic currency	Endogenous fiduciary base. Inflation targeting (Bank of England after 1993).	Endogenous fiduciary base. Limits imposed on credit. France, 1970s–1987.

Monetary Policy Doctrines

Monetary policy doctrines are closely linked to conceptions of money and thus to the theories of value on which these conceptions are founded. This brings us back, then, to our discussions in Chapter 1.

When we studied the courses that money has taken throughout history, we observed a theoretical divide that opposes external or exogenous conceptions of money to internal or endogenous ones (Table 6.1).

For those who adhere to the external money (currency) principle, the monetary base determines the total money supply on the basis of a stable and predictable monetary multiplier. If the ultimate liquidity is metallic, it must be pegged to a metallic rule of convertibility, whereas if it is fiduciary (issued by the central bank) it must respect a quantitative rule of convertibility. As the experience of the Bank of England has made abundantly clear, this does not prevent a highly active discretionary tactic being used in the short-term handling of financial tensions.

Essentially, the 'external' conception of money postulates that economic agents' demand for money results from stable behaviours, because money is endowed with an individual utility that is itself stable. The demand for money is thus assumed to be a stable function of individuals' wealth and of the opportunity cost of holding onto money. Those who argue this postulate a direct transmission between money and the economy. If the real quantity of available money is higher than the demand, individuals' attempt to spend the excess money supply will have inverse repercussions on other markets (of goods and factors of production) on account of the imbalances of excess demand. The markets adjust, in turn correcting these disequilibria. There is a rise in the price of all goods, and thus in the general price level, and in turn a fall in money's real value (its purchasing power for buying goods and services) until equilibrium is re-established on all the markets. This balance is re-established when the general rise in prices has completely absorbed the excess nominal money supply. This is why the quantitative theory of money asserts that inflation is a monetary phenomenon. The monetary policy that it advocates is the direct consequence of this assertion: the money supply must be made to evolve in tandem with the real demand for money, as desired by economic agents as a whole. This is necessary in order to guarantee price stability.

Then there are the partisans of 'internal' money (the banking principle). In their view, the demand for money is integral to the behaviour of the financial actors subject to bubbles and crises – to the intrinsic instability of finance.[7] We have already seen many examples of this instability in our study of financial crises across history. The demand for money is affected by the ambivalent character of liquidity. The money supply thus has to be flexible in order to prevent socially costly economic upheavals. Rules and discretion must therefore interact. The result is a concept of constrained discretion. As we showed in Chapter 1, there is nothing neutral about a monetary economy, because there is no system of relative equilibrium prices independent of money. Economic agents discover relative prices on the basis of nominal prices. Recognising inflation is an ambiguous problem; not all increases in nominal prices are evidence of inflation. They may express variations in relative prices, for example when there are temporary shocks affecting food prices or the price of raw materials. They may represent a cyclical – and thus reversible – movement in

7   Hyman P. Minsky, 'The financial instability hypothesis, capitalist processes and the behavior of the economy', in Charles P. Kindleberger and Jean-Pierre Laffargue (eds), *Financial Crises, Theory, History and Policy*, Cambridge: Cambridge University Press, 1982, pp. 13–39.

nominal prices, resulting from the business cycle. When economic agents identify such movements for what they are, these movements do not threaten confidence in the unit of account. If the slide in money's purchasing power is totally and unanimously accepted, then it is of no importance. Price stability is maintained, so long as private indexation processes do not flare up.

In this context, control by prices consists of the central bank's estimation of the price evolutions not influenced by temporary variations ('underlying inflation'), and the orientation of its policy rate in line with some target for how this underlying inflation should evolve. This means setting a target for so-called medium-term inflation – meaning, in effect, a horizon of between two and five years. Nonetheless, this orientation does not take account of the financial imbalances that result from excess credits. These latter can cause dangerous speculation bubbles on certain assets, even without having any effect on underlying inflation. This can be counteracted, however, in two different ways. The first method, within the framework of control by prices, is to estimate the indicators of financial tensions and to adjust the policy interest rate according to these indications. The interest rate thus deviates from what it would have been if the central bank had strictly followed its own inflation target. The second method is to use the interest rate to maintain an inflation target and, in combination with this, to use quantitative tools to contain financial tensions. Both methods are means of limiting the excessive expansion of credit, and they can be either applied to banks in general or targeted at certain types of credit (for example, real estate) which have a particularly destabilising effect in certain circumstances. Different techniques can thus be applied in order to maintain oversight over credit.

In general, we might say that confidence in the unit of account results from an attempt at coordination, which can bring about multiple possible equilibria. It is thus up to monetary policy to fix the focal point around which agents implicitly coordinate their expectations. This means providing them with a framework that rules out all possible equilibria outside of a given range. This means of coordination involves constraining monetary policy's short-term discretionary action through some medium-term rule for action, which can assure price stability. This stability is defined as a viable range of future inflation rates. When inflation remains within this band, central banks' actions will benefit from economic agents' confidence, no matter what the objectives motivating these actions. This framework brings into play a renewed monetary doctrine: flexible inflation target-ing, in which flexibility incorporates the methods described above.[8] Preserving flexibility means recognising the full importance of discre-tionary action, for no doctrine can give any precise prescription as to how monetary policy should be conducted in each situation. Only learning through experience – through trial and error – can generate a stable rule of conduct. Let us now see how each of the two doctrines describes the influence of monetary policy conducted according to its own precepts.

QUANTITATIVE DOCTRINE: THE PROBLEM OF
CONTROLLING THE MONETARY BASE

An extreme interpretation of the quantitative doctrine holds that the central bank can and should control the monetary base M_0, which is to say the central bank's monetary liabilities, in order to determine M_3, the total aggregate money, and therefore the general level of prices. Indeed, according to the quantitative doctrine, the money supply directly influences the general level of prices and influences this vari-able alone. This is consistent with the postulate that money is neutral. This hypothesises that there are known and stable relations between the monetary base, the mass of money, and the general level of prices.

Central bankers reject this dogmatic view, which they consider contrary to the defining features of a modern banking system. As has been evident since the beginning of financial liberalisation in the 1980s, the short-term variation in demand for cash is unpredictable. Setting a predetermined objective for the monetary base will bring excesses or insufficiencies of free reserves, with the rebound effect of huge day-to-day variations in the interest rate.[9] So it is impossible to

8   Ben Bernanke and Frederic Mishkin, 'Inflation targeting: A new framework for monetary policy?', *Journal of Economic Perspectives*, vol. 11, no 2, 1997, pp. 97–116.
9   Charles A. E. Goodhart, 'What should central banks do? What should be their macroeconomic objectives and operations?', *Economic Journal*, vol. 104, no. 427, 1994, pp. 1424–36.

impose tight controls on the quantity of the monetary base, unless we accept senseless variations in short-term interest rates.

Between October 1979 and August 1982, Paul Volker used the monetary base to bring inflation to a halt. He thus attempted to impose oversight over credit. This found no great success, in a financial system as complex and diversified as the American one. He established a formula through which the short-term interest rate would vary in accordance with the monthly variation of the monetary base. This was one form of information among others, and not a form of direct control over the monetary base. The initiative nonetheless caused gigantic variations in the American short-term rate, the rebound effect of which was a global recession. The Mexican financial crisis can be directly attributed to Volker's moves. Indeed, when the crisis broke out in August 1982, this initiative was immediately abandoned.

The real question is how the central bank operates in response to the information that it receives. How should it adjust short-term interest rates? According to what indicators? We saw that in the classical era, the Bank of England fulfilled this task admirably. So, did we lose the art of central banking at the end of the 1970s? Or has the structure of macroeconomic relations profoundly changed?

THE QUANTITATIVE DOCTRINE INCORPORATED INTO ORDOLIBERALISM: THE BUNDESBANK EXPERIENCE

The guiding idea in this case is the hypothesis that money is neutral 'in the long term', meaning that the inflation rate is proportional to the rate at which the quantity of money grows. If the central bank chooses a given monetary norm – a long-term trajectory for M_3 – and its action inspires confidence, then the hypothesised stability in the demand for money will guarantee that the norm chosen coincides with the corresponding long-term equilibrium inflation rate.

For the Bundesbank, the quantitative doctrine is not a panacea unto itself. Monetary policy can only succeed in stabilising inflation if it is based on the social culture of stability that ordoliberalism provides. This entails an implicit pact between citizens and the central bank. When the central bank publicly announces a medium-term quantitative objective, it appeals to economic agents' responsibility. What allows it to do so is a certain principle of sovereignty, designed to hold all arbitrary powers in check.

The Bundesbank deployed a procedure that was neither an automatic rule nor a series of discretionary actions. It did have a principle of action to guide the manner in which it exercised its judgement. This principle was put into effect as the Bundesbank chose an intermediary equilibrium in the growth of the quantity of money. Announcing this choice provided an orientation both to private agents and the government, who had to set their demand within this framework, for the Bundesbank would not tolerate the price drift that would have resulted if a bidding war had built up. This prevented the formation of inflationary spirals.[10]

This policy operates in a society in which macroeconomic adjustments depend on the search for compromise, and in which such compromises are sealed by way of institutional mediations that are themselves guided by the social acceptance of the central bank's conduct. The interest groups that make demands on GDP distribution take account of the limits that the central bank considers it reasonable to set on overall demand. The fact that this common reference point is taken into account in negotiations on income sharing and setting offer prices allows for inflationary pressures to be eased, without excessive losses in production or employment.

The Bundesbank thus maintained its reputation as the guardian of monetary stability. Indeed, those who held money validated its policy. These behaviours extended far beyond the economic calculations so dear to the theorists of pure economics. The only thing that enabled this outcome was a conception of sovereignty in which money was linked to the integrity of the social order. But how, then, can we conduct monetary policy in societies that are ridden by conflict, where these mediations do not work?

REGULATION IN ENDOGENOUS MONEY: WICKSELL'S
APPROACH AND INFLATION TARGETING

Knut Wicksell was the first theorist to introduce, in terms important to the development of monetary policy, the idea that money supply

10 Otmar Issing, 'Theoretical and empirical foundations of the Deutsche Bundesbank's monetary targeting', *Intereconomics*, vol. 27, no. 6, 1992, pp. 289–300.

depends on the rhythms of growth in production capacity.[11] This means that, contrary to the money-neutrality hypothesis, supply depends on a real economic variable. Money is never neutral in the long term; it influences the paths of growth, and the cost of making it available to economic agents in turn depends on this growth. The true pivot of the macroeconomic dynamic is not the real demand for money, but the natural interest rate or the neutral real rate.

This rate reflects the anticipated yield rate on newly produced capital goods. It is neutral when projected investment at this marginal yield rate is equal to the savings desired by economic agents as a whole. It is thus the real interest rate that realises the best possible macroeconomic balance for a given level of marginal capital profitability. When the central bank's nominal interest rate is equal to this natural rate, augmented by the inflation target, and economic actors align to this policy rate, GDP is at its potential. This means that the level of economic activity, and thus also of employment, is at a level where the society is making the best possible use of the resources available to it. The neutral real rate (r^*) is thus the rate for which the curve of the savings/investment equilibrium is stationary whereas the GDP is at its potential Y^* (Figure 6.1). This is a medium-term equilibrium which corresponds to the horizon of monetary policy itself. It follows from this that the monetary authority should set its policy rate (its nominal rate) at a level equal to the natural rate, in order to achieve price stability (zero inflation). If that is the case, then the real rate on the money market will be equal to the nominal rate. In fact, when the real rate on the money market is lower than the natural rate, companies have an interest in overinvesting and prompting an overuse of productive resources. This causes overheating, and inflation accelerates. If the opposite is the case, then productive capacities are underemployed and inflation decelerates. So, if the central bank can accommodate the private sector demand for liquidity at this rate, this will avoid an excessive expansion of credit and rate-induced inflation. At the same time, this approach avoids a shortfall in credit supply, a recession in production and rate-induced deflation.

----

11   Knut Wicksell, 'The influence of the rate of interest on prices', *The Economic Journal*, no. 17, 1907, pp. 213–20.

However, a capitalist economy does not only face short-term imbalances. Capitalist accumulation is essentially a process that creates persistent disequilibria through structural changes in production, consumption and employment. As the Austrian school emphasised, movements of large amounts of money closely interact with changes in relative prices. The natural rate changes over time, along with everything that influences the anticipated yield on future investment, or with what Keynes called 'animal spirits'. In a capitalist economy where competition stimulates innovation, this is a highly uncertain variable. This is why a non-contingent rule for fixing the policy rate, founded on an estimation of a supposedly stable neutral rate, would itself be a factor for destabilisation when economic conditions change.

Figure 6.1
Potential GDP and Neutral Real Rate

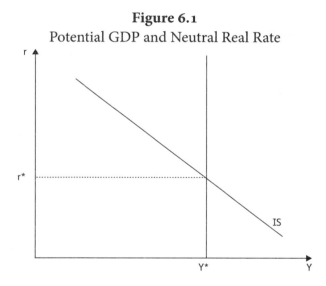

When we speak of rules, these must always be conditional on the state of the economy. Such a rule can be *ad hoc*, or it can derive from a loss function of the central bank, representing the arbitration between its own objectives. Different types of rules for interest rates can be used. Those readers interested in mathematics can see a definition of these rules in Box 6.1. These rules are ways of describing a discretionary monetary policy, which is constrained by situations of uncertainty. These are systems of constrained discretion, in which the rule is used as a safeguard.

Box 6.1
Interest rate rules

1) The Wicksellian norm which the Rilskbank used to break out of inflation in the 1930s set a target for price levels and not inflation rates. It is associated with the rates rule $it = \bar{i}t + \varphi pt$ in which pt = the log of the price index that is be stabilised. $\bar{i}_t$ follows a stochastic process that is independent of price movements but is correlated to the exogenous fluctuations in the natural rate r_t. The relationship defining the equilibrium nominal rate is $it = rt + Etpt+1 - pt$.

Eliminating i_t we get:

$$p_t = \frac{1}{1+\varphi} E_t p_{t+1} + \frac{1}{1+\varphi}(r_t - \bar{i}_t)$$

If we separate out the processes followed by r^t and $\bar{i}_t$ then p_t has a single solution:

$$p_t = \sum_{j=0}^{\infty} (\frac{1}{1+\varphi})^{j+1} E_t (r_{t+j} - \bar{i}_{t+j})$$

It follows that prices fluctuate around a long-term level:

$$\bar{p} = \frac{1}{\varphi}(\bar{r} - \bar{i})$$

The long-term value of the general level of prices is independent from demand for money. Price fluctuations explicitly depend on fluctuations in the natural rate, and thus on the expectations among entrepreneurs, to the extent that they are not compensated by adequate changes in the central bank's target.
2) The simple Taylor rule. It targets a nominal rate $i^* = r^* + \pi^*$, in which r^* is an estimate of the natural rate, making it a moving average of real market rates over the long term. π^* is the famous inflation target, while yt is the log of GDP level in the previous quarter, y^* the log of potential GDP, and πt the rate of variation in the log of the price index calculated

according to the Wicksellian rule. α and β are the quantities representing central bank arbitrage in correcting imbalances. This rule is represented in the equation:

$i = i^* + \alpha(y - y^*) + \beta(\pi - \pi^*)$

3) Dynamic adjustment by smoothing out interest rates. Here $x\,t = (y_t - y^*)$.

The rule is defined by the following two equations:

$\bar{\imath}_t = i^* + \beta\,(\pi_t - \pi^*) + \alpha\,(x_t - \gamma x_{t-1})$

$i_t = (1 - p_1)\bar{\imath}_t + p_1 i_{t-1} + p_2(i_{t-1} - i_{t-2})$

$\gamma > 0$ designates a persistance effect in which the operational objective of interest rates reacts to the past variations in the output gap.

4) Expectations targeting. As above, the rate adjustment is smoothed out. But the target interest rate depends on the expected inflation and output gap.

$$\bar{\imath}_t = i^* + \beta\left[\pi_{t+1} - \pi^*\,\middle|\Omega_t\right] + \alpha E_t\{x_{t+1}\,|\Omega_t\}$$

Where Ω_t is the whole set of information that the central bank employs in order to make its forecasts.

THE FEDERAL RESERVE TAKES STRUCTURAL CHANGE INTO ACCOUNT: THE GREENSPAN METHOD

In the mid-1980s, the Fed's managers understood that financial liberalisation had made the demand for money unstable, and a totally unsuitable guide for monetary policy. Indeed, financial liberation multiplied the instruments for investing savings and for developing and interconnecting financial markets. This significantly increased the possibilities for arbitrage. Financial portfolios – whether for private or institutional savings – diversified. The volume of financial transactions swelled much faster than GDP grew, and it required new forms of money linked to the intersecting commitments between financial intermediaries. The result was that the relationship between nominal GDP and the mass of money – what we call the speed of money's circulation – became erratic. Monetarism thus had to be shelved along with the other archaic pieces of monetary policy. While this doctrine did continue to operate in Germany, in the highly tempered form we described above, this was because in this period Germany steered well clear of any headlong rush into financial liberalisation.

The Fed thus found itself bereft of a monetary doctrine. But it continued to maintain the objectives that its status had conferred upon it. The Fed's missions – namely, to keep the economy at sustainable full-employment and to preserve a reasonable rate of inflation. In its wisdom, the legislature did not try to impose any quantitatively defined objectives. In any case, the 1980s were dominated by the financial instability that came in the wake of liberalisation. From the first savings bank crisis in 1982 to the second in 1988–9 – not to mention the impact of the banking crises in Latin America – the Fed was occupied with preventing systemic risk. When Alan Greenspan became chairman, he experimented with risk management. It was only in the 1990s that Wicksell's theory of macroeconomic regulation finally prevailed, in the form of the Taylor rule. However, during the recession at the beginning of the 1990s, Greenspan took liberties with the reaction function deriving from the Taylor rule. During the 1991–2 recession, he pushed down his interest rate a good deal further than this function would indicate (Figure 6.2) and, most importantly, he kept it at a low level relative to what the rule would suggest, even nearly two years after the recovery. This approach was repeated, to an even greater extent, during the recession of 2001–2002.

Figure 6.2
Fed funds and Taylor's rule

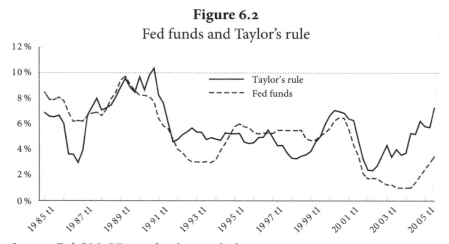

Sources: Fed, BLS, BEA, authors' own calculations.

Risk management is entirely compatible with Wicksell's theory. It is a means of conducting monetary policy that also takes account of financial imbalances. For financial instability rebounds on the economy and causes fluctuations in the natural interest rate. So, in recessions, marginal capital profitability, and thus the natural or neutral real interest rate, falls. If the Fed does not react, real market interest rates could climb above the neutral rate. This would perpetuate the insufficient demand and underemployment. It is thus necessary to push down the rates that condition the cost of capital, and to do so for long enough that companies can make favourable forecasts for the profitability of their future investments.

Looking at Figure 6.2, we can see that American monetary policy is flexible on two counts. From 1995 to 1999, the Fed funds rate was systematically above the rate that would have corresponded to the application of the Taylor rule.

This era demonstrated the pertinence of Wicksell's theory. Contrary to the hypothesis that money is neutral, this theory allows us to take into account the impact that structural change has on money.

So, what did happen? After an average annual rise of 1.4 percent over the 1973–95 period, the growth in labour productivity accelerated to a 2.5 percent rise in the 1995–2001 period. In 1995, Greenspan understood that the dominant opinion holding that productivity gains would remain very slow was in fact incompatible with other statistical observations: weak price increases, growing profits, the sharp rise in the Stock Exchange, as well as scattered information on high-tech investment.

What did monetary policy have to do to adjust to this structural change? If productivity grows faster than would be expected on the basis of past data, this means that these data have led to an underestimation of production potential. Since the production observed is in fact below its potential, there is a production deficit relative to the Fed's mission of realising the best possible level of sustainable employment. The chronic production deficit feeds the inflation slowdown which we can observe. This should lead the Fed to keep interest rates low.

On the other hand, if the profit rate has risen, this means that the neutral real rate is higher than had been believed. This means that the market real rates have fallen below the neutral rate. It is necessary, therefore, to push these rates up in order to rediscover the rate balance most compatible with the production potential. During the transitional phase, after it is announced that rates are going to increase, it is in companies' best interests to increase their investment, to enable them to consolidate productivity gains. This more efficient supply pushes down the sustainable unemployment rate, without accelerating inflation (NAIRU, or non-accelerating inflation rate of unemployment). Rather than taking a given NAIRU, the Taylor reaction function has to consider and estimate a bearish rate for NAIRU. This has led the Fed to attribute greater weight to the output gap than to the gap in inflation relative to a conventional target.

The Fed's flexibility was again on display in the recession of 2001–2003, and then in the recovery of 2004–2005. It conducted an active stabilisation policy in order to keep inflation and unemployment rates as close as possible to its own long-term objectives. It acted gradually, making a series of small changes (twenty-five base points) to the interest rate, each of them in the same direction. There were two reasons why it preferred such gradualism. The first was uncertainty over the channels for transmitting monetary policy. It was preferable to make a series of small doses of change in the same direction, and watch what happened as a result. The second was the need to smooth out rate variations in order to avoid long-term rates being disturbed by inopportune variations in short-term rates.

In a world of financial markets that are quick to unleash self-referential logics, central banks are averse to policy reversals that might polarise the markets and endanger their own reputation.

Macroprudential Policy

Since the 1970s, there has been an enormous explosion of financial assets. This was particularly true during the financial globalisation of the 1990s. This flourishing array of funding instruments constitutes a wholesale liquidity market ruled by the broker dealers (investment banks and the trading departments of universal banks). These new forms of liquidity are largely detached from retail banking and thus from deposit insurance. Fed by 'money market funds', this wholesale market provides a basis for shadow banking with enormous leverage and a systematic 'mismatch' of maturities, without any liabilities-side stability. Up until the general crisis in 2008, this market inter-mediation system operated through opaque risk transfer chains, unknown to market regulators and central banks. Trends in credit drive far-reaching cycles in the prices of financial assets. When these trends are reversed, financial crises are prompted.

Figure 6.3 portrays the macroeconomic sequences of this ampli-fication process. At the beginning of the cycle, the low cost of finan-cial intermediation is self-sustaining. Through its interaction with the fall in the price of risk, and the leverage and speculative valorisa-tion of assets, the expansionist boom is nourished. This boom spreads to the real economy through the increased wealth of non-financial agents.

Market actors are financed on credit, against a collateral which is the speculative asset itself. They, like those lending to them, have an interest in maintaining momentum, because there is no fundamental value in playing the role of an incontestable benchmark for the market. This is why debt leverage grows at the same time as the asset price rises, reaching levels that will later appear excessive.

Figure 6.3

The chain of the expansive phase of the financial cycle

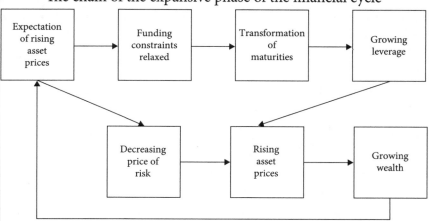

The banks' credit supply and the speculators' credit demand increase at the same time (Figure 6.4). The credit spread does not increase, even though exposure to the borrowers' debt increases with the rise in the credit supply. An insolvency risk builds up on balance sheets, but it remains concealed as long as the momentum continues. It resides in the invisible probability that the bubble of speculation will burst. One of the most spectacular characteristics of the enormous expansion of indebtedness that financed real estate speculation in the lead-up to the crisis was the sharp reduction of credit spreads during the 2003–06 period. This would later appear as a gross underevaluation of risk, but it was itself the consequence of the endogenous fall in the price of risk. This did not attract regulators and central banks' attention while the process was playing out. Given their theoretical framework, the latter had every reason to believe that financial innovations were making markets – and thus the opportunities to disseminate risk – more complete, and that rational agents would be able to grasp this in optimal fashion. The fact that the hidden risk builds up even as it remains concealed within balance sheets, and more generally within the multiple forms of exposure to asset price vulnerability, is inherent to the logic of momentum. The concept of financial efficiency denies this. Yet in these crisis situations, the underestimation of risk results from the lack of a benchmark external to the self-referential asset valorisation which finance produces. This risk is inscribed in balance sheets by means of the lever of indebtedness. It is not only an individual risk, for balance sheets are interdependent. It develops in the form of financial vulnerabilities.

Figure 6.4

Interdependency of credit supply and demand

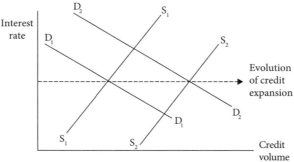

The Price of Risk and Financial Vulnerabilities: The Foundation of Macroprudential Policy

It is illuminating to employ a stylised representation of the relations between the price of risk and financial vulnerabilities.[12] Let us call the price of risk p, financial shocks s and the level of vulnerability to systemic risk V. Shocks emerge and intensify when there is a reversal in the financial cycle. According to the theory of financial instability, p is a function of s and V. It is a growing and convex function of s, and it is all the more convex as vulnerabilities rise during major shocks. We see such major shocks when the momentum of leverage has fed a large bubble of speculation. On the contrary, when there are benign shocks at the beginning of the phase of financial expansion, the price of risk perceived by market participants – p – is all the lower for the fact that the latent but hidden vulnerabilities are so high. This is because these vulnerabilities bring the sequence shown in figure 6.3, which produces the momentum in asset valorisation. Hence the monetary policy dilemma represented in Figure 6.5: a policy that favours a heavy fall in the price of risk, because inflation is low, causes vulnerabilities that will make the price of risk jump even further.

Figure 6.5
Sensitivity of the price of risk to shocks, adjusted by level of vulnerability

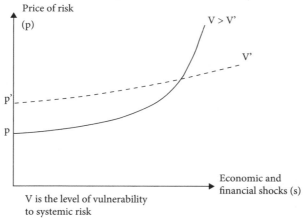

12   Tobias Adrian, Daniel Covitz and Nellie Liang, 'Financial stability monitoring', in *Federal Reserve Bank of New York Staff Report*, no. 601, 2013.

We can thus understand why financial crises break out unpredictably, even though the conditions for these same crises are implacably maturing, even during the euphoric phase. Such crises result from a failure of the financial markets, because the latter operate in a way that makes financial intermediaries incapable of coordinating a moderate, financed growth trajectory by way of robust strategies that prevent vulnerabilities from developing. When the level of shocks is low, the price of risk is lower if the financial system is built on greater vulnerabilities: $p < p'$ for $V > V'$ when s is low. Financial actors thus have an interest in joining and remaining within the bubble that increases their capital gains due to cheap leverage. *The crisis is inevitable, but it is impossible to predict the moment when it is going to break out.*

When bubbles develop, there is a major increase in the probability of an explosion, and thus in the probability of large-scale shocks. The vulnerabilities that have accumulated within this financial regime can transform the reversal in asset prices into a systemic crisis. What we saw in 2008 was an extremely far-reaching form of such a crisis.

In order to understand what is happening, we need only follow the sequence portrayed in Figure 6.3, albeit this time in reverse. The prices of speculative assets collapse, and the price of risk leaps up. The vulnerabilities inherent to the financial system explain how depressive sequences are amplified. With the dizzying fall in collateral values, the shadow banks' debt leverage can no longer be renewed. This leads to disorderly attempts at debt reduction, with firesales of assets. These in turn spread the sharp fall in values to all at-risk assets. The chains of intermediation transmit this debt reduction in a cascade effect. What follows is a run on state bonds, which are perceived as a last refuge. Non-financial agents indebted against asset purchases suffer a collapse in their wealth. This provokes a recession in the real economy. Commercial banks are affected in three ways: through paralysis in the wholesale liquidity market, because they have extended their credits far beyond their deposits; because they have bought up securities and derivatives resulting from the securitisation of credits; and because they have directly made loans to non-financial agents in distress. It is at this point that central banks are forced to intervene. They do so as a lender of last resort for the commercial banks, whom it is their mission to support. But they also intervene in the chains of shadow banking, both to replace the liquidity wholesale market that has become totally paralysed, and to come to the aid of the broker dealers. All monetary policy is, at this point, engaged in extraordinary strategies.

Macroprudential policy is a new tool that seeks to avoid the central banks being forced into *a posteriori* rescue bids, whose extent or duration cannot be arranged *a priori*. It is a tool dedicated to maintaining the stability of the financial system as a whole. In a sense, it is an intermediary between traditional prudential regulation and monetary policy. Its theoretical foundation flows from the analysis illustrated in Figure 6.5. Macroprudential policy does not seek to predict what shocks could potentially happen. In fact, uncertainty renders any such guesswork illusory. It does not enter into the intractable debate on whether or not the asset price dynamic is a speculative bubble. But it recognises momentum and seeks to bring together means of action that can soften the social cost of a future reversal in the financial cycle. In order to fulfil this objective, macroprudential policy has to maintain the risk price at a sufficiently high level in the phase of financial expansion in order to avoid it rising destructively during the turnaround phase. It is thus a matter of influencing the arbitration *between risk price and the probability of systemic crisis* that is inherent to finance's intrinsic instability. Modifying the conditions of this arbitration requires action on the underlying structural and dynamic vulnerabilities.

Structural vulnerabilities stem from the interconnections and complexities of market intermediation. Forms of risk exposed to the failures of coordination are the nests of systemic risk. These include synthetic, not completely replicated ETFs (Exchange Traded Funds); tripartite Repurchase Agreements (repos) exposed to forced collateral sales and excessively dependent on clearing banks' intra-day credit to broker dealers; uninsured ABCP (Asset-Backed Commercial Paper) and FCP (*Fonds communs de placement*); aggressively yield-seeking money market funds, whose liabilities are presumed to be equivalent to money; and the products of non-standard securitisation, negotiated in opaque over-the-counter chains.

Dynamic vulnerabilities refer to the high leverage of shadow banks (broker dealers, hedge funds, special purpose vehicles and conduits) and the maturity transformations incorporated into derivatives products. In the case of options, repos and short sales, leverage and maturity transformations operate in concert.

Identifying vulnerabilities rather than potential shocks enables greater attention to be paid to the systemic impact of shocks if they do indeed take place.[13] The detection instrument at the heart of macroprudential policy is the realisation of macroeconomic stress tests.

MACROPRUDENTIAL POLICY AND MONETARY POLICY

One mistaken conception considers macroprudential policy as something completely separate from monetary policy. If that were the case, then macroprudential policy would itself entirely achieve the objective of financial stability, and there would be no reason to change monetary policy doctrine. This view implies that there is no interference between the two. Monetary policy would, then, simply be a matter of reworking the monetary rate in order to achieve the inflation target and to keep the economy pinned to this objective. The extraordinary measures that central banks have taken since 2010, even when the policy rate has fallen to zero and remained there for several years, are evidence enough of how inane such a claim is.

We would misunderstand macroprudential policy if we believed that it had the objective or the ability entirely to compensate for financial shocks, dissipating their momentum. In fact, macroprudential and monetary policy both influence the financial markets, agents' balance sheets, and macroeconomic aggregates. These policies can thus have certain synergies. A rise in asset prices induced by more favourable profitability – the famous productivity shock – drives an acceleration of the demand for credit. Monetary policy must be able to accommodate this, if it is not to block growth. But a targeted macroeconomic policy must contain debt leveraging in order to avoid credit ballooning. What was missing during the stock market boom of the turn of the century was this second aspect. However, the coordination of the two types of policy is not automatic. Macroprudential policy has a longer reaction time, and the channels through which it is transmitted are less well known than those of monetary policy.

----

13   Nellie Liang, *Implementing Macroprudential Policies*, Conference on Financial Stability Analysis, Federal Reserve Bank of Cleveland and the Office of Financial Research, May 2013. https://financialresearch.gov/conferences/files/implementing_macroprudential_policies_may31-2013.pdf.

In principle, structural vulnerabilities are dealt with by static, or permanent, means: these include more demanding capital and liquidity obligations for the big banks, an authority that can resolve bank collapses in an orderly way, the centralised clearing of derivatives, and means of avoiding runs on money market funds. Yet even all of this is not enough to bypass the financial cycle. Innovations always exceed the limits established by the existing regulations. As we have seen, the financial system is strongly pro-cyclical and thus develops dynamic vulnerabilities of a macroeconomic character. It is necessary to be able to keep watch over the variations in the price of risk that result from lenders' and borrowers' strategic interactions. Only this way is it possible to halt the cyclical vulnerabilities that develop with the fall in the price of risk. The operational method deployed here is that of macroeconomic stress tests.

All central banks that adopt this procedure can use the tools of macroprudential policy in a dynamic way, as well as combine them with monetary policy. This allows them to reduce the span of the financial cycle and moderate the frequency and severity of crises. Three macroprudential tools have macroeconomic effects, and are thus able to complement monetary policy: requirements for counter-cyclical capital buffers; limits on loans relative to value of real estate assets (loan-to-value ratios) and on debt relative to household incomes (debt-to-income ratios); and required reserve ratios.

Capital ratios adjusted to the financial cycle must not rise either too early or too late in the growth phase. Hence the need for the handling of these instruments to be connected to the information provided by stress tests. These ratios must fall after the cycle goes into reversal, so as to preserve flows of credit from the banks to the economy even when losses are materialising in the banking system itself. This may have an asymmetrical effect: a modest impact in terms of slowing credit momentum, but also an amortisation of the credit rationing due to underperforming loans. In this way, the macroprudential toolbox can bring relief to the central banks, who will now have less need to follow ultra-accommodating monetary policies.

The instruments devoted to the real estate market are justified by the fact that speculation followed by real estate crisis is particularly devastating, owing to the extent of the wealth lost, the length and difficulty of debt reduction, and the recessionary effects transmitted to the economy as a whole. This is consistent with our empirical findings in the first section of this chapter: the principal driving force of the financial cycle is household indebtedness for the sake of real estate purchases. If well-judged limits can be placed on the expansion of credit in the euphoric phase of real estate speculation, then it is possible to put the brakes on price rises. A 10 percent fall in the loan-to-value limit ratio could reduce the appreciation of real estate prices by between 8 and 13 percent. These tighter controls on indebtedness also have an effect after the cycle has reversed. This is because they limit borrowers' defaults and the losses these impose on lenders. Recessions can be shorter, and central banks can avoid being constrained by the 0-level rate barrier. This means that they can take recourse to exceptional measures.

Compulsory reserves are an instrument of monetary policy that has been abandoned by Western central banks, but which has been successfully used in certain emerging countries, especially China. Central banks would be well advised to rehabilitate this instrument. It can be used in terms of quantity, in the form of a ratio variation; or in terms of price, in the form of a remuneration of banking reserves at a rate lower than the central bank's policy rate (which corresponds to a tax on credit, since the banks will pass the loss to be made up onto their clients).

Monetary Policy in Low-Inflation Situations

Contemporary economies universally use endogenous banking money. In our study of the implementation of monetary policy, we showed that the guide for monetary policy in these economies is the natural interest rate. This rate expresses the net anticipated profitability of new investment in production. It thus orients the business projects whose fulfilment depends on access to finance. The cost of accessing the means to finance the new capital goods that replace used or out-of-date means of production is the capital cost. The central bank influences the interest rates for the financial supports through which savings are made available to business projects. Insofar as it exercises this influence, the central bank is the regulator of this adjustment. It tries to ensure that the point of adjustment between aggregate savings and investments takes place at the level of economic activity which most efficiently employs the available human and material resources. But as we showed in Chapter 5 when we analysed the recurrence of financial crises, this adjustment is far from an easy ride. We have demonstrated in some detail that finance is moved by the logic of the momentum realised in long-term cycles. The reversal of a long phase of financial euphoria brings an overhang of debt relative to the production of new value and a rise, through speculation, in stock and real estate prices. This always triggers a financial crisis. This crisis may be a systemic one, if financial excesses have built up severe and widespread weaknesses among financial intermediaries. Such was the case of the expansive cycle that took off in the mid-1990s and culminated in 2007, unleashing a systemic crisis the following year. This cycle turned into a depressive phase, in which the world economy is still languishing. What can monetary policy do, when numerous private agents are seeking massive debt reduction and when there is great reticence about investing in production? Of course, the result is chronically insufficient demand and lasting low growth rates. This owes essentially to the cumulative fall in investment in production. This 'low-pressure' macroeconomic balance is called secular stagnation. In response, central banks attempt to revive confidence. But they encounter a sizeable obstacle in the general disappearance of inflation and, in particular, in the falling prices in the economic sectors most linked to the production of means of production (the prices of raw materials, the prices of the intermediate products of first-stage processing, and the prices for producing industrial products).

In a systemic financial crisis, the main problem is debt reduction among the economic and financial agents who had been exposed to excessive leverage. If the private sector seeks to reduce its debts as quickly as possible and in disorderly fashion, then the systemic risk will spread to the whole economy. Fire selling assets will push up interest rates even though the economy is already in recession. For in this situation, the lack of financial coordination is at its maximum.

This is what happened from September 2008 onwards. The banks did not have enough capital in reserve for them to be able to absorb the losses in their assets' market value. They were entirely dependent on the refinancing in the last resort by the central bank. The central bank's policy rates were thus no longer a tool for controlling inflation or economic activity, but instead aimed to keep the banking system solvent. The rate best able to ensure the solvency of the banking system is equal to the interest rate on the stock of previously accumulated loans minus the average rate of probable losses. If there was a low interest rate on the credits accorded in the euphoric phase (since monetary policy was accommodating and the price of risk was low), and the probable losses rose very high, then the theoretical equilibrium refinancing rate would have to be negative in order to keep the banks afloat. But how can there be a negative nominal interest rate?

Figure 6.6

US natural interest rate, 1970 Q1 – 2014 Q4

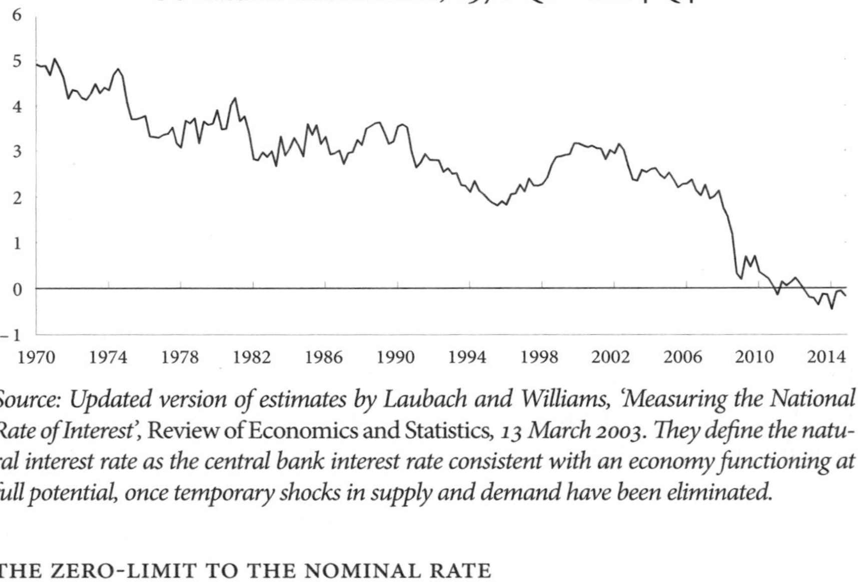

Source: Updated version of estimates by Laubach and Williams, 'Measuring the National Rate of Interest', Review of Economics and Statistics, 13 March 2003. They define the natural interest rate as the central bank interest rate consistent with an economy functioning at full potential, once temporary shocks in supply and demand have been eliminated.

THE ZERO-LIMIT TO THE NOMINAL RATE

As we have explained, the money issued by the central bank is absolute liquidity. Indeed, it is the universally accepted debt into which all other debt is converted. In a 'normal' economic situation, the central bank determines its policy rate in such a way as to make private actors' anticipations converge around the target it has announced. It ensures that the real rate that results (policy rate-inflation norm) is compatible with the natural rate, or in other words, that a gap does not develop in either direction large enough to cause an inflation bubble or chronic underemployment.

Yet the systemic financial crisis immediately had drastic effects for the banks and other financial intermediaries. The central banks had to inject liquidity by raising all the conditions on which they normally accorded liquidity to the banks. They also had to supply liquidity to the banks at the lowest possible cost. But a systemic crisis rebounds across the whole economy and profoundly alters all economic actors' attitudes towards risk. Such a crisis brings a generalised and lasting sense of caution. This is what we see with secular stagnation. The incentive to invest is weakened, for capital's net marginal yield (the real interest rate) falls very low or even below zero. This is what happened in the United States; according to the IMF, the natural rate has fallen close to zero in the OECD countries as a whole. Here we can see the impact of the systemic crisis. The natural rate immediately fell from 2 percent to close to 0 percent. Subsequently, the self-sustaining fall in growth brought inflation down towards zero. Figure 6.6 measures the natural rate in nominal terms (natural rate = net marginal capital productivity + inflation rate trend, considered as an approximation of the anticipated rate of inflation). The inflation rate slowly declined, bringing the nominal natural rate down to zero, and even below.

Here we see the trap in which monetary policy finds itself. Given that the money issued by the central bank is absolute liquidity, whoever holds short-term financial securities without credit risk (for example, Treasury bonds) has the option to convert them into cash, at no cost and without limit. It follows that the nominal money market rate, directly influenced by monetary policy, incorporates an option that results from this zero-rate floor constraint. After all, cash is an absolute and anonymously held liquidity, which bears no interest. Here we find the trait that lies at the heart of money. As the foundation of value and social medium *par excellence*, money is the base for the whole structure of debts and assets that constitute the interdependencies of the economy over time. We can formulate as follows the relation that determines the central bank's policy rate at very low natural-rate values, liable even to become negative:

$$\text{Nominal rate} = \max \{0, \text{virtual rate}\}$$

This equation represents the fact that if the natural rate is positive, the central bank works to fix its policy rate at the level of the natural rate expressed in nominal value. If the natural rate is negative or nil, the central bank sets its policy rate at zero. This equation can be written as:

$$\text{Nominal rate} = \text{natural rate} + \max\{0, -\text{natural rate}\}$$

The nominal natural rate is the rate that monetary policy would determine if it were following a standard rule known on the financial markets, at a moment when GDP is at full potential (full and effective employment of productive resources). The central bank's policy rate also encompasses situations in which there is a negative natural rate. It becomes the return on a synthetic financial product. It comprises a security which returns the natural interest rate combined with the purchase of a *put* option whose exercise price is zero. This option guarantees the zero floor when the natural interest rate becomes negative (Figure 6.7). It is implicitly sold by the central bank on the opposite of the virtual rate.

Figure 6.7
The future short rate as an option on the expected natural rate

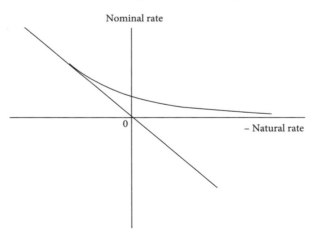

'Non-Conventional' Policies for Circumventing the Zero-Rate Barrier
When the option's intrinsic value is positive, the observed nominal rate is too high in relation to the natural rate that the central bank should fix in order to bring the economy back towards optimal

production (an output gap of zero). The economy is stuck in a liquidity trap. The result is that the curve of the short-term interest rate heads to close to zero, on account of the attractive power of the zero floor. The central bank thus finds its action constrained, if it is indeed committed to influencing the economy on the basis of the short-term rate. It loses its ability to transmit its impulses to the economy. It must, therefore, invent other means of action, which involve attempting directly to influence long-term rates. How does it do this?

The effect of the interest rate floor extends across the whole interest rate curve. For an option has a time value. When low inflation is expected to last, there is a non-negligible possibility that the anticipated future short-term rates will become negative, and thus virtual. The short-term rates (for example, three-month rates) that can be observed on the rate curve thus incorporate the option value for the term considered, in conformity with the following equation:

Three-month rate in one year = anticipated natural rate + term premium + option value

The option value thus has repercussions for the long-term rate:

Rate at R years = average anticipated short-term rates + risk premium + option value

The risk premium expresses the effect of the volatility of future short-term rates. The final term is the collision with the zero-rate barrier if the volatility of future rates causes the virtual rate to fall below zero. Since the option's time value rises with the volatility of future short-term rates, which itself grows over time, the rate curve is deformed. The information content of the rate curve is thus altered (Figure 6.8).

The central bank tries to have an effect on long-term rates by influencing anticipated short-term rates. It does this by making a commitment to preserve the short-term rate at zero while certain stated employment and inflation conditions are not met. This is the policy of guiding future interest rates (forward guidance). If the central bank's commitment is credible, then the anticipation-element of long-term rates will remain low. Forward guidance also allows a reduction in the

Figure 6.8

Deformation of the rates curve on approach to zero nominal rate

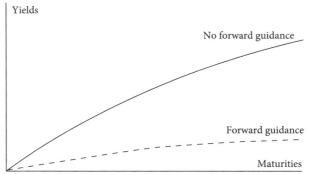

influence that the volatility of future short-term rates has on the price of risk. It thus pushes down the rate curve as a whole (Figure 6.8).

The rise in the price of risk also reflects the weakened liquidity of the assets held by financial investors (a weakening linked to the risk of heavy value losses, should it appear necessary to liquidate these assets). The central bank will make targeted purchases of long-term assets in order to place beyond market stress that asset which is the pivot of the financial markets, namely, the state bonds at various different maturities. This allows it to flatten the gradient of the rate curve and thus to complement forward guidance with control of the term premium. It can also buy up certain long-term assets that are particularly affected by the crisis, like mortgage securities in the US and UK, and more recently in the eurozone, or even certain company bonds. These are targeted asset purchases.[14]

If the central bank makes unlimited purchases of certain types of assets, it changes the liquidity of the securities chosen in relation to other securities, and thus the term premiums. The weaker the possibility of substituting one asset for another, the greater the possibility of changing the yield structure. The central banks hope thus to incentivise long-term investors to reduce their risk aversion and to redeploy

14   Christian Pfister and Natacha Valla offer a recent synthesis of central banks' innovative means of fighting the fall in the natural rate which leads to secular stagnation. See Christian Pfister and Natacha Valla, 'Les politiques monétaires non conventionnelles', in Sébastien Jean, Françoise Lemoine and CEPII, *L'Économie mondiale 2016*, Paris: La Découverte, 2015, pp. 40–56.

their portfolios in favour of other long-term categories of securities with a positive effect on real investment (reviving the real estate market and a bringing about a recovery in productive investment). This is monetary policy's portfolio channel.

CONCLUSION: CENTRAL BANK INDEPENDENCE, AT THE HEART OF ECONOMIC POLICY

If it is to guarantee the legitimacy of money, the central bank must appear to stand above the partisan interests which clash over the management of liquidity. This external position must remain credible, but it must not prevent the bank from playing its proper political role in regulating money. It must not, therefore, prevent it from taking the necessary discretionary actions. Hence, independence is a monetary principle integral to sovereignty, and not an operational rule transforming the central bank into some kind of automaton. The foundational texts should invest the central banks with the mission of maintaining price stability. But in all their great wisdom, these texts should hold back from specifying what price stability is. For this would deny the central bank its own capacity for judgement in the face of unforeseeable contexts. Independence is a symbol that works if the central bank can adopt flexible policies to respond equitably to a variety of imbalances, without being suspected of threatening price stability.

Central bank independence is by nature a symbolic guarantee, but its practice inserts it deep into the economy. For this reason, it is fundamentally important that a constitutional order is legally formalised that avoids any confusion between the levels of representation and of action. That is why we have to think about central bank independence in the form of an overlapping hierarchy. The central bank must be endowed with a mandate that guarantees its independent fulfilment of its mission, as well as the independence of its means. But this mission cannot be detached from the whole set of policies that citizens entrust to their representatives, in order to work for the well-being of society. Indeed, this is why the central bank must remain in dialogue with the other powers that execute economic policy and why it must be accountable to the people's representatives, demonstrating that it is fulfilling its mandate.

Part IV

The Enigma of International Currency

We think we know what international currency is. But we never find concrete examples of it. In a world of nations, we only ever encounter national currencies. If there is a single lesson to take from our extensive theoretical and historical analysis, it is that there is no money that is not invested with sovereignty. And there exists no universal sovereignty. So how can we deal with this problem? In Part II we showed that these famous virtual currencies are just private means of payment without any fiduciary peg, and that in no case are they fully functioning currencies. If they did aspire to play a role in the real economy, they would be required to undergo the test of conversion into national currencies. Much more interesting are local currencies. If these are indeed more than fleeting means of payment that appear during monetary crises, they are the monetary vehicles of a complex and multilevel sovereignty that is still taking form.

Nonetheless, the expansion of capitalism does not respect national borders. It plays on the ambivalent character of money. It is through the international projection of national currencies in market transactions, especially financial ones, that a global finance is constituted in certain eras. The space in which some currencies circulate extends beyond the space of economic relations that is set under the authority of national sovereignty. We then have exchange relations in which national currencies come face to face, becoming currency within spaces of sovereignty outside of their own. Under what conditions can we claim that these relations make up a system? For a system would imply rules and a mode of regulation that preserve these relations over time.

This poses the question of what rules would allow us to identify an international monetary system. When we speak of a 'system', we presume that there is an efficient sequencing of all kinds of exchange relations across national boundaries. We know that if such an efficient organisation does exist, it expresses itself in the payment system. A payment system is efficient if it advances the circulation of debts over time in such a manner that payments are irrevocable and final. This logic extends to the international space. This implies that there must be a single ultimate liquidity; indeed, this is the consequence of the hierarchy that sovereignty establishes. What does this mean in terms of international monetary relations? As we shall now show, a hierarchy must necessarily be established between currencies. What conditions must be met for this configuration to remain stable?

Following the method used thus far in this book, we will turn to history in order to confirm or invalidate the ideas that come from theory. There are two eras widely recognised as having had an international monetary system. First is the gold standard in the classical age of capitalism's financial expansion, which lasted for around forty years up until World War One. Then there was the Breton Woods system in the era of labour societies, which lasted for almost three decades after World War Two. We will show how different these systems were in terms of the rules that defined them and the contradictions that ultimately swept them away.

This historical detour should also enable us to find some bearings for the era of financial globalisation that has followed the disappearance of the Bretton Woods system. If we do not have accepted rules, is there a system or not? Does the dominant role set for the dollar in the Bretton Woods system endure today? If so, how? In this era, international relations have been affected by something of an Unidentified Flying Object in the monetary landscape: namely, the euro. This is a supranational currency that claims to be uniting nations monetarily but does not rest on any sovereignty compatible with the space in which it circulates. The incomplete nature of the euro has had a major impact on the development of the contemporary crisis of financial globalisation, for it has handicapped Europe's position within international relations.

Other powerful forces are also helping to remodel international monetary relations. Most important is the displacement of productive capacities, and thus of international exchange, towards Asia. This displacement particularly revolves around the rise of Chinese power, bringing onto the international scene a major currency that is supported by a principle of sovereignty very different to the prevalent ones in the West.

International monetary prospects for the next decade convey the spontaneous idea of multi-currency systems. This is more a slogan – the end of hegemonies, the end of key currencies – than any kind of rigorously elaborated notion. Doubtless, if the humanity of this present century is indeed to survive, then its future lies in sustainable growth. This must proceed by way of the production of global public goods. International liquidity is a global public good that has never found its necessary institutional solution. Competition among currencies is no substitute for this, because it crashes up against the need for a single ultimate liquidity.

When Lord Keynes presented his vision for the postwar monetary order in 1942, he conceived of a system of rules for international payments that would neutralise the question of ultimate liquidity at the international level. His vision was to take the logic of the banking principle to its extreme conclusion, through a hierarchically organised system of credits and payments whose rules would make it impossible for private actors to accumulate international liquidities. At the highest level, the scourge of money's ambivalent character would thus be banished, through a system of credits among central banks that obeyed common rules managed by an international institution.[1] Money would return to being what Aristotle had considered it to be: a pure social relation, or pure Law. When nation-states were first established, Keynes's discourse was nowhere to be heard. At a moment when it is everywhere apparent how incapable the nation-state form is of dealing with the challenges of human development, Keynes's ideas deserve to be reconsidered.

----

1   John Maynard Keynes (1942–3), 'The Keynes Plan', in J. Keith Horsefield (ed.), *The International Monetary Fund 1945–1965: Twenty Years of International Monetary Cooperation*, vol. 3, Washington, DC: IMF, 1969.

7

International Currency
Faced with the Test of History

Sovereign states have the ability to control their residents' international exchanges in various ways: restrictions on foreign trade or capital movements, limits on the purchase of foreign currencies, or taxing deposits in such currencies. When they do this, international exchange is left fragmented and restricted. The adaptation of international exchange to a means of payment that each partner can accept operates essentially by means of bilateral deals between countries. We cannot, then, speak of an international currency.

If an international currency were to exist, it would have to be a public good that satisfied money's general characteristics in regulating credits and debts. It would have to do so, moreover, from the perspective of the finality of international payments. For that to be possible, there would need to exist an ultimate form of liquidity in a market of credits and debts united by the freedom of capital movements. The international currency would need to be issued in a form and at a volume appropriate to the needs of international transactions: this would be a fundamental condition for the currency's recognition. But as we shall see, this condition has rarely existed in the monetary regimes that have followed one another throughout history.

Analysts of international monetary relations mostly settle for a functionalist approach. They observe that the usual functions of money are here divided into two, because they concern exchanges between residents and non-residents, whether they are private or public (Table 7.1).

Table 7.1

The functions of international money

Functions	Private sector	Public sector
i) Unit of account	– Main invoicing currency – Cash on world markets (in raw materials, derivatives, etc.)	– Anchor currency for setting exchange rates
ii) Exchange intermediary	– Settlement of trade and financial transactions – Intermediary on the currency exchange market	– Currency for exchange intervention
iii) Reserve of value	– Currency for non-residents' investments – Banking markets, bonds, etc.	– Official exchange reserves

While there are divergences in the ways in which private and public agents use international money, the choices each make tend to reinforce one another. Indeed, the private sector's choices are often guided by government choices. For example, in a country whose currency is pegged to the dollar, private businesses will more readily invoice their exports in this same currency. Similarly, the different functions of international money are not independent of one another. A currency, like the dollar, that often serves as an intermediary for exchange will also tend to serve as a unit of account and a reserve of value.

Taken as a whole, the choices that public and private agents make with regard to international tendency will tend to converge towards one dominant currency.

THE INCOMPLETE NATURE OF INTERNATIONAL CURRENCY

The existence of currencies that fulfil payment functions at the microeconomic level of international exchange is not enough to assure the existence of an international currency. Given that the payment system is the operator of value, finality of payment must be established across the ensemble of international exchanges for the macroeconomic coherence of these exchanges to be established.

What Is an Efficient International Monetary System (IMS)?

For the 'standard' theory of financial efficiency, there is no complication. It is necessary and sufficient that the prices of all goods equalise across all their sites of sale (at purchasing power parity) and that the expected yields on all assets equalise. This amounts to an equalisation of anticipated real capital yield rates, wherever in the world this capital is invested. It is as if capital were everywhere homogeneous! We find, here, the same aporia as in the theory of pure economics, highlighted in Chapter 1. It is presumed that there exists some general equilibrium – in this case extended to the global level – for this theory is constructed as if there were just one single economic agent and one single commodity in the world, and thus one single country.

There are three conditions for the equalisation of anticipated real capital yields:

– The difference in interest rates between any pair of currencies on the capital markets must be equal to their forward exchange rate, such that the nominal interest rates adjusted by exchange variation – as it is measured on the forward exchange markets – are equalised. This condition stems from capital mobility and arbitrage. It could supposedly be realised through the disappearance of controls on capital movements.

– There must be financial efficiency on the currency markets, extended across all of the world's currencies. This means that the exchange rate variations observed on forward markets are unbiased estimates of anticipated variations in these rates. It follows from this that the forward markets offer the best possible forecasts of future exchange rates.

– The nominal prices on goods markets, corrected by exchange rates, must be the same for all baskets of goods and for all currencies. Purchasing power parity is the name for the general integration of markets and goods, meaning that there is a single world price for each good or service.

It goes without saying that, in empirical terms, these conditions are never realised. But this is not what is at stake here. The essential thing is that, in theoretical terms, this definition of economic and financial integration outlines a world without money, for it does not take account of what is exclusive about money and what distinguishes it from financial assets: namely, liquidity. Indeed, as we have seen, in any monetary system established under a form of sovereignty, the monetary unit is the unit for measuring values. It follows that all financial assets have prices that can vary in terms of the unit of account, whereas liquidity has a fixed price equal to 1.

In principle, the worldwide integration of all financial markets across different assets – in other words, the equalisation of their yields – implies the adjustment of two types of variables: namely, currency exchange adjustment and the adjustment of assets' relative prices at the global level. This latter adjustment results from the variation in the relative demand for different financial assets according to their prices. Movement in these prices causes variations in their anticipated yields. The same is not true of ultimate liquidity, for its price is always equal to 1 in whatever unit of account it is expressed. So, if financial integration is to be complete, there must be only one form of liquidity in the world, on which demand is focused. This gives rise to an impossibility theorem: *if two currencies are competing to be the basis for ultimate liquidity in the world economy, then their exchange rate is indeterminate.*[1] Box 7.1 presents a simplified demonstration of this. Liquidity is a public good and the object of unanimous confidence. No market will ever determine an equilibrium price for something that is the object of unanimous confidence, and thus not subject to any arbitration.

Box 7.1
The indeterminacy of exchange rates in a world of perfect financial integration

Let's consider a world in which there are two currencies (1 and 2) competing to supply international liquidity. By its very nature, liquidity is singular, for it expresses money's status as a public good. The equilibria between the supply and demand for money in the two countries, expressed in real terms, are as follows:

---

1   John Kareken and Neil Wallace, 'On the indeterminacy of equilibrium exchange rates', *Quarterly Journal of Economics*, vol. 96, no. 2, 1981, pp. 207–222.

$$\log M_1 - \log P_1 = \theta_1 \log Y_1 + \alpha(r_1-r) + \sigma(r_1-r_2)$$
$$\log M_2 - \log P_2 = \theta_2 \log Y_2 + \alpha(r_2-r) - \sigma(r_1-r_2)$$

where $M_{1,2}$ is the supply of money, $Y_{1,2}$ is total income in each of the two countries, $r_{1,2}$ is the real yield on the two currencies and r is the real yield on a financial asset that can be assumed to be common, since the financial markets are totally integrated.

There is also total integration in the markets of goods and thus PPP. From this we can deduce the equilibrium equation of the exchange rate:

$$e = \log P_1 - \log P_2 = e^* - \eta \, (r_1-r_2)$$

where $e^* = \log[(M_1/Y_1 \, \theta)/(M_2 /Y_2 \, \theta)]$ and $\eta = \alpha + 2\sigma$

The difference in the two currencies' real yields is

$r_1-r_2 = \delta = (R_1-R_2) - \hat{e}a$, where $\hat{e}a$ is the expected variation in the exchange rate between the two currencies. R_1 and R_2 are the nominal exchange rates in the two countries, expressed in their respective currencies. So the equilibrium exchange rate between the two currencies is

$$e = e^* - \eta\delta = e^* - (\alpha+2\sigma)\delta$$

If the two currencies become perfectly substitutable for one another, then the substitution elasticity is $\sigma \to \infty$. It follows that $\partial e/\partial \hat{e}a \to \infty$. Yet the two currencies can only circulate simultaneously if their prices in terms of purchasing power (for buying goods) are neither zero nor infinite. So they must have the same yield, meaning that $\delta = 0$.

So the equilibrium exchange rate between the two currencies is $e = e^* - 0 \times \infty$. This means that the exchange rate is indeterminate. Neither has been defined as the supplier of international liquidity.

Leaving such mathematical demonstrations aside, the intuitive reason is clear. The market cannot determine the equilibrium price between two candidates for the same public good. For unlike in the case of demand for financial assets, the demand for currencies cannot be separated out. Here, money's nature as a collective good is decisive.

In the real world, this means the following: the more two currencies can be substituted for one another, the more unstable their exchange rate becomes. The smallest differences between the monetary policies governing them, or any kind of events that shift beliefs regarding their future exchange rate, trigger capital movements between them. This is true because the demand for money is not an individual demand for a good. Rather, it is a collective demand for a payment system. It is collective because an individual's demand for the services of the payment system is an increasing function of others' demand.

This conclusion is the pivot of any serious theory of international currency. In the absence of any universal sovereignty, it explains why international liquidity concentrates around one dominant currency. We can thus more seriously pose the question: what is an effective international monetary system (IMS)?

If an IMS is indeed organised, it must necessarily be organised around a dominant currency, whose ultimate liquidity supply must in turn depend on non-residents' participation in international exchanges. The freedom of capital movements, however, sets currencies in competition. So these economic actors must be virtually sure that this dominant currency will preserve its status. This is far from self-evident if there exist serious competitors whose economic policies are not coordinated. Yet direct policy coordination is inconceivable in a universe of free capital movements. Given the intrinsic instability of the financial markets, there are too many elements pointing to the separate or even divergent interests among the different countries. But there can be agreement on common principles and rules that define an international system. An international system is thus an international agreement with the legal force of a treaty. This agreement concerns the nature of the rules inserted into the IMS. The virtue of having such a system is that it establishes rights and duties for the participating countries, imposing limits on the divergent conduct that would be liable to produce an international liquidity crisis. These rights and duties are all the more acceptable if the participating countries can draw mutual advantages from them. Such advantages owe to the macroeconomic efficiency of the system taken as a whole.

Macroeconomic efficiency can be defined in terms of an intertemporal worldwide equilibrium. Indeed, there is no reason why countries' balance of payments accounts should be zero in any given period. They should be able to be deferred in time, just as in national monetary systems, due to common confidence in liquidity. Legitimate credit and debt deferral can indeed define an intertemporal worldwide equilibrium, but only if several conditions are satisfied:

– Balance of payments deficits and surpluses must come from structural differences in different countries' saving and investment behaviours, for example, differences owing to populations' age structures or growth rates. They must not come from the vicious cycles between debt leverage and temporary asset price rises on certain globalised markets (stocks, real estate, raw materials).

– Financial investors must be able to correctly evaluate the future yields and risks that assets bear across international borders, so that there is no momentum or speculative drift, despite the fact that this is the financial markets' *raison d'être*, for it is here that the capital gains (on which capitalist enrichment depends) are made.

– Stabilising monetary adjustments must prevent shocks from accumulating by rebounding between countries.

If these conditions are not met, then the deficits in the balance of payments that result from financial excesses will be a force for destabilisation. Financial vulnerabilities result from the accumulation of foreign debts, bubbles in the price of assets financed on credit, and financial techniques that produce intersections of commitments among international financial counterparties that bear a hidden systemic risk.

Balance of payments surpluses are disequilibria, if they create externalities stemming from asymmetrical adjustments. They reduce demand and economic activity in other countries when, for various reasons, adjustment via interest and exchange rates does not work for different reasons: liquidity traps, inflexible currency exchange, or deflationary pressures.

What, then, are the principles of international organisation revealed to us by history? Which principles allow us, if not to prevent financial disorder, then at least to contain it for a certain number of years – allowing us to take advantage of the improvements in monetary regulation at the national level that we studied in Chapter 6?

One of these principles was the international gold standard in the classical era of capitalism. This, in a sense, resulted from a 'spontaneous' convergence around a rule of convertibility. This accompanied the first process of financial globalisation, before ultimately coming up against World War One. The other was the Bretton Woods system, which was a heavily institutionalised international system. Contemporaneous with the rise of the labour society, it specified the dollar as the key currency and thus the bearer of international liquidity. This was an international means of organisation that defined precise rules for exchange as well as oversight by an international institution, the International Monetary Fund (IMF). This institution regulated the currency exchange system and mutualised the financing necessary to settling balance of payments accounts.[2]

In both cases, therefore, there was a hierarchically organised international monetary system with a single, stable form of ultimate liquidity. If there are no explicit rules, then financial disorders proliferate and end up combining in a global crisis. That is what happened in the Great Depression (1929–38) and the Great Stagnation (2008–?).

INTERNATIONAL FINANCIAL INTEGRATION UNDER THE GOLD STANDARD, AND ITS DESTRUCTION

The international gold standard was the monetary system that came closest to a universal sovereignty, at least on the ethical if not the political level.[3] It was called an unwritten monetary constitution. For minted gold – a form of money that was not the debt of any country – played the role of an ultimate liquidity external to all countries. Indeed, governments worked to make sure that national currencies were convertible to gold without limit, both for residents and for non-residents. It is worth remembering that this convertibility was legitimised by the dominant principle of sovereignty known as the 'natural order'. Convertibility was the norm in a supposedly universal society

---

2   For a wide retrospective of views on the Bretton Woods system and its extensions, see the collective work edited by Thierry Walfaren, *Bretton Woods. Mélanges pour un cinquantenaire*, Paris: Association d'Économie Financière, 1994.

3   Michel Aglietta, *La Fin des devises-clés*, Paris: La Découverte, 1986.

founded on private property and respect for contracts: a society called bourgeois society. Indeed, the internationalisation of capital in the second half of the nineteenth century gave it a universal character, although its roots were in England and the Netherlands.

Convertibility was a lot more than an arithmetical relation linking each national unit of account to the declared price of the weight and fineness of gold in which that unit was defined. It was also the belief that the concern to preserve the nominal value of private contracts stood at a higher ethical level than the political objectives that governments could achieve by manipulating their currencies. At the monetary level, an unbreakable confidence in the permanence of convertibility made the money supply sensitive to variations in gold reserves.

The hierarchical character of the monetary system made the pound sterling the pivot of the international system. This allowed the Bank of England to direct international interest rates (see Chapter 6), and avoided any destabilising capital movements.

Identifying these formal characteristics is essential to understanding that ethical confidence in the gold standard engendered hierarchical confidence in the Bank of England and then projected this onto a transnational level. But we need more than this to understand the persistence of this order over time. Indeed, when we studied money's historical trajectories, we showed that any monetary order founded on a well-defined principle of sovereignty is mortal. Yet, as we know, having taken a bimetallic approach, France converged with the gold standard in the 1860s. So how did the gold standard remain resilient for half a century?

The second half of the nineteenth century was the period of the second industrial revolution and the rise of the United States, Germany and Japan. The international gold standard was unable to prevent the long deflation from 1873 to 1896 and the multiple financial crises that marked this period. Yet it was only at the beginning of the twentieth century, above all after the terrible financial crisis of 1907, that the Bank of England's dominant position began to be eroded.

As we have shown, money is never neutral; it is transformed in tandem with the transformations of economic and financial structures. Thus, if we are properly to grasp what the international gold standard was, we need to understand how it adapted itself to the trajectory of capitalism in this period.

The International Allocation of Savings and the Alternate Phases of Long-Term Investment

There have been two great processes of financial globalisation. The first took place in the second part of the nineteenth century, during the classical age of capitalism; the second has been unfolding since the 1980s. The fundamental traits of these two processes could hardly be more opposed. In the first case, savings moved from developed countries to developing countries, from the rich countries (the United Kingdom and France) towards poor ones – in other words, the areas that were being colonised. Emigration by the European population followed the flows of capital. In the second case, savings have essentially moved from poor countries to rich ones, and the flow of manpower has followed in the same direction. This makes development very difficult. In the first period, international capital flows were long-term in orientation and not in competition: English savings were transferred to the non-European world far beyond Britain's own empire; French savings went to Europe, the Middle East and, very gradually, its own colonies. In the second globalisation process, capital movements have essentially been a matter of speculation, driven by a mode of competition based on mimicry. So it is not surprising that the relations between money and finance have been very different in the two cases.

Indeed, the geographical division of the capital stocks held by Europe's two great powers in the post-1870 period shows that rather than competing with one another, they shared out the world among themselves (Table 7.2).

From the mid-1860s, and particularly after the 1870s, the English savings channelled by investment banks left Europe in favour of the lands of empire and the virgin or little-settled territories of the Americas and Oceania. Conversely, 70 percent of the capital accumulated by France in 1914 was to be found in Europe and the Middle East.

The most important characteristic of this period, apart from this carving-up of the world, was the complementary relationship between capital flows moving to the areas that were being colonised and the massive emigration towards these same areas. The United Kingdom, the dominant country of this period, saw 3 percent of its population emigrate in the 1880s, 5.2 percent in the depression-hit 1890s, and another 2 percent in the first decade of the twentieth century, which was marked by growth. This constituted an unprecedented addition to the population of the countries to which they were migrating. In the United States, on top of the rise owing to natural growth, 9 percent of the population came from immigration; the corresponding figure for Australia was 17 percent, and for Argentina 25 percent.

Table 7.2
Division of global long-term capital markets
by the United Kingdom and France

United Kingdom			
By destination area (%)	1854	1870	1914
Europe	55	25	6
Latin America	15	11	24
British Empire	5	34	29
United States	25	27	29
Rest of the world	—	3	12
Out of a total of (£m)	260	770	4,107
France			
By destination area (%)	1851	1881	1914
Europe	96	71	58
Middle East	—	20	11
French colonies	—	4	9
Americas	4	5	16
Rest of the world	—	—	6
Out of a total of (£m)	98	688	2,073

Source: Kenwood and Lougheed, Growth of International Economy, 1971.

The complementary relationship produced by these flows of capital and manpower fed a global growth regime. A young and productive European labour force was attracted by the higher wages or the incomes they could draw as business owners in the colonies. Thanks to this emigré population, rapid technological advances in rail and sea transport transformed into low-cost inputs for European industries, either directly or via the lower cost of subsistence goods. The long-term investment flows coming from advanced capitalist countries that had large savings were thus the vehicles of a global growth regime that closely linked the areas that exported workers and capital with the areas that imported them.

Figure 7.1

Long-term international interdependencies under the gold standard

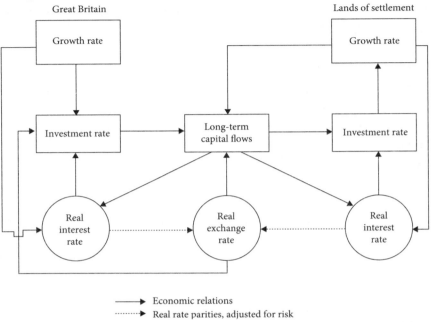

- ⟶ Economic relations
- ⋯⋯▸ Real rate parities, adjusted for risk

The combination of capital accumulation in Britain with investment abroad played a crucial role in the global growth of the classical age (Figure 7.1). When investment opportunities weakened in Britain, British savings were invested in the areas being colonised. The capital flows to these regions increased the supply of raw materials from mining and, especially, agricultural production. At the same time, stagnation in Britain reduced demand. The prices of the imported food products began to fall. Living standards in British agriculture were reduced and the population was thus pushed to move to the cities. The concomitant low cost of subsistence goods and the excess labour force increased capital profitability. An investment boom took off in Britain. It lasted until the increase in employment levels and the rise in the cost of subsistence goods pushed up wages to the point that profitability again began to decline. This was all the more likely to happen given the fact that agricultural imports were increasing rapidly, whereas investments abroad had weakened on account of the high profitability levels in Britain itself. There followed, therefore, a situation in which capital profitability in Britain weakened and increased in the areas that were being colonised. This prompted another cycle of capital exports, driving workers to emigrate while unemployment increased at home.

International financial integration and stability of long-term rates
The most spectacular characteristic of the gold-standard period is the great stability of long-term nominal interest rates. Long-term rates are not sensitive to fluctuations in short-term rates. The comparison between the 1880–1913 and 1960–97 periods is enlightening in this regard (Table 7.3).

Table 7.3
Variability of interest rates (standard deviation in monthly variance)

Country	1880–1913		1960–1997	
	LT	ST	LT	ST
United Kingdom	0.21	1.16	2.84	3.07
France	0.30	0.67	2.85	3.11
United States	0.33	2.56	2.60	3.35

LT = Long Term, ST = Short Term

Source: R. Contamin, Transformations des structures financières et crises. Les années 1990 au regard de l'étalon-or classique, *dissertation, Paris-X-Nanterre, 2000.*

Each of the two eras compared here saw a long phase of inflation and a long phase of falling inflation (and deflation in the 1890–96 period). However, the average variability of long-term rates was around ten times lower under the gold standard. Short-term rates also varied less, but here there is a much less significant gap with the 1960–97 period. It thus had two different structural characteristics. Conversely, prices and incomes were strongly cyclical and thus much more variable than in the economies of the latter half of the twentieth century (Table 7.4). This meant that the purpose of economic policy was very different in the classical age to what it was in labour societies, as we saw in Chapter 6 when we studied monetary regulation. Short-term cycles were heavily correlated with the determining influence of the Bank of England policy rate, while there was alternation in the phases of long-term investment. So, the world economy fluctuated in the short term and was stable in the long-term. We can see the strong correlation of monetary rates in Table 7.5.

Table 7.4.
Comparison of economic indicators of stability,
for the United Kingdom and the United States of America

	1879–1913		1946–79	
	UK	USA	UK	USA
Price variation coefficient	14.9	17.0	1.2	1.3
Income variation coefficient	2.5	3.5	1.4	1.6
Money supply variation coefficient	1.6	0.8	1.0	0.5

Source: Cooper (1982).

Table 7.5
Correlation of the variations in monetary interest rates

	UK	Germany	France	Austria
UK	1	0.83	0.90	0.76
Germany		1	0.89	0.93
France			1	0.83
Austrial				1

Source: Vidal (1989).

THE LONG-TERM STABILISATION OF BALANCES OF PAYMENTS

One sharp macroeconomic difference between the two globalisation processes is that the first saw no drift in current account balances, a characteristic of growing structural imbalances. Indeed, long-term capital exports were positively correlated to exports of British commodities and negatively correlated to internal investment and domestic economic activity, and thus to imports. Given that the balance of long-term capitals was negatively correlated to the balance of trade, Britain's basic balance stabilised. This lack of fluctuation in the basic balance meant that Britain did not accumulate long-term structural debt. This was totally at odds with the US situation under Bretton Woods, and indeed in the period of the imbalances of the 1980s and 2000s. Remaining constantly in long-term surplus, Britain had short-term creditors that were compelled to lend to its banks. Their counterparty was the export of long-term investments. The product of these investments provided the means of payment for the commodities that were exported by Britain or by European countries who accepted bills of exchange in sterling, which was the universal means of payment for international trade.

Moreover, price movements and volumes headed in the opposite direction to variations in the trade balance (in value terms), thus cushioning the latter. When domestic investment increased, the British terms of trade also increased, as we showed above. But import volumes increased more quickly than export volumes. When the rise in wages and imports accelerated agricultural price movements, the terms of trade reduced. Nonetheless, the profitability of investment in Britain weakened and economic activity fell. Import volumes thus fell as well. But the flow of investment abroad took up the slack and provided means of buying British commodities. Export volumes increased and the balance of trade (in volume) headed higher into surplus. Table 7.6 depicts these stabilisation mechanisms.

Table 7.6
Long-term stabilisers of the UK balance of payments

Variables	Phase of growing UK investment	Phase of falling UK investment
Growth rate of UK Gross Fixed Capital Formation	↗	↘
Growth rate of long-term capital exports	↘	↗
UK terms of trade	↗	↘
Variations in the balance of trade	↘	↗

The result of this set of endogenous rebalancing mechanisms was that the international monetary system operated with a very low need for gold. As the pivot of the gold standard system, the United Kingdom was the country with the least gold reserves. As we know, this resulted from the opposite levers that its policy rate exerted on the issuance of bills of exchange in sterling, and the foreign banks' liquid deposits in British banks. Because confidence in convertibility prevented speculative movements, variations in short-term capital always had a stabilising effect. They offered a flexible means of financing the temporary imbalances in the basic balance.[4]

The Great Deflation of the Classical Age, and the Death Throes of the Gold Standard

The great transformations of capitalism always begin with a major financial crisis. The crisis that initiated the end of the gold standard broke out in Vienna in May 1873 and spread across all of Europe. Its immediate cause was enormous real estate speculation, financed by debts issued on behalf of real estate companies by new branched banks. Incapable of recouping their mortgage credits, banks collapsed in their hundreds across the great cities of Europe, from Vienna, to Berlin, to Paris. The banking crisis immediately triggered a violent recession.

Banks that lacked liquidity could no longer command confidence. Interbank loans froze or became very expensive. The crisis immediately spread to the stock markets and to upstream economic sectors (steelworks, cement production). It also rebounded on the US railroads. The latter had financed themselves through bond issuance on the European financial markets and in Wall Street, which was also caught up in the crisis due to contagion. The crisis also spread to global agriculture and the food industries on account of the fall in consumption. It thus hit the immigration countries hard.

In the United States, the fragility of the banking system – which lacked any central bank – combined with dependence on foreign finance and the debts resulting from the Civil War to trigger a

---

4   Michel Aglietta, 'Intégration financière et régime monétaire sous l'étalon-or', *Revue d'économie financière*, no. 14, 2006, pp. 25–51.

monetary crisis. This crisis owed to the shortage of gold, which was aggravated by the desire of the Republican majority in Congress to redeem the greenbacks as quickly as possible by means of gold conversion.

The American financial system's fragility and its lack of flexibility in creating a central liquidity made deflation the essential characteristic of the continuing depression that lasted from 1873 to 1896 (Table 7.7). This depression was a long economic stagnation made up of resurgent financial crises. After an initial crisis lasting four years (1873–77) there were fresh banking crises in 1882–84 and then again in 1890–96. In Chapter 5 we referred to the Barings crisis, which required an international loan of last resort operation orchestrated by the Bank of England. In between these episodes of financial crisis, economies did see phases of growth. This growth amid deflation was above all the prerogative of the new industrial powers: Germany, Japan and the United States.

The Great Deflation prompted structural changes which transformed the international division of labour and thus weakened the economic structures that allowed the Bank of England to play its unique role. Indeed, the first response to deflation was industrial concentration. Outside of the United Kingdom, free trade was set onto the back foot, with the Méline tariffs in France and the MacKinley tariffs in the United States. The years in between the end of this deflation and World War One were a period of cartels, and one period in which Europe's great powers outbid each other to consolidate their colonial empires – or, in Germany's case, to create one. The United States established its own exclusive domain in Central America. The great powers also accelerated their carve-up of China, although they had to accept the Japanese presence in that country following its victory in the Sino-Japanese war.

All these developments irreversibly weakened the Bank of England's monetary lever over international payments. The only barrier to this power disappearing entirely was the fragile state of the US financial system, and above all its lack of a central bank. This meant that the creation of the Fed in 1913 was bound to put an end to the Bank of England's hegemony. The Federal Reserve Act brought a huge leap in the dollar, now a currency able to internationalise itself through

Table 7.7

Variation in wholesale prices, from mid-nineteenth century until 1913 (percentage change per period).

	1849–73	1873–96	1896–1913
United States	+67	−53	+56
United Kingdom	+51	−45	+39
Germany	+70	−40	+45
France	+30	−45	+45

Sources: US Department of Commerce, Statistical Abstracts from Colonial Times to 1970. For European countries, B. R. Mitchell, European Historical Statistics, 1978.

the expansion of US trade. Of course, World War One was a powerful accelerator for what had now become inevitable. The international gold standard could not survive the advent of rivalry among nations who shared no common conception of free trade.

The postwar world was very heterogeneous, and undermined both by the enormous public debts of the warring countries and the political instability in Europe and Asia. Keynes immediately grasped the dramatic consequences of the Treaty of Versailles in his *Economic Consequences of the Peace* (1919). The financial burden imposed on Germany could only destabilise its economy and unleash nationalist passions, the first episode of which was the German hyperinflation crisis studied in Chapter 5.

World War One thus completely transformed the global economy. The British and French leadership, however, did not want to hear of this. Their sole political aim was to re-establish the old order. Wartime inflation was far from cancelled out by the deflation of 1920–21. Inflation had been made possible by monetary creation that was itself linked to the inconvertibility of national currencies. Would restoring gold convertibility at prewar parity be enough to resuscitate the international monetary order?

From a quantitative point of view, the money supply rested on a much narrower gold base than it had in the prewar period. Reviving growth demanded a continuous expansion of credit and money. Re-establishing nominal convertibility at parity with 1913 meant imposing a real gold price much lower than it had been. This could only produce a depression in gold production. In order to avoid global deflation extending indefinitely, it was necessary to make up gold reserves with foreign currency, on a very large scale. This is precisely what the 1922 Genoa conference recommended: that is, to allow central banks to hold a large part of their exchange reserves in the form of liquid securities in foreign currencies, and to preserve as far as possible the gold convertibility of these currencies. This meant moving to a totally different monetary universe, albeit without recognising it openly. This was the Gold Exchange Standard.[5]

The Gold Exchange Standard seemed to be a satisfactory solution in terms of economic efficiency. It saved on the cost of using metal for monetary purposes, which had risen very high on account of the worsening metal scarcity. But this argument disregarded the very nature of a monetary system. The real question is: how secure can exchange reserves be, if they are held in the form of assets in foreign, rival financial centres? Here the problem of international liquidity returned in far greater dimensions. Before World War One, sterling reserves were held as receivables to London banks. These assets were considered absolutely safe. But by the 1920s, conditions were very different.

Re-establishing gold convertibility was not enough to rebuild the confidence rooted in an economic order that had now been irreversibly overturned. After World War One, there was a clash between national sovereignties. The first sovereign decision taken by the great powers was to declare an embargo on gold exports. They could not have taken a measure more incompatible with the gold standard that they were claiming to restore! In the 1920s the status of reserve money essentially flowed from political strategies. After 1919, the United States finally had a central bank with the authority to regulate money. But it did not have a doctrine of international monetary relations for a gold exchange system.

---

5   The Genoa conference lasted from 10 April to 22 May 1922. Organised on Britain's initiative, it brought together thirty-four countries, and resulted in the Genoa accords. It sought to re-establish the global monetary order that had been cast asunder by World War One. The accords culminated in the advocacy of a gold exchange standard in which sterling and the dollar were the reserve currencies substituting for gold. For the first time, the dollar rose to the status of an international currency.

The political structure of the United States had not been changed by the war. In Congress, national interests remained subordinate to local ones, and foreign policy to domestic policy. The rural states' bloc against the West and Midwest remained as important as ever. Successive US governments sought to influence the dilapidated state of the warring countries' finances by encouraging private American capital to internationalise. But investment banks in that period were no better able than they are today to guide American capital flows abroad in any long-term sense. They simply sought quick and easy profits in the form of exorbitant commissions. On the political side, the Republican-majority Congress was again obsessed with the repayment of war debts, and it put pressure on the Treasury to use private loans as means of influence. The thorniest problem was that of German reparations.[6] This question illustrated the failure of the US's limp policy and, moreover, implicated it in the global catastrophe. When we studied German hyperinflation we saw how it ultimately ended. The success of the *rentenmark* in November 1923, combined with the reorganisation of Germany's foreign debt through the Dawes plan in October 1924, precipitated a rush to borrow from German businesses and local authorities. American banks were attracted by the commissions on brokering, while savers were attracted by interest rates that were higher than domestic bond rates. Both were confident in the solidity of the *rentenmark*. These loans created a heavy financial burden, on top of that of reparations. One hundred and twenty-four issues of German securities were sold to the United States for a total of $1.5 billion. Added to that, the American banks made short-term advances to the German, Austrian and Hungarian banking systems. When speculation began to balloon on Wall Street in 1928, loans on

---

6   The Treaty of Versailles, signed on 28 June 1919, also contained financial dispositions. Germany was to pay France and Belgium the exorbitant sum of 132 billion *goldmarks*, as compensation for war damage; there were also several economic sanctions that seriously weakened the country. This cardinal error, perpetrated under French pressure, sowed the seeds of the hyperinflation of 1923, which produced a social and political crisis that was the crucible of the growth of Nazism. In mid-1919, Keynes demonstrated the dangers that the Treaty posed to the restoration of an international balance, showing that it was impossible for Germany to honour the commitments that had been imposed upon it. See Keynes, *The Economic Consequences of the Peace*, New York: Harcourt Brace, 1920.

securities became the fuel for this speculation. The interest rate on short-term finance (call loans) for share purchases, and on the trusts' pyramid operations, exceeded the yield that banks could achieve by lending to their counterparts in Central Europe. In consequence, the American banks did not renew their advances as they reached maturity, thus weakening the banking system in these countries.

The American financial crisis began with the crisis of the Florida real estate boom. Speculation had flown off the handle, and it was exacerbated by Charles Ponzi's fraudulent manoeuvres. The crisis exploded when the Fed ended up increasing its interest rate.[7] This crisis put a sudden stop to the rise in household incomes, and then spread to agriculture. After this first crisis, a purely financial boom took flight on Wall Street in 1928–29. The crisis of October 1929 was still, at that moment, one limited to these markets, and did not have a great effect on the real economy. But it weakened the banks, as well as other investment funds. Only in the autumn of 1930 did the American banking crisis first break out, bringing a violent contraction of credit. This drove borrowers to reduce their spending, and prompted a fall in both consumption and investment. The deflation that followed was so powerful that it destroyed financial stability and pushed the economy into depression. What made the economy so vulnerable was the borrower class's very high leverage during the phase of prosperity that had preceded 1929.[8] The reversal of the upward cycle precipitated a wave of bankruptcies across the economy, accelerating this reversal. Besides this direct spread of the crisis, it also spread – more importantly – by indirect means. Indeed, the deflation that accompanied this reversal effectively redistributed wealth from borrowers to creditors. The decline in borrowers' net wealth incentivised them to reduce their current and future spending, while those who held liquidity awaited a further fall in prices. This in turn aggravated the reversal. By March 1933, the real debt burden had thus increased by 40 percent on account of the fall in prices and incomes.

7   Barry Eichengreen and Kris Mitchener, 'The great depression as a credit boom gone wrong', *BIS Working Paper*, no. 137, 2003.
8   Irving Fisher, 'The Debt-Deflation Theory of Great Depressions', *Econometrica*, vol. 1, no. 4, 1933, pp. 337–57.

However, the sequence of events linked to the US's internal financial dynamic only partly explain the devastation of the Great Depression. International interdependence played a decisive role in determining the depth and the length of the crisis. American savings were heavily invested in Central Europe. The first wave of US bank collapses in autumn 1930 rebounded on their counterparts, at the same time as it provoked the massive withdrawal of capital from the London stock exchange. The British banks cut off their international finance, triggering a catastrophe in Central Europe. The collapse of the Austrian bank Credit Anstalt in May 1931 led to the general insolvency of Central Europe's banking systems and an economic depression with disastrous social and political consequences.[9] In 1931 and 1932, the effects of the economic and financial collapse in Central Europe strengthened the waves of US bank collapses.

Britain and France's return to gold convertibility – now nothing more than a ghost of the gold standard – shattered in the summer of 1931 with the mass demand to convert sterling deposits on the London stock exchange. This forced Britain off the gold standard, and drove the formation of the sterling zone in September of the same year. Following the British government's decision, France's obstinacy in sticking to the gold bloc brought only a massive overvaluation of the franc, accompanied by devastating inflation. This lasted until the Popular Front government devalued the franc in 1936. The international gold standard was thus subject to the definitive disappearance of internal convertibility in all countries.

Only in September 1936, after Léon Blum's government decided to devalue the French franc, was a tripartite monetary accord between the US, UK and France concluded for the purposes of containing competitive devaluations.[10] The three governments informally agreed to provide one another with credit settled in gold at an agreed price in order to stabilise exchange rates.

---

9   Charles P. Kindleberger, *The World in Depression 1929–1939*, Berkeley University of California Press, 1973.

10   For a presentation and an analysis of the tripartite agreement, see Ian M Drummond, 'London, Washington and the Management of the Franc, 1936–39', *Princeton Studies in International Finance*, no. 45, 1979.

The revaluation of the price of gold and the lowering of minimum reserves in numerous countries meant that an important share of gold stocks was freed up to strengthen international liquidity. After a 50 percent rise in the value of gold reserves, combined with the contraction in international trade, there were no longer shortages of international liquidity. The most important problem was that of adjustment. It was necessary to avoid a fresh wave of competitive devaluations. In three simultaneous declarations, the governments of the United States, the United Kingdom and France committed to ongoing cooperation via the intermediary of their respective exchange stabilisation funds. This would make it possible to ensure that their currencies' relative levels would develop in an orderly way. The currency acquired by central banks during these operations was settled in gold on a day-by-day basis, at a price fixed every twenty-four hours.

This was a system borne of circumstance, and it did not have time to prove its viability. The preparation of a fresh war marked its end. This was, however, a regime of monetary cooperation that could be resuscitated in the future with some international reserve asset other than gold. The 1920s had illustrated the failure of a monetary regime that revolved around key currencies and that was founded on gold as an international unit of account. The tripartite agreement defined a system for international settlements between central banks, by means of gold. This allowed it to manage a system based on three major currencies, each of which was attached to its own currency zone. This was, therefore, a three-currency system with a common means of settlement.

THE BRETTON WOODS SYSTEM: COORDINATION VIA THE INSTITUTIONALISED HEGEMONY OF THE DOLLAR

The end of World War Two saw new arrangements for international monetary relations inspired by the concerns of the United States' leadership, which were shared by the other powers of the Atlantic alliance. These leaders wanted to promote societies that were open to international exchange. It was necessary to do this within the context of new social priorities and the government's responsibility to ensure full employment.

This objective demanded innovation in the monetary domain: notably, the substitution of the automatic mechanisms that had existed under the gold standard. These would be replaced with principles of collective action that would guide adjustments in the countries that joined the system. These principles were transformed into rules and procedures under the aegis of a consultation forum set up for this very purpose: the International Monetary Fund (IMF). The IMF was created at the Bretton Woods conference as a common subsidiary of the member countries' governments. It had three responsibilities: to be the guardian of mutually accepted rules; to provide financial aid for the accepted adjustments; and to drive debates on monetary questions.

The Bretton Woods accords of July 1944 came at the end of long and complex negotiations. Indeed, these talks saw a clash between two visions for the future. On the one hand was the vision of the US Treasury under Secretary Harry White; on the other hand was that of Lord Keynes, who represented the UK Treasury. The pair did share two convictions. The first was that the dramatic economic distortions resulting from the war could only be resolved through monetary measures. It was necessary to organise money in such a way as to free up trade. This idea was in every sense the inverse of what Nazi Germany had implemented in its zone of influence; under the inspiration of Dr Schacht, trade had been organised precisely in order to bypass money. The second conviction shared by White and Keynes resulted from the experience of the monetary disorders of the interwar period. Unless there were commonly accepted international monetary rules, conflicts of interest would worsen. No adjustment would come of a laissez-faire policy alone.

The two negotiating parties had different conceptions of monetary regulation, however, guided by their contradictory interests. But their two shared convictions made possible the approach that resulted in the creation of the IMF. This was an institutional heritage that lasted even beyond the Bretton Woods system itself.

The Difficult Compromise Underlying the IMF's Creation[11]

At the beginning of this chapter, we saw the general obstacle that international money faces: the lack of universal sovereignty. From

---

11   On Keynes and White's rival expectations and conceptions, and the difficult reconciliation that led to the Bretton Woods accords, see Michel Aglietta and Sandra Moatti, *Le FMI. De l'ordre monétaire aux désordres financiers*, Paris: Economica, 2000.

this, the problem arises of how there can exist an ultimate liquidity that is not shared. A second problem is the existence of a means of adjusting balances of payments among nations. Such a means of adjustment must avoid cumulative imbalances in international payment flows, in exchange rates, or in both. Keynes and White each confronted these problems on the basis of the opposed situations of their countries after the war. They also expressed different philosophies regarding the fundamental problems of international money.

The Keynes plan was a proposal for a Payments Union. It combined three proposals, corresponding to three major ideas.[12] The first asserted that it was impossible to liberate international trade without organising a payment system that regularly supplies acceptable means of international payment, consistent with demand. The second called for symmetry in adjustments between deficit and surplus countries in order to prevent deflationary tendencies. In the 1920s the United States and France accumulated and sterilised gold reserves, severely handicapping London in its role as the mediator for international trade, especially given that the United Kingdom had made the error of seeking to re-establish parity with gold at the 1913 level. The third of Keynes's proposals involved the extension of the logic of banking money to the international level. He proposed that a third, supranational level be added to the hierarchy of the banking system.

These proposals were very consistent. The hierarchically organised system of payments was a public good, and it would be extended to the global level by way of an International Clearing Union. Exchange markets could thus be abolished, since the settlement of net foreign account balances would be realised between central banks. This would proceed via the cession of a reserve asset issued by an international clearing bank on whose books the national central banks would each have their own accounts. This reserve money would not be held by private agents. It would be expressed in an international unit of account (IUA), which Keynes wanted to call the 'bancor'. This would be the third-level currency, resolving the problem of international

12   John Maynard Keynes, 'Proposals for an International Clearing Union' (1941), in *The Collected Writings of John Maynard Keynes, XXV,* Cambridge: Cambridge University Press, 1980.

liquidity. National currencies would be defined by fixed but adjustable parities in bancor, on conditions that were mutually agreed by the rules of the system.

In effect, the central banks of the creditor countries would cede to the international clearing bank the net credits that they held on the central banks of the debtor countries. The counterparty of this 'net-net' position would be a credit for the same amount in IUA. This involved the creation of international money, issued by the Clearing Union's settlement bank. This bank would thus be a debtor of the creditor countries' national central banks. Conversely, and symmetrically, it would be a creditor of the debtor countries' central banks. The result would be a functional symmetry between surplus and deficit countries.

For this symmetry to function, it would be necessary to lay down adjustment rules that imposed symmetrical obligations on the two categories of country. If these rules were to be mutually acceptable, they had to be coupled with shared advantages. For the debtors, there was the possibility of borrowing in order to cushion the austerity that would come from restrictive adjustments. For the creditors, these rules offered a guarantee of limits on the debt that could be accumulated by the debtor countries' central banks. For the purposes of limiting debts, Keynes foresaw a system of quotas and alert indicators. These limits were accompanied by early-response corrective actions, which would force the governments of the debtor countries to take certain measures when a given percentage of the quota had been reached. These measures included devaluing the national currency in relation to the bancor. On the other hand, the governments of countries that issued too much credit relative to their quota could be compelled to revalue or to conduct more expansive budget policies.

Keynes's whole economic philosophy was concentrated on this plan for a new global monetary order, which would be instituted by the international political community. Before all else, it was necessary to exercise the deflationary demons of the past, through the controlled creation of money at a fully international level.

The White plan was of a completely different nature, because it was shaped by very different concerns. It suggested that it was first of all necessary to establish the preponderance of the dollar in institutional terms – and this would be a crushing preponderance, once international trade had recovered. Secondly, it was necessary to correct the flaws that had brought the monetary imbalances of the interwar period. For White, re-establishing multilateralism meant forbidding any discrimination against US exports. If competitive devaluations were to be avoided, it was necessary to re-establish convertibility among currencies and to establish fixed exchange rates that could be adjusted after collective consultation. Moreover, it was vital for the US financial community that capital exports encountered no barriers. This is why White proposed a staged reduction of exchange controls: convertibility would first be reduced to current operations, and then extended to non-speculative capital. Only the most volatile capital (hot money) would permanently continue to be controlled.

White proposed the creation of two institutions. He did this in order to both respect fundamental principles and achieve objectives contingent upon the situation of American hegemony that was now certain to be established. These institutions were an Exchange Stabilisation Fund – later to become the IMF – and an International Bank for Reconstruction and Development – later to become the World Bank – capable of supplying the necessary capital when private finance was found wanting. The Stabilisation Fund's role would be to generalise the experience of the tripartite accord that the three main central banks had reached in 1936. Its capital would be made up of gold, convertible currencies and the government securities of the participating countries. The United States would have the right to a veto in controlling the Fund. Obtaining dollars would require authorisation from the Fund and thus from the US government. This measure raised the dollar to the rank of an international money for official settlements.

These differences had to be flattened out if a single text was to be presented to the two countries' legislatures. The Americans also insisted that a global conference be convened. The process of meeting these two objectives led to sharp disputes, which lasted for almost two years. The major differences between the two plans concerned the nature of the initial quotas (whether these would be drawing rights on a bank, or subscription to a Fund's capital); the role of the exchange market and the extent of capital controls; and, finally, the symmetry or asymmetry of compulsory adjustments.

In Keynes's view, capital controls had to be permanent, since floating exchange rates were not capable of leading to an economically satisfying equilibrium in the balances of payments. The Clearing Union would much more effectively take over this role, just as the banking principle had unified currencies within nations by eliminating the dualist system of the Middle Ages, as well as the confusion among different units of account that resulted from it. Nonetheless, Keynes was well aware that the points on which the US Congress remained intransigent were unavoidable conditions for an agreement. For this reason, the Stabilisation Fund's capital would have to come from national contributions and it would have to contain a gold component. Strict limits would need to be placed on the credits accorded to the Fund and on its loans to debtors. The gold value of the dollar could not be changed without Congress's agreement.

Keynes used his theoretical schema to guide his negotiating tactics. He wanted to insert London's minimum requirements into White's own mechanism: that is, to secure the lowest possible subscription in gold and the greatest possible size for the total capital on which its lending capacity depended. Above all, Keynes wanted to insert a criterion that would prevent any opposition to a devaluation: the notion of a 'fundamental imbalance' in the current balance. This was accepted by the American side. On 8 October 1943, the two sides reached a procedural agreement to draw up a common Anglo-American text that would serve as the basis for what would be the first United Nations conference.

The Dollar as the Pivot of a New Monetary Order

The US Treasury Secretary, Henry Morgenthau Jr, had two major objectives. The first was to shift the centre of international financial power from the London and New York investment banks to the US Treasury itself. The American delegation was, therefore, intractable on the question of where the new IMF should be based. It had to be established in the capital of the country that had the largest quota. The second objective was to place the dollar at the heart of the international monetary system. The Americans won out on both points. The

IMF was indeed located in Washington, and each country had to declare its parity in gold or in a currency convertible into gold at the weight and fineness in force on 1 July 1944. Given that most of the countries lacked gold, they declared their parities in dollars.

Determining the quotas was also something of a struggle. White had to appoint a special committee for this purpose. In the end, reaching a compromise required an increase in the amount that was being shared out. The global conference at Bretton Woods was nonetheless one of a kind, in the sense that it did indeed produce results. None of the previous conferences, from Paris in 1865 to London in 1933, had managed to do so.

Of course, the system's rules were an expression of the situation of US dominance at the end of the war. There lay the seeds for problems that would later haunt the Bretton Woods system, when the European economies' restored competitiveness made it possible to re-establish current account convertibility from 1958 onwards.

In the absence of a common point of reference in a higher form of liquidity – other than a country's debt defined in IUA – there emerged the problem of the nth country. Between n countries linked by officially declared exchange rates, there can only be $n-1$ independent exchange rates. It followed that the United States could not have an exchange-rate target, when the dollar was the pivot of a fixed-exchange system. This is why the American monetary authorities did not intervene on exchange markets, nor keep foreign currency reserves. On the other hand, their commitments to foreign official institutions took the form of these institutions' own international reserves. But the American monetary authorities had to be responsible for keeping international liquidity in line with the global demand resulting from the financing of international trade.

There was thus a sort of dual division of labour between governments. This was a very imperfect substitute for the banking hierarchy that Keynes had envisaged for his International Clearing Union system. $N-1$ countries had to advance an exchange-rate target and accumulate dollar reserves to this end. Capital controls were indispensable for neutralising the monetary impact of variations in reserves levels, for a purely monetary sterilisation could not alone suffice. But this constraint entered into conflict with American businesses' desire to export their capital. They exerted pressure for controls to be lifted in the countries in which they planned to invest. The United States was in theory responsible for regulating the price of gold at thirty-five dollars an ounce. Yet this formal obligation did not play out in reality, because the foreign governments in the United States' political and military orbit did not demand the gold conversion of their dollar monetary assets.

When the capital controls were lifted, the system's Achilles heel quickly revealed itself. The US's monetary policy was not subject to any form of constraint from a global feedback mechanism able to regulate worldwide liquidity. This is the dollar's exorbitant privilege.[13] Exchange focused on the dollar, coupled with the fixed price of gold in dollars and the emptiness of the gold-convertibility constraint, made monetary expansion in the rest of the world subject to monetary expansion in the United States.

The Period of Preconvertibility (1947–58)

The Bretton Woods system went through two periods, 1947–58 and 1958–71, separated by the re-establishment of convertibility in Europe. The first sub-period was dominated by the Marshall Plan and the Korean War. The Marshall Plan was an exceptional response to the dilapidation of European economies after the war, and above all a means of containing communism after the Truman Doctrine was adopted in mid-1947. The absolute priority was to anchor Western Europe in the American sphere of political influence. To that end, it was necessary to take rapid action to strengthen Western Europe's industrial capacity.

The European Recovery Program known as the Marshall Plan was announced in May 1947. It was administered by a special US agency, the Economic Cooperation Administration (ECA).[14] Marshall Aid

---

13   Barry Eichengreen, *Exorbitant Privilege*, Oxford: Oxford University Press, 2011.

14   A conference at Bercy focused on the Marshall Plan and the recovery of the European economy. The contributions are collected in René Girault and Maurice Lévy-Leboyer (eds), *Le Plan Marshall et le relèvement économique de l'Europe*, Comité pour l'histoire économique et financière de la France, Conference, Bercy, 21–23 March 1991.

amounted to twenty times the IMF's resources. Nonetheless, even despite this aid, it remained impracticable to make European currencies convertible. It was thus necessary to establish a multilateral payments mechanism in order to develop the intra-European exchanges which were still held back by bilateralism and reciprocity. This mechanism would promote multilateral credits, thus saving on the use of the dollar in payments on commercial transactions between European countries. This was the European Payments Union (EPU), created in June 1950.[15]

The EPU was endowed with an initial capital drawn from Marshall credits. It was to provide the member countries of the Organisation for European Economic Co-operation (OEEC) a clearing and credit mechanism inspired by the ideas of Keynes's plan. This was doubtless the reason why it encountered the hostility of the US Treasury. It took all the State Department's powers of persuasion to get Congress to agree to match the EPU's capital through Marshall credits.

This also demanded huge devaluations. First came sterling, which devalued 30.5 percent relative to the dollar. It was then followed by twenty-three other European countries, who devalued in similar proportions. The trauma of these devaluations made governments hostile to parity alterations. The system drifted towards fixed parities, putting off adjustments for as long as possible. Salvation came from the Korean War, which broke out in June 1950. The resumption of large-scale military spending in the United States gave fresh impulse to industrial production in Europe.

At the end of the 1950s, the Bretton Woods system was finally in working order. It had to confront the two problems that any international monetary system must resolve if it is to be effective. It has to provide a global supply of international liquidities consistent with the needs of international exchange; and it has to assure that balances of payments are adjusted so as to balance out the offer and demand across the different currencies. The Bretton Woods system functioned

---

15   On the functioning of the European Payments Union, and its contribution to overcoming dollar scarcity, see the analysis produced soon after its creation by Michel Jaoul and Olivier Schloesing, 'L'Union européenne des paiements', *Revue économique*, vol. 5, no. 2, 1954, pp. 263–77.

in conformity with its statutes for a relatively short period, from 1958 to 1971, because it failed to deal with these two problems, and thus proved unable to adapt to the transformations of the world economy.

Global Monetary Expansion and the Triffin Dilemma

The problem that would undermine the Bretton Woods system was the permanent deficit in the US capital balance. Up until the end of the 1960s, the United States maintained an average annual current surplus of $2.4 billion. But net long-term capital exports and net short-term non-monetary capital outflows were much greater than the current surplus. As a result, the liquidity balance displayed a permanent deficit of more than $3 billion a year, rapidly rising at the end of that decade.

There were structural capital outflows, on account of the initiatives that American businesses were taking by implanting themselves in Europe. Liquid funds were deposited in European banks, who recycled them in international payments flows which supported commercial and financial operations in dollars. A deterritorialised dollar market was constituted: the euro-dollar market. Subject to arbitrage by liquid asset holders, and especially by the American banks, the euro-dollar rate was closely linked to the rate on the New York money market. From 1965 onwards, the United States government made a real attempt to counter this arbitrage by limiting banking capital outflows, albeit without success. So, if due to a recession or an expansive monetary policy the monetary rate in the United States fell below the monetary rates in European countries, an avalanche of dollars would inundate these countries' central banks. These liquid dollars were placed in official exchange reserves made up of securities on the US money market. What followed was a mutation in the monetary system, which transformed from a gold-dollar standard system to a *de facto* pure dollar standard system. The outflow of dollars from the United States increased the money supply in the rest of the world by way of the increase in foreign central banks' reserves. But investing the reserves in the US financial system made the dollars available to US residents again, with the effect that the US money supply was immunised from the liquidity outflow in dollars. Following the logic of the pure dollar standard, the global money supply was entirely determined by the United States, so long as exchange rates remained fixed.

Table 7.8 shows the average annual variation in official dollar exchange reserves from late 1959 to late 1972. The slide accelerated sharply after the devaluation of the pound sterling in November 1967.

Table 7.8
Annual mean variation in official foreign exchange reserves

	End 1959 to end 1967		End 1967 to end 1972	
	In billions of dollars	*As a percentage*	*In billions of dollars*	*As a percentage*
All countries	1.5	7.3	14.9	29.0
Industrialised countries	1.1	10.6	8.9	30.0

Sources: Ronald McKinnon. 'The Order of Economic Liberalization: Lessons from Chile and Argentina', Carnegie-Rochester Conference Series on Public Policy, Vol. 17, 1982. Data drawn from the IMF's International Financial Statistics.

The expansion of international reserves was constantly fed by the deficit in the US's external monetary position. Since the creation of money depended exclusively on the US's domestic policy objectives, the supply of international liquidity was not adjusted to demand. The excess of international reserves built up, and translated into monetary expansion in the rest of the world (Figure 7.2).

Figure 7.2
Global inflationary growth driven by US money creation (1958–71)

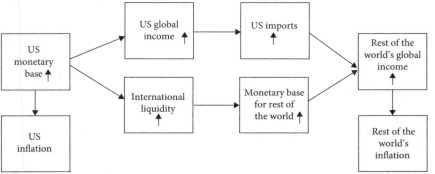

Table 7.9. portrays the monetary asymmetry mechanism produced by the Bretton Woods system under US monetary hegemony.

It is necessary now to study the consequences of an intervention by a foreign central bank, following the rules of the Bretton Woods system. Such an intervention was expressed in an acquisition of surplus dollars on the foreign exchange market, at the prevalent exchange rate. The intervention portrayed in Table 7.9 involves two operations: 1) the transaction on the exchange market; 2) the investment of the dollars acquired by the foreign central bank in assets that will bring returns.

Table 7.9
Asymmetrical effect of foreign central bank intervention on foreign exchange markets

Operation	USA			Rest of World		
	Fed	Commercial bank		Central bank		Commercial bank
(1)	– R$ + D$	– R$	– D$	+ D$	+ RW	+ RW – D$
(2)	– D$ + R$	+ R$	+ D$	– D$ + T$		
Total	–	–	–	+ T$	+ RW	–	–

In operation (1), the foreign commercial banks draw on their deposits with their American counterparts (D$) in order to buy the central money of their own country (Rw). The US commercial banks finance these withdrawals through an equivalent fall in their own free reserves (R$). After this operation, the monetary base falls in the United States and rises in the rest of the world by the same amount. The monetary effect of the intervention (in the strict sense) on the foreign exchange market is thus symmetrical. It is a transfer of money without any impact on the overall money supply.

In operation (2), the foreign central banks convert demand deposits (D$) acquired from the Fed into remunerative assets (T$), for example Federal Treasury bonds. The securities are sold by private American residents who increase their bank deposits through these sales. The American commercial banks can thus rebuild their reserves. In sum, the Fed's monetary base has remained intact while the aggregate monetary base of the rest of the world's central banks, expressed in dollars, has increased. The complete monetary effect of exchange interventions is asymmetrical, and it causes an increase in the overall monetary mass – an increase that is entirely subject to American policy.

Such are the terms of the dilemma which Robert Triffin identified in 1958.[16] There were two possibilities: the United States could fight its payments deficit under the constraint of the gold conversion of the exchange reserves held by foreign central banks, thus inducing a dollar scarcity which in turn would create deflationary pressures across the global economy; or it could tolerate the deficit by pursuing its own internal objectives and financing its international spending. It could thus promote its political and military hegemony, thanks to the tolerance shown by its allies. But this would eventually undermine confidence in the dollar's gold parity. The problem of international liquidity was thus closely bound to the problem of adjusting the balances of payments in such a way as to allow an equilibrium in the US monetary balance. But was no process through which to drive such an adjustment and make it conform to non-residents' dollar needs.

In 1960, the rise in global liquidity in dollars was reflected in the rise in private gold markets, pushing the price up to $40 an ounce. The US government had no responsibility over the private price of gold. However, speculation on gold was symptomatic of the concern over the dollar's pivotal role in the Bretton Woods rules. Thus, the US government reacted in two ways. Firstly, in 1960, it formed a network for swaps between central banks, by means of the Bank for International Settlements (BIS); secondly, in 1961, it formed the Gold Pool in order to maintain the market price for gold at the level of official parity, $35 an ounce. The gold sales made in order to keep this price caused the erosion of official gold reserves, further weakening the system's gold base. In the second half of the 1960s, gold reserves fell lower than not only the United States' foreign engagements, but even the US monetary authorities' own direct foreign engagements. There was no future for the Bretton Woods system unless it made far-reaching changes to its rules.

16   Robert Triffin, *Gold and the Dollar Crisis*, New Haven: Yale University Press, 1960.

The Impotence of Efforts at Reforming the Bretton Woods System
The Triffin dilemma worsened when the US ceased to conform to the price stability policy that the dollar's international role ought to have imposed upon it. There was instead monetary creation in order to finance the budget deficits associated with the Vietnam War and the social programmes of President Johnson's Great Society project. From 1965 onwards, the current balance worsened and inflation accelerated. Confidence in the dollar became more fragile, leading to increased interventions by European central banks and thus to an explosion in their dollar reserves.

What Valéry Giscard d'Estaing called the United States' 'exorbitant privilege' was challenged by President de Gaulle, fed by Jacques Rueff's nostalgic monetary thinking with its penchant for the gold standard. In the Germans' view, the United States was exporting its inflation to surplus countries. At the end of the 1960s, the swollen dollar reserves became increasingly difficult to sterilise. The IMF was impotent to deal with these developments. It had never been able to establish an agreement between the United States and the surplus countries over parity adjustment. The United States did not want a devaluation of the dollar that would have pushed up the price of gold, and their partners did not want to revaluate unilaterally. Thus, the question of adjusting the balances of payments remained unresolved. In this sense, the pound sterling was the weak link for the whole system. Speculative pressure against the pound built up after the Suez Crisis in 1956. The British monetary authorities were driven to re-establish convertibility so that London could recover its role as a global financial centre. But the sterling balances accumulated during the war proved a permanent obstacle to this aim. The constant threat to the pound sterling drove a series of central bank rescue plans, either through BIS intervention or the swaps network that the Fed had established with the Group of Ten (G10) European central banks. Nonetheless, these expedient measures only dealt with disturbances to the capital account. The chronic current balance deficit condemned the government to a stop-and-go policy. Any phase of expansion inevitably led to a deterioration of current payments, a diminution of exchange reserves and resumed speculation against the pound.

Up until the fateful devaluation of November 1967, the United Kingdom repeatedly drew on the IMF in order to finance its deficits.

The IMF was incapable of resolving the adjustment question, but busied itself with finding some means of increasing its resources so that it could finance these withdrawals. Since there could be no question of changing the quotas, General Agreements to Borrow (GAB) were created in 1962, at the same time as the G10, within the IMF. It was also decided to establish the Gold Pool. Within the IMF, the rich countries were empowered to increase the Fund's resources simply for the purposes of financing their own drawing requirements, or else in order to stabilise the market price of gold at around $35 an ounce. One last possible initiative was a radical monetary innovation at the international level. This was the invention of Special Drawing Rights (SDR). We will address SDR's possible role at the heart of international monetary system (IMS) regulation in the last section of this chapter, which is devoted to the transformation of the IMS. The objective of creating an international scriptural money – a radical innovation, because it was not any country's debt – was to set the IMF back at the centre of the global management of international liquidity. It was the Ossola report, produced by a G10 study group in 1965, that drew up the concept for this innovation. However, SDR would not be reserved to the G10 countries alone, since the hostility of developing countries and the pressure from the Fund's director-general imposed the decision to allocate this reserve asset to all IMF members. The agreement on the creation of SDR was approved by the IMF general assembly in Rio de Janeiro in 1967. The first amendment to the Fund's statutes, enacting the creation of SDR, came into effect in 1969. The first allocations were staggered between 1970 and 1972.

In such a context, speculators could hope that a more vehement attack would allow them to make up for the losses suffered during fruitless past attacks. This attack finally came in November 1967, in the wake of seriously disruptive events at both the international level (the Six-Day War in the Middle East) and the domestic level (the dockers' strike). Since Britain's official reserves were very low, the pound's position was vulnerable to speculation that exploited the payments intervals between exports and imports. Ultimately, on 18 November 1967, it was decided to make a concerted 14.3 percent devaluation.

Here, the IMF played a central role in convincing the British that there was no other way out, in determining the extent of the parity change, and in supplying the credits that were necessary for the stabilisation policy. But this consultation represented a failure that would ultimately sweep away the whole system.

Within just four years after the devaluation of the pound sterling, the Bretton Woods system would itself disappear. Gold speculation ran riot, and the Gold Pool was left powerless to resist. It was closed in March 1968, leaving the way open for a double market. The central banks continued to exchange gold at the official price. But the gap between this price and the floating price on the free market became the barometer of the lack of confidence in the dollar. The dollar's gold convertibility was effectively destroyed. There was thus nothing left to safeguard the dollar pivot in the exchange system other than the central banks' goodwill in absorbing dollar flows and thus indefinitely expanding their official credits to the United States.[17] Given that the US followed a unilateral policy, reserves ballooned. This situation became intolerable for the Bundesbank, the paragon of anti-inflationary virtue. In May 1971, it crossed the Rubicon by refusing to continue absorbing dollars, thus unilaterally allowing the Deutsche Mark to float upward. The Americans quickly counter-attacked. On 15 August, President Nixon unilaterally declared the indeterminate suspension of the dollar's gold convertibility. He imposed a temporary 10 percent surcharge on US gold imports. This dramatic American move demanded that a conference be held at Washington's Smithsonian Institute that December. The conference agreed on a complete overhaul of exchange rates, allowing a substantial devaluation of the dollar relative to most European currencies, even as adjustable and fixed exchange rules were maintained. This severed any link with gold.

---

17   Much has been written on this crucial period for international monetary relations. For a synthesis by an observer of the strategic interplay among the major powers, who himself took part in multiple negotiations, see Robert Solomon, *The international monetary system, 1945–1976: An Insider's View*, New York: Harper and Row, 1977. For a very detailed view of this historical era, see Michael Bordo and Barry Eichengreen (eds), *A Retrospective on the Bretton Woods System*, Chicago: University of Chicago Press, 1993.

For a short period, the international monetary system was officially governed by a pure dollar standard. This system released the United States from any consideration of international coherence. It did not take long for the Nixon administration to take advantage of this in the worst possible way. With the 1972 election approaching, Nixon ordered the Fed's chairman Arthur Burns to conduct an inflationary monetary policy, threatening to change the Fed's status if it were not implemented. Burns increased the money supply, inflation accelerated, and speculation against the dollar ran riot. After the pound left the exchange mechanism in May 1972, other currencies followed. Speculation against the dollar became irresistible. After the exchange markets closed for a week in early March 1973, when they reopened the world found itself faced with generalised floating exchanges.

The Failure of the Reform Attempt (1972–74) and the Jamaica Accords (1976)

The SDR were at the heart of the negotiations seeking to rebuild the international monetary system between 1972 and 1974. These negotiations took place within the Committee of Twenty (C20) and subsequently the IMF Interim Committee.[18] The SDR stood at the crossroads between two crucial questions: the demonetisation of gold and the future of the dollar. Firstly, with the establishment of floating exchange rates, in June 1974 the SDRs' value passed from being attached to gold to being attached to a basket of currencies. This matched with the US's desire to approve floating exchanges rather than return to a system of parities centred on SDR.

But, this being the case, there was an inherent contradiction in purporting to make SDR the main reserve asset. For it is impossible to separate the choice of reserve from the nature of the adjustment. The fundamental disagreement on the modalities of the adjustment inevitably spilled over into the disagreement on reserves, making the reform

---

18   On the attempt to reform the IMS after the disappearance of Bretton Woods, and the complete failure of these efforts, see the very strong analysis in John Williamson, *The Failure of World Monetary Reform, 1971–1974*, Nashville: Nelson and Sons, 1977.

attempt a total failure. Drawing inspiration from some of the ideas in Keynes's plan, the reform sought to construct a system of symmetrical adjustments in order to remedy the rigid aspects of the Bretton Woods system. It was necessary to develop rules that could deal with imbalances before they began to accumulate. The Americans proposed making reserves an indicator for decisions on altering exchange rates. The deficit and surplus countries would have to systematically alter their parities above or below a threshold level of reserves. But if this mechanism was to be accepted, agreement was still needed on the nature of the asymmetries to be corrected. The Americans saw the surplus countries as responsible for the asymmetries. For the Europeans, and above all for the Germans, the system's asymmetry owed to the dollar's status as reserve currency. For the Germans, the rise in global inflation was the proof that imbalances were not to be treated symmetrically. There were thus no grounds for an agreement on adjustment. As for the question of international liquidity, making SDR the main reserve asset implied the possibility of substituting them for dollar assets. Yet since the beginning of the 1970s, dollar assets had exploded. Moreover, there was no tantalising remuneration on SDR, and there were only weak opportunities for diversifying investments. In particular, developing countries wanted to establish a link between the creation of new reserves and aid for development. Finally, the Europeans and the Americans were opposed over restrictions on capital movements.

The Jamaica Accords buried modern history's first experience of worldwide monetary cooperation. The accords rubber-stamped each country's freedom to make an independent choice regarding its exchange regime, provided that it notified the IMF. In order to salvage the appearance of monetary consultation, the accords gave the IMF the task of keeping 'oversight' over member states' policies. For their part, the rich countries could make a mockery of this supposed monitoring, but the accords did allow the IMF to take on a new role as a mentor for indebted developing countries.

The true winners of the destruction of the Bretton Woods system were the international investment banks, who were able to arbitrate between currencies and throw themselves into credit distribution policies at the international level, with all the risks of financial crisis that this entailed. From the second oil shock in 1978 onwards, they swept across the whole world in an orgy of indebtedness that lasted thirty years, before once more opening up an era of financial crises.

The second financial globalisation process that resulted was very different from the first such process, because while the first had been inscribed in the gold standard monetary order, the second was coupled with a return to the international monetary jungle. Nonetheless, the consequences of this return to financial crises were cushioned by the new tools available to central banks in their role as lenders of last resort. These tools included the episodic collaboration among central banks in cases of acute international crisis. They were also very different on account of the IMF's adaptation to the new roles that resulted from the Jamaica Accords. Table 7.10 portrays the evolution of these roles after Bretton Woods, and the role that the IMF could have played if anything had come of the reform project studied by the C20.[19]

The essential questions are more pertinent than ever. How should we characterise the post-Jamaica Accords international situation? In what sense can there be said to be an international currency? Given the lack of any common rule, what can be said about exchange movements and the adjustment effects that they supposedly bring?

AFTER THE JAMAICA ACCORDS: THE DECENTRALISED
DOLLAR SEMI-STANDARD SYSTEM

The second financial globalisation process began with two almost simultaneous events: the failure of the C20's attempt to reform the international monetary system, and the first oil shock in 1973. This shock radically altered the extent and direction of international capital flows. There was now a polarisation between oil exporter and importer countries. The preservation of global growth demanded a powerful expansion of international credit. American investment banks and European universal banks sank into the breach opened up by governments' incapacity to reorganise the financing of development and by the extremely small volume of IMF resources in relation to the financing that was required.

---

19   The studies produced within the C20 are gathered in a book published by the IMF, *International Monetary Reform*, Committee of Twenty, 1974.

Table 7.10

Development of the IMF's roles

	Mutual assistance fund for currents running temporary deficits (Bretton Woods)	Agency issuing an international monetary asset (C20)	Financial intermediary for development (Washington Consensus)	International lender of last resort (new structure)
Structure of the monetary and financial system	Stable and adjustable parities, control of capital movements.	SDR as an international unit of account for defining parities.	Extension of flexible exchanges, and the development of sovereign debts.	Financial globalisation generalised to developing countries.
Nature of adjustments and the Fund's role	Current account balance constrained. Distinction between fundamental and temporary imbalances. Macro-economic monitoring and conditionality.	Symmetrical adjustments between countries in deficit and surplus. SDR reserves as an indicator of imbalances.	Solvency of developing countries' sovereign debts. Structural adjustment. Increased conditionality.	Brutal capital account imbalances owing to the instability of the financial markets. Intervention aimed at restoring confidence on the markets. Financial fragility as an indicator of imbalances.
The regulation of liquidity and the Fund's financial role	Financial aid strictly limited by quotas.	SDR as the main international reserve asset.	Proliferation of credit faciilities, lifting of access limits, deadlines extended.	Emergency liquidity, unconnected to quotas.
System governance	Inter-governmental concertation, following a principle of international insurance.	Increased supranational powers. Responsibility for issuing the reserve asset.	Mediator role between debtor states and their various creditors (the states of the Paris Club, international banks).	Constitution of an international lender of last resort, based on a variety of public and private actors.

Private finance set itself up in a commanding position by forming an international lobby with unprecedented power. This decisively altered the scope of national sovereignty. The result was four decades of expansion in international capital flows, making up part of a global financial cycle moved by the credit dynamic. Over the decades, the directions of capital flows changed as globalisation extended. Our purpose here, however, is not to describe the history of finance, but to study the interactions between finance and money in an era of financial deregulation in which private finance dominated the economy as a whole. To this end, it is useful to draw up a table synthesising these four decades leading up to the global financial crisis (Table 7.11).

Table 7.11

Decade	Main direction of net capital flows	Source of financial imbalance	Dominant mechanism for the transmission of finance capital	Nature of financial crises
1970s	South/South: from OPEC to Latin America and Asia.	2 oil shocks → unsustainable sovereign debts.	Recycling of oil revenues by international banks.	Sovereign debt crises in Latin America (Chile, Mexico, Argentina).
1980s	US/Germany and Japan. Differences of economic policy.	US deficit → exchange rates distorted. US interest rates very high then too low after the Louvre Accord of 1987.	US public debt market: Treasury bonds bought by institutional investors.	Stock market crises: Wall Street in 1987, Japan in 1990. Banking crises in developed countries.
1990s	Multi-directional: towards emerging markets until 1997, and then towards the USA (IT).	Excessive dollar debts/Asian banks, Russian and Latin-American governments/US share purchases.	Interbank credits and portfolio investment. Intensive use of derivatives.	Multiple crises: Asia, Russia, Latin America, banks and currencies. Stock market crash (2001).
2000s	Polarisation: US/Germany, Asia, oil producers.	Collapse of US savings/rising savings in emerging countries. Global imbalance.	All types of financial markets: stocks, bonds, securitised credits.	Global banking crisis starting from credit for mortgages.

What these four decades have in common is the financial cycle that has been highlighted by the Bank for International Settlements (BIS). The financial cycle resulting from the new global credit dynamic has profoundly transformed the macroeconomy in relation to what it was under the Bretton Woods system. The financial cycle has a much longer duration than the decision-making horizon of market participants and policymakers. This cycle extends beyond their capacity to adjust to financial instability. This is why macroeconomics spontaneously became pro-cyclical. Indeed, the most important trait of financial dynamics during these cycles is momentum, through which imbalances in asset stocks and indebtedness build up. These imbalances affect credit flows in both bearish and bullish phases of the financial cycle.[20] Figure 7.3 portrays the financial cycles and short-term business cycles in the main Western countries in which finance is entirely liberalised. These series are logarithms presented in real terms, deflated by the consumer price index. Only credit as a share of GDP is expressed as a percentage. The financial cycle corresponds to the average of these three standardised and filtered series.

The financial cycle is here measured on the basis of three financial variables: total credit to the non-financial private sector; credit as a share of GDP; and real estate prices. The series are in real terms, deflated relative to the consumer price index, in log form. Only credit as a share of GDP is expressed as a percentage. The financial cycle corresponds to the standardised mean of the three series.

We can draw three lessons from this. First of all, the financial cycle has continued to expand over the last forty years as a consequence of the financial liberalisation that began in the 1980s. This shift gave free rein to financial forces, first at the beginning of the 1990s and then in the 2000s, in the United States, the United Kingdom, Ireland and Spain. Financial crises thus appear to be increasingly correlated across the different countries. Only Germany appears as an outlier, with limited variation in its financial cycle over this whole period.

20   Claudio Borio, 'The financial cycle and macroeconomics: What have we learnt?', *Journal of Banking and Finance*, vol. 45, 2014, pp. 182–98.

Figure 7.3

Business cycles and financial cycles (1976 Q1–2014 Q3)

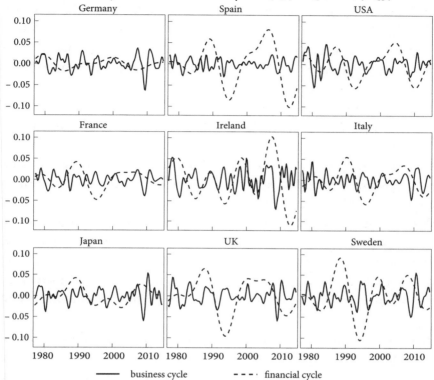

Sources: IBS and OECD. Calculations by Thomas Brand for Aglietta and Brand, 'La stagnation séculaire dans les cycles financiers de longue période' (2015). Legend: These estimates build on the work of Drehmann, Borio and Tsatsaronis, 'Characterizing the Financial Cycle: Don't Lose Sight of the Medium Term' (2012).

Secondly, we can see in Figure 7.3 that the financial cycle is not positively correlated to the short-term macroeconomic cycle. In most countries, the financial cycle is greater in periodicity and extent. Monetary authorities have ignored this, in conformity with their postulate that finance is self-regulating. Given that the doctrine of inflation-targeting saw this as a univocal process – with one instrument (the short-term rate) used to work towards one objective (the inflation target) – it was impossible to interact with the financial cycle and thus to cushion the disequilibria that were building up within it.

Thirdly, not all recessions in the business cycle can be explained in terms of a reversal in the financial cycle. Only the most serious crises in production are simultaneously combined with a reversal in the financial cycle. This allows us to understand, for example, why the bursting of the tech bubble at the end of the 1990s had less impact than in the current crisis, in which the real estate bubble was fed by credit. It is in these phases of prolonged indebtedness that the risks of secular stagnation are greatest.

We should not underestimate the real estate market's role in the *momentum* dynamic that drives the financial cycle. Momentum means that the trajectory of prices over time is the consequence of self-reinforcing interactions between market participants' anticipations and their attitudes towards risk. The real estate sector is all the more important in this regard, in that it is financed by bank debt, which is then largely transformed into bond securities. These financial operations are called securitisation. The indebtedness that results from finance for real estate involves a very large number of economic agents, households and businesses. This creates a close link with the indebtedness of financial intermediaries, who amplify their own loan capacities through very high leverage on their own equity. Before the crisis, this leverage was frequently above thirty, and could rise as high as fifty or sixty. We can thus conclude that the financial cycle results from a powerful interaction between the growth in private debt and the evolution of asset prices.

When we studied monetary regulation, we saw that before the great crisis of 2008, the big central banks were not endowed with macroprudential tools that could integrate financial stability into their monetary policies. They adopted these tools only after they saw the prolonged financial disorder provoked by that crisis. Nonetheless, financial globalisation allows for international capital movements to make sudden and drastic changes of direction. The systemic risk here is linked to international chains of counterparties involved in a global financial system much larger than the banking system in the strict sense. There can be no effective policy to block this systemic risk without monetary cooperation organised at the international level. Yet this cooperation was lacking in the forty years that preceded the great crisis. Financial cycles have also had disruptive effects on international monetary relations.

This fact is even more disturbing given that the tendency towards growth in international capital movements has not had a positive effect on long-term growth. This runs counter to the postulate advanced by the theory of efficiency, according to which greater financial integration automatically means greater efficiency in allocating savings. Studying a wide sample of developed and emerging countries, Dani Rodrik and Arvind Subramanian have shown that opening finance up internationally had no effect on growth over a twenty-year period (1985–2005).[21] More recent BIS studies conducted by Stephen Cechetti and Enisse Kharroubi have even suggested that the opening up of finance had a negative effect on global productivity.[22] What is happening looks like a 'bell curve'. If a closed economy is the starting point, the opening up of finance does benefit growth up to a certain point. But once that threshold has been passed, it becomes harmful.

It is not difficult to understand the disconnect between the hypothesis advanced by the theorists of financial efficiency and the empirical reality. In the first chapter, we showed that the theory of intertemporal price consistency – a theory on which financial efficiency depends – is a theory of an economy without money. We have demonstrated that, on the contrary, the efficiency or inefficiency of finance proceeds precisely by way of the monetary system. However, after the Jamaica Accords there was both an explosion in international indebtedness and a retreat in international monetary coordination. This meant a face-off between currencies lacking in any common rule. The inability to regulate the dual problem of the international liquidity supply and the adjustment of balances of payments – an incapacity which manifested itself in the global inflation under the Bretton Woods system – took the form of a cycle in the dollar. This was a highly disruptive phenomenon that propagated the financial crisis at the global level.

21   Dani Rodrik and Arvind Subramanian, 'Why did financial globalization disappoint?', *IMF Staff Papers*, vol. 56, no. 1, 2009, pp. 112–38.
22   Stephen Cecchetti and Enisse Kharroubi, 'Reassessing the impact of finance on growth', *BIS Working Paper*, no. 381, 2012.

The International Monetary System as a Dollar Semi-Standard

After the fall of Bretton Woods, countries could freely choose their own exchange regimes. That meant that a country could allow its currency to float according to supply and demand, set its rate relative to another currency, or adopt some intermediate arrangement between these two extremes. Even this was not a binding decision, for governments could change their choice at any moment in line with circumstances.

The system thus became a hybrid. A small number of developed countries opted for flexible exchanges and open capital markets. Exchange rates mainly varied under the effect of speculative funds and financial investors' asset diversification strategies, and were only partially oriented by economic fundamentals. Most currencies chose a more or less flexible dollar peg, and the respective countries preserved more or less rigorous capital controls.

The result has been two coexisting types of disequilibrium. On the one hand, there is momentum in the exchange movements between fully convertible currencies. This takes the form of a cycle in the dollar against all the flexible exchange currencies. On the other hand, there is an accumulation of financial disequilibria through the polarisation of current account balances. These disequilibria are amplified by capital movements. They lead, therefore, to an accumulation of exchange reserves in the expansive phase of the financial cycle, and to violent contractions during financial crises.

Figure 7.4 portrays the dollar's global cycle in terms of real exchange rates, relative to a large currency basket calculated by the IMF. Far from keeping parity relative to purchasing power, in forty years the dollar has lost 40 percent of its value. But this is anything but a regular trend. It has taken place through huge cycles, of great extent and duration, made up of phases of cumulative appreciation and phases of profound depreciation. Given that these are real effective exchange rates, there is a distortion of international exchange prices. There are over-evaluations and under-evaluations of the dollar in international trade. Clearly, these price misalignments create massive inefficiency in international trade, translating into persistent and global instability in the balances of payments.

Figure 7.4

The dollar cycle and its trend (real effective exchange rate)

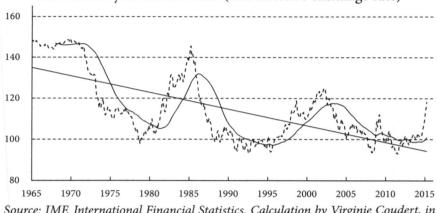

Source: IMF, International Financial Statistics. Calculation by Virginie Coudert, in Michel Aglietta and Virginie Coudert, 'Currency turmoil in an unbalanced world economy', CEPII Policy Brief, no. 8, 2015.

Figure 7.5 illustrates the massive disequilibria between the current balances of the United States, the eurozone and Japan, which have been the three most important currencies since the creation of the eurozone. This polarisation becomes even stronger in phases of real appreciation in the dollar, and then eases in phases of depreciation, albeit without disappearing entirely.

Figure 7.5

US, Japanese and Eurozone Current Account Balances (% of GDP)

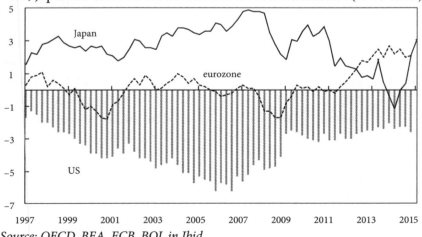

Source: OECD, BEA, ECB, BOJ, in Ibid.

We have seen that these heteroclite currency arrangements are unable to produce stability in the international monetary system. Given their incapacity to provide this public good, the following question arises: what explains the persistence of the dollar's dominant role as a key currency, i.e. as a provider of international liquidity? To answer this question, we must recall the fundamental conclusion established above. Ultimate liquidity is a collective good, in the sense that it results from the polarisation of the demand for protection against the uncertainty of financial crises. It cannot be the property of more than one currency at the same time. Essentially, then, the answer is that the dollar's very long-term persistence as the basis of international liquidity owes to the fact that there is no other currency to replace it.

The dollar has remained the dominant currency with respect to all of money's essential functions. Today it is totally dominant on the exchange markets (encompassing 87 percent of transactions); as a peg for foreign currencies (72 percent of countries who choose a foreign peg choose the dollar); in the make-up of official exchange reserves (61 percent); and even in bank loans (57 percent).[23] Unfortunately there has been rather less research into currencies' functions in invoicing and settling international trade. The available data is not always recent. Nonetheless, here again the dollar reigns supreme. It is easily dominant in the invoicing of both exports and imports. This dominance increased further still during the global financial crisis.[24] Eighty percent of Asian exports (excluding Japan), and 94 percent of Brazil's, are carried out in dollars.[25] Today, the dollar is still very heavily overrepresented if we compare its use in trade invoicing relative to the proportion of all transactions worldwide that involve the United States.

The eurozone economies themselves contribute to the dollar's resilience. The share of French export invoicing made out in dollars rose

23   For detailed quantitative information on the relative importance of the dollar and other convertible currencies in the different functions of international money, see Michel Aglietta and Virginie Coudert, *Le Dollar et le système monétaire international*, Paris: La Découverte, 2014.

24   Hiro Ito and Menzie Chinn, 'The rise of the redback: Evaluating the prospects for renminbi use in invoicing', in Barry Eichengreen and Masahiro Kawai, *Renminbi Internationalization*, Washington DC: Brookings Institution Press, 2015, pp. 111–58.

25   Daniel Gersten Reiss, 'Invoice currency in Brazil', *MPRA Paper*, no. 59412, University Library of Munich, 2014.

from 9 percent in 1974 to 18.6 percent in 1995 and 38.5 percent in 2012. Only Germany is able to more easily impose the euro's use (62 percent of its exports are made out in euros). The literature that seeks to explain the inertia in the dollar's position emphasises the network effects and the higher costs that come with a change of invoicing currency. This is particularly true on hydrocarbon markets, where almost all transactions are carried out in dollars, notwithstanding vague and often partly politically motivated bids to replace the dollar with some other currency. (Such was the case of Saddam Hussein's Iraq under sanctions; the Iranian project for a euro-based oil market; the euro-denominated oil contracts under Hugo Chávez's regime; and the Russian–Chinese gas deal in 2013.) Linda S. Goldberg and Cédric Tille emphasise exporter firms' involuntary 'coalition effect', which owes to their incentive to use the dominant unit of account.[26] This allows them to limit any possible fluctuations in their prices relative to those of their competitors. In other words, the dollar's inertial position in the invoicing of international trade can be explained in part by a self-referential logic at work within private actions. This logic emerges from the mimetic character of competing exporters' behaviour.

Even since the disappearance of the Bretton Woods system, the dollar has remained very stable as a proportion of exchange reserves over time. This illustrates the crucial importance that ultimate liquidity has for foreign governments (Table 7.12). When reserves are expressed in value, the dollar's share varies in line with exchange rates, especially as the dollar tends to vary against all the other currencies convertible at floating exchange rates. Hence, the dollar share increases when the dollar appreciates, and diminishes when it depreciates.

There are, of course, economic reasons for the enduring role of the dollar. First of all, full convertibility is not itself sufficient. There also has to be an economically sizeable country (in terms of GDP and its share of world trade) to create enough liquidity to finance the whole world's trade needs. After all, the economy of a small country could be destabilised by overly large demand coming from non-residents. A large country benefits from having a lesser degree of openness, which leaves

26   Linda S. Goldberg and Cédric Tille, 'Vehicle currency use in international trade', *Journal of International Economics*, vol. 76, no. 2, 2008, pp. 177–92.

Table 7.12
End-of-year exchange reserves by currency
(identified reserves as a percentage of the total)

Currency	1973	1995	2000	2005	2010	2013
US dollar	64.5	59.0	71.1	66.5	61.8	61.4
Yen	0	6.8	6.1	4.0	3.7	3.9
Pound sterling	4.2	2,1	2.8	3.7	3.9	3.9
Euro*	5.5	27.0	18.3	23.9	26.0	24.2
Others	25.8	5.1	1.7	1.9	4.6	6.6

Source: IMF annual reports.
*Pre-1999 figures are the sum of the Deutsche Mark, the French franc and the Dutch guilder

it less sensitive to external shocks and exchange movements. It is thus less liable to being destabilised by the international use of its currency. More important still is the development of the issuer country's financial markets. Non-residents must be able to borrow this currency with ease and invest their funds on its markets with a minimum of transaction costs. This demands deep and liquid financial markets, as well as derivatives markets on which the risks can be covered.

This final condition immediately designates the dollar as the main international currency, for the euro remains an incomplete currency whose government securities markets are not homogeneous and unified. The securities issued by the US Treasury and American government agencies offer an unrivalled guarantee of liquid and safe assets. The total volume of these securities exceeds $8 trillion, and their daily turnover is over $500 billion. One of the major explanations for the dollar's resilience thus lies in the United States' capacity to provide the liquidity and safety demanded by international financial actors. This is particularly the case when uncertainty is rising, for instance when faced with the prospect of slowing global growth, financial crises, geopolitical tensions, and so on.[27]

But the essential reason lies elsewhere. Non-residents' search for liquidity in situations of extreme stress is the search for a substitute for sovereignty. They think that they can find this substitute in the United

---

27   See Benjamin J. Cohen, 'The demise of the dollar? Plus ça change, plus c'est pareil', *Revue de la regulation*, no. 18, 2015; and David Fields and Matías Vernengo, 'Hegemonic currencies during the crisis: The dollar versus the euro in a cartelist perspective', *Review of International Political Economy*, vol. 20, no. 4, 2013, pp. 740–59.

States' political and military power, and in what they believe to be the quality of its macroeconomic governance, in the form of the Fed's record of 'risk management'.

The dollar's preponderance was thus strengthened in the wake of the crisis because of economic actors' preference for safe assets, as well as the fact that inflation was very low. The Fed's massive acquisition of Treasury bonds with a wide range of maturities – tripling the size of its balance sheet – gave the US public debt markets unparalleled liquidity. The dollar is a safe-haven currency in times of severe crisis.

The Paradoxes of the Financial Crisis and the Enduring Problem of the IMS

The immediate cause of the financial crisis was a generalised excess of indebtedness. The central banks faced an extremely large-scale systemic crisis, and the measures they took in response prolonged the rush toward indebtedness. They flooded economies with liquidity even before the conditions of profitability in the real economy had been re-established. Swelling central banks' balance sheets, such monetary policies in fact maintain the underlying financial vulnerabilities, and increase debts rather than reducing them. The rise in total (public and private) debts was generalised across the world (Figures 7.6a and 7.6b). Indeed, growth was far too weak for any robust debt-reduction process to be implemented.

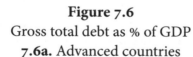

Figure 7.6
Gross total debt as % of GDP
7.6a. Advanced countries

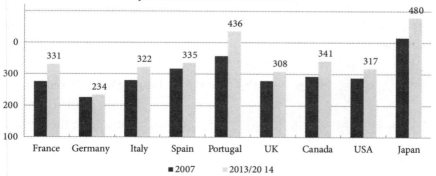

Source: M. Aglietta and V. Coudert, 'Currency turmoil in an unbalanced world', CEPII Policy Brief, *no. 8, July 2015, pp. 3–4.*

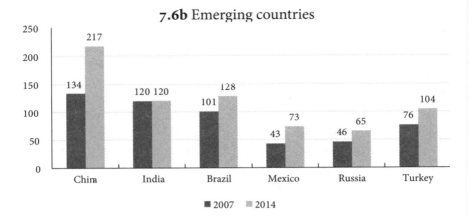

7.6b Emerging countries

■ 2007 ■ 2014

The capital-profitability conditions that would have been necessary to set economies back on the path of a robust accumulation of productive capital had not been met. According to the latest estimates, the natural interest rate, also called the neutral real interest rate – i.e. the marginal rate on new productive investment – in the United States has fallen into negative territory (see Figure 6.6). And despite the existence of floating exchange rates, the estimated average world real interest rate is closely linked to the American neutral rate.[28] This is characteristic of an era in which the obsession with liquidity dominates economic behaviour. Hemmed in by constraints on profitability worse than the United States' own, actors adjust by reducing investment volumes.

In the April 2015 World Economic Outlook, the IMF undertook a deeper study of the decline in productive investment and the fall in potential growth.[29] Productive investment has contracted in lasting fashion in all advanced countries. Since the crisis, it has fallen by an average of 25 percent relative to pre-crisis forecasts. Eighty percent of the general weakness of economic activity can be imputed to the fall in investment.

So, by no means is the preponderance of the dollar a factor for stability in the world economy. On the contrary, it plunged into

28   James D. Hamilton, Ethan S Harris, Jan Hatzius and Kenneth D. West, *The Equilibrium Real Funds Rate: Past, Present and Future*, Report by the US Monetary Policy Forum, New York, 27 February 2015.

29   IMF, World Economic Outlook, Chapter 3, 'Where are we headed? Perspectives on potential output', and Chapter 4 'Private investment: What's the holdup?', April 2015.

recession those emerging countries who had resisted the initial phase of the financial crisis. This was because the dollar's supremacy caused a flood of capital outflows. The emerging countries had deliberately built up excessive amounts of international reserves, which they considered a precaution and means of protecting themselves against financial crises or speculative attacks. This accumulation strategy, however, proved counter-productive. Not only did it fail to shelter them from crises and instability, but it was socially costly and penalised economic growth, as Dani Rodrik's empirical study shows.[30]

The dollar's supremacy perpetuates an imbalanced international monetary system that generates major asymmetries in international monetary relations. This is particularly true of the relations between the United States and the emerging economies.[31] The first of these asymmetries owes to the size and the structure of national economies' international indebtedness. Founded on a national currency, today's monetary architecture attributes an 'exorbitant privilege' to the country that issues the reserve currency.[32] This is because it allows it to import products and financial assets without giving anything back to the rest of the world in exchange. Following this approach, the United States could take on heavy or even almost unlimited debts in its own currency.[33] Conversely, the emerging and developing countries cannot take on international debts in their own currency. Their international debts are thus in foreign currency. This is the 'original sin' syndrome highlighted by Eichengreen, Hausmann and Panizza.[34]

---

30   Dani Rodrik, 'The Social Cost of Foreign Exchange Reserves', *International Economic Journal*, vol. 20, no. 3, 2006, pp. 253–66.

31   Jean-François Ponsot, 'The "four I's" of the international monetary system and the international role of the euro', *Research in International Business and Finance*, vol. 37, 2016, p. 299–308.

32   Eichengreen, *Exorbitant Privilege*.

33   It is only *almost* unlimited, for the mechanism only functions if the dollar inspires confidence and remains a universal currency by continuing to be accepted as such by the rest of the world. On the macroeconomic level, there is no payment (in the sense of redemption of a debt) in the operation of moving dollars out of the United States: the dollars issued for the rest of the world are but a simple recognition of a debt that remains universally recognised . . . for the moment.

34   Barry Eichengreen, Ricardo Hausmann and Ugo Panizza, 'Currency mismatches, debt intolerance and original sin: Why they are not the same and why it matters', *NBER Working Paper*, no. 10036, 2003.

The recent history of money shows that emerging countries' attempts at international issuance in their own currency are both rare and ineffective. One example is the experience of Brazil from 2005 onwards. This initiative was small in scale, and it was not crowned with success.[35] These countries are thus subjected to heavy financing constraints, foreign currency imbalances and exchange risk. One solution envisaged by the G20 and the IMF seeks to provide multilateral support for the development of more efficient domestic markets.[36] This would allow these emerging countries to overcome their financing constraints. However, in reality this is a far from optimal solution, because it does not remove the element of indebtedness in foreign currencies.

Today's architecture is also asymmetrical, because when there are persistent imbalances in the balances of payments, this architecture does not share out the burden of adjustment evenly. The issuer of the international currency does not have to concern itself with this problem as attentively as do the peripheral countries. The former offloads the burden of adjustment onto these countries, in particular if they are in deficit. This privileged situation puts the issuing country into the position of a business-cycle maker and generator of global shocks (for economic activity, raw materials prices, exchange rates, and so on). Conversely, the peripheral countries have to take on the burden of an asymmetrical adjustment. Their position as a business-cycle taker makes them vulnerable to exogenous shocks that they have to absorb. Here, too, they are incentivised to accumulate surplus foreign currency reserves as a precaution, and to implement restrictive neo-mercantilist policies focused on export-led growth.[37]

Finally, there is a profound asymmetry in terms of the autonomy of different countries' economic policy. On the one hand, the United

---

35 Jean-François Ponsot, 'Original sin', in Rochon and Rossi (eds), *The Encyclopedia of Central Banking*, pp. 392–4.

36 See the joint study by the IMF, World Bank, European Bank for Reconstruction and Development and Organisation for Economic Co-operation and Development, *Developing Local Currency Bond Markets: A Diagnostic Framework*.

37 Thomas I. Palley, 'Global imbalances: Benign by-product of global development or toxic consequence of corporate globalization?', *European Journal of Economics and Economic Policies*, vol. 11, no. 3, 2014, pp. 250–68.

States can conduct autonomous and counter-cyclical monetary poli-cies without worrying about the consequences these will have for the rest of the world. This fits with the famous saying: 'The dollar is our currency, but it's your problem.' There is only limited budget policy constraint, for as we have seen, the US Treasury's bonds are the instru-ment of ultimate liquidity for the international monetary system. On the other hand, the emerging economies do not have any real leeway in which to move: their monetary and exchange policies have to adapt to the decisions of the US Federal Reserve, which is what really sets the tone. Their budget policies have to be 'sustainable' in the eyes of the financial markets.

Events since the crisis have thus confirmed Rodrik's diagnosis.[38] A process of deep financial globalisation is incompatible with the diver-sity of national preferences in a multipolar context that lacks the insti-tutional cooperation framework abandoned since the failure of the C20 in 1974. The licence given to financial capital to circulate without limit stands in contradiction with countries' sustainable development needs. This condition can only intensify, and the ultimate result will be the deterioration of the dollar semi-standard.

Is it possible to conceive of a path to the kind of compromises that would create viable international monetary regimes? In the final chap-ter, we will try to set out the terms of the apparently unending quest for an international currency.

---

38   Dani Rodrik, *The Globalization Paradox*, New York: W.W. Norton & Co., 2011.

8

Transitioning to a New International Monetary System

We have now come back to the question posed as the starting point of Part IV. What is international money? A look across history has not provided the answer. From the Delian League to the international gold standard and the Bretton Woods system, there have been numerous attempts to provide greater legitimacy to arrangements between multiple currencies each legitimised by its own foundational sovereignty. Yet these attempts have never lasted more than a few decades: a tiny fraction of time compared to the several millennia over which money has charted its course. We can understand the theoretical nature of the problem. A money is necessarily a system in a given space where it represents and realises value. Its endurance over time is ensured by sovereignty. But given that the very idea of universal sovereignty makes no sense in the present era of the development of human societies, any international currency will necessarily be incomplete. It can only be realised in the form of the acceptance of one single currency's hegemony, or else in the form of voluntary arrangements between states called international monetary regimes.

A hegemony can be accepted if it is a benevolent one; that is, if, through the hegemon's regulation of money, it produces a worldwide arrangement that is compatible with the foreign interests of the dominated states, so that the authority of these states is not threatened. Yet as each hegemony develops it is eroded, because it engenders increasing social costs. The hegemonic state seeks either to rein in these costs or to finance them; in doing so, it inevitably ends up exploiting the advantages of its position. In the case of the dollar, the US government takes no account of the repercussions its policies will have on other countries, since its asymmetrical position immunises it from the rebound effects of the disruption abroad. This asymmetry inevitably produces rivalries when other political powers increase their influence in international exchange, but without bringing any alternative into being as a result. Instability takes hold of international exchange, as we saw with specific reference to the dollar in Chapter 7.

International monetary regimes are created by voluntary associations among states. Bretton Woods was a peculiar regime that aimed to create elements of international law and international institutions (the IMF, the World Bank) distinct from the associated countries themselves, in order to legitimise the dollar's hegemony. However, Keynes had already shown that it was possible to think about this problem differently, and to create a monetary structure that incorporated a symmetrical form of cooperation. Another example, at the regional level, is the association of states that created the euro. This has not resulted in a common sovereignty capable of giving the euro a direct democratic legitimacy. Instead, it has produced an incomplete currency which has exacerbated the asymmetries among the member countries. This is despite the fact that it has created common institutions that are unique worldwide, the most important of which is the European Central Bank.

Voluntary association among states looks like the only practicable way to break out of a degenerated hegemony, even while preserving globalisation through symmetrical cooperation – which is to say, a cooperation that goes beyond policy coordination (which, as in the case of the G20 in 2009, is a mere arrangement of circumstance). If a lasting international regime is to be created, states must be able to agree upon common values of equality, giving each member state, or set of member states gathered in influence groups, the ability to participate in the creation and political direction of the mediating international institutions. These latter institutions are responsible for ensuring the system's functioning, according to the principles that hold together the voluntary association of states.[1]

The first section of this chapter seeks to link these problems of political philosophy to the theoretical problems that economists have grasped in terms of Robert Mundell's impossibility theorem. It asks: on what conditions can a monetary regime based on international cooperation overcome the obstacle this theorem poses? The second section applies these analytical tools to the euro. It does this in order to illuminate possible ways forward, or ones capable of overcoming the impasses of the intergovernmental governance practised thus far. Finally, in the third section we will indicate paths to developing the existing international monetary institutions towards an international monetary system that promotes special drawing rights (SDR) as the ultimate reserve asset.

THE IMS: FROM THE HEGEMONY OF A KEY CURRENCY TO INSTITUTIONALISED COOPERATION

We know already that a system of generalised competition among currencies is unviable in a context of far-reaching financial globalisation. Indeed, such a system will be confronted by the indeterminacy of exchange rates. This itself flows from the unique character of the ultimate liquidity, a singularity implied by the complete integration of capital markets. This is a problem we already encountered in Box 7.1 of Chapter 7.[2]

The Indeterminacy of Exchange Rates in a System of Competing Currencies

According to the hypothesis of market efficiency – the hypothesis of an economy without money – financial globalisation treats international exchanges as if nations did not exist. Yet countries have economic borders that are recorded in their balances of payments.

---

1   Thomas Christiano, 'Democratic legitimacy and international institutions', in Samantha Besson and John Tasoulias (eds), *The Philosophy of International Law*, Oxford: Oxford University Press, 2010.

2   For a rigorous demonstration of this theorem, see Kareken and Wallace, 'On the indeterminacy of equilibrium exchange rates'.

This is the case because any production of value, and thus any issuance of money that recognises and is the vehicle for this value, is national. There thus results the following identity at the global level: Σ (net production) $\equiv \Sigma$ (domestic demands).

Since international exchanges do not themselves create any net value, the payments for these exchanges must not lead to any net creation of money. As Keynes insisted in his 1942 proposal, international money should be purely a vehicle. It should transfer income from importer countries to exporter countries. Yet this rule of international monetary circulation is violated by the international use of national currencies. As we saw with the Bretton Woods system, the total international means of payment may not line up with the needs of the international circulation of goods and services.

Indeed, the deficit countries who use their own currencies in international payments simply transfer their own debt over time. This is a debt, indeed, that never has to be settled. That is the significance of the key currency's 'exorbitant privilege' in a world of purely fiduciary national currencies. If there is no obligation to settle payment deficits in an ultimate money which is not the debt of any country, then *everything takes place as if the finality of payments had been indefinitely suspended*. If the structure of surpluses and deficits crystallises in the hands of the same categories of agents, then the latter will undergo a forced accumulation of liquid assets, beyond their cash requirements. The attempt to convert these liquid assets into financial assets will bring about direct exchanges of currency for currency. It follows from this that exchange markets are swollen by the conversion of currencies that are external to the balance of payments equilibrium. Rather, these conversions result from pure arbitrage on the best forms of holding liquidity. If two currencies are in competition within this arbitrage, the exchange rate that takes form is not the result of the forces that are induced by the transfer of income from a debtor to a creditor in the balance of payments equilibrium. It does not contribute to adjustment. Rather, if the currencies are strongly substitutable, then this exchange rate will tend towards indeterminacy, and thus has every chance of disrupting this adjustment. This is why the aggregate monetary value of purely financial transactions can expand out of all measure in relation to total international trade and world GDP.

This fundamental conclusion is partly recognised in the international macroeconomic literature, where it takes the name of Mundell's impossibility theorem.[3]

IMS Organisational Forms: Mundell's Impossibility Theorem

Mundell's theorem does in part grasp the consequences of money's character as a public good. It aspires to determine the IMS organisational forms that will resolve the problem of indeterminacy. The theorem states that it is impossible to reach the *first best*, which combines the advantages of fixed exchange rates, perfect capital mobility and autonomy of national policymaking. Indeed, perfect freedom for capital would totally constrain national policies to respect fixed exchange rates; if we want autonomy, we have to accept floating exchange rates, but then this leaves international liquidity undefined. This is a problem if we also want complete financial integration. If we want both fixed exchange rates and autonomous policies, then we need capital controls that are all the stricter the more autonomy we want. So, we then have to accept a limited financial globalisation. Here we are inevitably shifting between *second-best* arrangements. In order to identify these configurations, we need, first of all, to properly understand the significance of the three elements identified by Mundell.

Fixed exchange rates eradicate the risks associated with anticipating these rates. Through multilateral rules, they provide international trade with a huge degree of extra certainty. They represent a collective guarantee. Failing that, most countries' governments unilaterally set themselves rules for foreign exchange, accumulate exchange reserves out of the need for self-insurance, and intervene on exchange markets for fear of letting their currencies float freely.

The perfect mobility of capital movements is a notion associated with the hypothesis of efficient financial markets. Such a situation would lead to complete financial integration at the global level. If this hypothesis were indeed fulfilled, the very notion of an equilibrium (or lack thereof) in a country's balance of payments would lose all meaning. The equilibrium would instead be global and intertemporal. If

3   Robert A. Mundell, 'A Theory of Optimal Currency Areas', *American Economic Review*, November 1966, pp. 657–65.

that were the case, deficits and surpluses would come exclusively from structural differences in each country's savings and investments – in other words, differences resulting from agents' individual utility-optimisation behaviours. In this situation, investors would arbitrate between all investment opportunities worldwide according to their rationally anticipated yields and risks; macroeconomic and financial adjustments would prevent shocks from having any cumulative effect.

The financial efficiency hypothesis denies the uncertainty that produces the need for liquidity, as a protection against unknown future events whose probability is impossible to calculate. The demand for protection against unpredictable extreme events is a collective demand, because one can only protect oneself by demanding what others are also demanding.

The third element involved in Mundell's *first best* is the autonomy of national economic policies. Any government will aim for growth that supports the best possible use of the country's resources. It will thus seek to arrange the regulatory measures that ensure that the economy is fully employing its resources. If we assume that each government is indeed able to regulate its economy effectively, then it will be in every country's interest for international relations to restrict its policy as little as possible.

We thus arrive at Mundell's triangle, which synthesises possible types of IMS (Figure 8.1).[4] This is an equilateral triangle in which each side represents one of the three criteria, while each point represents one of the possible choices a country can take. As we move from any given side towards the opposite point, we move away from the full realisation of the criterion that this side represents. The three medians and the opposite sides mark out three segments defining three types of IMS: one is dominated by capital controls (vertex A), the second by fixed exchange rates (B), and the third by the independence of monetary policies (C). We can say that the IMS is coherent if countries with convertible currencies choose to situate themselves within the same diamond. The Bretton Woods system is close to the line AB (fixed exchanges), with a staggered pattern of capital

----

4   Robert Mundell's famous triangle appears in his 1968 textbook *International Economics*, London: Macmillan.

controls: these are low for the United States, high for France and very high for Japan. The large economic powers that had been close to the fixed exchange rate system (segment AB) have migrated towards segment BC by accepting greater capital mobility and thus floating exchanges. The major Western countries did this in the 1970s after the disappearance of the Bretton Woods system; Japan did so in the 1980s; and China did so after 2005. The European countries also followed this trend, albeit only as a group (the E08) brought together by the EMS and then the euro.

However, Mundell's triangle does not take into account uncertainty, nor the function that international liquidity exercises in keeping it at bay. This means that not all positions in Mundell's triangle are accessible to all countries at the same time. There must be consistency in the main countries' choices for international exchanges to be able to prosper, thanks to practicable adjustments in the balances of payments. This is why we see the three segments designating different types of IMS. Segment BaOc is a system of administered exchange rates and a capital mobility that is more restricted the closer we get to the centre of the triangle. Segment CaOb is an IMS dominated by flexible exchange rates. It is only viable if governments find the volatility in exchange rates tolerable. This means that capital mobility must be limited, and flexibility must be reduced, so that countries whose currencies are insufficiently convertible can insure themselves by holding abundant foreign exchange reserves. Segment AbOc depicts an IMS in which there are generalised capital controls (with limited convertibility at current exchange rates everywhere), or where certain countries have protectionist barriers.

This geography does not tell us how choices are made, nor how the main countries manage to establish a consistent position within one region of Mundell's triangle, if they do indeed manage to do so. It is necessary to take account of the paradox of currency competition, which drives polarisation when currencies become increasingly substitutable for one another. It follows from this that a regime of pure flexible exchanges with symmetrical currencies is only possible if globalisation is limited. Only this way can the international payment system function without strategic behaviours aimed at the accumulation of liquid reserves emerging. As Rodrik argues, such an evolution

Figure 8.1

Modes of international monetary organisation and the effects of globalisation: a shift towards flexible exchanges

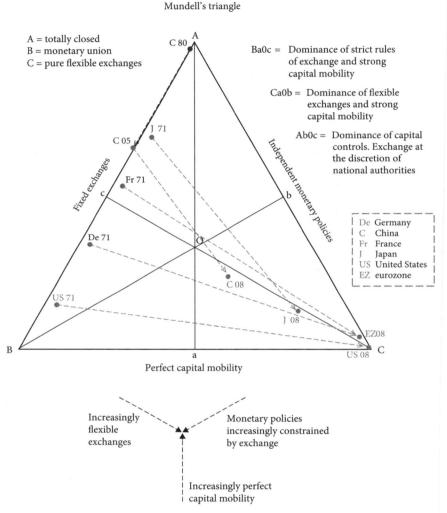

Mundell's triangle

A = totally closed
B = monetary union
C = pure flexible exchanges

Ba0c = Dominance of strict rules of exchange and strong capital mobility

Ca0b = Dominance of flexible exchanges and strong capital mobility

Ab0c = Dominance of capital controls. Exchange at the discretion of national authorities

De Germany
C   China
Fr France
J   Japan
US United States
EZ eurozone

Increasingly flexible exchanges

Monetary policies increasingly constrained by exchange

Increasingly perfect capital mobility

would imply a retreat of financial globalisation. This is also what happened historically in previous waves of globalisation, during the great discoveries of the sixteenth century and the classical age of capitalism. But if deep financial globalisation must persist, then it will involve the formation of international monetary regimes. The choice seems polarised: will this mean a regime under the hegemony of a key currency, or an institutionalised cooperation regime?

International Monetary Regimes: Hegemonic Stability

In the 1960s, the historian Charles Kindleberger introduced his influential conception of the 'hegemonic stability' of international monetary regimes.[5] He conceived this as the only possible type of stable regime. However, such a postulate remains open to dispute, being neither necessary nor sufficient, but rather simply derived from Kindleberger's recognition of the US hegemony that prevailed in a given historical period. After the Jamaica Accords, his postulate was criticised by the 'institutional liberal' current, which was very active in US political science. One of its leading protagonists was Robert Keohane. Here we will take inspiration from Keohane in our redefinition of international monetary regimes.[6]

The so-called 'realist' current upholds the thesis of 'hegemonic stability'. This current of thought considers that a stable international economic order can only come from the hegemony of a dominant power. For only the state is a real political force, able to gain mastery over the self-reinforcing interaction between power and wealth. Power is an actor's asymmetrical capacity to influence other actors' decisions. Exercised unequally, power leads to the formation of property rights, according to which wealth is produced, divided and accumulated. Conversely, wealth brings together the means of accumulation that transform power relations in the long term.

The relations between states are a test of these states' respective strength. This is because there are no complete and coherent international rules for the distribution of global income and the factors of production. Any coordination that takes place is necessarily the result of negotiations. Such negotiation is continuous; disagreements can never be completely eliminated, since each actor in the international political game seeks to pass adjustment costs onto other actors. There

---

5   For an exposition of the defenders and avatars of this theory, see Charles P. Kindleberger, *International Money: A Collection of Essays*, Crows Nest: Allen and Unwin, 1981.

6   Robert Keohane, *After Hegemony: Cooperation and Discord in the World Political Economy*, Princeton, Princeton University Press, 1984. For an overall view of the research inspired by this intellectual current, which was very active in the late 1970s and early 1980s, see the collective book edited by Stephen D. Krasner, *International Regimes*, Ithaca: Cornell University, 1983.

is an international regime when the negotiation is given form by specific international institutions and rules which influence states' practices by altering their preference functions. According to the theory of hegemonic stability, the greater the dominance of one nation, the stronger this configuration will be, and the more will it lead to cooperative relations.

Antonio Gramsci elaborated a less 'materialist' version of hegemony.[7] His vision is a subtler one, because it rejects any mechanical link between material (hard) power and leadership. Of course, the hegemonic power must have a military force sufficient to protect the international relations over which it dominates. But that does not mean that global military domination is required. Rather, what is needed is some capacity to dissuade any hostile nation that might seek to use military force to influence any of the crucial attributes of this leadership to its advantage, such as it is exercised within its own sphere of influence.

Hegemonic stability also has a place for soft power. Soft power emphasises both the links between economic and material forces and those between ethical values and political representations. There is leadership when the dominant group's political orientation succeeds in legitimising the objective structure of its dominant position. It achieves this when it succeeds in making the rules that define the international regime – of which this power is the centre – recognised as universal principles.

So, an international order is only hegemonic if those subordinate to it voluntarily recognise the criteria that constitute it as such. This means that an order is only hegemonic if the subordinate find greater advantage in conforming to its principles than entering into conflict with them. Unlike imperialism, hegemony is a flexible mode of control that operates by way of intermediate international institutions and market financing. This ensures the hegemonic system the allegiance of elites in the subordinate states. If it is to secure this allegiance, the

7   Gramsci elaborates his theory of hegemony by distinguishing political society, which brings together the set of legal public institutions and deploys legitimate coercion (hard power), from civil society, which brings together cultural institutions that spread an ideology whose goal is to secure majority allegiance based on accepted values (soft power). He develops this theory of hegemony in his *Prison Notebooks*.

ruling group in the hegemonic nation must have a long-term vision and enough cohesion to allow it to sacrifice immediate economic gains for the stability of the international order.

Only a hegemonic system is capable of regulating a world economy that has great freedom of capital movements. But, if this is the case, then the international monetary system will enter into crisis when the key currency is no longer able to play this hegemonic role to the benefit of all the countries that accept a multilateral system of exchanges. The transition is accompanied by either the re-establishment of the key currency's prerogatives, or the emergence of another key currency. This was what happened in the interwar period, as the dollar came to replace the pound sterling. So, if the dollar becomes less able to fulfil international monetary functions and no other currency establishes itself in its stead, this can only mean a retreat for the freedom of capital movement.

Nonetheless, this is not the only possible reading of history. Certainly, the long-term structural changes since the Jamaica Accords have weakened the dollar's predominance at the political level. Great continental powers have emerged that are not in the orbit of US soft power, and whose prosperity instead depends on a system of multilateral exchanges. Moreover, we face natural resource scarcity and the further degradation of these resources under the threat of climate change. This means that this will be the century in which producing global public goods becomes an essential condition of numerous populations' survival. In this context, the relations between nations cannot only be considered in terms of conflicts of interest. A distinction must be drawn between irreducible conflicts of interest that lead to wars and the simple lack of coordination between nations whose interests are indeed compatible. In this book, we have advanced the hypothesis that international monetary problems are situated within this second perspective. If this is not the case, and the interests of the great powers are truly conflictual, then we will need to prepare ourselves for a new Cold War, which threatens to escalate out of control in a world of scarce natural resources.

The lack of coordination of the international system is its congenital flaw. It claims to be global and to promote freedom of exchange, and yet the production of this international public good is placed in

358 THE ENIGMA OF INTERNATIONAL CURRENCY

the hands of a single country. This is the very essence of the Triffin dilemma. There is no mutually accepted rule that would compel the dominant country to uphold the collective interest, when its dominant monetary position immunises its financial system against external influences.[8] This lack of coordination itself takes on a leading role when the disruption caused by the lack of coordination rebounds on the country that issues the key currency.

If the coming decades follow the same tendencies that the OECD has detected within the 'shifting wealth' process, then a cooperative multi-currency system could well emerge. The dollar would not be supplanted by some other key currency, but rather incorporated as the most important currency in a rule-governed multi-currency system forming an international monetary regime. This possibility demands that we analyse how international monetary regimes founded on cooperation can take form.

Cooperation and International Regimes

From the 1980s onwards, a current of thought called institutional liberalism developed in the United States.[9] It argued that the difficulties of cooperation in the international monetary domain owed to the obstacles formulated in theory. Establishing a viable regime without a hegemon requires a unanimously accepted form of ultimate liquidity which is not the debt of any single country. It also requires the construction an international payment system rules that produce symmetrical adjustments in balances of payments. Is it possible to use political means to organise an international regime that bears these characteristics?

Theorists of international monetary regimes identify three different states of relations among states: harmony, cooperation and discord.

Harmony is the postulate advanced by the doctrine of pure economics. It signifies a configuration in which national divides are

---

8   Eichengreen highlights the elements that radically distinguish the issuer of the key currency from other countries. In Chapter 7 of his book, he describes the scenarios that could lead to the destruction of the dollar's dominant role. See Eichengreen, *Exorbitant Privilege*.

9   Its main founders were Joseph Nye, Robert Keohane and Stephen Krasner. This current of thought was introduced to France by Gérard Kébadjian. See Gérard Kébadjian, *Théories de l'économie politique internationale*, Paris: Seuil, 1999.

irrelevant, and in which individual agents automatically realise their mutual objectives by acting in their self-interest. This is a market characterised by pure and perfect competition, extended across the whole world. In this case, the political is completely separated from the economic. Cooperation is neither required nor desirable. Money does not exist, or it is neutral.

Cooperation is a process of coordination among nation-states' policies. It involves mutual adjustments between the decisions taken by different states. Thus, if one state takes decisions that have harmful consequences on other states, their impact will be cushioned or counterbalanced to some degree by way of adjustments.

Discord is a situation in which states consider other states as obstacles to the fulfilment of their own objectives. As far as the means that it is able to mobilise allow this, each state unilaterally seeks to bend the policies of the other states in line with its own interests. When the nations embroiled in this configuration are of similar strength, attempts at unilateral influence meet with resistance. Conflicts result.

The adjustments necessary for overcoming discord and establishing cooperation may be indirect; they may be limited to preventing adverse consequences from rebounding upon itself. Such an attitude stems from a recognition of the interdependence that develops when financial integration intensifies. Explicit adjustments may also be made through negotiation, pressure and dissuasion – means by which one state incites others to take actions consistent with its own policy. This is a permanent negotiation, in which objectives are knocked back and forth within a compromise framework. *Cooperation thus emerges from a conflict which has been placed under control.*

It takes more than this to create an international regime. Such a regime requires a higher ethical principle to legitimise it. This latter must be able to establish a doctrine of international relations based on the equality among nations of whatever size or resources. This principle or set of values is a shared belief in what international relations ought to be. It must guide states' strategies, determining their norms of behaviour in terms of their rights and responsibilities. From these norms, which influence states' strategies, there derive rules that represent prescriptions or proscriptions for action. Here we pass from the level of strategy to that of operation. Finally, the decision-making procedures for day-to-day policy tactics must follow recognised and accepted principles, such that collectively-made decisions can be implemented.

For an international regime to exist, there must be international institutions autonomous of states that can create structural links between these four logical levels. It is these institutions that give an international regime its coherence. Nonetheless, international regimes are weak institutional structures, because they rarely have legislative grounding in an entente among sovereign states. They affect economic relations by way of interstate deals, and through their effect in reorienting national economic policies. International regimes do not represent the beginning of an international order that stands above nation-states. They do not found a new, universal principle of sovereignty. This is why we would better speak of a voluntary association of states than an international legal order.

Nonetheless, given its layered structure, an international regime is indeed an institutionalised form of cooperation. The governments that associate through it have made 'investments of form' that enable them to reach agreements with greater mutual advantages than could otherwise be achieved through *ad hoc* circumstantial cooperation. This is the case when international institutions provide common reference points to which states conform, even though these institutions do not in fact hold authority over states. This reduces the uncertainty surrounding other states' behaviour and allows for the mutual adaptation of states' practices.

International institutions reduce the qualitative uncertainty over states' behaviour in their relations with other states. In this institutional context, negotiations are better codified and their conclusions can be used at a later date, allowing for a collective learning process. The existence of this formal framework means that the rules underpinning the regime do not have to be renegotiated every time specific new problems come under scrutiny. International regimes can thus help states to anticipate a narrower range of behaviours, now that states have adhered to a common higher principle. Finally, the close links between the governments and officials of the partner countries in handling these procedures encourage expectations of good faith. There is thus less of a disruptive effect from moral hazard. Moreover, the reference to common principles establishes links between questions that otherwise belong to distinct domains. The expansion of the field of negotiations can bring about profitable agreements which would not have emerged if there were only fragmented and *ad hoc* negotiations covering a narrower terrain.

The robustness of an international regime thus depends on the density of the communications that it establishes between actors. Future cooperation is nourished by the experience of past cooperation, which preserves a strategic balance. This protects a model of appropriate action, even if the conditions are no longer the same as those that motivated the creation of the institutions concerned. Thus, the institutions created at Bretton Woods survived beyond the Bretton Woods system itself; they adapted by developing their functions.

What we still have to do is to get a sense of prospects for the future, using these tools of analysis to question the IMS's possible futures. First of all, we must get the measure of a monster. In creating the euro, Europe's leaders established the most demanding and ambitious international monetary regime that has thus far been invented. Unlike the monetary unions of the past, the euro has abolished national currencies. However, it has not been possible to build a supranational sovereignty, nor to construct an international regime with symmetrical adjustments, nor indeed to benefit from a system in which one hegemon openly assumes the leadership role.

The failure to develop the euro's potential is a major warning for the future of international monetary relations. This warning regards both the possibility of sharing the attributes of sovereignty and the role that the euro could play in a future IMS.

THE EURO: HOPES AND DISILLUSIONMENT

The euro is a legal tender that was created by the Maastricht Treaty in 1991 and voted through the parliaments of those countries who adopted it over the course of 1992. Our goal here is not to study the eurozone and its problems. Mountains of studies have been written on this subject, in which we have ourselves participated in several books. We deliberately included our reflection on the euro in this final chapter, dedicated to the future of international money. Rather than postulate that the euro is equivalent to a national currency, before analysing in what sense is not the case, we will advance the hypothesis that the eurozone is an economic space lacking an international monetary regime, and explore how far this regime differs from those that preceded it.

In What Sense Is the Euro an Incomplete Currency?

The Maastricht Treaty created an unprecedented international institution: namely, a central bank. The European Central Bank (ECB) is not placed under the authority of a source of sovereignty. We know that in democratic societies, sovereignty is conferred by a constitutional order that formalises the foundations of coexistence. In modern nations, this constitutional order is the inextricable foundation both the state's power and confidence in the money issued by the central bank. No such constitutional order exists in the eurozone. The euro is not, therefore, a fully functioning currency that unites citizens under the authority of a sovereign parliament, which in turn gives the central bank legitimacy through its organic relations with the state. In this fundamental sense, the euro truly is an international currency.

The lack of any organic link between the single currency and a political sovereign has very serious consequences. We are living in a common monetary space that does not also have a public space. It thus lacks the institutions that could give rise to a democratic life, as the source of coordination and collective decisions. The ECB cannot, in principle, be the lender of last resort for any member state's public debt. This downgrades the member states' public debts to the rank of private debts faced with the settlement obligation. Any eurozone country could default on its debt; as we have seen in the Greek case since 2010, it is as if the euro were a foreign currency for its own member states. The result is a fragmentation of the monetary space: a euro deposited in a Greek bank does not have the same value as a euro deposited in a French or German bank.

This fragmentation takes on dramatic proportions when an important part of the national public debts is held by economic agents who belong to other eurozone countries but are non-residents in the country concerned. When the crisis revealed that Greece was insolvent, the panic among private lenders also struck the public debts of the creditworthy states, since the Maastricht Treaty's *ukases* prevented the monetary authority from playing its role as lender of last resort. In establishing this prohibition, the Treaty could only exacerbate the national rivalries that would develop between creditor and debtor countries in conditions of crisis. These rivalries irreparably led to the fragmentation of the same financial space that the euro was supposed to unify. That is why both the Council of heads of state and government and the ECB found themselves backed into a corner. The situation demanded urgent *ad hoc* institutional responses that could make up for the lack of an organic link between the currency and the states, taking a policy of small steps punctuated by the events of the crisis.[10]

However, the eurozone is unlike the monetary unions that we can find throughout history, such as the Latin union founded in December 1865 and the Scandinavian union created in May 1873. Unlike in these cases, in the eurozone national currencies have disappeared. It follows that the payment system is completely unified. Finality of payment is realised across the whole eurozone through a higher stage of clearing and settlement among the national central banks. This takes place on the ECB's books, and is called the TARGET2 system. The result is that households and businesses' confidence in the euro has not collapsed. This is despite the fact that the financial space has effectively been fragmented by banks' retreat into their own national territories as a consequence of the crises in the public finances. It was the TARGET system that preserved the unity of the payment system in spite of the dysfunction of the interbank market.[11]

However, this took place at the operational level of the payment system. The euro's incompleteness at the political level has serious consequences for the eurozone in terms of its macroeconomic policy. Given that the euro is not placed under political sovereignty in the space in which it circulates, member states' economic policies do not

10   These so-called 'non-conventional' measures are described in chapters 1 and 2 of Michel Aglietta, *Europe: sortir de la crise et inventer l'avenir*, Paris: Michalon, 2014.
11   TARGET's crucial role in the eurozone financial crisis is described in detail by Philippine Cour-Thimann, 'Target balances and the crisis in the euro area', *CESifo Forum*, vol. 14, 2013.

364 THE ENIGMA OF INTERNATIONAL CURRENCY

make up a single unit. This prevents the eurozone as a whole from having a coherent macroeconomic policy. The restrictions imposed by the Maastricht Treaty prevent Europe's mediating authorities – the European Commission, the Eurogroup, and the European Parliament – from exercising appropriate governance over economic policies at the aggregate level. Since the eurozone is not sovereign, it has no budgetary policy and no external monetary policy. There follow three contradictory negatives that affect the credibility of the Council of eurozone governments: there is no federal budget under the authority of the European Parliament; there are no budget transfers between states; and there is no government default. These three imperatives are untenable in a situation of severe financial crisis. The result is the political threat of divisions within member states, with the rise of so-called 'sovereigntist' forces. Perhaps more seriously, the shortcomings of eurozone economic performance drive a slow erosion of support for the currency among the citizens of all member countries.

Why Is the Euro An Incomplete Currency?

The French economists who sincerely favour the strengthening of the eurozone argue, quite rightly, that what is needed is a strengthening of European institutions. We saw above that this is compatible with a solid international regime, even if this does not go as far as full and total federal sovereignty. We have characterised such a regime as a voluntary association of states who establish an institutionalised mode of cooperation. What the eurozone is most lacking is not a radical political leap, but the will or capacity to cooperate. All those who have reached this point of the argument come up against the same conclusion: Germany and France do not trust each other! But perhaps there are structural reasons why this is the case, which we must understand if we are to know if and how it is possible to surpass this obstacle.

The euro was not born under favourable auspices. The upheavals prompted by the fall of the Berlin Wall forced a hurried compromise. Chancellor Kohl wanted to get the international community to endorse a rapid unification of Germany. President Mitterrand was frightened by the prospect of future German power, and wanted to use currency as a means of binding Germany to Europe. The compromise reached was that Germany would be given free rein for reunification, but would also have to abandon the Deutsche Mark and accept monetary union. Yet while Germany nominally abandoned the Deutsche Mark, it did not abandon the monetary doctrine that had given it such prestige. In Chapter 4, we showed that this aura owed to the fine balancing act that made the monetary order the pivot of the social-market economy. The French republican tradition stands diametrically opposed to this worldview. Transferring this doctrine to the ECB and applying it to very disparate societies could only cause misunderstandings and mutual incomprehension as to how it was to be applied.

The ambiguity persisted through the episodes of political deadlock that cropped up over time. This was the reason why, when the eurozone was faced with the devastating shock of the financial crisis, it had neither the common means of action nor, most importantly, the foresight among its political leaders (or still less, the democratic legitimacy) to assert the long-term interests of the European project. One suggestion that emerged from political debates was that of the need for a social contract for Europe. This would mean recognising the existence of a common good to be preserved and nurtured. That would be possible if we first created the political foundations of coexistence, and thus the political foundations of the consciousness that we belong to one same community of fate. But one cannot create this consciousness, or this community, by decree. It is citizens who become conscious, or not, of their common fate. Both the overly bureaucratic common institutions, and the policies that the states themselves adopt towards Europe, however, elude any democratic control at the European level. Lobbyists interfere with their activity. Executives' political responsibility is non-existent, while the European Parliament is not invested with any sovereign authority.

As long as this situation continues, the eurozone will be no more than an international monetary system defined by an intergovernmental treaty. Instead of remaining content to oversee a straitjacket of rules that produce asymmetrical adjustments, it must develop an institutionalised mode of cooperation capable of delivering symmetrical adjustments.

In the compromise on which the euro was founded, the political transformations that a common currency implies were carefully left to one side. It was in this sense that France and Germany's opposing political inheritances conducted a dialogue of the deaf.

As we showed in Chapter 4 when we studied the different forms of democratic sovereignty, the conception of political sovereignty prevalent in Germany today proceeds from the ordoliberalism that was formalised in the Basic Law of 1948. This Law condenses the moral values that unite the German people. This is a juridical order that seeks to prevent the rise of any arbitrary power, whether this comes from the state by way of a parliamentary majority or from coalitions of private agents (oligopolies, cartels or lobbies). The state's economic role is far from minimalist, but it must inscribe its actions within the institutional framework of the market. This institutional framework is not simply an amalgamation of market mechanisms – and its keystone is money. Monetary stability is a constituent element of a social order that transcends politics.

In France, on the other hand, sovereignty is based on the republican principle that emerged from the Revolution. The National Assembly represents the people's sovereignty. While in Germany universal suffrage flows from law, in France it is universal suffrage that institutes law. That is why the nationalisation of the Bank of France in 1936 made it a state body. Only in 1994 did it change in status, making it a clone of the Bundesbank in anticipation of the euro's introduction. Yet there is still a great chasm between these two conceptions of sovereignty. And the principles of sovereignty are not negotiated like commodities, for they give juridical form to societies themselves. Citizens individually agree to respect the constitutional law that they have collectively established. This is why governments do not have the power to establish a common order through political compromise. Only a European constituent assembly could do so. That is why a federal European state is highly unlikely to come to pass.

We therefore need to take a different path in order to make the euro a complete currency. For want of a common principle of sovereignty, we can only make the euro work on the basis of a partial pooling of sovereignty, able to secure the acceptance of European mediation institutions. The idea would be to evolve away from an overbearing set of rules that paralyse economic policy and towards collective action in the macroeconomic and budgetary domains. If political governance were able to direct an aggregate budgetary policy, this would relieve a major uncertainty for the ECB. For otherwise it only knows *ex post* what the aggregate eurozone budget was! It could thus conduct a policy of constrained discretion within the framework of a *policy mix*, meaning it would not be forced to invoke exceptional circumstances like the threat of inflation.

Overcoming the Paralysis in the Interstate Governance of the European Council

Intergovernmentality does not allow the pursuit of a collective European interest. An intergovernmental form can only be a play of strategies among states each pursuing their own national interests. For in their reciprocal relations states can only express their particular interests. There tend to be endless negotiations that result in compromises concluded 'on the brink of the abyss'. These compromises are the source of divergent interpretations that revive controversy, mutual distrust and the search for further compromises. Indeed, the compromises reached are non-cooperative equilibria between the different stakeholders.

This is the domain of *ad hoc* negotiation. Such negotiation is highly inefficient in comparison with institutionalised cooperation. The latter sets negotiations within a common institutional framework that brings out a collective interest. Obviously, the difficulty here lies in negotiating even a minimal institutional reform that can introduce European mediation into interstate governance. As ECB board member Benoît Coeuré put it: 'We urgently need to abandon this intergovernmental process in favour of a democratically legitimate, shared decision-making process founded on votes.'[12] If such a shared decision-making process is to succeed, it must not be confused with an abandonment of national sovereignty. It is indeed possible for sovereign states to decide to cooperate, rather than simply to compete with one another! Cooperation brings shared responsibility, which in turn strengthens reciprocal confidence. The European mediation institution allowing for such cooperation would be a eurozone

---

12   Benoît Coeuré, 'Il faut un ministère des Finances de la zone euro', *Le Monde*, 28 July 2015.

'Treasury' placed under the supervision of the eurozone states in the European Parliament.

It is thus necessary to identify those processes whereby sovereign rights can be transferred to the supranational level, while at the same time leaving national democratic processes intact. More precisely, within the eurozone, it is necessary to set down a means of formalising in European law the institutions that would be able to coordinate the relevant economic policies. The European Union is a curious hybrid. Unlike in the case of a confederation of nations, in the EU there is a European competition law that prevails over national legislation. But unlike in the case of a federal state, there is no constitutional authority. This is why, in the domains where there is a priority of European law, this priority is not hierarchically established. Rather, it is conceived as a constitutional alliance that delegates limited powers to the Union. Since the Union has been recognised as having a legal personality, there is such a thing as European citizenship, but this is a weak form of citizenship in terms of political organisation. Is it nonetheless possible to push further on this point, and to extend the domain of shared sovereignty to the macroeconomic level?

The major obstacle to this project is the German Constitutional Court. Germany's Basic Law poses a problem for any bid to subordinate national law to European law. All European law has to conform to the constitutional principles of the German Basic Law. This doctrinal position is clearly opposed to any supremacy of European law over national laws. Indeed, the German Basic Law is without parallel. It includes an 'eternity clause' which states that two of the articles of the Basic Law cannot be violated by any legislative measure: Article 1, which stipulates that human dignity is inviolable, and Article 20, which affirms the principle of democratic rule.

We might not think that such principles would pose obstacles to the elaboration of a European constitution. But the Court takes an extraordinarily broad interpretation of the eternity clause, conferring immense power upon it. Its manner of conceiving of human dignity is stretched to the degree that it incorporates economic and political questions. The Court is obliged to uphold the Basic Law, and this commits it to maintaining that the Bundestag must preserve its legislative powers over every decision that concerns fiscal receipts and public spending.

So, we can understand what kind of legal imbroglio the advance towards political union might provoke. The Court may insist that a European law is not applicable in Germany, even though it is valid in European law and thus applicable in the other member states. This would destroy the uniformity that European law needs if it is to establish its legitimacy, and thus block the integration process itself. Such legal contradictions have already punctuated the small steps forward, retreats and hesitations of the German government since the beginning of the euro crisis.

If sharing sovereignty by legal means is blocked, it is still possible for the EU to explore shared sovereignty in the for of a public power. The European budget accounts for only 1 percent of the EU's GDP. It is thus incapable of taking any action to secure macroeconomic stabilisation. Public investment is neglected and no impulse is given to the private sector to help it break out of stagnant productive investment. Such are, however, the responsibilities of a common public power endowed with its own monetary space.

The EU should equip itself with a borrower and an investor of last resort. A European economy threatened with secular stagnation is urgently in need of a major borrowing and investment policy. The member states are not themselves able to take on this responsibility, caught up as they are in the European obligation to clean up their budgets. The combination of climate emergency and the threat of stagnation offers the EU countries the opportunity to develop a common policy able to feed investment across a vast terrain, ranging from energy to transport, renovating buildings and regenerating territory through the circular economy.

Whether this means establishing a European treasury or developing the existing European budget, the essential thing is to arrive at a fiscal union that stands above the banking union that is on its way to being realised today.

The Incompleteness of the Euro
A banking union, complemented by an eventual union of capital markets, would allow the unification of the European financial space. The euro could potentially have a unified government securities market on a scale, depth and liquidity equivalent to that of the dollar. Budgetary

union would allow for the issuance of Eurobonds that would compete with US Treasury bonds, and thus the constitution of the liquid market that any front-rank international currency must necessarily have.

As we know, even if the euro could challenge the dollar's claim to ultimate liquidity, this competition would not in itself constitute a system. For the exchange rate would tend towards indeterminacy. The interdependency of interest rates would be biunivocal and influenced by exchange volatility, unlike in the dollar-dominated system, where it is univocal. The essential trait of American unilateralism in the monetary domain, i.e. the absence of feedback effects from the disturbances that its policy inflicts on other countries, would disappear. The US establishment might then begin to understand that financial globalisation leads to disruptive interdependencies that can only be mastered through political multilateralism.

A Europe that had achieved political autonomy and that had the objective of preserving multilateralism could play a very useful mediating role in building the international monetary governance necessary to oversee a multiple-currency system. This would require that the eurozone adopt an external monetary policy. Thus far, it has never had such a policy, for this would directly concern the problem of sovereignty; the objectives of such a policy could not be decided by a central bank.

Europe still has to be able to play a major role in making the IMF the authority that organises international monetary coordination, which it had to abandon after the disappearance of the Bretton Woods system. Since the multi-currency system is structured by monetary regions, the representation of individual eurozone countries must give way to the representation of the eurozone as a single entity.

This reform would put an end to a grotesque anomaly. Currently, a set of countries that no longer have national currencies sit separately in the IMF general assembly, while the second-most international currency has no representative to speak in its name. The result is that the Europeans have no official capacity to take the initiative in the debate on how the IMS ought to develop. The solution would be a merger of the eurozone countries' quotas and associated voting rights. This would bring a double benefit. Firstly, it would give the eurozone considerable aggregate weight. Secondly, given that a merger does not mean a mere addition, it would free up a substantial proportion of the quotas, which could be redistributed across the rest of the world, so they might be redeployed in emerging countries.

THE LONG MARCH OF CHINESE CURRENCY INTO THE IMS

China's economic opening process is closely linked to the gradual changes that have been introduced in its economy. Its internal and external transformations interact in multiple ways, and each corresponds to its development strategy. Its opening up to the outside world was conceived in order to encourage the strong growth that the internal market alone could not provide. Opening up has both advantages and disadvantages for development. The Chinese remember the century of decline they suffered from 1840 onwards, as the Western powers opened China up by force.

The socialist revolution cut political ties with the West and reduced economic relations to a minimum. The Cultural Revolution which followed entrenched the country's isolation, which continued up until the diplomatic détente at the end of the Vietnam War. Hence, no decision to open up the country's economy could be taken lightly. Nonetheless, the Chinese reform did succeed in transforming the country. In less than thirty years, it changed it from a closed economy to a major global trading power. In 1970–71, China's total foreign trade (exports and imports) stood at the very low level of 5 percent of GDP. By 2005 this figure had risen to 65 percent, an astonishing statistic for a country of this size, and far higher than what we see in other continental countries.

The aspect of the reform that concerned 'opening up to the outside' took two paths, founded on two parallel regimes. The one path represented was a vertical and intra-industry export-processing trade regime encouraged by liberalised rules and the massive recourse to foreign direct investment (FDI).[13] The other path took the form of

---

13   'Process trade' refers to a specific type of insertion into the division of labour. Profiting from its young, large and disciplined working class, China created special economic zones to which it attracted large quantities of foreign direct investment. It imported all the supplies necessary for the production of industrial consumption goods, especially electronics, textiles and chemical products. Chinese labour did the assembly work, and then the commodities were sold on markets in Western countries.

an ordinary and relatively protected trade regime. This dual path, which allowed for the transformation of the Chinese production system, was planned to gradually melt into a market economy. This would reduce the importance of the planning system, before dissolving it into an open market economy. The transition from the planned economy to the market economy continued up until the second phase of the reform, launched in the mid-1990s. It was from this period onwards that currency began to become important to China's foreign relations. Up until that point, there was the dual exchange rate system that had been introduced in 1986 in order to stimulate process trade. It was in 1992, at the initiative of Deng Xiaoping, that China's foreign policy changed. In October 1992, the Chinese Communist Party's Fourteenth Congress adopted the principle of a socialist market economy. Markets would be extended to all sectors and the 'dual path' would be abandoned. In parallel to this, China's decision to apply to join the WTO propelled the country towards an open market economy.

THE CONTRIBUTION OF THE EXCHANGE RATE
TO CHINA'S OPENING UP (1995–2012)

The first important decision was the unification of the exchange rate system on 1 January 1994. The exchange rate was depreciated to the lowest level on the secondary markets, bringing a heavy devaluation of the official exchange rate relative to the dollar. In mid-1995, the rate was fixed for ten years at 8.3 yuan to the dollar (Figure 8.2). The Chinese government then decided to revise the exchange regime, instead mounting regular appreciations of the currency. This appreciation was only temporarily interrupted, at the very height of the global financial crisis. Free access to foreign currencies could be obtained upon presentation of documents attesting to commercial transactions. This *de facto* realised the convertibility of money on the current account. This phase of automatic appreciation (except in the period of acute financial crisis) was then replaced by variation within a tight band, between 6.1 and 6.3 yuan to the dollar.

The stability and then the predictability of the nominal exchange rate regime in a shifting economic context had a considerable impact

Figure 8.2

The renmibi's nominal exchange rate against
the dollar, and the effective real exchange rate

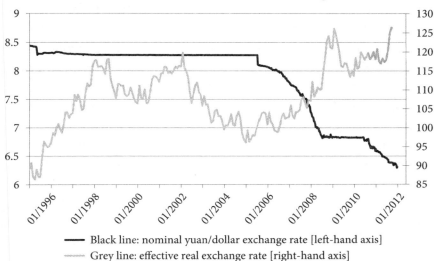

——— Black line: nominal yuan/dollar exchange rate [left-hand axis]
------- Grey line: effective real exchange rate [right-hand axis]

Source: CEIC.

on the real effective exchange rate, and thus on China's price competitiveness. Immediately after the unification of the exchange rates, Chinese prices were still absorbing the last traces of the enormous inflation of the late 1980s and early 1990s. At first China's competitiveness sharply deteriorated, falling by 20 per cent in two years. Then came the Asian crisis, which prompted heavy currency depreciation in the East Asian countries directly concerned. The Chinese government decided not to devalue the yuan, and in so doing agreed to a rise in the real effective exchange rate, in the name of monetary stability. This rate appreciated 10 percent further in a single year.

From late 1998 until China's entry into the WTO in 2001, competitiveness was the indirect result of fluctuations in the nominal exchange rates of its – above all Asian – competitor countries relative to the dollar. There followed two strongly contrasting periods which were closely linked to the exchange regime adopted by the Chinese government. From late 2001 until the change in the exchange regime in July 2005, China considerably benefited from the rise in its market share as a proportion of international trade. With the progress of intra-industry vertical trade (process trade), China became the 'workshop of the world'. And the sector of manufacturing industry brought increasing yields. The expansion of the world market for Chinese products led to a rapid rise in productivity. Given that manufacturing businesses could benefit from an infinitely elastic labour supply curve, wages did not increase as much as productivity did. Rising profits contributed considerably to financing capital accumulation, while prices remained stable. A circular process reinforced competitiveness, and this translated into very large trade surpluses. These developments were the Chinese-specific origin of the supposedly global imbalances that were used to force the Chinese government to appreciate its currency. In July 2005, it finally gave in to international pressure and returned to the creeping, informal revaluation of the yuan relative to the dollar.

This had a spectacular effect on China's price competitiveness. From mid-2005 to the end of 2011, the real effective exchange rate appreciated by 25 percent. While the trade balance did continue to expand up until the peak of the financial crisis in summer 2008, this in fact owed to the unsustainable bubble of demand fed by credit issued in the United States. When this ballooning credit capsized, prompting a violent contraction and then a slowdown in world trade relative to the prevalent tendencies in the pre-crisis period, China's trade surplus fell and the real effective exchange rate resumed its tendency to appreciate.[14]

The Debate on Global Imbalances and Its Consequences for China's Exchange Policy after the Crisis

Table 8.1 describes the structure of the worldwide savings–investment balance over the period in which the yuan tended to appreciate, up until the change of the exchange regime in late 2010. It shows that net savings in the United States remained negative over this whole period, while net savings in industrialised Asia as well as emerging Asia (including China) remained positive. In emerging Asia outside of China, this was the consequence of the 1997 Asian crisis. This crisis forced the governments of the affected countries to mount a radical

---

14　On the slowdown in world trade, see Sébastien Jean, Françoise Lemoine and CEPII, *L'Économie mondiale 2016*, Paris: La Découverte, 2015, pp. 87–102.

change in their growth policy, in order to get rid of their external debts and accumulate foreign currency reserves.

Up until 2004, China's current accounts surplus increased less than that of Japan or even other emerging and even industrialised countries. After this point, however, the Chinese surplus increased strongly as the real estate bubble ballooned in the United States. Between 2005 and 2008, China registered a savings surplus, and the United States an increasingly large deficit. Meanwhile the dollar depreciated, and the yuan appreciated, in real terms.

Table 8.1

Sources and uses of global savings. Net financial savings as a % of national or regional GDP

Country or region	Average for 1988–1995	1996–2003	2005	2007	2008	2009	2010
Advanced economies	– 0.7	– 0.3	– 1.0	– 0.8	– 1.3	– 0.7	– 0.3
USA	– 2.5	– 2.7	– 5.2	– 5.2	– 5.6	– 4.0	– 3.4
Eurozone (Germany)	n. d. (- 0.7)	+ 0.5 (- 0.1)	+ 0.8 (+ 6.4)	+ 0.8 (+ 10.4)	+ 0.1 (+ 9.9)	+ 0.1 (+ 6.8)	+ 0.7 (+ 7.9)
Japan	+ 2.3	+ 2.5	+ 3.6	+ 4.8	+ 3.2	+ 2.7	+ 3.1
Industrial Asia	+ 3.4	+ 4.1	+ 5.5	+ 6.4	+ 5.0	+ 8.6	+ 7.1
Developing and emerging countries	– 2.0	0.0	+ 4.1	+ 4.0	+ 3.5	+ 2.0	+ 1.6
Sub-Saharan Africa	– 0.9	– 2.3	– 0.3	+ 1.2	0.0	– 1.4	– 0.9
Latin America	– 1.2	– 2.5	+ 1.4	+ 0.1	– 1.2	– 0.6	– 1.3
Emerging countries in Asia (China)	– 2.4 (n. d.)	+ 1.4 (+ 2.6)	+ 4.1 (+ 7.1)	+ 6.9 (+ 10.6)	+ 5.8 (+ 9.6)	+ 4.1 (+ 6.0)	+ 3.0 (+ 4.7)
Central-Eastern Europe	– 1.4	– 3.2	– 5.1	– 8.1	– 7.8	– 2.4	– 3.7
Middle East	– 4.1	+ 3.8	+ 17.4	+ 15.3	+ 15.4	+ 3.5	+ 5.0
Russia and CIS	– 10.3	+ 4.7	+ 8.8	+ 4.0	+ 4.8	+ 2.8	+ 3.9

Source: IMF, World Economic Outlook, *October 2010 and earlier issues, Appendices. Table A16.*

Moreover, the United States wallowed in a deficit with respect not only to China, but almost every region of the world. The sole exceptions were the countries of Central and Eastern Europe. After the crisis, the US's deficit decreased somewhat, and the Chinese surpluses fell by more than half as a percentage of GDP. From 2010 onwards, Germany had easily the largest surplus among all countries.

In the mid-2000s, the fashionable explanation for all this was the overabundance of global savings. This explanation spread worldwide after Ben Bernanke's famous March 2005 speech. This reasoning was an intelligent way of sweeping aside the United States' responsibility and justifying the unilateralism of its policy. The Federal Reserve boss highlighted several independent factors that had encouraged savings in the rest of the world. For instance, in East Asia (except for Japan), the demographic structure had evolved in such a way as to increase the weight of strata with large numbers of savers (40–65 years of age). In China, this phenomenon was accentuated by the weak state of pension plans, driving a major turn towards savings as a precaution. Rises in the price of oil and gas stimulated savings in countries that exported raw materials (such as Russia and the Middle East). Countries with emerging markets undertook far-reaching policy changes in order to privilege a growth regime propelled by exports.

Identifying these excess savings, we might deduce that foreign investors continued to seek the attractive financial investments that the US financial system, presumed to be efficient – and this was indeed what people believed at the time – was happy to provide. This inflow of foreign savings pushed down long-term interest rates, produced a jump in real-estate prices, and encouraged American households to spend. In this view, the scale of the US's deficits meant that American households would act as consumers of last resort, in the name of global growth. Yet it is not at all true that there was an overabundance of savings in the world: IMF statistics show that global savings barely increased at all in the fifteen years leading up to the crisis.

Nonetheless, savings fell in the United States in the 2000s significantly more than they did in the other developed countries, with a few exceptions (UK, Ireland, Spain and Iceland) which had also experienced a long real estate bubble. In the second trimester of 2006, the net household savings rate in the United States fell to 1.5 percent of available income. In short, the main cause of the global imbalances came from the United States' economy. The pivot-currency status attached to the dollar was a condition that facilitated the persistence of financial polarisation. And it was no less a threat to the global economy.

The Management of the Yuan and the Accumulation of Exchange Reserves (2001–12)

In the 2000s, the conflict-ridden dollar semi-standard system that we studied in Chapter 7 was a one-way system. It left it up to the foreign central banks to absorb the overabundance of dollars discharged abroad by US residents' spending, which was far higher than their own country's production capacities. The People's Bank of China did this on a very considerable scale (Figure 8.3).

Figure 8.3

China's Exchange Reserves

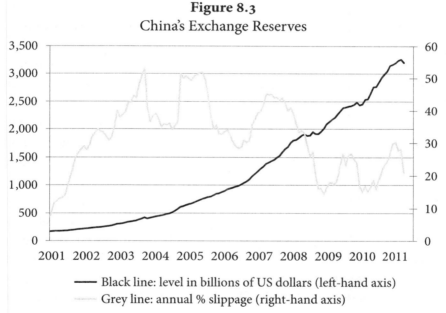

—— Black line: level in billions of US dollars (left-hand axis)
········ Grey line: annual % slippage (right-hand axis)

Source: Datastream. Groupama-AM calculations.

The regular appreciation of the yuan (by around 25 percent between July 2005 and December 2011) did not put the brakes on the accumulation of foreign exchange reserves over this period. On the contrary, it incentivised foreigners to buy up Chinese assets as much as controls on capital movements allowed. Moreover, the capital inflows that the central bank had to absorb were amplified by the rapid decline in the rate of Fed funds, which fell from 5.25 percent in August

2007 to 2 percent in mid-2008, and around 0 percent from September of that same year. In the United States itself, the Federal Reserve threw itself into a quantitative easing policy, flooding the planet with dollar liquidity. China's accumulation of reserves thus continued at an annual average rhythm of 40 percent, up until the recovery induced by the stimulus plan after May 2009. The pace of reserve accumulation significantly slowed and never recovered its previous rhythm, because the current account surplus had been considerably reduced.

After the crisis, capital controls became more porous, to the point of becoming the dominant factor in the accumulation of exchange reserves. The aggravation of the crisis in the second half of 2008 and the consequent fall in Chinese growth led to substantial outflows of volatile capital (hot money). After the launching of the stimulus plan and the rapid recovery for which it allowed, capital inflows resumed and had to be absorbed by an extra accumulation of reserves. The accumulation of currency reserves was thus partly disconnected from the balance of trade and even from the current account balance (Table 8.2).

The flows of volatile capital ('other' and unrecorded flows) had a considerable impact on the balance of payments. The latter was very sensitive to the uncoupling of the Chinese economy in 2009, which brought a reversal of the capital outflows that had taken place at the moment of the collapse in the final trimester of 2008. Capital flowed into China in order to profit from the expansion of asset markets induced by the stimulus plan. These inflows financed the stock market and the luxury real-estate market. When we compare the second half of 2008 to the second half of 2009, we see that the $120 billion fall in the balance of trade was more than compensated for by the $130 billion influx of volatile capital (hot money). This latter principally came from 'other' capital flows, essentially meaning short-term deposits and loans from the financial institutions of Hong Kong.

Given that China was becoming not only an economic power but a financial one as well, there was good reason to change the exchange rate management regime. In the short term, the Chinese government took the wise decision to suspend the nominal dollar peg. On 19 June 2010, the Chinese People's Bank announced that it was getting rid of

Table 8.2

China's Balance of Payments from 2008 to 2010
(in billions of dollars)

	2008		2009		2010	
Semester	S1	S2	S1	S2	S1	S2
Current account balance	191.7	244.4	134.5	162.6	124.2	179.7
Of which: Trade balance Capital revenues Current transfers	129.2 38.3 24.2	219.7 3.1 21.6	102.3 16.9 15.2	117.8 26.4 18.5	76.4 28.3 19.4	158.0 – 1.4 23.1
Capital account balance	70.3	– 54.4	59.6	81.2	87.5	60.7
Of which: Net foreign direct investment Net portfolio Others	40.8 19.8 9.7	53.6 22.8 – 130.8	15.6 20.2 23.9	18.7 18.5 44.0	37.0 – 7.3 57.8	63.5 31.3 35.9
Total balance	262.0	190.0	194.1	243.9	211.7	310.4
Errors and omissions	– 18.8	– 8.8	8.2	31.4	33.7	– 16.8
Exchange reserves	– 280.8	– 198.8	– 185.9	– 212.5	– 178.0	– 293.6

Source: CEIC.

this peg, and that it would instead be using a basket of currencies to serve as a reference point in a more flexible system of exchange rates. This decision heralded the gradual turn of the monetary policy framework towards national targets, as well as a first step towards yuan convertibility. The government has repeatedly decided on intraday fluctuation margins around the reference rates of ± 0.5 percent to ± 1.0 percent in May 2012 and ± 2 percent in March 2014. Moreover, the daily central rate and the band of rates that go with this do not constrain the central bank's action the following day. The central bank can determine the central rate as it wishes each day. That is what happened on 11 August 2014, creating a great deal of commotion in the international financial community. The Chinese People's Bank published a report announcing that, henceforth, the next day's reference exchange rate would depend on the rate upon the market's close the previous day. This would, moreover, be linked to the conditions of supply and demand on the interbank market, as well as the evolution of the exchange rates that counted for most in the basket of currencies determining the yuan's effective exchange rate. This prompted an immediate depreciation of 1.9 percent. This change of procedure was justified by the concern to put forward a central parity that was more guided by the market. This meant creating greater exchange volatility in order to suppress the one-way speculation and counter the effects of the depreciation of emerging countries' currencies. These technical measures made up part of the wider perspective of the yuan's gradual evolution towards convertibility.

First Steps in the Internationalisation of the Yuan

The financial crisis that struck the world in 2008 accelerated the changes already at work in the global economy. This crisis redefined China's economic and financial relations with the rest of the world. A long-term structural change is evident: an increasing proportion of China's trade concerns emerging markets in developing countries in Asia and the rest of the world, while its trade with Japan and the West has become relatively less important. In the 2000s, Chinese trade with the emerging world doubled from 15 to 30 percent of its total foreign trade. The dollar serves as a third currency for this type of exchange. It is only the chosen vehicle for the invoicing and settlement of exchanges if the transaction costs linked to using the dollar (which implies two conversions between the trade partners) are less than they would be if either of the two partners' own currency were used. Transaction costs can indeed be lower when a vehicle currency is used: this question essentially depends on the market liquidity of the currency to which the partners have access.

However, in 2008 dollar liquidity collapsed worldwide, and interbank credit suddenly dried up. The shortage of international means of payment prompted a sudden collapse, which hit global trade hard. This led to a major contraction in economic activity even in countries like China that were not caught up in Wall Street's financial storm. A shock of this scale was able to turn the system of international payments upside down. For example, a Chinese importer and a Brazilian exporter could find an advantage in invoicing and settling a transaction in yuan, as long as the yuan deposits resulting from the payment for the imports into China offered a competitive yield before being recycled in the payment for the import of Chinese products into Brazil. But the Chinese money market was closed to non-residents, with the exception of a handful of qualified foreign investors. So it was necessary that financial assets in yuan, including deposit accounts, should become available to non-residents outside of the continental Chinese monetary space. Hong Kong was the ideal financial hub to manage the financial services ensuing from the development of this embryonic offshore yuan.

The pilot system for invoicing and settling foreign trade in yuan was launched at the Hong Kong financial centre in 2009. It was based on a protocol between the Chinese People's Bank and the Hong Kong Monetary Authority, an agreement to guarantee and regulate liquidity. Non-financial companies and non-residential financial institutions were allowed to open yuan accounts at accredited Hong Kong deposit institutions, even if they were not directly involved in trade with continental China. This was the opening of the CNH (Chinese Yuan Hong Kong) market: the market of financial assets in offshore yuan.

In 2011, capital controls set up barriers to arbitrage between the offshore and onshore yuan: there was a dual exchange rate. Given that the offshore market had limited liquidity, the offshore exchange rate had a liquidity premium. This created an appreciation of around 2 percent over the onshore exchange rate. But the European crisis at the end of 2011 brought volatility in this premium. When worries over the euro's future prompted capital invested around the world to retreat to the US bonds market, this premium collapsed. This brought a sharp rise in the dollar. The same phenomenon took place in May 2013 when the Fed announced that it would soon be stopping its asset-buying policy, and again in summer 2014 with the worries produced by the rise in the Federal Reserve's policy interest rate. By 2015 these events led the new Chinese leadership, headed by Xi Jinping, to accelerate the move towards convertibility.

Financial Liberalisation and the Internationalisation of the Yuan

The internationalisation of the yuan makes up part of China's overall policy of opening to the outside world and liberalising its economic and financial system. This long-term strategy was formulated in the directives of the PCC Central Committee in November 2013 and approved by the National People's Congress in its March 2014 session.

In the new phase of the Chinese economic reform, financial liberalisation has become an immediate priority. It links the transformations being pursued in China's domestic economy and the transformations it seeks in its international relations. What is important for China, here, is to reduce resistance to structural change by eliminating the distortions in capital allocation caused by the collusion between the big banks and the big state enterprises. These distortions owe to financing conditions that discriminate in favour of these latter. Such a change proceeds by way of a liberalisation of interest rates, enacted in order to force financial institutions to evaluate their risks correctly. This involves the introduction of private capital into the ownership of state enterprises and the development of a multiplicity of forms of finance, designed to encourage the rise of an innovative private sector. All this implies the need to develop financial asset markets.

The second priority is to promote the yuan to the level of an international reserve currency by 2020, thus making it fully convertible. This priority forms part of China's shifting geopolitical strategy. During the high-growth period in which China was the 'workshop of the world', its key means of asserting itself internationally was to expand its trade. Yet today it is rearranging its economy with a view to the enrichment of its middle classes, the development of diversified consumption habits, and the promotion of innovation, enabling it to achieve global standards. All this will mean a transformation of China's international relations. The government is offering incentives to businesses to cast their nets abroad in order to assimilate the most advanced management practices and technologies, and thus to become global actors. This goal proceeds by way of capital exports and entering the stock exchanges in all the world's financial centres. Moreover, the Chinese government has made clear its desire to exercise an international financial influence. This will be an instrument for the commercial and financial integration of East Asia around the Chinese economy; for guaranteeing the supply of basic products; and for overseeing trade with Europe by way of the 'Silk Road'. The creation of the various banks for financing infrastructure, including banks dedicated to the Silk Road, as well as the BRIC bank, demonstrate China's desire to pursue a financial strategy that has global influence over the world economy.

This is the reason why this phase of reform, designed to re-establish China's historic place in the world – the position enjoyed by the Middle Kingdom – implies decoupling the yuan from the dollar. The Thirteenth Five Year Plan will draw out the roadmap for leading the yuan to full convertibility in 2020. The drive towards convertibility is strongly supported by the central bank. Indeed, the liberalisation of China's internal markets has changed the state's role with regard to finance. While it formerly exercised a direct influence, by fixing interest rates and making injunctions to banks to establish to whom and how much they were lending, This now makes way for an indirect influence at both the prudential and monetary levels. The structure of interest rates will, however, need some nominal anchoring, given that they will no longer be directly determined. This implies the need for the central bank to acquire a degree of autonomy, enabling it to conduct monetary policy in accordance with domestic macroeconomic objectives. The yuan must therefore decouple from the dollar and become a fully functioning international currency.

The yuan is thus on the way to becoming a global currency. The most recent stage of this advance came at the end of November 2015, with its inclusion in the basket that makes up the SDR. With a more flexible exchange rate and an open current account, China will no longer have to accumulate dollar reserves. Beyond the disruption of the summer of 2015, which resulted from China's inevitably jerky adjustment to financial openness – as was the case in all the countries that liberalised their financial systems before it – as economic reform progresses, the yuan will become a reserve currency. The IMF will be driven to give the yuan official validation as it develops its statutes, leading it to attribute more weight to emerging countries in its decision-making bodies. After the failure of the reform initiative in 2010, this is the *sine qua non* condition for the IMF's ability to recover the legitimacy it has lost. It is in view of this that we should try to understand the key guidelines of the future development of the IMS.

POSSIBLE TRANSFORMATIONS OF THE IMS

The twin problems of international liquidity and adjusting balances of payments cannot be solved when there is no hegemonic power capable of acting in the collective interest. This form of organising international relations must therefore recede into history. In the seventeenth century, this was the fate of the dualist system mediated by the Italian bankers, which was replaced by the hegemonic banking system founded on Bank of England.

In this early phase of the twenty-first century, the stability of the global economy is threatened by the decline of the dollar's hegemony. When liquidity becomes anarchic and indebtedness is allowed to grow indefinitely, the hegemonic power becomes unable to deliver the collective good of international adjustment. Its hegemony thus becomes dangerous. We can interpret this phenomenon in terms of the theory of the ambivalence of money, by generalising this theory to the global level. The weight of debts increases without relent when the continual issuance of liquidity allows these debts never to be settled. The hierarchically organised monetary system that backs up confidence in money thus instead degrades into a homogeneous system. In a world of free capital movements, the tension between collective rules on payments and the private desire to appropriate liquidity plays out at the global level. Indeed, the monetary hierarchy must have a higher stage at the international level. We have already seen that historically the key currency has constituted this stage, in the form of the sterling standard and then the dollar standard. Yet the latter is dysfunctional: it has begun to transform into a homogeneous system. Logically, a homogeneous system will produce a generalised inflation. We should not be misled by the particularly low prices of goods and services. The error, here, is to forget that the characteristics of financial globalisation have transferred inflation onto asset markets. We ought to be concerned by the anomaly that after a major financial crisis, the price of financial assets – whether debt titles or shares – has increased relentlessly after the initial fall following the crash, which was quickly reversed by the flood of liquidity. Worse still, this homogeneous-system logic has generalised to the emerging countries.

At the global level, this dysfunction is amplified by the growing disjunction between the United States' relative economic decline and its continuing monetary and financial supremacy. With the dollar semi-standard, the implicit dollar zone covers around 60 percent of world GDP and population, even though the US represents only 23 percent of world GDP and 12 percent of international trade. What is more, the United States' share of outstanding international investments has fallen to 24 percent, even as US investment funds administer 55 percent of institutionally managed international assets.[15] This means that the basis for the creation of the value monetised at the global level is increasingly disconnected from the currency that operates the circulation of this value. Consequently, the costs of the dollar's domination for the countries that accept it have begun to outweigh the advantages of the coordination it effects.

As a result of this divorce, asset prices and capital movements are subject to gigantic fluctuations in the very countries that have attached themselves to the dollar in the hope of securing stability. We have reached the point where the anticipation of a tiny increase in the Fed's policy rate will affect $9 trillion of debts and deposits, because the network of international banks and shadow banking is not content to redistribute the Fed's liquidity injections. Rather, it amplifies them out of all proportion in the wholesale liquidity market. The offshore dollar market has doubled in size since 2007.

The vulnerabilities created by this wholesale market create systemic risk, which is aggravated by the overlapping of shadow banking and the banking system. This risk arises through the intensification of a purely financial leverage that is incorporated into forms of liquidity creation outside of the creation of banking money.[16] The banks use shadow banking to increase leverage and to circumvent regulations on capital and liquidity, creating *ad hoc* structures to attract money market funds. These off–balance sheet structures relend liquidities, either to the banks who sponsor them or to investment funds seeking

15   Patrick Foulis, 'The sticky superpower', Special report on the world economy, *Economist*, 3 October 2015.
16   Derivatives in the form of repos and loans on securities, tripartite swaps, the securitisation of derivatives products, and leveraged ETFs (Exchange Traded Funds).

speculative arbitrage on financial markets around the world. This circulation of liquidity for speculative purposes leads to violent capital inflows and refluxes in the emerging countries. We are seeing these movements, which can destabilise entire economies, take place increasingly frequently.

The question posed, then, is the following: how long will sovereign countries link their finances to a currency issuer whose political system is undermined by partisan fragmentation, and which increasingly uses its financial power as a political instrument? If we think that the world is evolving towards polycentrism and away from a key currency system, then we would search in vain for any substitute for the dollar. The alternatives are either a retreat of financial globalisation – and history has repeatedly seen this before – or the transcendence of the key currency system. In the latter case, we face the following question: how can we envisage the higher stage of money at the global level in the absence of a universal sovereignty to legitimise it?

Answering this question demands that we look back over the terrain already prepared by Keynes, in order to spell out the proposals capable of advancing multilateral cooperation. We showed earlier that approaches that proceed by way of negotiating *ad hoc* political compromises will fall short due to their lack of institutionalisation. If we are to get beyond these aporias, it is necessary to establish regulatory institutions capable of preserving decentralised behaviours in a global economy. Indeed, this is an economy in which there is an increasingly diversified set of interdependencies, as regions previously on the edges of the international game now converge with it. Bretton Woods lasted for a quarter of a century because negotiations could make use of an institutional framework that had been legitimised by treaty. But the system declined because its rules ossified. This prevented it from being able to maintain the flexibility necessary for a cooperative approach in the face of a variety of economic conjunctures. As for our own time, there is no need to create the site of institutionalisation: it already exists. The IMF must recover the monetary role it lost after the Jamaica Accords, and become a body capable of resolving sovereign debt crises. *The IMF must again become the governing body of an international monetary regime.*

Let us recall the essential properties of an international regime. Such a regime articulates principles, rules and procedures for maintaining permanent coordination.[17] Its principles are those of multilateral exchange that emerged from the Bretton Woods framework. In the twenty-first century, these principles include the recognition of the need to produce global public goods. These principles legitimise both cooperation as an aim and the need for this cooperation to be continuous. Its rules are the orientations and the constraints guiding the mutual commitments that governments sign up to, meaning that the influences countries exert on one another are internalised in the policies pursued. The procedures of an international regime are the means of action, information and oversight through which the institution that mediates multilateral governance facilitates the application of the rules and defuses potential conflicts.

Institutionalised Cooperation: A Compromise for an International Monetary Regime

The deep globalisation that results from the complete integration of capital markets is incompatible with the diversity among nations' social preferences that we see in a multipolar world. In a multicurrency system, flexible exchange rates cannot establish market equilibrium prices to adjust these preferences. For the competition between currencies confronts international liquidity's character as a public good. In these conditions, the quasi-homogeneous system that the IMS has become, now that it is flooded with an overabundance of dollars, can turn into its opposite. That is to say, it can become a fragmented system of national currencies or groups of national currencies, whose competition over international liquidity must be restrained if we are to avoid exchange rate indeterminacy.

Destabilising financial dynamics, expressed in global financial imbalances, were an essential factor in the build-up of vulnerabilities that led to the systemic crisis. It follows that international financial regulation must be a major pillar of any reform. This regulation must include capital controls, in order to deflect the most harmful effects of the financial excesses that will inevitably reappear despite even the

---

17   Benjamin J. Cohen presents the theory of international monetary regimes in Krasner (1983), *International Regimes*.

most demanding prudential rules. This implies a need for compromise agreements over the system's institutional framework.

The first compromise is based on the tendencies towards the regional integration of international trade. It is possible to institutionalise zones of monetary cooperation on the basis of these tendencies, with each zone based on the currency that is preponderant in that region. These zones could have a considerable sphere of influence. As well as the dollar – whose zone of preference extends across a large part of the Americas – there are two currencies that have the stature of dominant regional currencies. These are the euro, whose influence could extend across the Mediterranean and the Middle East, and the yuan, as a pivot money for East Asia. Such forms of regional monetary cooperation should include solidarity in providing emergency financing in the face of external financial shocks. This will make it possible to reduce the need for countries to self-insure by accumulating dollar reserves.

These spaces of monetary cooperation would introduce a principle of subsidiarity, in a two-level IMS. Many financial shocks could be absorbed within the framework of regional monetary arrangements. At a higher level, the negotiation of international monetary rules would involve a reduced number of partners, each representing a group of countries. This negotiating structure would make acceptable compromises more achievable, for the recognition of the mutual influences between large zones would reduce the incentive for freeriding.

The second compromise involves strengthening financial regulations and making them mutually compatible. This is an immense task, and one which financial lobbies continue to challenge. It has already been undertaken within the framework of the Basel III negotiations, under the aegis of the committee of G20 central bankers. This reinforced prudential regulation brings together many different elements. The first is the need to impose order on shadow banking, without which it is impossible to establish any financial stability. The second is the creation of macroprudential regulation compatible across the big central banks. This includes a counter-cyclical regulation of the capital and liquidity ratios of financial institutions of systemic influence, whether banks or otherwise. Systemic risk boards should be set up in all international financial centres, tasked with blocking any build-up of speculation on credit and asset prices. The 'too big to fail' syndrome must be eradicated through predefined compulsory restructuring procedures for fragile financial bodies, and there should be an absorption of any eventual losses by their creditors. The third element is a transformation of central banks' monetary doctrine, which must put financial stability on the same footing as price stability in the conduct of monetary policy. For the moment, this condition has not been realised. We see this in the return to excessive volatility in the global financial markets, which central banks do not seem able to get a handle on, and instead feed via their asset purchase policy.

Finally, the third compromise is the construction of an international form of monetary governance appropriate to a multi-currency system. The G20 could be a promising forum in this domain, if it contributed to strengthening the legitimate international monetary authorities. It has indeed already begun to play a positive role in this regard, for it has decided to considerably increase the IMF's resources and to broaden its tasks. In transforming the Basel Financial Stability Forum into a Financial Stability Board, and widening the participation therein, it has opened the way to closer collaboration among central banks in promoting macroprudential regulation that follows common principles. But more is needed. The IMF is the only institution with the necessary legitimacy and expertise to control the aggregate credit in the world economy, to detect the germs of systemic risk in international financial interdependency, and to analyse and supervise the channels through which financial fragility is transmitted. The IMF must rediscover its central role in international monetary governance, in the spirit of Bretton Woods.

For an IMS with More Symmetrical Adjustments

Transforming international monetary relations in the direction of an institutionalised cooperation framework is one of the necessary responses to the financial instability endemic to globalised finance. These developments would change political attitudes with regard to interdependence and provide an apprenticeship in international cooperation in the macroeconomic and financial domains. Moreover, possible competitor currencies to the dollar, like the euro and the yuan, could expand their field of attraction if the structural problems of China and the eurozone could be properly overcome. At Bretton Woods, the United States' political and monetary domination prevented the formation of a system able to deal with the problems of adjusting balances of payments and endowing the world with a fully international liquidity. By around 2020, that dominant position will stand still more at odds with the United States' declining economic weight. The US will no longer be immunised against financial shocks and economic fluctuations in the rest of the world. When this point arrives, it will become possible to envisage a substantial reform in international monetary governance. With regard to the adjustment of the balances of payments, the important thing is to prevent the repercussions that result when unilateral economic policies like the Fed's monetary policy propagate shocks. Since the Jamaica Accords, long-term exchange rate cycles have amplified these repercussions rather than cushioned them. This is because such cycles have facilitated the pursuit of destabilising credit policies in the United States, which have in turn been amplified at the global level by the international banking lobby.

We can envisage two rules for re-establishing symmetrical adjustment within a multilateral consultation framework. Without such a framework, nothing is possible. One of these rules is an adjustment by prices – in other words, by the ordered variation of exchange rates. The other is an adjustment through capital flows that preserves the sustainability of balances of payments over time, avoiding the intensification of global financial disequilibria like the ones we saw in the 2000s.

This first adjustment involves the co-management of floating exchange rates on the basis of reference exchange rates, following the method proposed by John Williamson back in the 1980s.[18] This is a flexible method appropriate to detecting long-term distortions in real exchange rates. It is compatible with the multilateral surveillance mission that the G20 has assigned to the IMF. These are not target rates with margins of fluctuation, which would mean corridors that

18   John Williamson and Marcus Miller, *Targets and Indicators: A Blueprint for the International Coordination of Economic Policy*, Policy Analysis in International Economics, no. 22. Washington, DC: Institute for International Economics, 1987.

limit the variation of exchange rates. Rather, they are bearings for the IMF's multilateral surveillance and for periodic consultation forums within the IMF framework, which would be staged by the member countries with the greatest political responsibility.

These reference exchange rates and the associated stabilisation mechanisms must above all facilitate growth in the developing countries that the OECD categorises as 'converging' countries. They must allow previously fragile countries to enter this group. Purchasing power parity (PPP) is a very poor guide for estimating real exchange rates. The exchange rates of converging countries, whose growth owes to a rapid increase in productivity in their manufacturing industries, are bound to be underestimated relative to PPP. The reference real exchange rate is an increasing function of the ratio between the GDP per capita of the country concerned and the leading country. It regularly appreciates as the gap in GDP per capita closes. This is the trajectory that China followed between 2005 and 2014, and Japan and Korea before it.

The other method for guiding adjustments is to make use of reference current balances. This method would consist of adopting and adapting the work the C20 carried out in its abortive attempt to reform the Bretton Woods system.[19] This method consists of estimating the investment requirements necessary to sustaining the capital growth compatible with the long-term trajectory of countries' potential growth. It must also analyse the structural differences between countries' savings rates, following a single homogeneous method. Only the IMF can devote itself to such an investigation; and indeed, it already does so on a bi-annual basis, albeit without this leading to any consultation among the member countries. The current balances that result from the structural investment–savings balance would then be adjusted by taking into account conjunctural variations in production capacity utilisation rates and the degree to which inflation deviates from countries' target levels. We would then end up with reference current balances, to be included among the indicators for multilateral surveillance.

19   The C20's work is expounded in Williamson, *The Failure of World Monetary Reform, 1971–1974.*

Promotion of SDR as an International Ultimate Liquidity

It is only possible to re-establish symmetrical adjustments by creating an ultimate liquidity into which all important currencies are convertible, and which is at the same time a flexible-supply fiduciary money. This money already exists potentially, even if it has been deliberately neutralised. This money is Special Drawing Rights (SDR). SDR is an allowance within a specific department of the IMF. It is not an engagement by any financial institution any more than was monetised gold. So it is not debt, but a purely fiduciary asset. SDR opens up a right of credit in any currency, which can be fully utilised by any IMF member. When an IMF member sells SDR in order to buy a currency, this creates a credit in SDR for the buyer who is counterparty to the transaction. This credit is compensated by a mirroring debt written up in the IMF's own SDR department. Following their reciprocal transactions, the IMF member countries will have net debts or credits with the SDR department, depending on whether their SDR holdings are higher or lower than their allocation. These net credits and debts yield market interest rates.

There are three good reasons further to develop the SDR. The first is to make up for the disadvantages of the dollar semi-standard by reducing the incentives for central banks whose currencies are weakly convertible to buy up dollars as self-insurance. The second is to allocate sufficient amounts of SDR to avoid fluctuations between the excess or lack of dollars, such as would rebound on exchange rates. Achieved with the aid of a collectively-agreed issuance rule, this could resolve the Triffin dilemma. If the issuance rule is counter-cyclical, this will make the IMF an embryonic international lender of last resort. The third reason to develop the SDR is to create a substitution account within the IMF that would allow countries overloaded with dollar reserves to diversify them in an ordered way, without having to pass through the exchange markets, and thus without risking prompting the kind of fluctuations in exchange rates that are liable to spark monetary crises.[20]

20 When the substitution account was seriously envisaged in 1979, the IMF director's advisor Jacques Polak made a reasoned appeal for SDR to be put at the centre of the IMS. See Jacques Polak, 'Thoughts on an IMF based fully on SDR', Pamphlet Series, no. 28, International Monetary Fund, 1979.

The SDR's current role is very modest, since it has been artificially constrained by its conditions of usage. This is because the US government, and above all, Congress, want to prevent it from overshadowing the dollar. Moreover, the allocations are made according to quotas that date back to 1944! Consequently, the countries that are most in need of SDRs are also those that receive the least; only 3 percent of the total allocated is assigned to low-income countries. There have only been three allocations since the SDR's creation in 1968. The first one in 1971–72 amounted to 9 billion, the second one in 1979–81 amounted to 12 billion, and finally the third one in 2009, right in the middle of the financial crisis, amounted to 182 billion. A quite different mechanism would be needed to make the SDR the world's ultimate reserve asset: this would require allocations of 150–250 billion a year. These could be constant, or ideally, counter-cyclical. SDR transfers should become the IMF's only financing mechanism. The quotas should be significantly altered in order to represent developing countries on an equitable footing. A rule for the continuous allocation of SDRs as an international ultimate liquidity could gradually be reformed into a rule for the issuance of an endogenous money. The SDR would lose its status as a basket of currencies and instead become the unit of account in which national currencies are defined.

What are central banks currently doing with the SDRs allocated to their countries? For some of them, they constitute a passive reserve that can become a means of financing in periods of crisis. Others use them to repay the country's debts to the IMF. Yet others are intermediaries – a sort of market makers – who buy and sell SDRs in order to accommodate the needs of their counterparts. Finally, others make their allocation of SDRs into a diversification asset.

There is no technical obstacle to making the SDR the reserve asset for a symmetrical multi-currency IMS, in which the SDR replaces the key currency as the universal ultimate liquidity. If governments do indeed want to pursue the adventure of economic globalisation, it is necessary – and sufficient – that they become conscious of their political responsibility. But there is another function that needs taking on: namely, the emergency financing of balances of payments when the repercussions of uncontrolled disequilibria activate systemic risk.

Someone has to fulfil the function of an international lender of last resort. After the series of crises in the 'emerging' countries between 1994 and 2001, the IMF created a certain number of emergency credit lines, albeit without success. No country stepped forward to take advantage of this. It was the Fed itself that played this role, with the bilateral swaps used by Mexico, Korea, Singapore and Brazil during their respective crises.

The IMF made two further unsuccessful attempts to render its means of finance more flexible. These were the introduction of the Flexible Credit Line in March 2009, and the Precautionary Credit Line in August 2010. It is not too difficult to see why this did not work. These credit facilities were coupled with structural conditions (including solid fundamentals and intrusion into the countries' domestic policies). This was an utter negation of lending in the last resort. For the latter refers to an injection of liquidity that everyone accepts in order to avoid a systemic crisis causing the implosion of the endangered countries' financial systems, or even – as we saw in the autumn of 2008 – threatening to bring down the whole international financial system. Moreover, financing lines of credit takes time, because it operates by way of central banks making loans in convertible currencies – and these loans have to be accepted by governments. Conversely, the coverage for last-resort liquidity needs to be instantaneous. This is not at all inflationary, for last-resort money creation exists in order to counter the deflation caused by the shortage of liquidity. Moreover, the new SDRs created would in any case be cancelled out when the loans are repaid.

The only effective solution is a multilateral last-resort financing mechanism, self-financed by the IMF through an *ex nihilo* creation of SDRs. This would set the IMF, as international lender of last resort, within the same logic as central banks in their role as national lenders of last resort. This is the only way to avoid a generalisation of self-insurance – a behaviour which feeds persistent instability in the balances of payments. Moreover, the SDRs that are issued thanks to allocations-by-quota, but which countries do not use, could usefully be deployed to lend to countries that have unsatisfied liquidity needs. In this sense, they could serve as a counter-cyclical financing instrument.

IMF Governance

If SDRs were developed in these ways, the multi-currency system would become coherent, thanks to its basis in a fully international reserve and settlement asset. All member countries could unconditionally make use of a drawing facility, up to a certain limit. The IMF would become the source of a collective insurance, which would resolve the Triffin dilemma. This would also mark a great step towards eliminating the iniquities that deliberately hold back numerous countries' convergence in order to preserve the privileges enjoyed by Western countries.

If IMF reform did go this far, there would be no reason to maintain the historic separation between the general resources department and the SDR department within the Fund. This separation only exists in order to prevent SDR from becoming a true international currency. The merger of these two departments is indispensable if the IMF is to become a monetary actor again. As for quotas, these should no longer be rigid distribution criteria, but instead simple indicators of limits on indebtedness.

This transformation of the IMS will take place over the long term. It will become the mode of monetary regulation compatible with the current transformation of the world economy, under the effect of forces that are redistributing wealth and power between countries. The IMF can only become the central institution of international monetary governance if it stops the Western countries monopolising its powers.[21] If it is to assume the dual mission of preventing discordance in macroeconomic policies and maintaining oversight over the common factors for financial instability, the IMF must broaden its

---

21   One recent, and indeed spectacular, consequence of this anomaly accompanied the US Congress's refusal to ratify the increase in the Fund's capital, decided by the IMF general assembly four years earlier. This move sought to double the Fund's quotas in order to give the emerging countries a larger place in international governance. This was an extremely serious affront to the G20 and the US government itself. It is difficult to see any better example of how the advance of international relations is thwarted by the very country that is supposed to be the international leader. The same aggressive and discriminatory attitude again emerged when Congress expressed its hostility to the yuan being included in the SDR currency basket. Nonetheless, the IMF did end up including the yuan in this basket in November 2015.

political base. This will entail a profound change in the distribution of power and responsibilities among its member countries. It must considerably increase the political weight of non-Western countries and strengthen the political support of its executive director.

Substantial revisions of the quotas, extending far beyond the homeopathic changes accepted thus far, are indispensable if the IMF is to become the institution that ensures the monetary regulation of the international financial system. The criteria employed to define these quotas and the associated voting rights must definitively and totally abandon the heritage of the negotiating parties and alliances that were powerful in 1944. This inheritance must be replaced by an objective formula based exclusively on economic and financial factors.

Since the multi-currency system is structured by regions, As we argued above, the individual representation of the eurozone countries must give way to the representation of the eurozone as a single body. Another necessary change is to amend the blocking-minority threshold that defines the qualified majority necessary to take decisions that alter the Fund's statutes. This qualified majority level currently stands at 87.5 percent. This was calculated at Bretton Woods in order to allow the United States to arrogate a blocking-minority vote to itself, allowing it alone to veto decisions. This arrangement is politically intolerable and economically anachronistic.

Finally, if the Fund is to be able to play the central monetary role defined above, it will need to be able to make emergency decisions. Its executive director must, therefore, have the effective political support of a leadership body that can be rapidly convened, and which has a high enough political standing to be able to make demands on the member countries. This implies upgrading the executive committee to the rank of a political board, bringing together high-level officials mandated by their respective governments. This board should meet every month, and whenever necessary in emergency situations. The executive director role should cease to be the exclusive preserve of the Europeans. Defining an open selection process that is exclusively based on criteria of competence is a long overdue reform.

Such are the desirable changes in monetary governance today. If the IMF is to assume the monetary role that its founders ascribed to it

– a role that it has never truly fulfilled – it must be endowed with political leadership. This leadership must have the capacity to take action and reflect its members' common interest in getting a grip on global crises and pursuing the adventure of globalisation.

CONCLUSION

At the end of this long trek through the arcana of international money, we can clearly see the reasons for the deficiencies in the IMS. Our system is unable to fulfil its very *raison d'être*: the adjustment of the balances of payments among the sovereign countries that take part in international exchanges. Its dysfunction has worsened since the 2008 crisis. The proliferation of unlimited liquidities from the US Federal Reserve has continued to spread across an ever-greater number of countries. These liquidities are exchanged for one another in order to realise speculative surplus value on the financial products that constitute the wholesale liquidity market. The new prudential regulations imposed on banks have opened the way for shadow banking to intermediate this market.[22]

The conclusion of these investigations is that the usual methods of regulating actors through the provision of capital and liquidity are constantly being circumvented by new financial arrangements that bring the emergence of new and unregulated actors. Transactions, and not only the actors engaged in them, must be regulated in order to contain the proliferation of activities that supply wholesale liquidity. This means forbidding chains of over-the-counter transaction. This can be achieved by imposing a rule that transactions on the wholesale liquidity market must be channelled through centralised clearing and settlement systems. Central clearing houses must control the day-to-day coverage of at-risk positions; they should be supervised by regulators who only accept products whose risks can be interpreted and calculated.

----

22   There has already been a dissection of existing shadow banking operations for the purposes of their eventual regulation by the Financial Stability Board (FSB) located in Basel. An overview document was published in March 2015. See Financial Stability Board (2015), 'Assessment Methodologies for Identifying Non-Bank, Non-Insurer Global Systematically Important Financial Institutions'. fsb.org.

The disorder on the wholesale liquidity markets is fed, more fundamentally, by the failure of international liquidity regulation. This is why we must adopt the perspective opened up by Keynes, and understand, firstly, that all value is produced in a sovereign monetary space; and has as its counterparty a creation of liquidities which allow the realisation of this value through the finality of payments. International economic exchanges, then, are transfers of value between entities located in different monetary spaces. This means that *no extra creation of liquidity is required in order to realise these payments*.

This is why no universal sovereignty is required in order to found an international currency. This currency must be issued for the purpose of (and on account of) adjustments in the balance of payments, thus realising a functional connection that does not exist in a world of national currencies competing on wholesale liquidity markets. Notably, this currency does not need to be held by private actors. It would be issued by a supranational monetary institution as a currency common among the central banks. In integrating payment systems at a worldwide level, this currency would complete the logic of money as a global public good. The important thing, here, is that there has to be institutionalised cooperation between states in order to define the conditions of this body's management, in conformity with the principle of value transfers between nations. Let us call this money SDR, issued by the IMF. The Fund would, then, finally become what it was created to be: the common monetary institution in a hierarchically organised monetary system, covering all payments worldwide. Under these conditions, the SDR would change in character. It would no longer be a currency basket, but the highest level of fiduciary money. National currencies would define their parities in terms of SDR. The very long historical evolution of money would have found the form of organisation consistent with its essence: the universal form of the representation of value.

This proposal suggests an answer to the question at the very heart of this book. Money is the social relation that structures the debts so decisive to the dynamics of societies. In the twenty-first century, globalisation has shown itself to extend far beyond finance. Globalisation now concerns global public goods like the climate, the integration of the economy and ecology, technical progress, and investment in human capacities across the whole planet. Inclusive and sustainable development is our necessary purpose today, for in its absence, our civilisation may well perish.

The form of sovereignty inherited from the ideological upheavals stretching from the Renaissance to the Enlightenment is that of the democratic nation-state. Today, the nation-state is contested from below due to the renewed importance taken on by territories as sites of public debate – public debate threatened by the return of communalism. It is also challenged from above, by interdependencies that markets are far from able to control by themselves, and by the emergence of global public goods that imply unprecedented forms of cooperation.

Money is co-substantial with sovereignty, and it is thus directly affected by these transformations. The new technologies that promise to transform payment systems, the territorial sovereignties that promise to develop local currencies, and the emergence of a new universal form of liquidity will all take part in the transformation towards a global and differentiated society. This global society will be reflected in the permanence of the monetary principle, for in all its plurality of forms, money is the expression of value.

Bibliography

Adrian, Tobias, Daniel Covitz and Nellie Liang (2013), 'Financial stability monitoring', in *Federal Reserve Bank of New York Staff Report*, no. 601.

Aglietta, Michel (1986), *La Fin des devises-clés*, Paris: La Découverte.

——, (1992), 'Genèse des banques centrales et légitimité de la monnaie', *Annales, Économies, Sociétés, Civilisations*, no. 3, May–June, Librairie Armand Colin, pp. 675–98.

——, (2006), 'Intégration financière et régime monétaire sous l'étalon-or', *Revue d'économie financière*, no. 14, pp. 25–51.

——, (2014), *Europe: sortir de la crise et inventer l'avenir*, Paris: Michalon.

Aglietta, Michel and Thomas Brand (2013), *Un New Deal pour l'Europe*, Paris: Odile Jacob.

Aglietta, Michel and Jean Cartelier (1998), 'Ordre monétaire des économies de marché', in Michel Aglietta and André Orléan (eds.), *La monnaie souveraine*, Paris: Odile Jacob, p. 131.

Aglietta, Michel and Virginie Coudert (2014), *Le Dollar et le système monétaire international*, Paris: La Découverte.

——, (2015), 'Currency turmoil in an unbalanced world economy', *CEPII Policy Brief*, no. 8.

Aglietta, Michel, Etienne Espagne and Baptiste Perrissin Fabert (2015), 'Une proposition pour financer l'investissement bas carbone en Europe', *France stratégie. Note d'analyse*, no. 24.

Aglietta, Michel and Sandra Moatti (2000), *Le FMI. De l'ordre monétaire aux désordres financiers*, Paris: Economica.

Aglietta, Michel and André Orléan (1982), *La violence de la monnaie*, Paris: PUF.

Aglietta, Michel, Pepita Ould Ahmed and Jean-François Ponsot (2014), 'La monnaie, la valeur et la règle', *Revue de la régulation*, vol. 16, no. 2.

Ahmed, Pepita Ould (2003), 'Les transitions monétaires en URSS et en Russie: une continuité par-delà la rupture?' *Annales: Histoire, Sciences Sociales*, vol. 5, pp. 1107–35.

——, (2008), 'Le troc: une forme monétaire alternative', in Frédéric Lordon (ed.), *Conflits et pouvoirs dans les institutions du capitalisme*, Paris: Presses de Sciences-Po, June, pp. 143–71.

——, (2010), 'Can a community currency be independent to the state money? A case study of the credito in Argentina (1995–2008)', *Environment and Planning A*, vol. 42, no. 6, pp. 1346–464.

Ament, W. S. (1888), 'The Ancient Coinage of China', *The American Journal of Archaeology and of the History of the Fine Arts*, vol. 4, no. 3, pp. 284–90.

Andreau, Jean (1998), 'Cens, évaluation et monnaie dans l'Antiquité romaine', in Aglietta and Orléan (eds), *La monnaie souveraine*, pp. 213–50.

——, (2007), 'Crises financières et monétaires dans l'Antiquité romaine entre le IIIe siècle avant J.- C. et le IIIe siècle après J.- C.', in Théret (ed.), *La Monnaie dévoilée par ses crises*, vol. I, pp. 103–29.

Bagehot, Walter (1873), *Lombard Street: A Description of the Money Market*, London: H.S. King.

Bank of International Settlements (BIS) (2012), *Innovations in Retail Payments, Report of the Working Group on Innovations in Retail Payments*, May. www.bis.org/cpmi/publ/d102.htm.

Beaujard, Philippe, Laurent Berger and Philippe Norel (eds) (2009), *Histoire globale, mondialisations et capitalisme*, Paris: La Découverte.

Bejin, André (1976), 'Crises des valeurs, crises des mesures', *Communications*, no. 25.

Bernanke, Ben and Frederic Mishkin (1997), 'Inflation targeting: A new framework for monetary policy?', *Journal of Economic Perspectives*, vol. 11, no 2, pp. 97–116.

Bloch, Marc (1953), 'Mutations monétaires dans l'ancienne France', *Annales ESC*, vol. 8, pp. 145–58.

Bordo, Michael D. (1990), 'The Lender of Last Resort: Alternative Views and Historical Experience', *Federal Reserve Bank of Richmond Economic Review*, January–February.

Bordo, Michael and Barry Eichengreen (eds) (1993), *A Retrospective on the Bretton Woods System*, Chicago: University of Chicago Press.

Borio, Claudio (2014), 'The financial cycle and macroeconomics: What have we learnt?', *Journal of Banking and Finance*, vol. 45, pp. 182–98.

Borio, Claudio, Craig Furfine and Philip Lowe (2001), 'Procyclicality of the financial system and financial stability: Issues and policy options', *BIS Papers*, no. 1, pp. 1–57.

Borio, Claudio, N. Kennedy and Stephen Prowse (1994), 'Exploring aggregate asset price fluctuations across countries', *BIS Economic Papers*, no. 4.

Boyer-Xambeu, Marie-Thérèse, Ghislain Deleplace and Lucien Gillard (1986), *Monnaie privée et pouvoir des princes*, Paris: Presses de Sciences-Po.

Braudel, Fernand (1979), *Civilization and Capitalism, 15th–18th Centuries*, 3 vols, London: Harper and Row.

——, (1985), *La dynamique du capitalisme*, Paris: Arthaud.

Brender, Anton and Florence Pisani (1997), *Les Taux d'Intérêt. Approche Empirique*, Paris: Economica.

Breton, Stéphane (2002), 'Monnaie et économies des personnes', introduction to special issue of *L'Homme*, no. 162.

Burbank, Jane and Frederick Cooper (2010), *Empires in World History: Power and the Politics of Difference*, Princeton: Princeton University Press.

Caillé, Alain (2002), 'Quelle dette de vie?', in *L'Homme*, no. 162, pp. 242–54.

Cailleux, P. (1980), *Revue de Synthèse*, no. 99–100.

Callu, Jean-Pierre (1969), *La politique monétaire des empereurs romains de 238 à 311*, Paris: De Boccard.

Carrié, Jean-Michel (2000), 'Les crises monétaires de l'Empire romain tardif', Paris: Éditions de l'EHESS, September, republished in Théret (ed.), *La Monnaie dévoilée par ses crises*, vol. I, pp. 131–69.

Cecchetti, Stephen and Enisse Kharroubi (2012), 'Reassessing the impact of finance on growth', *BIS Working Papers* no. 381.

Christiano, Thomas (2010), 'Democratic legitimacy and international institutions', in

Samantha Besson and John Tasoulias (eds), *The Philosophy of International Law*, Oxford: Oxford University Press.

Cleveland, Harold Van B. (1976), 'The international monetary system in the interwar period', in Benjamin M. Rowland (ed.), *Balance of Power or Hegemony: The Interwar Monetary System*, Lehrman Institute, New York: New York University Press.

Clower, Robert and Peter Howitt (1996), 'Taking markets seriously: Groundwork for a post-Walrasian macroeconomics', in David Colander (ed.), *Beyond Microfoundations: Post-Walrasian Macroeconomics*, Cambridge University Press, pp. 21–37.

Cohen, Benjamin J. (2015), 'The demise of the dollar? Plus ça change, plus c'est pareil', *Revue de la regulation*, no. 18.

Coeuré, Benoît (2015), 'Il faut un ministère des Finances de la zone euro', *Le Monde*, 28 July.

Cour-Thimann, Philippine (2013), 'Target balances and the crisis in the euro area', *CESifo Forum*, vol. 14.

Daumas, François (1987), *La civilisation de l'Égypte pharaonique*, Paris: Arthaud.

De Roover, Raymond (1953), *L'Évolution de la lettre de change, XIV–XVIIIe siècles*, Paris: Armand Colin.

Desmedt, Ludovic (2007), 'Les fondements monétaires de la révolution financière anglaise: le tournant de 1696', in Théret (ed.), *La Monnaie dévoilée par ses crises*, vol. I, Paris: Éditions de l'EHESS, pp. 311–38.

Drummond, Ian M. (1979), 'London, Washington and the Management of the Franc, 1936–39', *Princeton Studies in International Finance*, no. 45.

Duby, Georges (1973), *Guerriers et Paysans*, Paris: Gallimard.

Dupré, Denis, Jean-François Ponsot and Jean-Michel Servet (2015), 'Le bitcoin, une tragédie du marché', Report by the Mission d'études sur les monnaies locales complémentaires, pp. 18–22.

Dupuy, Claude (1992), 'De la monnaie publique à la monnaie privée au bas Moyen Âge', *Genèses*, no. 8, pp. 25–59.

Dupuy, Jean-Pierre (2012), *L'Avenir de l'économie: sortir de l'écomystification*, Paris: Flammarion, pp. 75–150.

Dumont, Louis (1983), *Essais sur l'individualisme*, Paris: Seuil.

Eichengreen, Barry (1985), *The Gold Standard in Theory and History*, London: Routledge.

——, (2011), *Exorbitant Privilege*, Oxford: Oxford University Press.

Eichengreen, Barry, Ricardo Hausmann and Ugo Panizza (2003), 'Currency mismatches, debt intolerance and original sin: Why they are not the same and why it matters', *NBER Working Paper*, no. 10036.

Eichengreen, Barry and Kris Mitchener (2003), 'The great depression as a credit boom gone wrong', *BIS Working Paper*, no. 137.

European Central Bank (ECB) (2012), *Virtual Currency Schemes*, October. www.ecb. europa.eu/pub/pdf/other/virtualcurrencyschemes201210en.pdf.

Fama, Eugene (1976), *The Foundations of Finance: Portfolio Decisions and Securities Prices*, New York: Basic Books.

Feiertag, Olivier (ed.) (2005), *Mesurer la monnaie. Banques centrales et construction de l'autorité monétaire (XIX–XXe siècle)*, Paris: Albin Michel.

Fichte, Johann Gottlieb (2012), *The Closed Commercial State*, New York: SUNY.

Fields, David and Matías Vernengo (2013), 'Hegemonic currencies during the crisis: The dollar versus the euro in a cartelist perspective', *Review of International Political Economy*, vol. 20, no. 4, pp. 740–59.

Financial Stability Board (2015), 'Assessment Methodologies for Identifying Non-Bank, Non-Insurer Global Systematically Important Financial Institutions'. fsb.org

Finley, Moses I. (1975), *Économie antique*, Paris: Éditions de Minuit.

Fisher, Irving (1933), 'The Debt-Deflation Theory of Great Depressions', *Econometrica*, vol. 1, no. 4, pp. 337–57.

Foulis, Patrick (2015), 'The sticky superpower', Special report on the world economy, *The Economist*, 3 October.

Frankel, Herbert (1977), *Money. Two Philosophies: The Conflict of Trust and Authority*, Oxford: Blackwell.

Garcia, Gillian and Elizabeth Plantz (1988), *The Federal Reserve: Lender of Last Resort*, Cambridge, MA: Ballinger Press.

Gernet, Louis (1968), *Anthropologie de la Grèce antique*, Paris: Gallimard.

Gillard, Lucien (2005), *La Banque d'Amsterdam et le florin européen au temps de la République néerlandaise (1610–1820)*, Paris: Éditions de l'EHESS.

Girard, René (1972), *La Violence et le Sacré*, Paris: Grasset.

Girault, René and Maurice Lévy-Leboyer (eds) (1993), *Le Plan Marshall et le relèvement économique de l'Europe*, Comité pour l'histoire économique et financière de la France Conference, Bercy, 21–23 March 1991.

Glassner, Jean-Jacques (2002), *La Mésopotamie*, Paris: Les Belles Lettres.

Goldberg, Linda S. and Cédric Tille (2008), 'Vehicle currency use in international trade', *Journal of International Economics*, vol. 76, no. 2, pp. 177–92.

Goldfinger, Charles (2000), 'Intangible economy and electronic money', in OECD (ed.), *The Future of Money*, Paris: OECD Publications, p. 87–122.

Goodhart, Charles (1994), 'What should central banks do? What should be their macro-economic objectives and operations?', *Economic Journal* vol. 104, no. 427, pp. 1424–36.

——, (2000), 'Can Central Banking Survive the IT Revolution?', Special Paper, Financial Markets Group, London: London School of Economics.

Graeber, David (2011), *Debt: The First 5,000 Years*, Brooklyn: Melville House.

Gramsci, Antonio (1978), *Cahiers de prison*, Paris: Gallimard.

Grandjean, Catherine (2005), 'Guerre et crise de la monnaie en Grèce ancienne à la fin du Ve siècle av. J.-C.', in Bruno Théret (ed.), *La monnaie dévoilée par ses crises*, vol. I, Paris: Éditions de l'EHESS, pp. 85–102.

Hahn, Frank (1982), *Money and Inflation*, Oxford: Basil Blackwell.

Hamilton, James D., Ethan S. Harris, Jan Hatzius and Kenneth D. West (2015), *The Equilibrium Real Funds Rate: Past, Present and Future*, Report by the US Monetary Policy Forum, New York, 27 February.

Hawtrey, Ralph George (1932), *The Art of Central Banking*, London: Longmans Green.

Hirschman, Albert O. (2006), *Bonheur privé, action publique*, Paris: Hachette.

IMF (1974), *International Monetary Reform*, Committee of Twenty.

——, (2015), World Economic Outlook, April.

IMF, World Bank, EBRD and OECD (2013), *Developing Local Currency Bond Markets: A Diagnostic Framework*.

Issing, Otmar (1992), 'Theoretical and empirical foundations of the Deutsche Bundesbank's monetary targeting', *Intereconomics*, vol. 27, no. 6, pp. 289–300.

Ito, Hiro and Menzie Chinn (2015), 'The rise of the redback: Evaluating the prospects for renminbi use in invoicing', in Barry Eichengreen and Masahiro Kawai, *Renminbi Internationalization*, Washington DC: Brookings Institution Press, pp. 111–58.

Jaoul, Michel and Olivier Schloesing (1954), 'L'Union européenne des paiements', *Revue économique*, vol. 5, no. 2, pp. 263–77.

Jean, Sébastien, Françoise Lemoine and CEPII (2015), *L'Économie mondiale 2016*, Paris: La Découverte, pp. 87–102.

Kalecki, Michal (1962), 'A model of hyperinflation', *Manchester School of Economics and Social Studies*, vol. 30.

Kareken, John and Neil Wallace (1981), 'On the indeterminacy of equilibrium exchange rates', *Quarterly Journal of Economics*, vol. 96, no. 2, pp. 207–222.

Kébadjian, Gérard (1999), *Théories de l'économie politique internationale*, Paris: Seuil.

Keohane, Robert (1984), *After Hegemony: Cooperation and Discord in the World Political Economy*, Princeton, Princeton University Press.

Keynes, John Maynard (1920), *The Economic Consequences of the Peace*, New York: Harcourt, Brace and Howe.

——, (1941), 'Proposals for an International Clearing Union', in *The Collected Writings of John Maynard Keynes, XXV* (1980), Cambridge: Cambridge University Press.

——, (1942–3), 'The Keynes Plan', in J. Keith Horsefield (ed.) (1969), *The International Monetary Fund 1945–1965: Twenty Years of International Monetary Cooperation*, vol. 3, Washington, DC: IMF.

Kindleberger, Charles P. (1973), *The World in Depression 1929–1939*, Berkeley: University of California Press.

——, (1978), *Manias, Panics and Crashes*, New York: Basic Books.

——, (1981), *International Money: A Collection of Essays*, Crows Nest: Allen and Unwin.

Kiyotaki, Nobuhiro and Randall Wright (1991), 'A Contribution to the Pure Theory of Money', *Journal of Economic Theory*, vol. 53, no. 2, pp. 215–35.

Krasner, Stephen D. (1983), *International Regimes*, Ithaca: Cornell University.

Liang, Nellie (2013), *Implementing Macroprudential Policies*, Conference on Financial Stability Analysis, Federal Reserve Bank of Cleveland and the Office of Financial Research, May. https://financialresearch.gov/conferences/files/implementing_macro-prudential_policies_may31-2013.pdf.

Landes, David S. (1969), *The Unbound Prometheus: Technological Change and Industrial Development in Western Europe from 1750 to the Present*, Cambridge: Cambridge University Press.

Le Maux, Laurent (2001), 'Le prêt en dernier ressort. Les chambres de compensation aux États-Unis durant le XIXᵉ siècle', *Annales, Histoire et Sciences Sociales*, vol. 56, no. 6, pp. 1223–51.

——, (2012), 'The Banking School and the Law of Reflux in General', *History of Political Economy*, vol. 44, no. 4, pp. 595–618.

Le Maux, Laurent and Laurence Scialom (2007), 'Antagonismes monétaires et constitution d'une banque centrale aux États-Unis', in Théret (éd.), *La monnaie dévoilée par ses crises*, Paris: Éditions de l'EHESS, pp. 339–68.

Le Rider, Georges (2001), *La naissance de la monnaie: Pratiques monétaires de l'Orient ancien*, Paris: PUF.

Livius, Titus, *History of Rome*, Book 27.

Lucas, Robert (1972), 'Expectations and the neutrality of money', *Journal of Economic Theory*, vol. 4, no. 2, pp. 103–24.

Magnen, Jean-Philipe and Christophe Fourel (2015), *D'autres monnaies pour une nouvelle prospérité*, Report by the Mission d'étude sur les monnaies locales complémentaires et les systèmes d'échanges locaux.

Mairet, Gérard (1997), *Le Principe de souveraineté. Histoires et fondements du pouvoir moderne*, Paris: Gallimard.

Marie, Jonathan (2014), 'Hyperinflation argentine de 1989: une interprétation post-keynésienne', *Revue de la régulation*, vol. 15, no. 1.

Marques-Pereira, Jaimes (2007), 'Crecimiento, conflicto distributivo y soberanía monetaria en Argentina', in Rober Boyer and Julio Neffa (eds), *Salida de crisis y estrategias alternativas de desarrollo, la experiencia argentina*, Buenos Aires: Miño y Dávila, pp. 177–207.

Marx, Karl (1992), *Capital: A Critique of Political Economy*, Vol. 1, trans. Ben Fowkes, London: Penguin.

Mauss, Marcel (1973), 'Essai sur le don: Forme et raison de l'échange dans les sociétés archaïques', *Année sociologique* (1923–1924), republished in Marcel Mauss, *Sociologie et anthropologie*, Paris: PUF.

Menu, Bernadette (2001), 'La monnaie des Égyptiens de l'époque Pharaonique', in Alain Testard (ed.), *Aux origines de la monnaie*, Paris: Éditions Errance, pp. 73–108.

Minsky, Hyman P. (1982), 'The financial instability hypothesis, capitalist processes and the behavior of the economy', in Charles P. Kindleberger and Jean-Pierre Laffargue (eds), *Financial Crises, Theory, History and Policy*, Cambridge: Cambridge University Press, pp. 13–39.

Moen, John R. and Ellis W. Tallman (2000), 'Clearinghouse membership and deposit contraction during the panic of 1907', *Journal of Economic History*, vol. 60, no. 1, pp. 145–63.

Mundell, Robert A. (1966), 'A Theory of Optimal Currency Areas', *American Economic Review*, November, pp. 657–65.

——, (1968), *International Economics*, London: Macmillan.

Muth, John (1961), 'Rational expectations and the theory of price movements', *Econometrica*, vol. 29, no. 3, pp. 315–34.

Orléan, André (1984), 'Monnaie et spéculation mimétique', *Bulletin du Mauss*, no. 12, December, pp. 55–68.

——, (2007), 'Crise de souveraineté et crise monétaire: l'hyperinflation allemande des années 1920', in Théret (ed.), *La monnaie dévoilée par ses crises*, vol. II, pp. 177–220.

——, (2011), *L'Empire de la valeur. Refonder l'économie*, Paris: Seuil.

Palley, Thomas I. (2014), 'Global imbalances: Benign by-product of global development or toxic consequence of corporate globalization?', *European Journal of Economics and Economic Policies*, vol. 11, no. 3, pp. 250–68.

Patinkin, Don (1965), *Money, Interest and Prices*, New York: Harper and Row.

Pesin, Fabrice and Christophe Strassel (2006), *Le Modèle allemand en question*, Paris: Economica.

Pfister, Christian and Natacha Valla (2015), 'Les politiques monétaires non conventionnelles', in Sébastien Jean, Françoise Lemoine and CEPII, *L'Économie mondiale 2016*, Paris: La Découverte, pp. 40–56.

Picard, Olivier (1978), 'Les origines du monnayage en Grèce', *L'Histoire*, no. 6, pp. 13–20.

——, (2008), *Guerre et Économies dans l'Alliance Athénienne, 490–322 av. J.C.*, Paris: SEDES.

Ponsot, Jean-François (2007), 'Dollarisation et banque centrale en Équateur', in Elsa Lafaye de Michaux, Eric Mulot and Pépita Ould Ahmed (eds), *Institutions et développement. La fabrique institutionnelle et politique des trajectoires de développement*, Rennes: Presses universitaires de Rennes, p. 233–58.

——, (2015a), 'Currency boards', in Louis-Philippe Rochon and Sergio Rossi (eds), *The Encyclopedia of Central Banking*, Cheltenham: Edward Elgar Publishing Limited, pp. 130–2.

——, (2015b), 'Original sin', in Rochon and Rossi (eds), *The Encyclopedia of Central Banking*, pp. 392–4.

——, (2016), 'The "four I's" of the international monetary system and the international role of the euro', *Research in International Business and Finance*, vol. 37, p. 299–308.

Polak, Jacques (1979), 'Thoughts on an IMF based fully on SDR', Pamphlet Series, no. 28, International Monetary Fund.

Price, Martin Jessop (1968), 'Early Greek bronze coinage', in Colin M. Kraay and G. Kenneth Jenkins (eds), *Essays in Greek coinage, presented to Stanley Robinson*, Oxford: Clarendon Press.

Rawls, John (2001), *Justice as Fairness: A Restatement*, Cambridge, MA: Belknap Press.

Reiss, Daniel Gersten (2014), 'Invoice currency in Brazil', *MPRA Paper*, no. 59412, University Library of Munich.

Robinson, Joan (1960), 'The Theory of Distribution', in her *Collected Economic Papers*, vol. II, Oxford: Basil Blackwell.

Rodrik, Dani (2006), 'The Social Cost of Foreign Exchange Reserves', *International Economic Journal*, vol. 20, no. 3, pp. 253–66.

——, (2011), *The Globalization Paradox*, New York: W.W. Norton & Co.

Rodrik, Dani and Arvind Subramanian (2009), 'Why did financial globalization disappoint?', *IMF Staff Papers*, vol. 56, no. 1, pp. 112–38.

Rosanvallon, Pierre (2011), *La Société des Égaux*, Paris: Seuil.

Rothbard, Murray (2007), *The Mystery of Banking*, Auburn: Mises Institute.

Sayers, R. S. (1976), *The Bank of England 1891–1914*, Cambridge: Cambridge University Press.

——, (1987), *Central Banking after Bagehot*, Oxford: Oxford University Press.

Schumpeter, Joseph A. (1939), *Business Cycles*, New York: McGraw-Hill.

Selgin, George A. (1988), *The Theory of Free Banking*, London: Rowman and Littlefield.

Sen, Amartya (2009), *The Idea of Justice*, London: Allen Lane.

Servet, Jean-Michel (1984), *Nomismata: État et origines de la monnaie*, Lyons: Presses Universitaires.

Sharpe, William (1964), 'Capital Asset Prices: A Theory of Market Equilibrium under Conditions of Risk', *Journal of Finance*, vol. 19, no. 3, p. 425–42.

Silver, Morris (1995), *Economic Structures of Antiquity*, Westport: Greenwood Press.

Simmel, Georg (1978), *The Philosophy of Money*, London: Routledge and Kegan.

Solomon, Robert (1977), *The international monetary system, 1945–1976: An insider's view*, New York: Harper and Row.

Théret, Bruno (ed.) (2007), *La monnaie dévoilée par ses crises*, vols I and II, Paris: Éditions de l'EHESS.

Thierry, François (2001), 'Sur les spécificités fondamentales de la monnaie chinoise', in Testard (ed.), *Aux origines de la monnaie*, Paris: Éditions Errance, pp. 108–44.

Thomas, Jean-Gabriel (1977), *Inflation et nouvel ordre monétaire*, Paris: PUF.

Thornton, Henry (1939), *An Enquiry into the Nature and Effects of the Paper Credit of Great Britain*, 1802, Introduction by Friedrich August von Hayek, London: Allen & Unwin.

Triffin, Robert (1960), *Gold and the Dollar Crisis*, New Haven: Yale University Press.

Trautman, Thomas R. (1987), *Lewis Henry Morgan and the Invention of Kinship*, Berkeley: University of California Press.

Veenhof, Klaas Roelof (1997), 'Modern features in Old Assyrian trade', *Journal of the Economic and Social History of the Orient*, vol. 40, no. 4, pp. 336–66.

Veyne, Paul (1976), *Le pain et le cirque. Sociologie historique d'un pluralisme politique*, Paris: Seuil.

Vilar, Pierre (1974), *Or et monnaie dans l'histoire*, Paris: Flammarion.

Walfaren, Thierry (1994), *Bretton Woods. Mélanges pour un cinquantenaire*, Paris: Association d'Économie Financière.

Walras, Leon (2010) *Elements of Pure Economics, or The Theory of Social Wealth*, London: Routledge.

Warnier, Jean-Pierre (2009), 'Alliance, filiation et inaliénabilité: le débat sur le don à la lumière de l'anthropologie de la parenté', *Sociétés politiques comparées*, no. 11, January.

Weiner, Annette (1992), *Inalienable Possessions: The Paradox of Keeping-While-Giving*, Berkely: University of California Press.

Wicker, Elmus (2005), *The Great Debate on Banking Reform: Nelson Aldrich and the Origins of the Fed*, Columbus, OH: Ohio State University Press.

Wicksell, Knut (1907), 'The influence of the rate of interest on prices', *The Economic Journal*, no. 17, pp. 213–20.

Williamson, John (1977), *The Failure of World Monetary Reform, 1971–1974*, Nashville: Nelson and Sons.

Williamson, John and Marcus Miller (1987), *Targets and Indicators: A Blueprint for the International Coordination of Economic Policy*, Policy Analysis in International Economics, no. 22. Washington, DC: Institute for International Economics.

Willms, Johannes (2005), *La Maladie allemande. Une brève histoire du présent*, Paris: Gallimard.

Woodford, Michael (2000), 'Monetary Policy in a world without cash', *International Finance*, vol. 3, no. 2, pp. 229–60.

Wright, Robert E. (2008), *One Nation Under Debt: Hamilton, Jefferson, and the History of What We Owe*, New York: McGraw-Hill.

Index

b denotes box; *f* denotes figure; *t* denotes table

A

ABCP (Asset-Backed Commercial Paper), 273

absolute liquidity, 37, 38, 61, 101, 152, 156, 278, 279

abstraction, 72, 83, 89, 93, 108, 110, 114, 116, 117, 148, 150

abstract units of account, 108, 109, 117, 195

accounting, 6, 32, 33–4, 83, 85–6, 168, 199, 227

accounts and payments, 33–5. *See also* accounting; payment system(s); unit of account

Addresses to the German Nation (Fichte), 129

ad hoc compromises/cooperation/ negotiation/structures, 360, 361, 363, 367, 385, 386

agrarian empires, money and state in, 85–6

Aldrich–Vreeland Act of 30 May 1908, 219

Alibaba, 156

alienable goods, 67

alternative theory of value, 81

American natural interest rate, 278*f*

Andreau, Jean, 72n9, 99n19

annuities, 192, 200, 205, 206, 207

antiquity

crises in metal-based systems of, 191–5

money and state in, 85–6

antoninianus, 103, 104, 193

Argentina crisis (2002), 243

Aristotle, 32, 91, 95, 102, 287

Arrow, Kenneth, 165

as, 98, 99, 192

Asian crisis (1997–98), 237

Asset-Backed Commercial Paper (ABCP), 273

auctioneer, as Walras metaphor, 19–20, 21, 31, 38

aureus, 99, 103, 111, 112*t*

Austrian school, 55, 56, 57

autonomisation of political/sovereignty, 70, 71, 73*f*, 83

B

Bagehot, Walter, 211, 212–15, 246, 250

balance of payments

adjustment of, 313, 319, 323, 324, 335, 353, 358, 384, 390, 397

China from 2008 to 2010, 379*t*

deficit in/surplus in, 243, 295

emergency financing of, 393

equilibrium, 316, 350, 351

impact on, 378

instabilities/imbalances in, 257, 336, 344, 394

long-term stabilisers of UK balance of payments, 303*t*

settlement of, 296